Fountas&Pinnell

Phonics, Spelling, and Word Study Lessons

GRADE **K**

Irene C. Fountas
Gay Su Pinnell

HEINEMANN
Portsmouth, NH

Heinemann
361 Hanover Street
Portsmouth, NH 03801-3912
www.heinemann.com

Offices and agents throughout the world

Grateful acknowledgment to the following schools for generously allowing Heinemann to photograph their students, teachers, and classrooms: Henry Wilson Elementary School, Manchester, NH, and Northwest Elementary School, Manchester, NH.

Cataloging-in-Publication Data is on file at the Library of Congress
ISBN: 978-0-325-09289-8

Editorial: David Pence, Alana Jeralds
Production: Victoria Merecki
Cover design: Suzanne Heiser
Interior design: Monica Ann Crigler
Typesetter: Technologies 'N Typography, Inc.
Manufacturing: Erin St. Hilaire

Printed in the United States of America on acid-free paper
3   4   5   6   MP   22   21   20   19
March 2019 Printing

PWS Contents

Introduction *1*

What Is Phonics? *1*

What Do Kindergarten Children Need to Know? *2*

Where Does Phonics Instruction Fit in the Design for Literacy Learning? *9*

Reading Contexts in the Kindergarten Classroom *11*

Writing Contexts in the Kindergarten Classroom *15*

Independent Literacy Work *17*

Designing an Environment to Support Letter, Sound, and Word Learning *20*

What Are Some Ways of Working Effectively with English Language Learners? *23*

Using the *Fountas & Pinnell Phonics, Spelling, and Word Study System* in the Kindergarten Classroom *30*

Materials and Resources in the System *30*

An Annotated Lesson and Its Features *31*

Planning and Implementing Effective Phonics Lessons *35*

Routines and Instructional Procedures for Effective Teaching *36*

Phonics Lessons in the Daily Schedule *42*

Nine Areas of Learning Across the Year: Early, Middle, Late *44*

Nine Areas of Learning Across the Year (Chart) *46*

A Suggested Sequence for Phonics Lessons *48*

Master Lesson Guide: Suggested Sequence for Phonics Lessons (Chart) *50*

PWS Lessons

EARLY LITERACY CONCEPTS *73*

ELC 1 Recognize Your Name *75*

ELC 2 Recognize Your Name *79*

ELC 3 Match a Spoken Word with a Group of Letters *83*

ELC 4 Match a Spoken Word with a Group of Letters *87*

ELC 5 Connect a Name to Other Words *91*

ELC 6 Understand First and Last in Written Language: Letters *95*

ELC 7 Understand First and Last in Written Language: Letters and Words *99*

ELC 8 Understand First and Last in Written Language: Words *103*

PHONOLOGICAL AWARENESS *107*

PA 1 Hear and Say Rhyming Words *109*

PA 2 Hear and Say Rhyming Words *113*

PA 3 Hear and Connect Rhyming Words *117*

PA 4 Hear and Generate Rhyming Words *121*

PA 5 Hear and Generate Rhyming Words *125*

PA 6 Hear, Say, and Clap Syllables *129*

PA 7 Hear, Say, and Clap Syllables *133*

PA 8 Hear, Say, and Clap Syllables *137*

PA 9 Blend Syllables *141*

PA 10 Hear and Say the Same Beginning Sound in Words *145*

PA 11 Hear and Say the Same Beginning Sound in Words *149*

PA 12 Hear and Say the Same Beginning Sound in Words *153*

PHONOLOGICAL AWARENESS (*continued*)

PA 13 Hear and Say the Ending Sound in a Word   *157*

PA 14 Hear and Say the Same Ending Sound in Words   *161*

PA 15 Hear and Say the Same Ending Sound in Words   *165*

PA 16 Change the Beginning Sound to Make a New Word   *169*

PA 17 Hear and Say the Middle Sound in a Word with Three Phonemes   *173*

PA 18 Hear and Say the Same Middle Sound in Words   *177*

PA 19 Hear and Divide Onsets and Rimes   *181*

PA 20 Blend Onsets with Rimes   *185*

PA 21 Hear and Say Two Sounds in a Word   *189*

PA 22 Hear and Say Three Sounds in a Word   *193*

PA 23 Hear and Say Four or More Sounds in a Word in Sequence   *197*

PA 24 Blend Three or Four Sounds in a Word   *201*

PA 25 Delete the Beginning Sound of a Word   *205*

PA 26 Delete the Beginning Sound of a Word   *209*

LETTER KNOWLEDGE   *213*

LK 1 Understand That Words Are Formed with Letters   *215*

LK 2 Recognize the Distinctive Features of Letter Forms   *219*

LK 3 Recognize the Distinctive Features of Letter Forms   *223*

LK 4 Recognize Letters and State Their Names   *227*

LK 5 Recognize the Distinctive Features of Letter Forms   *231*

LK 6 Recognize Letters and State Their Names   *235*

LK 7 Recognize Letters and State Their Names   *239*

PWS Lessons *(continued)*

LETTER KNOWLEDGE *(continued)*

LK 8 Recognize Letters and State Their Names *243*

LK 9 Understand That Words Are Formed with Letters *247*

LK 10 Recognize the Sequence of Letters in a Word *251*

LK 11 Recognize Letters and State Their Names *255*

LK 12 Recognize Letters and State Their Names *259*

LK 13 Form Letters with Writing Tools *263*

LK 14 Form Letters with Writing Tools *267*

LK 15 Make Connections Among Words by Noting the Position of a Letter *271*

LK 16 Categorize Letters by Features *275*

LK 17 Categorize Letters by Features *279*

LK 18 Form Letters with Writing Tools *283*

LK 19 Form Letters with Writing Tools *287*

LK 20 Recognize Uppercase Letters and Lowercase Letters *291*

LK 21 Distinguish the Differences Between Uppercase and Lowercase Forms of a Letter *295*

LK 22 Recognize That Letters Can Be Consonants or Vowels *299*

LK 23 Recognize the Order of the Alphabet *303*

LK 24 Recognize the Order of the Alphabet *307*

LETTER-SOUND RELATIONSHIPS   *311*

LSR **1** Recognize Beginning Consonant Sounds and the Letters That Represent Them   *313*

LSR **2** Recognize Beginning Consonant Sounds and the Letters That Represent Them   *317*

LSR **3** Recognize Beginning Consonant Sounds and the Letters That Represent Them   *321*

LSR **4** Recognize Beginning Consonant Sounds and the Letters That Represent Them   *325*

LSR **5** Recognize Beginning Consonant Sounds and the Letters That Represent Them   *329*

LSR **6** Recognize Beginning Consonant Sounds and the Letters That Represent Them   *333*

LSR **7** Recognize Beginning Consonant Sounds and the Letters That Represent Them   *337*

LSR **8** Recognize Ending Consonant Sounds and the Letters That Represent Them   *341*

SPELLING PATTERNS   *345*

SP **1** Recognize and Use the CVC Pattern   *347*

SP **2** Recognize and Use Phonograms: *-an*   *351*

SP **3** Recognize and Use Phonograms: *-at*   *355*

SP **4** Recognize and Use Phonograms: *-ay*   *359*

SP **5** Recognize and Use Phonograms with a VC*e* Pattern: *-ake*   *363*

SP **6** Recognize and Use Phonograms with a VC*e* Pattern: *-ine*   *367*

SP **7** Recognize Letter Patterns   *371*

PWS Lessons *(continued)*

HIGH-FREQUENCY WORDS *375*

HFW 1 Recognize and Use High-Frequency Words with One, Two, or Three Letters *377*

HFW 2 Recognize and Use High-Frequency Words with One, Two, or Three Letters *381*

HFW 3 Recognize and Use High-Frequency Words with One, Two, or Three Letters *385*

HFW 4 Recognize and Use High-Frequency Words with Three or More Letters *389*

HFW 5 Recognize and Use High-Frequency Words with Three or More Letters *393*

HFW 6 Recognize and Use High-Frequency Words with Three or More Letters *397*

HFW 7 Locate and Read High-Frequency Words in Continuous Text *401*

WORD MEANING/VOCABULARY *405*

WMV 1 Recognize and Use Concept Words: Color Names *407*

WMV 2 Recognize and Use Concept Words: Color Names *411*

WMV 3 Recognize and Use Concept Words: Number Names *415*

WMV 4 Recognize and Use Concept Words: Number Names *419*

WMV 5 Recognize and Use Concept Words: Days of the Week *423*

WMV 6 Recognize and Use Concept Words: Days of the Week *427*

WMV 7 Recognize Related Words *431*

WORD STRUCTURE *435*

WS 1 Hear, Say, and Identify Syllables *437*

WS 2 Understand the Concept of a Contraction *441*

WS 3 Understand the Concept of Plural *445*

WS 4 Recognize and Use Plurals That Add -s *449*

WORD-SOLVING ACTIONS *453*

WSA ❶ Recognize and Find Names *455*

WSA ❷ Recognize and Read Known Words Quickly *459*

WSA ❸ Change the Beginning Sound or Sounds to Make and Solve a New Word *463*

WSA ❹ Change the Beginning Sound or Sounds to Make and Solve a New Word *467*

WSA ❺ Hear Sounds in Sequence *471*

WSA ❻ Use Onsets and Rimes in Known Words to Read and Write Other Words with the Same Parts *475*

WSA ❼ Use Onsets and Rimes in Known Words to Read and Write Other Words with the Same Parts *479*

WSA ❽ Change the Ending Sound or Sounds to Make and Solve a New Word *483*

WSA ❾ Change the Ending Sound or Sounds to Make and Solve a New Word *487*

Glossary *491*

References *497*

Introduction

When you teach this collection of one hundred phonics lessons, you invite children to join you in exploring an exciting subject—language and how it works. We often think that phonics applies only to using letters and sounds in reading; in fact, knowledge of the building blocks of words is useful to children across all literacy learning. And, in turn, engaging in reading, writing, and talking propels learning in phonics.

In this book, you will find guides for the explicit, systematic teaching of aspects of language through lessons outside of continuous text; but you will also find suggestions for explicit systematic teaching as children read and write texts. The goal of these lessons is to help children expand and refine their reading and writing powers; but, we hope that they will also become enthusiastic explorers of words—investigating their meanings, seeing patterns, puzzling out simple and more complex letter-sound relationships, taking words apart and connecting them in an active way. In this way, they learn *how to learn* aspects of words and develop efficient and powerful word-solving strategies.

We believe that it is essential for all readers and writers to have a wide range of word-solving strategies—possibly hundreds—that they can use rapidly, flexibly, and in a largely unconscious way as they read and write. This flexible range of strategies enables them to keep their attention focused on the meaning as they process text. Of course, children in kindergarten are just developing these in-the-head strategies, so they need to learn to look closely at words and build their ability to solve them.

What Is Phonics?

Phonics is more than relating a letter to a sound. Learning phonics is complex. According to Clay (1991), a competent reader "uses not just the sounds of letters but phonological information from several levels of language. He can provide phonological identities for letters, digraphs, clusters, syllables, prefixes and suffixes, root words, phrases, and non-language strings. He will select a larger rather than a smaller unit for efficiency and may check one source of information against another" (290).

Let's look at the term *phonics,* which we often use as a kind of "shorthand" for everything Clay described above. But there are more precise definitions for the understandings children are developing. Here are some relevant terms:

- The **phonological system** is the sound system of oral language.
- A **phoneme** is a unit of sound that makes it possible to distinguish one word from another. For example, a single sound can make the difference, as in *pat* and *bat.*
- **Phonological awareness** refers to an individual's sense of the phonological structure of words, for example, rhymes, onsets (beginning part of a one-syllable word) and rimes (the rest of the word), syllables, and individual phonemes. It refers to awareness of *sound,* not letters.

- **Phonemic awareness** is an individual's ability to hear, identify, and manipulate the individual sounds—or phonemes in a word. Phonemic awareness (or **phoneme awareness**) is a subset of phonological awareness.
- A letter, or **grapheme,** is a written character in an alphabetic system of writing. The **alphabetic principle** is the understanding that sounds and letters are related.
- A **phonogram** is a common word ending that appears in many words or syllables (-*am* in *Pam, ham, jam*).
- **Phonics** is a method for teaching that involves developing learners' ability to hear and manipulate sounds and to learn the correspondence—both simple and complex—between sounds and letters as well as between sounds and larger units.

So, when we identify our one hundred lessons (including many that are generative because they are used over and over to teach a variety of letters, sounds, phonogram patterns, and word parts), we are referring to specific areas of learning about phonics, spelling, and word study—all of which are important for children to understand as they explore language and how it works.

What Do Kindergarten Children Need to Know?

Most kindergarten children are at the beginning of their knowledge of phonics, although for many, a great deal of learning has already taken place. From hearing books read aloud and exploring electronic media, they probably understand that you read the words (not the pictures); that a story is the same every time you read it; that words are made up of letters; and that there is some relationship between letters and sounds. They read, write, and explore their own names, learning much in the process. We cannot, however, take all of that for granted.

The Fountas & Pinnell Comprehensive Phonics, Spelling, and Word Study Guide (2017) is the key to the phonics lessons. This comprehensive volume is a meticulously constructed picture of the linguistic and language knowledge children develop on their journey to become highly expert and flexible word solvers. Most important for teaching kindergarten children are the areas identified as "in process" and "under control" during this first year of school. Complex learning takes time over many examples, and few concepts are simply "taught" in one lesson and do not need further development. Nevertheless, the period of time from beginning to the end of kindergarten represents a massive acquisition of knowledge.

We know that as teachers we simultaneously help children expand their oral language capabilities while we work with them on the understandings needed for literacy. At the heart of literacy is a language process in which children use what they know about the language they speak and connect it to print (Clay 1991). The semantic (meaning), syntactic (structure or grammar), phonological (sound), and graphemic (letters) systems all work together as the child is becoming literate. Decades of research have shown that when they are meaningfully engaged in using print, children develop early awareness of the relationships between these systems (Read 1971; Treiman 1985). Most children, however, need explicit teaching that focuses their attention to the use of letters, sounds, and word parts to solve words (Adams 1990; Armbruster, Lehr, and Osborn 2001; Clay 1991, 1998, 2001; Juel 1988; Juel, Griffith, and Gough 1986; Moats 2000; National Institute of Child Health and Human Development 2001; Pressley 1998; Snow, Burns, and Griffin 1989). The challenge for teachers is to organize their own knowledge and design systematic ways to engage the children in constructing their understandings and help them use them effectively and efficiently in their reading and writing.

We have identified nine areas of learning about phonics, spelling, and word study; for each area of learning, lessons are provided in this book. The continuum is based on research in language and literacy learning; we have asked linguists, researchers on literacy education, and many teachers to provide feedback on the phonics and word study section. We found surprising agreement on the knowledge needed to become an expert word solver.

Let's look at the nine areas of learning in more detail.

Nine Areas of Learning About Phonics, Spelling, and Word Study

Early Literacy Concepts Most early literacy concepts are developed through early reading and writing experiences, so we include only a few explicit lessons in this area. These concepts include distinguishing between print and pictures, understanding the concepts of letters and words, and learning that print has directionality (in other words, in English, we read from top to bottom, left to right). We also provide some basic lessons that will help children use their own names as resources in learning about sounds, letters, and words.

Phonological Awareness We recommend extensive work in reading aloud and shared reading to develop phonological and phonemic awareness. Songs, rhymes, and poetry give children the background and examples to participate fully in your lessons in this area. The development of phonemic awareness is basic to other learning about literacy in kindergarten; often you will want to extend these lessons by studying letters as well as sounds to make use of the way the two areas of knowledge complement each other.

Letter Knowledge Children need many different experiences with letters in order to learn "what to look for" when distinguishing one letter from another. They learn that there are many different letters in the set called the alphabet, that each letter has a different name, and that each letter is just a little different from every other letter. Some letters look alike in that they have similar features. Each letter also has an uppercase form and a lowercase form; sometimes these forms look almost alike and sometimes they are different.

Letter-Sound Relationships Letter-sound learning is also basic in kindergarten and is one of the explicit goals of the curriculum. Your lessons in this area will help children develop an organized view of the tools of literacy. For kindergarten, we emphasize consonants, but we also explore easy-to-hear vowels.

Spelling Patterns The patterns in regularly spelled words are especially helpful to kindergartners. As they explore simple phonograms and words that have highly reliable letter-sound correspondence, they learn the first strategies for decoding. Solving larger parts of words helps them read and write more efficiently and also gives them access to many words.

High-Frequency Words High-frequency words are also learned in many other components of effective and coherent design for literacy teaching. Lessons on high-frequency words help children develop a useful core of known words that they can use as resources to solve new words, check on their reading, and read and write fluently.

Word Meaning/Vocabulary Children need to know the meaning of the words they are learning to read and write. It is important for them constantly to expand their vocabulary as well as develop a more complex understanding of words they already know. This section of the continuum describes understandings related to the development of vocabulary—labels and concept words, such as colors, numbers, and days of the week.

Word Structure Word structure deals with the underlying rules for understanding contractions, compound words, plurals, prefixes, affixes, possessives, and abbreviations. Since most of these concepts are beyond kindergarten, we have not included lessons that address them. You can, however, incidentally point out such patterns to children during interactive writing and shared reading.

Word-Solving Actions Readers and writers use a variety of word-solving strategies to decode words when reading or writing continuous text. They also use parts of words and search for patterns they can connect. These strategies are invisible, "in-the-head" actions, although we can sometimes infer them from overt behavior. For example, children will sometimes make several attempts at words, revealing their hypotheses. Or they may work left to right on a word (traditionally called "sounding out"). Or they may make connections with other words. Proficient readers tend to use these in-the-head word-solving actions to read more smoothly, more sensibly, and more accurately. They orchestrate systems of information, always searching for a "fit." Most kindergartners are only beginning to assemble these sophisticated systems, but they are reaching for them. It is especially important for kindergartners to understand that every bit of information they learn is very useful in literacy processes.

While all areas are important, some are of critical significance in your kindergarten teaching of phonics. A guiding question in the selection of lessons is: What are the essential literacy concepts children need to understand to become accomplished readers and writers by the end of kindergarten? There is little disagreement on these essential areas:

Essential Literacy Concepts Every Kindergartner Should Know

Phonological Awareness

Kindergarten children are learning to

- recognize pairs of rhyming words;
- produce rhyming words;
- identify initial consonant sounds in single-syllable words;
- identify onsets and rimes in single-syllable words;
- blend onsets and rimes to form words;
- identify separate phonemes in words.

Letters and Sounds

Kindergarten children are learning to

- recognize and name most letters;
- recognize and say the common sounds that are connected to most letters;
- write many letters to match spoken sounds;
- use their knowledge of sounds and letters to produce early approximated writing.

Reading Words

Kindergarten children are learning to

- read a small core of high-frequency words quickly and automatically;
- use letters and sounds to figure out a few simple, regularly spelled single-syllable words;
- recognize easy spelling patterns in words (we, me).

Early Reading Concepts

Kindergarten children are learning to

- use information from pictures to help them learn about the print;
- move left to right across print (within a word and across the lines of a text);
- return to the left margin to read the next line;
- match one spoken word to one word in print, as defined by space;
- notice and isolate words within a text;
- read simple one- to three-line texts using high-frequency words and letter-sound relationships to monitor their reading and solve new words;
- have high expectations of print—that it will make sense and sound like the language;
- use their own background experience to make sense of a text;
- build vocabulary by noticing new words, discussing word meaning and visual structure, and collecting the words they encounter in books.

Phonological Awareness

We communicate by putting sounds together into words, phrases, and sentences that can be understood by other speakers. Children learn oral language easily and interactively within their homes and communities. To take on written language, children must realize that the words they speak are made up of individual sounds, or *phonemes*. They also begin to realize that visible signs (letters or *graphemes*) have been created to represent these sounds. In alphabetic systems (many languages), there is a relationship (although not a perfect one) between sounds and letters. Once a child grasps this "alphabetic principle" the door is open to "cracking the code."

It's important to help kindergarten children notice and connect sounds, recognize sounds, recognize rhyme (to make connections between words), hear onsets and rimes, and hear the syllables in words. This *phonological awareness* means that children develop extra sensitivity to the sounds of language and it is the basis for the more specific development of phonemic awareness. The lessons in this book use songs, poems, and rhyming words to develop phonological awareness.

The more narrow term *phonemic awareness* involves noticing and thinking about the individual sounds in words. It includes children's understanding that words are made up of sequences of sounds, which is basic to sound-letter connections in words. Phonemic awareness involves conscious attention to sounds, sometimes isolating them, identifying them, and manipulating them. In the phoneme chart below you see forty-four phonemes. Remember that the actual sounds the speaker makes can vary by regional dialect, idiosyncratic ways of articulating words, and other factors. In English, however varied they may sound, all dialects are mutually intelligible (so they are more alike than different).

Phoneme Chart

We examine forty-four phonemes. The actual sounds in the language can vary as dialect, articulation, and other factors in speech vary. The following are common sounds for the letters listed.

Consonant Sounds

b /b/ box	k /k/ kite	s /s/ sun	ch /ch/ chair
d /d/ dog	l /l/ leaf	t /t/ top	sh /sh/ ship
f /f/ fan	m /m/ mop	v /v/ vase	wh /hw/ what
g /g/ gate	n /n/ nest	w /w/ was	th /th/ think
h /h/ house	p /p/ pail	y /y/ yell	th /TH/ the
j /j/ jug	r /r/ rose	z /z/ zoo	ng /ng/ sing
			zh /zh/ measure

Vowel Sounds

/ă/ hat	/ā/ gate	/o͞o/ moon	/û/ bird
/ĕ/ bed	/ē/ feet	/o͝o/ book	/ə/ about
/ĭ/ fish	/ī/ bike	/ou/ house	/ä/ car
/ŏ/ mop	/ō/ boat	/oy/ boy	/â/ chair
/ŭ/ nut	/ū/ mule	/ô/ tall	

Fountas & Pinnell Phonics, Spelling, and Word Study Lessons, Kindergarten

The extent of a child's phonemic awareness when he enters kindergarten is one of the best predictors of how quickly he will learn to read, because hearing the sounds makes it easier to connect to letters and letter clusters. But if children have not attended to the sounds in words, you can help them learn quickly with the lessons in this book.

Letters and Sounds

At the same time they are learning about sounds in words, children are becoming familiar with the orthographic system, or the letters. Through many experiences with the letters of the alphabet, they learn the distinctive features that make each letter different from every other letter, and they learn the names of letters, which gives them a way to talk about them with others. When a child can identify a letter by its features, he can attach a sound to it. By the middle of the year, we expect that kindergartners will be able to recognize the alphabet letters and articulate the common sounds attached to them. Their own names are a powerful source of information as they begin this learning. They learn that "my name is a word and it is always written the same way." They learn to read their names as words, notice the letters, and connect them to other words.

Sometimes, phoneme awareness instruction focuses *only* on oral activities and we do include a number of lessons that have that focus. For example, children sort pictures by the beginning sounds of objects, animals, etc. They play oral games with rhymes and they learn to break down words into single sounds through phoneme changes or deletions. But when phoneme awareness is connected to letter knowledge, it becomes phonics. Children learn how to map the sounds they hear onto the letter or letters that represent them. Phonics as an instructional approach focuses on this relationship.

In a sense, children are building two bodies of knowledge that come together as they grasp the alphabetic principle. They begin to predict letters in words by connecting them with the sounds they hear; they learn to look at a printed word and make the sound of the beginning letter. They can say words slowly and identify the letters that spell the word.

Reading Words

Through a wide range of reading and writing activities, kindergartners soon acquire a small core of words that they know "by sight." That is, they recognize them as whole entities quickly and automatically. The first word a child recognizes is probably his name, but words such as *the*, *it*, *I*, *an*, and *to* follow quickly because they are ubiquitous in the language. Kindergartners also begin to use letters and sounds to solve a few simple, regularly spelled single-syllable words and in doing so become familiar with easy spelling patterns (*cat* and *mat*, for example). What's more, they can then use beginning and ending sounds to monitor and check on their reading of longer words. As they experience print and work with words, kindergartners notice patterns. For example, they

- connect words that start alike;
- notice that some letters appear together frequently;

- ▶ notice that some words begin or end with clusters of letters;
- ▶ notice that some letters are doubled.

After they understand that patterns exist and are useful in figuring out words, children begin to search for them. Children rapidly expand their oral vocabularies in kindergarten, especially if they have many conversations with adults and hear a great deal of written language read aloud. Vocabulary acquisition is important in word learning because it is very difficult to decode a word that you do not know, have never heard, and cannot say. To solve new words efficiently, children need to know how to use the letter-sound information inherent in the high-frequency words they automatically recognize. Many kindergartners are simultaneously learning concepts, labels for the concepts (color names, number words, days of the week, for example), and the printed symbols that represent the labels. This is even truer for children whose first language is not the language of instruction. We need to recognize the complexity of this learning in order to provide support. Kindergartners who are encountering English for the first time will require a great deal of oral language experience along with their work with print. It is especially important that they continually expand their speaking and listening vocabularies.

Early Reading Concepts

Although phonemic awareness, letter-sound knowledge, and word knowledge are important, we would not want to wait until children had "mastered" this body of information before having them experience the power and joy of reading. They learn to read by reading. Through shared reading and then by reading very simple texts themselves, kindergartners learn the left-to-right directional movement that is basic to reading, as well as the return sweep to the left. They learn that there is a relationship between spoken words and the clusters of letters on a page that are defined by white space. They learn to recognize and locate words that are embedded in continuous text.

Combining the knowledge they have of language, words, letters, sounds, and the way print works, kindergartners begin to read very simple texts of one or two lines. This active processing of text enables children to simultaneously put into action all of the information they have been gathering about sounds, letters, and words and to learn more about them. They begin, as Clay (2001) has said, to "assemble working systems" for constructing meaning from print. These beginners, often called "emergent readers," have high expectations of print. They expect it to make sense, sound like language, and be enjoyable; they show these expectations by their consistent search for meaning even as they get better at decoding words. All the time, they are expanding their oral and reading vocabularies through the words they hear in read-alouds as well as through the books they explore on their own.

Where Does Phonics Instruction Fit in the Design for Literacy Learning?

Phonics instruction means explicitly teaching children about the relationships between letters and sounds; for us, it includes the nine areas previously mentioned because they are all interrelated and important in children's learning to read and write. We further distinguish between phonics instruction within the context of continuous text and phonics instruction that is out of the context of continuous text (see Figure 1). Both can be systematic; both can be explicit; both are essential. The lessons in this book provide explicit phonics instruction *out of text*; but each lesson provides many suggestions for extending the learning through explicit instruction *in text*. For example, they include specific suggestions to use in interactive read-aloud, shared reading, guided reading, modeled writing, shared writing, interactive writing, and independent reading and writing. The list below provides the framework for Phonics/Word Study out of text.

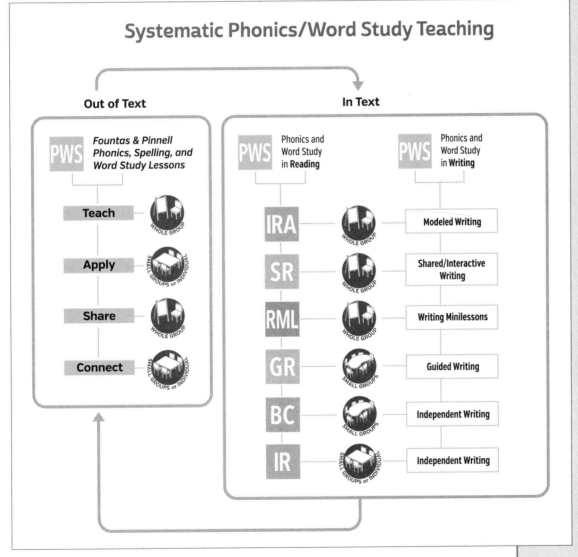

FIGURE 1 *Systematic Phonics/Word Study Teaching*

Each lesson includes:

1. **Teach** whole-class lesson based on a principle related to phonics. Each principle is listed and explained in *The Comprehensive Phonics, Spelling and Word Study Guide*; and each incorporates an element of inquiry. The inclusion of inquiry, where possible, rivets children's attention to discovering something about language; it makes the lesson enjoyable, even exciting! Children become pattern seekers and word discoverers, which we hope will be a lifelong habit.

2. **Apply** the principle through hands-on practice. Through this hands-on and often kinesthetic practice, children learn a great deal more. Each hands-on activity provides an experience in constructing their own knowledge. You may have them work in a small group at literacy centers or the whole class can engage in the activity with a partner or as individuals. Often, teachers use this application activity as part of children's independent work and it takes place while the teacher is working with small groups in guided reading lessons.

3. **Share**, as children meet briefly in a whole-class meeting, to talk about the discoveries they made. This brief sharing time gives you a chance to assess the effectiveness of your lesson, return to the principle and summarize the learning, and link to reading and writing so children know how to use what they have learned.

Your explicit phonics lessons are ideally embedded in a design for responsive literacy teaching that offers a coherent, organized combination of experiences, each of which contributes uniquely to children's literacy development.

Look carefully at the key and look along the right-side of the diagram A Design for Responsive Literacy Teaching (see inside back cover). Notice how this design also includes the teaching of systematic phonics lessons that focus directly on the specific aspects of sounds, letters, and words that are appropriate for children to learn at their grade level. The chain of blocks to the right represents these short and direct lessons, and that is what the lessons in this book are about. They offer systematic opportunities for explicit instruction out of the text. They are not embedded in other instructional contexts. But you will also notice those gray lines surrounding many of the other blocks, showing that phonics, spelling, vocabulary, and word study teaching is also embedded in many instructional contexts across the day. This phonics instruction is also explicit and offers opportunities to teach children how to apply letter-sound/word vocabulary in continuous text.

Each of these instructional contexts is explicitly related to *The Fountas & Pinnell Literacy Continuum: A Tool for Assessment, Planning, and Teaching*, Expanded Edition (2017). Here you will find Characteristics of Texts and detailed Goals (behaviors and understandings to notice, teach, and support) for each context. The phonics lessons in this book are linked to these goals in each of the nine areas. Let's move briefly through each instructional context to understand the comprehensive literacy design.

Reading Contexts in the Kindergarten Classroom

Interactive Read-Aloud In interactive read-aloud, the teacher selects and reads a fiction or nonfiction text to the group (usually in a whole-class setting); children have the opportunity to discuss the story and often to extend it through inquiry, art, science, vocabulary study, or writing about reading. By hearing stories and nonfiction texts read aloud, children learn about the structure, or syntax, of written language, which is different in many ways from oral language. It is especially important to read to kindergartners because the patterns and specialized vocabulary children encounter are the foundation for their learning to read for themselves. They build their background knowledge and a body of shared literary knowledge that will support all learning.

Many read-aloud books in the *Fountas & Pinnell Classroom™ Interactive Read-Aloud Collection, Kindergarten* (2018) have language that will delight children because of the way the writer plays with rhymes and sounds; and these help children develop an inner sense of the sounds in words—or phonological and phoneme awareness. And certainly, you can choose books from your favorites in the classroom or school library that also have this feature. You will find alphabet books, books with rhyme and alliteration, and books with onomatopoetic words.

Children enjoy hearing the language of books and poems. They enjoy repetition and rhyme; they love to chant, sing, or say poems together. Listening to poems and rhymes provides a foundation for learning about sounds, letters, and words because it invites children to explore all aspects of written language.

Interactive read-aloud is key to developing a strong oral vocabulary. When children hear texts read aloud and have the opportunity to discuss them, they take on the language of books—not only individual words but syntactic patterns. Vocabulary lessons on the meaning of words are more effective if children have heard the word used and understand something about it. As they hear and internalize words, they learn their meaning and start to be aware of the structural patterns in words.

You will notice that every phonics lesson has specific connections to the texts that you read aloud to children. You can identify these texts quickly by noticing the IRA tiles in the Connect Learning Across Contexts section of each lesson in this book.

Shared Reading Closely related to interactive read-aloud, shared reading offers strong support for children's growing awareness of the qualities of written language, including syntax, vocabulary, letters, and sounds in words. Shared reading has the additional benefit of an enlarged text that children can see. The teacher reads the books to the children, but the books are designed for repeated reading that allows the class to join in on the reading and follow the print. In this way, children have the opportunity to participate in a powerful demonstration of reading. They can see and analyze the details in the illustrations. They can attend to print. Shared reading is usually used with the whole class but may also be used in a small group.

Functioning as readers with the support of the group, children develop important early-reading behaviors, begin to recognize high-frequency words, and learn to use sounds and letters as critical and important information (see Holdaway 1987; Hundley and Powell 1999). Shared reading *leads* reading development so that children develop many strategic actions before they are expected to use them in guided or independent reading (see our book *Guided Reading: Responsive Teaching Across the Grades,* Second Edition 2017). Also, they have become familiar with many of the phonics concepts in this book, which makes lessons more effective.

Our *Fountas & Pinnell Classroom™ Shared Reading Collection, Kindergarten* (2018) includes carefully constructed original texts that offer children opportunities to try themselves out as readers. Small individual versions of each big book give children a chance to read again and again these familiar texts or listen to the audible version, each time noticing more about print. Shared reading lessons specifically draw children's attention to how to locate words in a text by connecting sounds and letters, how to connect words by features, and how to notice word parts.

Reading Minilesson Notice in A Design for Responsive Literacy Teaching (see inside back cover) that interactive read-aloud contributes directly to the four blocks below it. The reading minilesson is a brief, specific lesson on anything related to reading—genre, characters, setting, problem and solution, text organization, writer's craft, nonfiction features like graphics, and so on. The minilesson emerges from the connected text sets that children have heard, discussed, and responded to in interactive read-aloud.

The reading minilesson forms the first part of a structure: (1) minilesson; (2) independent literacy work, guided reading or book club; (3) group share. You will want to use minilessons across the year, beginning after children are accustomed to the routines of interactive read-aloud and have a repertoire of text knowledge on which to build. The first minilessons might have to do with routines for just about everything related to working together and engaging in literacy learning—from choosing and returning books to tubs to engaging in productive discussion with a partner and then with a small group. Our professional book, *The Reading Minilessons Book, Kindergarten* (2018) includes a complete set of reading minilessons for kindergarten, organized into categories such as Management, Literary Analysis, Strategies and Skills, and Writing About Reading.

Guided Reading As kindergartners participate in shared reading, they begin to notice letters and words, read left to right, and match word by word. They also learn to monitor their reading, making sure they are saying one spoken word for each written word. They learn to look at the right place as they read. When they know and can use a few high-frequency words as anchors and can use some letter and sound knowledge in shared reading, and independent reading, you will want to begin by asking them to read very easy texts in small guided reading groups. We usually recommend pulling three children together so you can observe each one carefully. (Also, you will have done an assessment for reading level, which is likely to be A or B.) But by the end of the year, many children will be reading Level D or above in instructional groups. In general, you will want to phase the children into working with little books in guided reading partway through the school year, with a goal of all children participating in guided reading by mid-year or just a little later. (This process will be slower in half-day kindergarten.)

Guided reading is small-group instruction (generally for three, four, or five children in the primary grades) in which teachers provide specific teaching for effective strategies (word solving, for example) that support comprehension. Guided reading groups consist of individuals who are alike enough that it makes sense to teach them together, which is necessary for efficiency. Because you know the reader's instructional level, you can select books that are more challenging than they can process independently and can provide the skilled teaching that enables them to read the new book with proficiency. All children read the same book, which the teacher selects from a leveled text set. A part of *The Literacy Continuum* provides text characteristics and goals for each level, A to Z. *Fountas & Pinnell Classroom*™ provides a collection of original fiction and nonfiction texts, with lessons, for kindergarten. You can also use books from many other sources (see the *Fountas & Pinnell Leveled Books Website*, www.fandpleveledbooks.com).

The structure of guided reading is: (1) book selection by teacher; (2) book introduction; (3) book reading by individual children; (4) book discussion; (5) teaching point by the teacher; and (6) letter/word work. While children are reading individually (softly to themselves in kindergarten), you may sample some oral reading and interact briefly. Sometimes, children may extend their responses to the book through writing or art.

As you work with children, you have many opportunities to look for effective reading behaviors (including but not limited to, the application of phonics principles). You can help them apply the principles you are teaching them in this book.

Book Club [Small-Group Instruction] Even kindergarten children can learn to participate with others in discussions of books, and they do so enthusiastically! But, like other instructional settings, having a good book club requires teaching and practice. *The Reading Minilessons Book, Kindergarten* includes lessons in the conventions of choosing books and turn taking, as well as listening to and looking at others. Also, there are minilessons on what you can talk about, on preparing for the discussion, and for self-assessment afterwards. After children are comfortable with the routines of interactive read-aloud, can work independently and can choose books, you can begin some book clubs, which at first will be quite short.

An effective book club might use this structure: (1) the teacher selects four books; (2) children choose the book they want to talk about; (3) children read and prepare for the book club; (4) children meet and talk about the book; (5) children self-assess how the book club went. Each child holds and refers to a copy of the book. The teacher guides and supports the group by supporting the process and encouraging them to engage in a line of discussion.

Books for book club are selected by the teacher for their potential to engage children and for appropriateness to the age group—NOT by level. In fact, these books are not leveled. Children choose (from the limited set), and they can either read it themselves or listen to an audio recording. Book clubs enable you to work with a small group of diverse children to help them learn how to think and talk about age-appropriate, grade-appropriate books regardless of their reading level.

Our book club collection includes texts that are organized in groups of four, most of which are related to the text sets in Interactive Read-Aloud. For each title, the teacher has a Book Club card to support the process.

Group Share (Reading) For the reading, writing, and word study elements shown in A Design for Responsive Literacy Teaching (see inside back cover), it is useful to engage in a short group share to bring closure to the instructional period. For each, you will want to return to the minilesson principle to extend the learning and add to an anchor chart or as a reminder to children. You invite children to share something they noticed or discovered in the book they are reading, in their writing, or in the word study application. The group share for word study might be held immediately afterwards if children participated in the application activity as a whole group. Group share for reading comes at the end of guided reading or independent reading; for writing, it comes at the end of independent writing.

Group share takes only two or three minutes. Not every child needs to share something every day. Also, you can have them share with a partner or in threes. Children can also self-assess how the period of time went.

Independent Reading and Conferring Independent reading involves children reading individually and independently reading books of their choice. Of course, children in kindergarten may read (or reread) several short books. But as they grow in reading ability, you want them to choose books for themselves and, sometimes, to respond to these books with drawing or writing. They may even keep a list of books that they have read, although you wouldn't want to do this before they can write titles quickly. Around the middle of the year, you may want to introduce the concept of reader's notebook and teach children to record aspects of their reading.

The books for the classroom library and student choice should be chosen for appeal and accessibility to kindergarten children. These books should accommodate a range of readers, from very early beginners to more advanced. Independent reading helps children build a repertoire of high-frequency words that they can recognize quickly and without effort, reserving more attention for challenging solving of new words.

You can confer with readers while the other children are engaged either in independent reading, in writing or drawing about reading, or in other independent literacy activities. Conferring is your chance to do some quick individual teaching and also to gather some valuable assessment data.

Reading conferences consist of the teacher and child sitting side by side at a desk or table and having a meaningful conversation about the child's book or her reader's notebook. In the *Fountas & Pinnell Classroom™ Independent Reading Collection*, we have provided one short "conferring card" for each book that will give you ideas for engaging the child in discussion even if you are not completely familiar with the book. In addition, we have included some generic conferring cards that you can use with any title to focus on literary elements, genre, or other area.

You may want to listen to a little oral reading to see how it is going and whether the child has chosen an appropriate text, but it is not always necessary to do this. You are really using the time to gather information about the child's thinking regarding his reading and also to do some quick teaching if the opportunity arises. You may reinforce the reading minilesson by helping the child apply it to this book (for example, animal characters that act like people). You may reinforce the phonics lesson by pointing out an example. Often, you will find out something that you can invite the child to say in group share.

Writing Contexts in the Kindergarten Classroom

Modeled Writing In modeled writing, the teacher demonstrates the process of writing for a variety of purposes and audiences. Children learn how a writer gets ideas down on paper and makes decisions.

Shared/Interactive Writing In shared and interactive writing, the teacher is able to demonstrate the writing process, from thinking of what to write to writing it word by word to rereading it. In shared writing, a group of children participate in composing a common text; together, the teacher and children develop a meaningful text, and then, with input from the children, the teacher writes the text on a chart, which is reread many times. Often, children contribute illustrations. This cooperatively constructed text becomes a classroom resource. Children can use it for independent reading or as a reference for their own writing. The writing can take many forms—"news of the day," a note or letter, response to a book from interactive read-aloud, a science, social studies, or math project. Shared/interactive writing is often used in reading minilessons, as a response in interactive read-aloud, guided reading, and shared reading.

Interactive writing is identical to shared writing and has all the same benefits, with one difference. At points in the construction of the text, the teacher may invite an individual child to come up and "share the pen." So, the teacher writes some of the print (usually words that children know very well or words that are too difficult for them at this time); the children write some words or parts of words. These "share the pen" occasions have high instructional value. (For a detailed description of shared and interactive writing, see McCarrier, Pinnell, and Fountas 2000.)

Shared and interactive writing are especially powerful tools in kindergarten because they expose the writing process in a very explicit way. They also give children the opportunity to put their knowledge of sounds, letters, and words into action for a real purpose. They say words slowly and make connections to sounds and letters. They learn to write word endings and phonogram patterns quickly. They use the high-frequency words they have just learned. And, they learn to reread their writing. Interactive writing is used often in this book under Connect Learning Across Contexts.

Writing Minilesson The writing minilesson is a short lesson on some aspect of writing—craft, conventions, or process. The writing minilesson forms the first part of a structure that is similar to the reading minilesson: (1) minilesson; (2) independent writing with conferring or guided writing; (3) group share. The writing minilesson gives you the opportunity to demonstrate principles related to the conventions and craft of writing. The first minilessons may involve management, showing children procedures for using the paper and other writing materials, for example. For kindergartners, writing minilessons will focus on simple topics, such as how to choose a topic for drawing or writing, how to tell stories, where to start writing on a page, how to say words slowly, how to use spaces, how to create illustrations that match your story, or how to write words to tell about your illustrations. Children then apply the principle to their own pieces of writing and they tell about it in group share.

Independent Writing and Writing Conferences In independent writing, children work individually on their own pieces of writing, usually on a topic of their choice. Writing helps children build a repertoire of high-frequency words they can write quickly. They also get a great deal of practice saying words slowly and thinking about how they are spelling. In fact, everything you teach in these phonics lessons will be applied as children write for their own purposes. Remember that many other contexts provide for writing about reading and offer models, which influence independent writing.

When children are drawing and writing independently, you can take the opportunity to hold short conferences with individual children. Writing conferences involve the teacher and child sitting side by side at a desk or table with the child's current work in progress and writing folder in front of them. The conference can focus on anything related to writing—conventions like spacing, craft such as using sound words and illustrations, or the process of writing. Most kindergartners will write expressive pieces and illustrate them and that will be completion. Often they make books about their experiences or topics that interest them. (They may choose some pieces to put into a writing folder.) But, towards the end of the year, they may want to improve a draft and copy it over. Or, they may want to display it (which in our view is the kindergarten way of publishing). This may require reconsideration of a piece. The writing conference helps you know where the child is in writing and this will give you information about what he knows about letters, sounds, and words as well as his ability to compose language.

Guided Writing Sometimes, during independent writing time, you may choose to bring together a small group of children, all of whom need to learn something in common about writing. It could be anything to do with writing—conventions, craft, or process. This grouping has nothing to do with reading level. It emerges from your observations of children as writers. The children are all working on their own pieces of independent drawing and writing, but they can apply your short lesson to what they are doing. This is an efficient way to support several writers. Sometimes, it might be saying words slowly to predict the letters or reminding children to use word parts they know, so it may be directly linked to what the children are learning about letters or words in *Phonics Lessons*.

Group Share (Writing) At the end of a writing period, it is useful to engage in a short group share to bring closure to the instructional period. Group share takes only two or three minutes. Children can talk about something they learned about writing today, or they can share part of what they wrote. You can take the opportunity to reinforce the writing minilesson. Children can also self-assess how the period of time went.

Independent Literacy Work

Independent work takes place *while* you are working with small groups in guided reading or guided writing or conferring with individual children. It is necessary for children to be engaged in productive and purposeful independent work for a part of the day. This gives you a chance to zoom in more closely in your instruction than you can while working with the whole group. In addition, it builds self-management and self-determination as children begin to realize that they can make choices and be responsible for their own behavior. Each of these independent settings, however, takes careful organization and teaching.

Here, children engage in self-directed work related to literacy. They may be assigned to a list of activities or have a limited choice. Some examples of productive literacy activities are

- independent reading from "browsing boxes" or "individual book boxes or bags" filled with little books that are very easy for children because they have been read in shared or guided reading;

- listening to audio recordings of books while looking at them;

- writing and drawing about books they have heard or read or content they are learning;

- painting or collage in an art center (often in response to a book from interactive read-aloud);

- reading books from the classroom library;

- building and rereading familiar poems in pocket charts;

- rereading a big book with a partner;

- gluing a familiar poem in a personal poetry book, rereading it, and illustrating it;

- working on a word study application related to the current phonics lesson.

All of the activities listed above are on the "quieter" side. But at another time in the day you will want to have other important center choices like dramatic play, blocks, water and sand that are essentials of an early childhood classroom.

In *Guided Reading,* you will find detailed descriptions of a "simple" system for independent work and for the use of "centers" to support managed independent learning. We have seen both work extremely well. We have also provided procedural minilessons in *The Reading Minilessons Book, Kindergarten,* as well as for writing about reading.

What Are Some Effective Ways to Manage Independent Literacy Work?

The first priority is to find an effective way for you and your children to work together. Too much time can be lost when you have to constantly direct traffic, and you want to teach for independent, self-directed behavior. Below we describe two "systems," one simple (or "beginning") and one more complex. For detailed descriptions of classroom organization and management see *Guided Reading*.

A Simple System For application activities and other independent work, you may engage children in the same four or five activities every day. Of course, there is change for the child because the books change and they draw and write on different topics. As mentioned before, you may want to engage children in working as partners to try out the application activity, but you may also have them do it as independent activity (after they have overlearned the routine and know exactly what to do). A simple list with pictures will remind them of four things they need to do during the thirty to sixty minutes of independent work time. (You'll start the year with shorter periods of time that you actively support.) Independent work could be, for example:

1. **Read a book.** Children have their own choice books from the classroom library, or they read from a tub of books that have been read before in guided or shared reading.

2. **Listen to a book.** It's quick and easy to record a book on a device, and children can listen to it play softly while they look at the book.

3. **Work on words.** Here children can engage in the application activity for today's phonics lesson or one that they have participated in recently.

4. **Work on drawing and writing.** Kindergarten children love to draw, talk about their drawings, and to begin to write about them. They also like to make books.

Putting this system into practice requires organized supplies and teaching of routines. *The Reading Minilessons Book, Kindergarten* provides 150 minilessons, many of which are "management" in that they show how to teach young children routines for how to work independently. In addition, each phonics lesson in this book has a section advising on how to teach children the Apply activity.

Using Centers A center is a physical space organized for specific learning purposes. You can have "permanent" centers such as the classroom library, an art table, a letter/word center, etc. You can also have "temporary" centers related to what children are studying, for example, a science center with growing plants. The temporary centers may focus on a class project. A center has comfortable working space for four or five children, and it contains all the materials they need to work there.

Children can do all of the activities in the "simple" system at a center location. In addition, you may add centers focused on

- drawing and painting,
- poetry,
- listening, and
- writing.

If you can teach children to use centers—even a few—they will learn something valuable about self-regulation that will serve them well in school and other settings. Below are some suggestions for using centers effectively.

- Clearly organize supplies so that only one kind of material is in a single container.
- Label supplies with both words and pictures.
- Using words and pictures, label the place on the shelf where the container is stored. Have all supplies that children will need for a given activity organized and available.
- Teach children routines for getting and returning materials.
- Establish and explicitly teach the routines that will be needed for a learning activity. Post simple directions in the center using both words and pictures.
- Limit the number of routines children are expected to follow—a few essential activities can be varied to explore different principles (for example, sorting).
- Stick to a consistent schedule.
- Introduce only one new application activity each day—typically, children will engage in one activity related to a principle over a period of one to five days.
- Place needed resources (such as charts or a word wall) on the wall near the center so that they will be available.
- "Walk through" the activity so that you can accurately estimate the time it will take.
- Allocate an appropriate amount of time for selected activities and teach children the routines so that they can perform them at a good rate.
- Teach children to speak softly while working independently, and model this behavior by speaking softly yourself.
- Have regular meetings with children to self-evaluate the productivity of work in the word study center.

FIGURE 2 *Reading Time Activities*

Designing an Environment to Support Letter, Sound, and Word Learning

You can make your teaching more efficient and effective by making sure you have a rich array of tools available. That includes the materials children need to work independently as well as displays that serve as resources. It pays to think analytically about materials and tools and to organize them for maximum student independence. With good organization and careful teaching of routines, kindergarten children can learn to get, use, and put away supplies such as crayons, pencils, markers, scissors, and glue. They can select books and return them to the appropriate bins. They can use resources such as shared poetry charts, big books, the classroom library, and individual book boxes. Many routines are described in these lessons. You can also find detailed descriptions of classroom organization and suggestions for classroom management in *Literacy Beginnings: A Prekindergarten Handbook* (2011) and *Guided Reading*. Below are some suggestions.

A Meeting Area

You will want to establish a meeting area for whole-class teaching. It should be a clearly defined space that is large enough for children to sit comfortably in a circle or in rows without touching each other. All children should be able to see and hear when you read aloud or engage them in shared reading. If possible, have a carpet for children to sit or use carpet squares that they can stack and retrieve.

In the meeting area you will need an easel with chart paper, a whiteboard (preferably magnetic so that you can demonstrate using magnetic letters), and references like a name chart, poetry charts, and the Alphabet Linking Chart. You will also need a pocket chart on which you can post letters or words on cards large enough for the whole group to see. Shared reading books should be handy, as well as the books you are planning to read aloud for a week or two-week period. Here you can also store any phonics lessons charts that you have made with the children.

A Print-Rich Environment

A classroom that is alive with print is a rich resource for teaching and learning. Of course, you want your classroom to look beautiful and inviting, with bright colors, but you can also be aware that everything you put on your walls can be a teaching tool or a resource for children. You will want

- alphabet charts of several kinds;
- charts of poems and songs, with illustrations;
- labels and directions for using materials at various centers, such as poetry and listening;
- the class schedule of the day;
- a list of "Books We Have Shared";
- word charts of various kinds (phonograms, words sorted by letter);

- a class name chart;
- stories, messages, lists, letters, records of science experiments, and other written materials produced through shared and interactive writing;
- helpers', or workers', charts for the classroom "jobs";
- a word wall;
- word study charts with principles;
- a rack of personal poetry books where each child's book can be kept and displayed;
- pocket charts with stories and poems on sentence strips;
- whiteboards to which magnetic letters and magnetic word cards will stick
- the classroom library with a variety of tubs labeled with categories.

It is not necessary to spend money on commercially produced posters or other decorative elements. Nor should you be working every night to preprint and decorate charts. The best resources are those you and the children make together. And almost everything on the list above can be an "in process" document. Elsewhere we have said:

> Teachers don't preplan and make attractive charts to decorate the room; our word walls and charts are *working documents* created by the teacher and children together. While the general plan and the principles repeat year after year {in *Phonics Lessons*}, the charts reflect the unique thinking of any one group of children; the examples they discover, the order in which they produce them, the way they organize them…When we recognize our word walls and charts as working documents that change and develop over time, we realize that they are also a living record of the teaching and learning that has taken place in our classroom program.
>
> —Fountas and Pinnell (1998, 52-53)

Books add to the quality of the environment. For example, big books with colorful and interesting colors can be displayed face out on a rack. The classroom library can have colorful tubs and books with covers facing out. Shared poetry charts can be posted on the wall or easel (or hung on a rack). Children can have personal book boxes, or you can place books in colorful "browsing boxes."

Three Vital Print Resources for the Classroom

Below are a few print resources that we think are very important and are referred to in the phonics lessons.

Name Chart One of the first charts you will want to make is the name chart, which displays the first names of every child in the class. (Most teachers have more than one name chart. You can print this ahead of time and complete it by placing a small picture of each child at the appropriate name. This will enable you to start by having children match their names to the names on the preprinted chart.)

You can give each child a card with his name. The print should be large enough to be seen by everyone in the meeting area. Children can place their names in a pocket chart to create their first name chart. Children will enjoy reading the name chart together so that they learn not only to recognize their own names but those of everyone in the class. You can also play a number of games with the chart.

▶ *Clap when we come to your name.*

▶ *I'm thinking of someone whose name starts with (ends with) D.*

▶ *Find a name on the chart that has a letter like your name.*

You will find the name chart to be a very valuable reference during phonics lessons. For example, children can be an "authority" on the first letter of their names. You can quickly find words that have similar patterns or first letters as the words you are using in the lessons.

Alphabet Linking Charts An alphabet linking chart is a poster that is large enough for children to see in the meeting area. On the poster, you will see each letter of the alphabet, the uppercase and lowercase forms, a picture that shows a key word for each letter, and the label attached to the picture.

You can purchase good alphabet linking charts to post in the meeting area, and this is useful because you can also duplicate these in small form so that every child can have one to use. But it is also a good idea to create one with the children, starting with a blank chart and building it with the children (gluing on and coloring the picture cards as letters are introduced).

FIGURE 3 *Alphabet Linking Chart*

Fountas & Pinnell Phonics, Spelling, and Word Study Lessons, Kindergarten

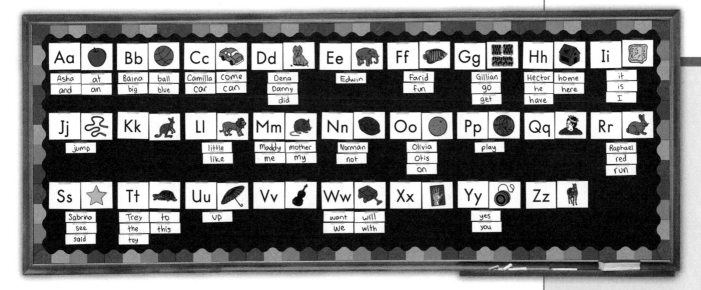

FIGURE 4 *A Word Wall in a Kindergarten Classroom*

Word Wall You can use any large clear space to create a word wall—a section of chalkboard, a wall section, a large piece of heavy cardboard. Just be sure that the word wall can be viewed from any place in the classroom. The purpose of the word wall is to create a reference tool that children can use during independent reading and writing time. You can also refer to it during interactive read-aloud, small-group guided reading, and phonics lessons.

The word wall is divided into squares, with an alphabet letter in each square (Aa, Bb, etc.). Words are added to the wall, a few at a time, under the appropriate letter. In kindergarten, you can put children's names on the word wall, along with color words and number words as you teach them in lessons. You can also place on the wall some high-frequency words as you teach them in lessons. (Use words like *I, a, an, and, at, but, come, can, for, get, go, have, in, is, it, look, make, me, my, no, not, or, play, said, see, she, he, the, then, they, this, to, up, we, went, with, you*.) As you work with phonograms, you will be making lists, but you can put one example of each pattern on the word wall.

We have described a comprehensive approach to authentic literacy learning. In this design, children spend their time thinking about books, reading books, talking about books, writing about books and learning how letters and words work. It is important to engage every child in learning successfully. Next we provide some general suggestions for working effectively with children who are building a literacy system in English as a new language.

What Are Some Ways of Working Effectively with English Language Learners?

You are likely to have many children in your class who not only can speak one language but are learning a second or even a third language. And that is a great thing. If English is an additional language, then it will be important that you understand and value the child's expansion of both home and school language. Usually, it takes several years for young children to learn English as a second language and to read, write, and think consistently in their new language.

You will want to adjust your teaching to make sure that English language learners have access to your teaching about sounds, letters, and words. Often, these adjustments are minor and easy to implement, but they are necessary to promote essential understandings on the part of these learners. In addition, many of these adjustments will help all of the children in your classroom because they help to make instruction more explicit and clear. But we should make it clear that meeting the needs of English language learners doesn't simply mean "teaching more." It means teaching (and even thinking) in a different way about your teaching. Put yourself in the position of someone who is learning another language. What could be confusing about concepts and directions? What should be demonstrated instead of simply "told"?

For each lesson in this book, look for a section on the first page labeled Working with English Language Learners. In this section, you will see one or two suggestions specifically related to the implementation of that lesson. On the following pages, we have placed some general suggestions for oral language, for reading, for writing, and for phonics and word study. It is obvious that these four areas overlap and are interconnected. Work in one area will tend to support learning in all other areas as well.

Oral Language

▶ Show children what you mean when you give directions. You may need to act out certain sequences of action and have children do it while you coach them. Have them repeat directions to each other or say them aloud as they engage in the activity. Support them during their first attempts rather than expecting independence immediately.

▶ Give English language learners more "wait and think" time. You could say, "Let's think about that for a minute" before calling for an answer. Demonstrate to children how you think about what you are going to say.

▶ Paraphrase and summarize for children. Repeat the directions or instructions several different ways, watching for feedback that they understand you. Paraphrase until you can see that they understand.

▶ Use pictures and objects that children understand and that connect to their homes and neighborhoods. At the same time, avoid examples that may be completely strange to children and to which they have difficulty bringing meaning.

▶ Use short, simple sentences in shared reading, interactive writing, and oral conversations. Avoid complex, embedded sentences that children will find hard to follow if they are just learning English. When a complex sentence is used (for example, in read-aloud or shared reading), watch for evidence of confusion on the part of children, and paraphrase with simpler sentences when necessary.

▶ Bring children's familiar world into the classroom through family photos, holiday souvenirs, and objects from home. Expand children's world by bringing in other objects that will give them new experiences.

Fountas & Pinnell Phonics, Spelling, and Word Study Lessons, Kindergarten

- Demonstrate using language structures while talking about familiar topics. Provide oral sentence frames when needed. Involve children in games that require repeating these simple language structures, for example: "My name is _____." "_____ has two brothers." "I like to eat _____." "Josiah likes to _____ (verb)."

- Make instruction highly interactive, with a great deal of oral language surrounding everything children are learning.

- Expand the activities using children's names. Be sure that you are pronouncing all children's names correctly and clearly as you draw their attention to the particular word that is a child's name. Help children learn the names of other children in the class by using them in sentences and placing them on charts.

- Engage English language learners in repeating and enjoying songs, rhymes, and repetitive chants. Incorporate body movements to enhance children's enjoyment of songs, rhymes, and chants and help them remember and understand the language better.

Reading

- Provide an extensive collection of simple alphabet books so that children can encounter the same letters in the same sequence, with picture examples in different texts.

- Read aloud often to children; in general, it is wise to increase the amount of time that you read aloud and discuss books with children. Be sure that the material you are reading to children is comprehensible, that is, within their power to understand with your support.

- Stick to simple and understandable texts when you read aloud to children. Watch for signs of enjoyment and reread favorites. Rereading books to children will help them acquire and make use of language that goes beyond their current understandings.

- Be sure that children's own cultures are reflected in the material that you read aloud to them and that they read for themselves. They should see illustrations with people like themselves in books. They should see their own cultures reflected in food, celebrations, dress, holidays, everyday events, and so on.

- Understand that shared reading involves children in a great deal of repetition of language, often language that is different from or more complex than they can currently use in speech. This experience gives children a chance to practice language, learn the meaning of the words, and use the sentence structure of English.

- Use a shared reading text over and over, inserting different names or different words to vary it. Rhythmic and repetitive texts are beneficial to English language learners. This repetition will give children maximum experience with the syntax of English and will help them to develop an implicit understanding of noun-verb agreement, plurals, and other concepts. Once a text is well known in shared reading, it can serve as a resource to children. Revisit shared reading texts for examples of language structure and for specific words and their meaning.

▶ As soon as English language learners can join in easily in shared reading, know some high-frequency words, and independently read shared reading texts with high accuracy, consider including them in guided reading groups. Guided reading is a very valuable context for working with English language learners because you can scaffold their reading and their language through an introduction that clears up confusion and you can observe them closely to gain information as to the accuracy and ease of their reading. Through observation and discussion, you can find what is confusing to them and respond to their questions.

▶ Be sure to use oral language, pictures, concrete objects, and demonstration when you introduce stories to help children untangle any tricky vocabulary or concepts they are reading in texts for themselves in guided and independent reading. They may encounter words that they can "read" (which really means decode) but do not understand.

▶ Help them in guided reading to relate new words to words they already know. During and after reading, check with children to be sure they understand vocabulary and concepts; build into lessons a time when they can bring up any words they did not know.

▶ Include word work on a regular basis in the guided reading lessons for English language learners. Make strong connections to what they have been learning in phonics.

Writing

▶ Value and encourage children's drawing, as it represents thinking and connects their ideas to early writing.

▶ Have children repeat several times the sentence they are going to write so that they will be able to remember it. If the sentence is difficult for children to remember, that may be a sign that it is too complex for their present level of language knowledge; consider simplifying the structure or rephrasing the sentence so that it is easier for children.

▶ Focus on familiar topics and everyday experiences in interactive writing so that children can generate meaningful sentences and longer texts. Reread the piece of interactive writing many times, encouraging fluency as children gain control over the language.

▶ Guide children to produce some repetitive texts that use the same sentence structure and phrases over and over again, so that children can internalize them.

▶ Know that once a text has been successfully produced in interactive writing and children can easily read it, this text is a resource for talking about language—locating specific words, noticing beginning sounds and ending sounds, noticing rhymes, and so on.

- Encourage English language learners to write for themselves. Demonstrate how to think of something to write, and repeat it so that you remember it. Demonstrate how to say words slowly, providing more individual help and demonstration if needed.

- Surround children's independent writing with a great deal of oral language. Talk with them and help them put their ideas into words before they write. Encourage them to tell their stories and share their writing with others and extend their meanings through talk.

- Provide a great many models of writing for English language learners—interactive writing, shared reading, charts about people in the room or their experiences. Encourage children to reread and revisit these models to help them in their writing. In the beginning, they may use phrases or sentences from charts around the room, varying their own sentences slightly. Gradually, they will go beyond these resources, but models will be a helpful support for a time.

- Learn something about the sound system of the children's first language. That knowledge will give you valuable insights into the way they "invent" or "approximate" their first spellings. For example, notice whether they are using letter-sound associations from the first language or whether they are actually thinking of a word in the first language and attempting to spell it.

- Accept spellings that reflect the child's own pronunciation of words, even if it varies from standard pronunciation. Notice the strengths in the child's attempts to relate letters and sounds. Show that you value attempts rather than correcting everything the child writes.

Phonics and Word Study

- Use many hands-on activities so that children have the chance to manipulate magnetic letters and tiles, move pictures around, and work with word cards and name cards.

- Be sure that the print for all charts (ABC charts, name charts, shared writing, picture and word charts, etc.) is clear and consistent so that children who are working in another language do not have to deal with varying forms of letters.

- Make sure that English language learners are not sitting in an area that is peripheral to the instruction (for example, in the back or to the side). It is especially important for these learners to be able to see and hear all instruction clearly.

- Provide a "rehearsal" by working with your English language learners in a small group before you provide the lesson to the entire group. Sometimes they may find it more difficult than other children to come up with words as examples; however, only a few minutes (for example, thinking of *s* words) will help these learners come up with responses in whole-group settings. It will not hurt them to think about the concepts twice, because that will provide greater support.

- Use real objects to represent pictures and build concepts in children's minds. For example, bring in a real lemon that children can touch and smell rather than just a picture of a lemon. When it is not possible to use real objects to build concepts, use clear pictures that will have meaning for children. Picture support should be included whenever possible.

- Be sure to enunciate clearly yourself and accept children's approximations. If they are feeling their own mouths say (or approximate) the sounds, they will be able to make the connections. Sounds and letters are abstract concepts, and the relationships are arbitrary. It will be especially complex for children whose sound systems do not exactly match that of English. They may have trouble saying the sounds that are related to letters and letter clusters.

- Accept alternative pronunciations of words with the hard-to-say sounds and present the written form to help learners distinguish between them. Over time, you will notice movement toward more standard English pronunciation. Minimal pairs (sounds that are like each other, have similar tongue positions, and are easily confused, such as /s/ and /sh/, /r/ and /l/, /sh/ and /ch/, /f/ and /v/) are often quite difficult for English language learners to differentiate. English language learners often have difficulty with inflected endings (-s, -ed).

Fountas & Pinnell Phonics, Spelling, and Word Study Lessons, Kindergarten

- Speak clearly and slowly when working with children on distinguishing phonemes and hearing sounds in words, but do not distort the word so much that it is unrecognizable. Distortion may confuse English language learners in that it may sound like another word that they do not know.

- Use the pocket chart often so that children have the experience of working with pictures and words in a hands-on way. They can match pictures with words so that the meaning of words becomes clearer.

- Work with a small group of English language learners to help them in the application activity and make your instruction more explicit. Notice concepts that they find particularly difficult and make note to revisit them during word work.

Children work with magnetic letters in a kindergarten classroom.

Using the *Fountas & Pinnell Phonics, Spelling, and Word Study System* in the Kindergarten Classroom

Materials and Resources in the System

The *Fountas & Pinnell Phonics, Spelling, and Word Study System* includes a range of materials and resources designed to help you plan and implement effective literacy instruction. At the core of the system are the one hundred lessons found in *Phonics Lessons*. The lessons are organized in the nine areas of learning for phonics, spelling, and word study. Each lesson is constructed on one principle detailed in *The Comprehensive Phonics, Spelling, and Word Study Guide*, which is also included in the system. Additionally, *Student Sets* are available for purchase on the Heinemann website. These pre-assembled resources can help you avoid cutting and assembling picture and word cards as you tailor a lesson to a particular group of students, extend an activity, or create a new lesson based on a generative lesson in *Phonics Lessons*. Additional ideas for enriching and extending phonics content can be found in *Sing a Song of Poetry, Kindergarten*, Revised Edition, an entire volume of poems, songs, and rhymes with teaching suggestions. A number of organizational ideas outlined in the next few pages of this book (such as the Master Lesson Guide and the Nine Areas of Learning Across the Year) can be implemented in a variety of ways using the labeled folders and dividers provided with the system.

Fountas & Pinnell Phonics, Spelling, and Word Study Lessons, Kindergarten, containing 100 brief lessons for whole-group instruction that help children attend to, learn about, and efficiently use sounds, letters, and words.

Fountas & Pinnell Phonics, Spelling, and Word Study Ready Resources

Online Resources

Sing a Song of Poetry: A Teaching Resource for Phonemic Awareness, Phonics, and Fluency, Kindergarten, Revised Edition

The Fountas & Pinnell Comprehensive Phonics, Spelling, and Word Study Guide

Lesson Folders

An Annotated Lesson and Its Features

Over the next several pages you will learn more about how to use an array of features of a lesson.

What do your children already know, and what do they need to learn next? Your insights about your own children will guide your choice of lessons and help you plan instruction that targets your children's learning needs.

Each lesson title reflects the content of the lesson using precise language taken from *The Fountas & Pinnell Comprehensive Phonics, Spelling, and Word Study Guide.*

Hear, Say, and Clap Syllables

PHONOLOGICAL AWARENESS 8

EARLY MIDDLE LATE

Plan

▶ **Consider Your Children**

If clapping syllables is new to children, begin with one- and two-syllable words only. Clapping syllables will be a new concept for many of the children early in the year. This technique will be very useful as they learn to take words apart, but it may take some practice to coordinate saying and clapping the words. Be sure that they can listen to you say the word and then repeat it after you. The contrast of words with one part and two parts will help them understand the concept you are demonstrating.

▶ **Working with English Language Learners**

Be sure to use English words the children can understand or learn easily from the pictures. Articulate the words slowly and carefully, and provide many opportunities for children to repeat the words and clap them. Invite children to say and clap their first and last names as well as some words in their own languages. For example, *cat* is *gato* in Spanish, and *gato* could be placed in the two-syllable column.

Typically, it takes several years for young children to learn English as a second language and to learn to read, write, and think consistently in their new language. As you adjust the lesson for English language learners, your instruction becomes clearer and more explicit in ways that help all of your children.

YOU WILL NEED

PWS Ready Resources
▶ PA 8 Pocket-Chart Picture Cards

Online Resources
▶ PA 8 Action Tags
▶ PA 8 Picture Cards
▶ PA 8 Two-Way Sorts

Other Materials
▶ pocket chart
▶ glue sticks

Generative Lesson ✓
A generative lesson has a simple structure that you can use to present similar content or concepts. You can use this lesson structure to teach children to hear, say, and clap words with a different number of syllables.

All materials needed for the Teach, Apply, and Assess sections of the lesson are listed. Lesson-specific materials are provided as reproducibles in Online Resources. If children are rotating through a center, you need only enough materials for one small group to work with at a time. If they are working individually, as partners, or in simultaneous small groups, you will need additional copies.

Generative lessons provide a recurring structure you can use with similar items with a knowledge set. As children acquire knowledge, they build systems for similar learning that accelerate the learning.

We help you understand the language principle underlying each lesson so you can teach with clarity and a well-defined purpose.

UNDERSTAND THE PRINCIPLE

Hearing the syllables in words helps children learn how to break words into parts that can be represented with letters and letter clusters. It also helps children learn how to match their oral language to the written language as they begin to read.

EXPLAIN THE PRINCIPLE

Words can have one or more parts.

Listen for, say, and clap the parts in a word.

Comprehensive Phonics, Spelling, and Word Study Guide

Refer to: page **19**, row **6**

Each lesson highlights a key principle from *The Comprehensive Phonics, Spelling, and Word Study Guide.*

Concise, clear language "rings inside children's heads." Avoid jargon and technical labels; use a common language that enables you to reach your readers and writers simply and easily. Sometimes you will show children examples and invite them to think of the principle; other times, you will state the principle, give a few examples, and invite the children to add examples.

Easy-to-use organization (referenced to Nine Areas of Learning Across the Year as well as the Master Lesson Guide) shows the area of learning, the lesson number within the area, and the approximate time of year to teach the lesson. This information helps you find and select appropriate lessons for your children.

8 PHONOLOGICAL AWARENESS

EARLY MIDDLE LATE

ACTIVITY: PICTURE SORT

INSTRUCTIONAL PROCEDURE

SAY AND SORT

See page 36 for detailed descriptions of Instructional Procedures.

Each Teach activity is based on a specific activity that can be used with a larger group of children.

EXPLAIN THE PRINCIPLE

Words can have one or more parts.

Listen for, say, and clap the parts in a word.

Comprehensive Phonics, Spelling, and Word Study Guide

Refer to: page **19**, row **6**

We repeat the principle in language suitable for children that you may refer to during your teaching.

We take you through the lesson step by step, suggesting effective language you might use. Sometimes, the lesson is oral only, without written examples. Make frequent use of the pocket chart to hold pictures, letters, and words (or use chart paper on an easel). Occasionally, you may write the principle on the chart before the lesson and generate examples with children during the lesson, but in kindergarten this is done infrequently as the concepts are simple and best stated verbally.

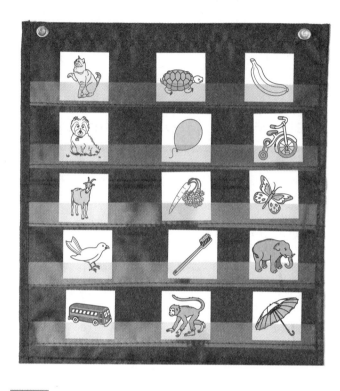

Teach

1. Tell the children they are going to clap the parts of words.

2. Begin by showing the picture representing the first one-syllable word. Ask children to say and clap the word. *When you say words, you can clap the parts you hear.* Demonstrate with *cat. How many parts do you hear in* cat? *You hear one part and you clap once.*

3. Say and clap the rest of the one-syllable words.

4. *Some words have two parts that you can hear.* Demonstrate with *turtle. You hear two syllables and you clap two times.*

5. Continue through the rest of the two- and three-syllable words.

6. Saying and clapping the words may be enough for one lesson. If you feel the children can continue, move to the next part of the lesson.

7. Display a pocket chart with three columns.

8. Go through the pictures again. This time, have children tell you where to place the picture under 1, 2, or 3, according to the number of syllables. Say and clap words as many times as needed for children to hear the syllables.

Modify the steps for implementing the lesson to fit your own group of children. Much will depend on your children's experience and how well you have taught routines.

In many lessons, a gray dot (•) indicates an opportunity to pause for children's responses.

In each Apply section, we provide a photo showing an example of the product or process children will engage in as they practice and apply what they've learned.

Each Apply activity is based on a specific activity that is sometimes the same as—but sometimes different from—the Teach activity.

Each Teach activity and each Apply activity are built around one of ten instructional procedures to develop children's knowledge of words and how they work.

Children work independently (individually, with partners, in small groups) to apply and practice what they've learned in the lesson.

PHONOLOGICAL AWARENESS 8

EARLY MIDDLE LATE

ACTIVITY: PICTURE SORT

INSTRUCTIONAL PROCEDURE

SAY AND SORT

See page 36 for detailed descriptions of Instructional Procedures.

ACTION TAGS

say

sort

glue

read

The lesson routines are identified in concise words on tags that you can post in the word study center to remind children of what to do. If you are not using centers, you can post the tags where everyone can refer to them as they work. Tags help your children become independent learners.

Apply

Have the children use two-way sorts to say and sort pictures representing two- and three-syllable words. Alternatively, give them two-column sorts and pictures to say, sort, and glue. They should read their final lists to a partner.

Share

As a review, have children choose a word of their own and clap the syllables. You may want to give them a category: for example, food, clothes, animals.

Assess

- Observe the children's ability to say and clap the syllables in words.
- Notice whether children recognize and use syllables when writing.
- You may wish to use Phonological Awareness Assessment B or K.

Use the guidelines to reinforce the principles and help children share their learning. In many lessons, we suggest behaviors to notice and support.

Assess the impact of the lesson and application in ways that are informal and integral to the work children are doing. For some lessons, we suggest using the more formal and systematic procedures in Online Resources to help you determine children's needs for further lessons.

Using the Fountas & Pinnell Phonics, Spelling, and Word Study System

For each lesson, we provide read-aloud titles from *Fountas & Pinnell Classroom™* chosen specifically to support the principle and work of each lesson.

If children need more experience, you can repeat the lesson format using these suggestions for variations, different examples, or more challenging activities.

These are not homework assignments; rather, they are ways you can help family members and caregivers make connections between home and school.

Connect learning across an effective and coherent design for responsive literacy teaching through interactive read-aloud, shared reading, interactive writing, and independent writing. Your observations across learning contexts will help you think of specific connections you can bring to your children's attention; add your own notes to enhance the lesson.

8 PHONOLOGICAL AWARENESS

EARLY MIDDLE LATE

Connect Learning Across Contexts

Interactive Read-Aloud When you find an interesting two- or three-syllable word in a book you are reading aloud, ask children to say and clap it.

RA *A Visitor for Bear* by Bonnie Becker

RA *When Sophie Gets Angry* by Molly Bang

Shared Reading See "Puppies and Kittens" in *Words That Sing* (2019). If you don't have these poetry charts, enlarge the print of this poem or other poems such as "Little Jack Horner" or "Open, Shut Them" in *Sing a Song of Poetry*, and point out two- and three-syllable words and have children say and clap them. You might have them use highlighter tape to mark rhyming words. You may also wish to use the following Shared Reading title from *Fountas & Pinnell Classroom™*.

SR *Ten Big Elephants* by Susan F. Rank

Interactive Writing Say and clap some words when writing them, or revisit the text to clap words.

Independent Writing Encourage children to say and clap words to identify the parts so that they can hear the sounds and connect them to letters as they write.

Extend Learning

■ Repeat the lesson with other words: for example, *book, bus, top, house, grapes; lemon, wagon, football, flower, hammer, pencil, pumpkin, water; dinosaur, icicle, kangaroo, tornado, strawberry*.

■ You may want to clap four-syllable words (*alligator, caterpillar, escalator, motorcycle, pepperoni, watermelon*) as an oral activity.

▶ **Connect with Home**

Show family members how to say and clap syllables with children. The caregiver might say a word and have the child beat a pan with a wooden spoon or clap the number of syllables he or she can hear in the word. They can clap words in the supermarket or in the kitchen while cooking. Suggest starting with the names of family and friends.

Planning and Implementing Effective Phonics Lessons

While the Teach section of the phonics lesson is explicit and structured, it also involves children in inquiry and encourages them to become "noticers" of the features of letters and words. What they discover is memorable and results in deeper learning. They are always learning an important principle they can apply to their reading and writing.

Lessons should be conversational. State the principle clearly at the beginning of the lesson (or at the end, if you think it is appropriate for children to derive it through inquiry and example). Your tone should be that of *I'm going to show you something interesting about how words work* or *What do you notice about these words?* Invite children to make connections to their names and anything else they know. Invite them to contribute further examples, and recognize and praise their thinking even if the examples don't quite fit. Always try to understand their thinking and build on a partially correct response.

Remember that a lesson is brief. Don't let it go on too long. Depending on the particular principle, you'll need only a few examples to make an understanding clear. Your goal is for children to integrate some of these examples into their own thinking so they can connect them to new learning when they are working on their own. At the end of the lesson, summarize the understanding you are trying to instill and take another moment to restate the principle. If appropriate, place an example on the word wall. Then explain and demonstrate the application activity.

You may choose to have all children do the Apply activity simultaneously immediately after the lesson (especially at the beginning of the year). But they also may be able to rotate to a word study center to engage in the activity during independent work time as they develop the ability to manage their own learning.

- Present the lesson to the entire class and then involve all children simultaneously in the Apply activity. They can work individually or with partners as you circulate around the room. Immediately follow the activity with sharing.

- Present the lesson to the entire class but involve children in application activities in small groups that you supervise. Have the rest of the children involved in independent reading/writing activities. Follow the activity with sharing as soon as all groups have completed it.

- Present the lesson to the entire class and explain the application activity. Have children complete it first (simultaneously for the whole group) and then move to another independent activity. Work with small groups in guided reading or writing while children work independently.

- Present the lesson to the entire class and explain the application activity. On the same day, have children rotate to a word study center to complete the activity. Have a brief sharing at the end of the period.

- Present the lesson to the entire class and explain the application activity. Over several days, have children rotate to a word study center to complete the activity. Have a brief sharing at the end of each day. Ask the children who participated to talk about what they learned.

At the end of an Apply activity, children meet for a brief group share of something they have learned about letters, sounds, and words.

Routines and Instructional Procedures for Effective Teaching

In the lessons we have designed for kindergarten, there are ten instructional procedures to develop children's knowledge of words and how they work. You will have noticed one of these routines used twice in the sample.

Most procedures engage children in inquiry to generate an important principle. For example, children might be shown a group of words and asked to notice a common feature (e.g., all words ending with silent *e*). However, in some early lessons inquiry is not included because children have not yet learned enough about letters and words to notice the similarities.

SEE AND SAY Efficient word solvers look for and find visual patterns in the way words are constructed. Recognizing familiar patterns helps children notice and use larger parts of words, which makes word solving faster and easier. The See and Say procedure described below helps children examine and identify familiar patterns in words, such as CVC and CVCe patterns, and learn to make new words by putting a letter or letter cluster before the familiar pattern. Used frequently in lessons in the areas of Letter Knowledge and Letter-Sound Relationships, the See and Say procedure generally follows this sequence:

1. Show words that have a common visual feature. [*man, fan, van, pan*]
2. Children search for visual patterns. [They all end the same.]
3. Help children articulate the principle. *You can look at a part or pattern to read a word. You can make new words by putting a letter or letter cluster before the pattern.*
4. Children work with words to apply the principle. [Children write words with the pattern.]
5. Summarize the learning by restating the principle.

FIND AND MATCH You will use Find and Match to help children discover connections between sounds, between letters, and between sounds and letters. The example provided below focuses on ending consonant sounds, but you'll also use Find and Match to support children in matching sounds or letters at the beginning or end of words, locating and connecting rhyming words, matching letters and pictures of words that begin or end with the same sound, or pairing words that start and end with the same sounds.

1. Show pictures, words, or pictures and letters that go together. [pictures: bed, cup, dog, girl, drum, goat; letters: *b, c, d, g*]
2. Children look for the connection between the pictures and words, or pictures and letters. [The letters stand for the sounds heard at the end of the words that the pictures represent.]
3. Help children articulate the principle. *You can hear the last sound in a word. You can match sounds and letters at the end of a word.*
4. Children work together with pictures and words, or words and letters to apply the principle. [Children match each picture with a letter that represents the ending sound in the picture's name.]
5. Summarize the learning by restating the principle.

Children can use *see and say* to recognize beginning consonant sounds and the letters that represent them.

Children can use *find and match* to understand that words are formed with letters.

36

SAY AND SORT Sorting helps children look closely at features of letters or words and make connections between them. Using Say and Sort, children form categories of pictures, letters, or words that are similar by sound, feature, word pattern, or word part. In the following example, children sort pictures by the number of syllables in the words they represent, but across the lessons children will sort by other features as well, such as rhyming words; beginning, ending, and medial sounds; recognizing letters and their features; and distinguishing consonants and vowels.

1. Show and say words or show pictures and say the names of the pictures that have a common feature. [words/pictures: *cat, bus, dog; turtle, balloon, carrot; banana, butterfly*]
2. Children search for the common feature. [They have one, two, or three parts.]
3. Help children articulate the principle. *You can hear and say the syllables in a word. Words can have one or more syllables.*
4. Children work with words or pictures to apply the principle. [Children sort the words or pictures according to the number of syllables.]
5. Summarize the learning by restating the principle.

HEAR AND SAY You will use Hear and Say to help children hear the sounds in words and eventually connect those sounds to letters, a key process in building literacy. In early Phonological Awareness lessons, Hear and Say is primarily an aural task. As children develop their understandings of how words work, they may be asked to represent the sounds they hear by constructing words with magnetic letters or in writing. Although the example given below centers on rhyming words, you also will use Hear and Say to support children's work with rhyming words; syllables; beginning, middle, and ending phonemes; and onsets and rimes. Hear and Say typically employs the following sequence:

1. Say words that are connected by the way they sound. [*man/can, me/he, hot/pot*]
2. Children search for phonological patterns. [The words sound the same at the end.]
3. Help children articulate the principle. *Some words have parts at the end that sound the same. They rhyme.*
4. Children work with words to apply the principle. [They say word pairs and tell whether the word pairs have end parts that sound the same (rhyme).]
5. Summarize the learning by restating the principle.

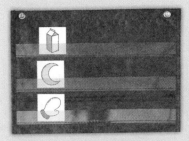

Children can use *say and sort* to hear and say the same beginning sound in words.

Children can use *hear and say* with sentences containing rhyming words.

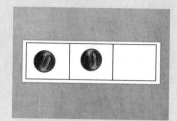

Children can use *sound and letter boxes* to hear and say three sounds in a word.

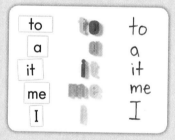

Children can use *words to know* to recognize and use high-frequency words.

HEAR, SAY, AND WRITE: SOUND AND LETTER BOXES D.B. Elkonin, a Russian psychologist, developed sound and letter boxes to help children become more aware of the sounds and letters in words. The technique has also been used by Marie Clay and by other researchers and educators. You can use the structure of sound boxes to help children listen for and identify each sound in a word. You can model by drawing the boxes and then support children in using them. Early in kindergarten, you can introduce sound boxes in the absence of letters to help children identify individual sounds. This is particularly helpful when children are not yet able to hear the sounds in sequential order. Draw a box (or use the page of sound boxes in *Ready Resources*) for each sound in the word. Have children say the word slowly, sliding a marker into each box in sequence. The goal is for children to learn how to use the boxes for sounds by saying words slowly and listening for each sound in sequence. Using the procedures below, you'll make one box for each sound (not each letter) in each word. Children may need to learn these a step at a time.

1. Model saying a new word slowly (*r-u-n* for *run*), being careful not to distort the individual sounds.

2. Children say the same word slowly and listen for each sound as they run a finger under the boxes (or push a marker into each box).

3. After they can easily do steps one and two, children write a letter for each sound they hear, one letter per box, with your guidance. In the beginning, you'll accept letters that are not in the correct sequence (but put them in the right boxes), focusing instead on whether children can connect letters to sounds.

4. Children say words slowly and write letters in sequence independently.

5. Summarize the learning by restating the principle. (You can say words slowly to hear sounds and write the letters.)

WORDS TO KNOW You will use this procedure to help children build and work with a collection of high-frequency words. Children need to be able to recognize high-frequency words quickly and easily. These words are enormously beneficial to beginning readers, who can use them to understand the concept of a word as letters with white space on either side, to understand the concept of a word in language, to monitor voice-print match, to monitor accuracy, to self-correct, to notice letter-sound relationships or word parts, to notice connections between words to solve words, to begin to write words correctly, and to read and write at a good rate. In many of the lessons that feature high-frequency words, you'll use the following procedure:

1. Show a group of high-frequency words, reading each one while running your pointer finger under it, left to right. [*a, I, in, is, of, to, and, the*]

2. Children look at each word to see if they recognize it.

3. Help children understand the principle. *Some words have one letter. Some words have two letters. Some words have three letters. You see some words many times when you read. You need to learn words that you see many times because they help you read and write.*

4. Children work with high-frequency words to apply the principle. [Children read, say, and write high-frequency words.]

5. Summarize the learning by restating the principle.

Fountas & Pinnell Phonics, Spelling, and Word Study Lessons, Kindergarten

NOTICE PARTS Efficient word solvers notice particular features of words, including visual patterns in the way words are constructed. Recognizing common features and familiar patterns helps children notice and use larger parts of words, which makes word solving faster and easier. Notice Parts helps children examine and identify onsets, rimes, and other common features in words. It is used frequently in lessons in the areas of Letter Knowledge, Spelling Patterns, and Word-Solving Actions. The Notice Parts procedure generally follows this sequence:

1. Show a group of words with a common feature. [*big, pig, dig*]
2. Children search for the common feature. [the phonogram *-ig*]
3. Help children articulate the principle. *You can look at a part or pattern to read a word. You can use the part or pattern to write a word. You can make new words by putting a letter or a letter cluster before the pattern.*
4. Children work with words to apply the principle. *You can read and/or write words by using the spelling pattern. You can make new words by adding a letter or letter cluster before the pattern.*
5. Summarize the learning by restating the principle.

SAY AND WRITE You will use Say and Write to help children begin to make the shapes of letters. The procedure allows children to understand that using efficient and consistent motions to form a letter can be broken down into discrete steps. Moreover they begin to understand that they can articulate these steps themselves. This procedure is used frequently in lessons in the area of Letter Knowledge, as well as occasionally in Early Literacy Concepts, Phonological Awareness, Letter-Sound Relationships, and Word-Solving Actions. The Say and Write procedure may follow this sequence:

1. Show children letters written in manuscript form. [*o, h, x, f, e; G, D, H, S, Z*]
2. Children say the name of each letter.
3. Help children articulate the principle. *You can make the shape of a letter. You can say the steps you use to make a letter. You can check to see if a letter looks right.*
4. Children work with letters to apply the principle. [Children use efficient and consistent motions to form letters in manuscript print with writing tools.]
5. Summarize the learning by restating the principle.

MAKE WORDS This procedure can help children build words (including contractions) through the use of discrete tactile materials such as magnetic letters, letter tiles, or letter cards. Make Words appears in lessons in Spelling Patterns, Word Structure, and Word-Solving Actions and may follow this sequence:

1. Show and say a word that contains a common phonogram. [*not*]
2. Children identify the beginning phoneme in the word. [/n/]
3. Help children articulate the principle. *You can change the first sound in a word to make a new word.*
4. Children work with words and letters to apply the principle. [Children change the first sound in a word to make a new word.]
5. Summarize the learning by restating the principle.

Children can use *notice parts* to understand first and last in written language.

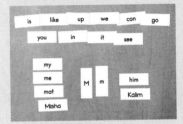

Children can use *say and write* to form letters with writing tools.

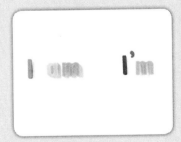

Children can use *make words* to understand the concept of a contraction.

Children can use *map words* to recognize and use concept words.

MAP WORDS Children need to know the meaning of the words they are learning to read and write. Map Words can help children read and write the names of concept words (e.g., number words, days, months, seasons) and related words. This procedure, which appears in lessons in the area of Word Meaning/Vocabulary, may follow this sequence:

1. Show a word map with a concept word in the center, and say the concept word. [*color*]
2. Children think of words that relate to the concept word. [names of colors]
3. Help children articulate the principle. *A color has a name. You can read and write the names of colors. You can find the names of colors.*
4. Children work with words to apply the principle. [Children say color words, and you write them on the word map.]
5. Summarize the learning by restating the principle.

A Few Further Suggestions

We recommend using black or dark-colored markers on white chart paper for constructing the charts. You may want to use colored transparent highlighter tape to emphasize certain words or letters, but, in general, it is better not to clutter up the examples with color-coding, which is usually a distraction for kindergartners. Also, it may confuse them; you want them to look at the distinctive features of letters—not the color! If you have set up centers in your classroom, be sure that all of the necessary materials are readily available in the word study center where children will use the application. If children work at their own tables, arrange materials in a central area or on each table. If the activity is new or difficult, place a model in clear view so that children can check their results. Below are more suggestions.

▶ Focus on one principle that is appropriate and useful for children at a particular point in time.

▶ State the principle in simple, clear terms in the Teach section of the lesson.

▶ Be sure that all children can see and hear as you demonstrate the principle or write examples on a chart.

▶ Invite children to connect the principle and examples to their names; use names as examples when possible.

▶ Share examples and add examples from children (if children are unable to provide some examples, then either the principle is not clearly stated or it is too difficult).

▶ Place an example on the word wall for the children's response when teaching lessons on words.

▶ Check for understanding by asking children to locate and talk about examples. Summarize the lesson by returning to the principle and stating it again.

▶ Engage the children in inquiry—getting them to notice important aspects of words and construct an important principle.

▶ Use a conversational rather than a lecture style. Promote interaction so children can be active, engaged learners.

Fountas & Pinnell Phonics, Spelling, and Word Study Lessons, Kindergarten

- Invite interaction so that children bring their own knowledge to bear on the application of the principle.

- Use a few good examples that you select in advance so that you have them ready to show the children.

- Clearly state the principle at the end as children come to their own conclusions from examples, or make a clear statement of the principle as you begin the lesson.

- Provide an Apply activity that children can do independently (after being taught routines), and that will be productive in their learning.

- Demonstrate the Apply activity explicitly so that you know children can perform it independently.

- Provide all necessary materials for the Apply activity in one place—for example, the word study center or a clearly defined and organized materials center.

- Provide Apply activities with potential multilevel learning that permits advanced students to apply the principle to more sophisticated examples and to make more discoveries and allow children who are less experienced to develop the understandings with simple examples.

- Convene children for a brief sharing period so that they can comment on what they have learned and you can reinforce the principle again.

- Make connections to previous word study lessons or understandings and discoveries made in any other component of an effective, coherent design for responsive literacy teaching.

- Keep lessons brief; a few examples are enough.

The Assessment Guide

There is a time to use systematic, planned tasks that are designed to gather information about particular aspects of children's growing word knowledge. Performance-based assessment may involve observation, but it also represents more formal structured experiences in which the tasks are standardized. Standardization of the procedure creates a reliable assessment situation that is more objective than daily ongoing observation. The goal is to get a picture of what each child can do independently. Usually you do not actively teach during a performance-based assessment, but you may make teaching points after the neutral observation.

The Assessment Guide (found in Online Resources) includes more formal, performance-based assessment tasks across the nine areas of learning. You can use these tasks in multiple ways: as diagnostic tools to determine what children know and need to know; as monitoring tools to help you keep track of your teaching and children's learning; and as documentation of the teaching and learning you and the children have accomplished. You and your colleagues may even decide to place some of the summary sheets in your children's permanent cumulative folders as a way to create a school-wide record of the phonics and word study program.

As noted, the opportunities for informal assessment are embedded in each lesson in the Assess feature.

Phonics Lessons in the Daily Schedule

There are many ways to organize your schedule. It depends on your school schedule, the times you must reserve for special areas like music or library, and, of course, on whether you teach full-day or half-day kindergarten!

Remember that phonics lessons are short—often, five minutes is enough time. Application also will take no more than five to ten minutes and after children become proficient and know routines, they can perform them independently or with a partner. The extent to which you use the suggestions for extending phonics lessons is a teaching decision; and most of these involve integrating phonics with other classroom work that you are doing anyway.

Obviously, you can do more in a whole day than a half day; but we know that schedules are tight even if teachers have a full day. You have to plan carefully to include everything you want to do and everything that is required. And every kindergarten child needs plenty of time to play and to choose some of his own activities.

Take a look at an example of the contexts that you may want to "fit together" in the management of your schedule for literacy learning (Figure 5).

Make a frame for your day with the times that school begins and ends, a space for lunch and recess, and then begin to "slot in" what you want to do. If you have very limited time, you may not be able to do everything every day. When you have created what you think will be a workable schedule try it. You can make adjustments, but once you find an excellent schedule, stick to it! Having a predictable schedule is very important for kindergarten children. There will always be some interruptions (assemblies, field trips, and so on), but try to keep them to a minimum. Children should walk in the door with a good idea of what their work and play will be.

In the pages that follow, you will see two different options for planning and organizing lessons across the year. These two organizational tools are Nine Areas of Learning Across the Year and the Master Lesson Guide: Suggested Sequence for Phonics Lessons.

Kindergarten • Full Day

FITTING IT ALL TOGETHER
Start with this suggested framework, or design your own

INSTRUCTIONAL CONTEXT		ACTIVITY OPTIONS	MINUTES EACH DAY
GROUP MEETING		• Bring the classroom community together to introduce/discuss the day and set goals.	5
INTERACTIVE READ-ALOUD LESSON	IRA	• Teacher reads aloud a book from a text set and children share their thinking. The text experience often leads to writing about reading in the *Reader's Notebook*.	15
SHARED READING	SR	• Teacher engages children in shared reading using enlarged print books and shared poetry charts and often leads to shared/interactive writing.	10
PHONICS, SPELLING, AND WORD STUDY LESSON	PWS	• Teacher provides an explicit, inquiry-based lesson on a phonics principle that children can apply to reading and writing.	10
BREAK			
READING MINILESSON	RML	• Teacher provides an explicit minilesson for children to apply to their independent reading and writing about reading/drawing.	10
SMALL-GROUP INSTRUCTION	GR	• Teacher meets with 3 Guided Reading groups each day.	60
	BC	• Teacher initiates Book Clubs as appropriate, and they meet about once per month.	

INDEPENDENT LITERACY WORK	IR	• Rotate through Literacy Centers *OR* engage in four tasks:
		  1. Read a book
		  2. Listen to a book
		  3. Work on writing
		  4. Work on letters/words (application from Phonics lesson)	

GROUP SHARE		• Gather children together to reflect on and share learning.	10
BREAK			
CENTERS AND/OR CHOICE TIME		• Children rotate through a variety of centers; dramatic play, sand/water table, art, blocks, music/movement, computer, science table, math, etc.	30

Suggested time allotments shown are for utilizing the instructional contexts of *Fountas & Pinnell Classroom™* within a full-day kindergarten classroom. Visit www.fountasandpinnell.com/fpc for an alternative half-day kindergarten suggested schedule.

TOTAL: 2.5 HOURS

FIGURE 5 *Fitting It All Together*

Nine Areas of Learning Across the Year:
Early, Middle, Late

We have organized the kindergarten lessons by nine areas of learning (see *The Fountas & Pinnell Comprehensive Phonics, Spelling, and Word Study Guide*) and by suggested time of year (early, middle, or late).

EARLY KINDERGARTEN The beginning of kindergarten is an exciting time for both you and your new students. For many children, kindergarten is their first experience with large-group instruction. The first three months of kindergarten are critical for turning this group of twenty or more individuals into a community that works together cooperatively and productively. You want children to share with and support one another and to treat you, their materials, and one another with respect. Your work with them on classroom routines is very important and time well spent. You will want to have a very predictable schedule and a highly organized classroom and to teach children gradually and explicitly how to move about the room, use materials, and follow directions. The first two months of school are when you "set the scene" for learning.

MIDDLE KINDERGARTEN During the middle three or four months, most children will have settled into the routines of kindergarten and be able to perform them automatically. They can sustain independent work for longer periods of time and be responsible for themselves and for materials. You will still need to be explicit and clear in your demonstrations and to reteach routines if things are falling apart for some children.

LATE KINDERGARTEN During the last three months of the year, children will be integrating their knowledge of reading, writing, and how words work. Learning accelerates as you connect word study with children's work in reading and writing. Your children will have established a strong foundation as emergent readers and writers to continue their learning.

In creating this overview or map (see pages 46–47), we considered how children's experiences are likely to build across the year as a result not only of the direct teaching of principles related to sounds, letters, and words but also of their daily experiences hearing written language read aloud and participating in shared, independent, and guided reading and interactive and independent writing.

This map shows a continuum of easier to harder principles. It will help you think in broad strokes about the program you are providing for the children in your classroom, which must always be considered in light of your observations and assessments of what the children know and can do at any given point. If children are very knowledgeable and experienced, you may decide that some lessons can be abbreviated or omitted. If children are very inexperienced in a given area, lessons may need to be repeated using different examples.

Reflecting on the map will help you be aware of the entire body of knowledge that is important for kindergarten children to acquire as a foundation for literacy learning.

The overview contains two kinds of information.

▶ Using the rows, you can take one area of learning and follow children's development of a principle from easier to harder throughout the year. For example, lessons on phonological awareness begin with songs, rhymes, and chants. You'll help children become more sensitive to the sounds of language by having them match rhyming pictures and listen for the parts in words. Later in the year you will give closer attention to individual sounds in words and help children develop insights into the structure of words by identifying and manipulating these sounds. Each area of learning offers room for growth throughout the year.

▶ You can look down the columns to get a sense of the understanding children are building across the entire continuum. Working across categories, you ensure that children not only develop phonological awareness but also learn to look at print—distinguish letters and learn their names—as well as think about word meanings and become familiar with some high-frequency words that will help accelerate their learning.

Look at the map both ways. Children might be more advanced in one area than another. It is obvious that planning instruction is not always neat and tidy; however, the concept of easier to harder, in combination with assessment, should allow you to make effective decisions for children. Your understandings will allow you to

▶ make the most of what children know by allowing them to work at the edge of their knowledge;

▶ ensure clear, explicit teaching and meaningful practice to deepen conceptual knowledge;

▶ ensure that principles do not have to be taught again and again;

▶ avoid spending time on teaching what children already know.

If you wish to have a copy of the Nine Areas of Learning Across the Year for reference or recordkeeping, you can find it in Online Resources.

Nine Areas of Learning

1 Early Literacy Concepts   ELC

Early		Middle		Late
ELC 1	Recognize Your Name	ELC 5	Connect a Name to Other Words	
ELC 2	Recognize Your Name	ELC 6	Understand First and Last in Written Language: Letters	
ELC 3	Match a Spoken Word with a Group of Letters	ELC 7	Understand First and Last in Written Language: Letters and Words	
ELC 4	Match a Spoken Word with a Group of Letters	ELC 8	Understand First and Last in Written Language: Words	

2 Phonological Awareness   PA

PA 1	Hear and Say Rhyming Words	PA 13	Hear and Say the Ending Sound in a Word	PA 19	Hear and Divide Onsets and Rimes
PA 2	Hear and Say Rhyming Words	PA 14	Hear and Say the Same Ending Sound in Words	PA 20	Blend Onsets with Rimes
PA 3	Hear and Connect Rhyming Words	PA 15	Hear and Say the Same Ending Sound in Words	PA 21	Hear and Say Two Sounds in a Word
PA 4	Hear and Generate Rhyming Words	PA 16	Change the Beginning Sound to Make a New Word	PA 22	Hear and Say Three Sounds in a Word
PA 5	Hear and Generate Rhyming Words	PA 17	Hear and Say the Middle Sound in a Word with Three Phonemes	PA 23	Hear and Say Four or More Sounds in a Word in Sequence
PA 6	Hear, Say, and Clap Syllables	PA 18	Hear and Say the Same Middle Sound in Words	PA 24	Blend Three or Four Sounds in a Word
PA 7	Hear, Say, and Clap Syllables			PA 25	Delete the Beginning Sound of a Word
PA 8	Hear, Say, and Clap Syllables			PA 26	Delete the Beginning Sound of a Word
PA 9	Blend Syllables				
PA 10	Hear and Say the Same Beginning Sound in Words				
PA 11	Hear and Say the Same Beginning Sound in Words				
PA 12	Hear and Say the Same Beginning Sound in Words				

3 Letter Knowledge   LK

LK 1	Understand That Words Are Formed with Letters	LK 9	Understand That Words Are Formed with Letters	LK 18	Form Letters with Writing Tools
LK 2	Recognize the Distinctive Features of Letter Forms	LK 10	Recognize the Sequence of Letters in a Word	LK 19	Form Letters with Writing Tools
LK 3	Recognize the Distinctive Features of Letter Forms	LK 11	Recognize Letters and State Their Names	LK 20	Recognize Uppercase Letters and Lowercase Letters
LK 4	Recognize Letters and State Their Names	LK 12	Recognize Letters and State Their Names	LK 21	Distinguish the Differences Between Uppercase and Lowercase Forms of a Letter
LK 5	Recognize the Distinctive Features of Letter Forms	LK 13	Form Letters with Writing Tools	LK 22	Recognize That Letters Can Be Consonants or Vowels
LK 6	Recognize Letters and State Their Names	LK 14	Form Letters with Writing Tools	LK 23	Recognize the Order of the Alphabet
LK 7	Recognize Letters and State Their Names	LK 15	Make Connections Among Words by Noting the Position of a Letter	LK 24	Recognize the Order of the Alphabet
LK 8	Recognize Letters and State Their Names	LK 16	Categorize Letters by Features		
		LK 17	Categorize Letters by Features		

4 Letter-Sound Relationships   LSR

		LSR 1	Recognize Beginning Consonant Sounds and the Letters That Represent Them	LSR 6	Recognize Beginning Consonant Sounds and the Letters That Represent Them
		LSR 2	Recognize Beginning Consonant Sounds and the Letters That Represent Them	LSR 7	Recognize Beginning Consonant Sounds and the Letters That Represent Them
		LSR 3	Recognize Beginning Consonant Sounds and the Letters That Represent Them	LSR 8	Recognize Ending Consonant Sounds and the Letters That Represent Them
		LSR 4	Recognize Beginning Consonant Sounds and the Letters That Represent Them		
		LSR 5	Recognize Beginning Consonant Sounds and the Letters That Represent Them		

Across the Year

5	Spelling Patterns SP		
Early	**Middle**		**Late**
	SP 1	Recognize and Use the CVC Pattern	SP 5	Recognize and Use Phonograms with a VCe Pattern: -ake
	SP 2	Recognize and Use Phonograms: -an	SP 6	Recognize and Use Phonograms with a VCe Pattern: -ine
	SP 3	Recognize and Use Phonograms: -at	SP 7	Recognize Letter Patterns
	SP 4	Recognize and Use Phonograms: -ay		

6	High-Frequency Words HFW		
HFW 1 Recognize and Use High-Frequency Words with One, Two, or Three Letters	HFW 2	Recognize and Use High-Frequency Words with One, Two, or Three Letters	HFW 4	Recognize and Use High-Frequency Words with Three or More Letters
	HFW 3	Recognize and Use High-Frequency Words with One, Two, or Three Letters	HFW 5	Recognize and Use High-Frequency Words with Three or More Letters
			HFW 6	Recognize and Use High-Frequency Words with Three or More Letters
			HFW 7	Locate and Read High-Frequency Words in Continuous Text

7	Word Meaning/Vocabulary WMV		
	WMV 1	Recognize and Use Concept Words: Color Names	WMV 4	Recognize and Use Concept Words: Number Names
	WMV 2	Recognize and Use Concept Words: Color Names	WMV 5	Recognize and Use Concept Words: Days of the Week
	WMV 3	Recognize and Use Concept Words: Number Names	WMV 6	Recognize and Use Concept Words: Days of the Week
			WMV 7	Recognize Related Words

8	Word Structure WS		
	WS 1	Hear, Say, and Identify Syllables	WS 2	Understand the Concept of a Contraction
			WS 3	Understand the Concept of Plural
			WS 4	Recognize and Use Plurals That Add -s

9	Word-Solving Actions WSA		
WSA 1 Recognize and Find Names	WSA 2	Recognize and Read Known Words Quickly	WSA 5	Hear Sounds in Sequence
	WSA 3	Change the Beginning Sound or Sounds to Make and Solve a New Word	WSA 6	Use Onsets and Rimes in Known Words to Read and Write Other Words with the Same Parts
	WSA 4	Change the Beginning Sound or Sounds to Make and Solve a New Word	WSA 7	Use Onsets and Rimes in Known Words to Read and Write Other Words with the Same Parts
			WSA 8	Change the Ending Sound or Sounds to Make and Solve a New Word
			WSA 9	Change the Ending Sound or Sounds to Make and Solve a New Word

A Suggested Sequence for Phonics Lessons

The phonics lessons are organized into nine areas of learning. Within each area, lessons are organized from easier to harder, although some lessons are just about equivalent and are learned within the same time period—early, middle, or late in the year. Also, the lessons are designed to build on each other. So you can see the suggested sequence within each area of learning from the beginning of the year to near the end. (Some areas will be under good control by the middle of the year.) But you will want to create a yearlong sequence that works across the nine areas, taking easier principles first and building on them. A tremendous amount of learning goes on in the area of word study and phonics.

To help you plan your year and make good decisions about the children you teach, we have created a suggested sequence for teaching Phonics Lessons, Kindergarten. The suggested sequence, from 1 to 100, includes

- lesson titles and lesson numbers across the nine areas of learning;
- designation as a generative lesson (see page 31);
- specific suggestions for extending learning of the principle;
- specific suggestions for working with children who find the principle difficult;
- page numbers for each lesson so that you can find them in the lessons book quickly;
- blank space for your notes (you'll want to note whether you used the lesson and in what way).

You'll notice that the lessons are sequenced by typical appropriateness within each of the nine areas, so there is variety in the kinds of lessons that fall early in the year, then in the middle, and then late in the year. This sequence will serve simultaneously as a planning document and as a record of teaching. Use it to plan lessons for the coming week and to keep a record and notes of the lessons you have taught. Here are some suggestions for using the sequence effectively.

- Think about what children already know as you select and plan lessons. You may want to use some simple assessments. The Assessment Guide (in Online Resources) will help you consider children's strengths and needs. You'll also be gathering information as you work with children in lessons and as you observe them in application activities and group share. If a principle is firmly established, skip the lesson.
- Children may have learned a great deal in shared reading and early guided reading lessons so that early literacy behaviors are well established. You might not need to use all of the lessons in this area.
- You may identify a small group of children who need more support in establishing a principle. You can hold a brief small-group meeting to repeat the lesson and help them with the application activity.
- Remember that you can repeat the lesson using other examples if you think your whole class needs more work on the principle.

Fountas & Pinnell Phonics, Spelling, and Word Study Lessons, Kindergarten

- Some lessons may need to be repeated or extended over several days because there is a great deal of content to be covered—for example, consonants and related sounds.

- You can make adjustments in the sequence. If you are working on a series of lessons on one topic (for example, phonogram patterns), you may want to stick with it for a few more days to get it firmly into place.

- It's important to remember that you can skip over lessons if children already understand and can apply the principle. Don't teach a lesson just because it is there.

In the first column, we provide a sequence for the lessons.

In the second and third columns, you see the number and title of the lesson.

The ✓ icon identifies generative lessons.

In the fourth column, we provide suggestions for your consideration in teaching the sequence of lessons. This information will help you think about whether or not to repeat or extend the lesson with your students. You will also want to consult *The Comprehensive Phonics, Spelling, and Word Study Guide.*

In the fifth column, we have left space for you to enrich your planning and organization with your own notes.

Also in the fifth column, you can see the first appearance of each area of learning.

#	Lesson	Title	Teaching Suggestions for Extending Learning	Teacher Notes
			EARLY IN THE YEAR	
1	ELC 1 page 75	Recognize Your Name	There may be a few children in your class who do not yet recognize their names. Repeat the lesson with a small group, reducing the number of names to make it easier. Have them trace the first letter and tell what they notice about their names. Work until each child can find his name rapidly, without hesitation.	Start of ELC
2	ELC 2 page 79	Recognize Your Name	Repeat the lesson using the name chart made in Lesson ELC 1. Play a game matching the name card to the name on the chart. Give each child an individual copy of the name chart and have children quickly circle their own names and then point to names of others in the class. Use the name chart as a constant resource for interactive writing, and encourage children to use it in their independent writing.	
3	PA 1 ✓ page 109	Hear and Say Rhyming Words	Repeat the lesson with a variety of rhymes. Use *Sing a Song of Poetry* or *Words That Sing*. Have children highlight words that rhyme. They may notice that sometimes the endings look the same and sometimes they don't. Have children highlight ending parts of rhyming words that look the same.	Start of PA
4	PA 2 ✓ page 113	Hear and Say Rhyming Words	Use shared reading to help children enjoy poetry. After a poem is familiar, have them identify and highlight rhyming words. You may want to say a word and have children think of a word that rhymes. You can use this game as children line up or come to group meeting.	
5	PA 3 ✓	Hear and Connect Rhyming Words	Repeat the lesson with a small group of children who need more support. If the whole group needs more work on sorting, repeat the lesson with other	

MASTER LESSON GUIDE

#	Lesson	Title	Teaching Suggestions for Extending Learning	Teacher Notes
			EARLY IN THE YEAR	
1	ELC 1 page 75	Recognize Your Name	There may be a few children in your class who do not yet recognize their names. Repeat the lesson with a small group, reducing the number of names to make it easier. Have them trace the first letter and tell what they notice about their names. Work until each child can find his name rapidly, without hesitation.	*Start of ELC*
2	ELC 2 page 79	Recognize Your Name	Repeat the lesson using the name chart made in Lesson ELC 1. Play a game matching the name card to the name on the chart. Give each child an individual copy of the name chart and have children quickly circle their own names and then point to names of others in the class. Use the name chart as a constant resource for interactive writing, and encourage children to use it in their independent writing.	
3	PA 1 ✓ page 109	Hear and Say Rhyming Words	Repeat the lesson with a variety of rhymes. Use *Sing a Song of Poetry* or *Words That Sing*. Have children highlight words that rhyme. They may notice that sometimes the endings look the same and sometimes they don't. Have children highlight ending parts of rhyming words that look the same.	*Start of PA*
4	PA 2 ✓ page 113	Hear and Say Rhyming Words	Use shared reading to help children enjoy poetry. After a poem is familiar, have them identify and highlight rhyming words. You may want to say a word and have children think of a word that rhymes. You can use this game as children line up or come to group meeting.	
5	PA 3 ✓ page 117	Hear and Connect Rhyming Words	Repeat the lesson with a small group of children who need more support. If the whole group needs more work on sorting, repeat the lesson with other pictures. Use simple poems in shared reading. Have children identify and highlight rhyming words. Play a game by saying two words. Children stand and clap if the words rhyme.	
6	LK 1 ✓ page 215	Understand That Words are Formed with Letters	Repeat the lesson as needed until most children can make their names. Bring together a small group of children who still need more support in making their names. Have them work with the name puzzle until they can do it and check it letter by letter. Have children sit in a circle with name puzzles in front of them. They can tell what they notice about their names and the names of their friends.	*Start of LK*

Suggested Sequence for Phonics Lessons

#	Lesson	Title	Teaching Suggestions for Extending Learning	Teacher Notes
			EARLY *(continued)*	
7	WSA 1 ✓ page 455	Recognize and Find Names	Notice children who have difficulty recognizing their names and convene them in a small group. Make a quick name chart with the children. (This will limit the number of names and make it easier.) Repeat the lesson and play a short Lotto game with them if time allows. Recognizing one's name in many contexts is an exercise in quick letter/word recognition. When there is a great deal of print in the room, you can have children (or half of the group) move quickly without talking to a place that has their names. They read the name and say the first letter. Then they go quickly to a word that starts the same. Possibilities are word wall, name charts, helpers chart, pieces of interactive writing.	*Start of WSA*
8	LK 2 ✓ page 219	Recognize the Distinctive Features of Letter Forms	Repeat the lesson using other letters. Refer to Ways to Sort or Match Letters in Online Resources. Set up a sorting area where children can play at sorting letters.	
9	LK 3 ✓ page 223	Recognize the Distinctive Features of Letter Forms	For children who need more support making letters, work with them in a small group. Have them trace letters and use the Verbal Path for the Formation of Letters in Online Resources. They can say it aloud as they trace letters or make them on the table using larger movements. They can also write on the chalkboard using the verbal path, said aloud as they write. (Children will learn more about the verbal path in LK 5.)	
10	LK 4 ✓ page 227	Recognize Letters and State Their Names	You may wish to repeat the lesson using other letters. Work with a small group of children if needed to teach them to use a model to recognize like letters quickly and to group them together.	
11	ELC 3 ✓ page 83	Match a Spoken Word with a Group of Letters	Repeat the lesson, generating other sentences, cutting them up, putting them in the pocket chart and reading them word by word. As a free-time activity, children can reconstruct the sentences. Work with a small group of children who have difficulty coordinating this task. Be sure to stress crisp pointing under the words.	

#	Lesson	Title	Teaching Suggestions for Extending Learning	Teacher Notes
			EARLY *(continued)*	
12	ELC 4 ✓ page 87	Match a Spoken Word with a Group of Letters	Repeat the lesson with other sentences. You can use some familiar sentences from interactive writing or shared reading. As children draw, have them dictate a sentence about their drawings. Write it quickly on a sentence strip while they read it. They can put together their sentence several times and glue it on the picture.	
13	LK 5 ✓ page 231	Recognize the Distinctive Features of Letter Forms	Bring together a small group of children who need more practice making letters. Observe their formations of letters closely. Encourage them to use large movements to write on the chalkboard saying aloud the verbal path (see the Verbal Path for the Formation of Letters in Online Resources). In interactive writing, use the verbal path as children contribute letters to a piece.	
14	LK 6 ✓ page 235	Recognize Letters and State Their Names	Repeat this lesson several times until children develop automatic recognition of all the letters and can easily read their individual Alphabet Linking Charts. Work with a small group if needed. Use the enlarged version of the chart until you can point to a letter without saying it and ask children to "read" the letter and pictures. Use the chart as a resource in interactive writing. Place a copy of the chart in each child's writing folder.	
15	LK 7 ✓ page 239	Recognize Letters and State Their Names	Tape an alphabet strip to the top of every place at the table or to the top of each child's desk. Repeat the lesson until children can quickly and easily match magnetic letters to the alphabet strip in the pocket chart. Play a line-up game in which children have a letter for a "ticket." The child places the letter on an alphabet strip to get in line.	
16	LK 8 ✓ page 243	Recognize Letters and State Their Names	You may have a number of children who have trouble recognizing their names and/or who look only at the first letter. Meet with them in a small group and have them sit in a circle with the name puzzle envelope in front of them as a model (see LK 1). They mix up the letter cards of their names–with a partner sitting next to them–and play "alphabet soup" using the model. Have each child tell what she notices about her name and her partner's name. Challenge children to tell more than the first letter. Have each child go up to the Alphabet Linking Chart and locate a letter than is in her name (any letter): "Here is an *e*. My name has two *e*'s."	

#	Lesson	Title	Teaching Suggestions for Extending Learning	Teacher Notes
			EARLY *(continued)*	
17	PA 4 ✔ page 121	Hear and Generate Rhyming Words	Identify a small group of children who have trouble hearing rhyme. Emphasize listening to words in the absence of print. Take several rhyming patterns that make it easy to generate words than rhyme—for example, *rat, run, hat, goat.* Go around the table. The first child (or teacher) says, "*run/sun.*" The next child says "*run/sun/fun.*" Each child repeats the full string of words; help as needed. Work with rhymes in this way until children are sensitive to hearing and identifying them.	
18	PA 5 ✔ page 125	Hear and Generate Rhyming Words	Work with a small group of children who have trouble hearing rhyme. Emphasize listening to the words in the absence of print. Take a set of Lotto cards that have been cut apart, and spread them on the table one by one as you and the children say the names of the pictures. Then have them take turns "spying" two pictures that represent words that rhyme. They can keep it up until all pictures are matched. Repeat as needed until children can match pictures very quickly.	
19	PA 6 ✔ page 129	Hear, Say, and Clap Syllables	Repeat the lesson using different picture cards to sort into two groups: one-syllable words and two-syllable words. Add some three-syllable words if children find this very easy. Clap words into syllables when you add them to interactive writing. In shared reading, have children identify words with two syllables.	
20	PA 7 page 133	Hear, Say, and Clap Syllables	Repeat the lesson using another short poem from *Sing a Song of Poetry* or *Words That Sing.* Have children build sentences in the pocket chart and read them, keeping the pointer under each word (no matter how many syllables it has). Give children individual copies with lines helping them cut the lines of the poem apart. They can then reassemble them and read them.	

#	Lesson	Title	Teaching Suggestions for Extending Learning	Teacher Notes
			EARLY *(continued)*	
21	PA 8 ✓ page 137	Hear, Say, and Clap Syllables	Notice children who have difficulty clapping syllables accurately and work with them in a small group. They can look at an array of pictures, choose one, and clap it. Notice how they do when not working in unison with other children. Then say, "Who can find a word with three parts?" Continue until children have chosen all of the words and clapped them. Divide up pictures and have them work in pairs to sort them into one-, two-, and three-syllable words.	
22	PA 9 ✓ page 141	Blend Syllables	Identify children who have trouble blending and separating sentences. Bring them together and repeat the lesson. Have them generate two- and three-syllable words. Play Lotto with them to help them perform the analysis more rapidly. In interactive writing, clap words and then say them in syllables before writing them. Write three-syllable words a syllable at a time.	
23	PA 10 ✓ page 145	Hear and Say the Same Beginning Sound in Words	Work with a small group of children who have difficulty sorting the pictures by sound. Use the same pictures and observe children as they work in pairs. Then spread out the pictures and have children take turns placing a picture in the middle for others to match. Have them say the phoneme in an isolated way, followed by the word: /b/, *bear*. In interactive writing, have children predict the first sound of a word they want to write.	
24	PA 11 ✓ page 149	Hear and Say the Same Beginning Sound in Words	Lessons PA 10 and PA 11 require children to think of one beginning sound (using pictures to represent words with that begin with that sound). The emphasis is on hearing sounds in the absence of print. Repeat this lesson with other beginning consonant sounds that are easy to hear: /b/, /k/, /h/, /d/, /f/. You will not need to do this with every letter, as the idea is for children to learn *how* to hear beginning sounds that are alike. You can also play a line-up game: "I'm thinking of something that begins like *hand*." "I'm thinking of something that begins like *Jason*." In shared reading, invite children to say the word and say the first sound as an isolated phoneme.	

#	Lesson	Title	Teaching Suggestions for Extending Learning	Teacher Notes
			EARLY *(continued)*	
25	**PA 12** ✓ page 153	**Hear and Say the Same Beginning Sound in Words**	Use a poem with alliteration with the class. Teach the poem first, without looking at print, and have children identify words that sound the same at the beginning. Play a game by saying two words. If both words begin with the same sound, the children clap. If they don't, they stay still. Note children who have trouble coming up with examples, and play the game again in a small group. Use interactive writing with the small group so that children can say the word and then say the first sound before predicting the letter. After writing, have children highlight and say two words that start with the same sound. Do the same in shared reading.	
26	**HFW 1** ✓ page 377	**Recognize and Use High-Frequency Words with One, Two, or Three Letters**	Repeat the lesson using words from the word wall that children are just learning. By this time you may have words like *to, in, the, go, he, can, like*. Select words with two, three, and four letters. Work with the group to place the words in columns according to the number of letters. If children find this very easy, you can ask questions like, "Who can point to the second letter in a word?"	*Start of HFW*

MASTER LESSON GUIDE

#	Lesson	Title	Teaching Suggestions for Extending Learning	Teacher Notes
			MIDDLE OF THE YEAR	
27	LK 9 page 247	Understand That Words Are Formed with Letters	To help children who recognize fewer words, limit the choice and work with them in a small group. Give each a set of word cards and sort words by those they know quickly and those that they are not sure of. They can read those word cards several times and look for a part they want to remember.	
28	LK 10 page 251	Recognize the Sequence of Letters in a Word	Use the name puzzle again (see LK 1) to extend learning. If children find the name puzzle very easy, you may want to add their last names. Have them sit in a circle on the floor with the name puzzle envelope in front of them. They make the name puzzle and check it. Talk about the sequence of letters in a word and how it is always the same. Have each child tell how many letters are in their first names. (If last names are too long, don't tell the number.) Play a quick *ABC* game. "Raise your hand if you have an *a* in your name. Touch the *a*." Continue with all of the letters. Children will notice that some letters do not appear in any name. Invite individuals to name a letter, and have someone else find the letter on the Alphabet Linking Chart.	
29	LK 11 page 255	Recognize Letters and State Their Names	While children are working independently to read their letter books, work with a small group of children who have low letter recognition. They read the letter book in a shared way and find the letter on the Alphabet Linking Chart. Read the chart to help them realize that it is a resource.	
30	LK 12 page 259	Recognize Letters and State Their Names	Extend this lesson by working with the Alphabet Linking Chart, which you can read in a number of ways (see LK 6). After reading it several times, point to a letter without saying it. "Everyone whose name starts with this letter, stand up and say it." Vary the game by pointing to a letter and invite children to say a name that starts with that letter.	
31	WS 1 page 437	Hear, Say, and Identify Syllables	Repeat the lesson, adding more picture cards to those that children have already sorted. Set up a sorting tray that children can use independently. If some children have difficulty distinguishing between one and two syllables, bring them together in a small group and help them sort quickly.	

Start of WS

Fountas & Pinnell Phonics, Spelling, and Word Study Lessons, Kindergarten

Suggested Sequence for Phonics Lessons

#	Lesson	Title	Teaching Suggestions for Extending Learning	Teacher Notes
			MIDDLE *(continued)*	
32	LSR 1 ✓ page 313	Recognize Beginning Consonant Sounds and the Letters That Represent Them	If you have a group of children with low knowledge of letter-sound relationships, work with them in a small group at the pocket chart to repeat the matching. Work until each child can do it quickly. Continue on to LSR 2, but realize you will probably use LSR 1 and LSR 2 in repeated forms in several following lessons, choosing two or three letters at a time.	*Start of LSR*
33	LSR 2 ✓ page 317	Recognize Beginning Consonant Sounds and the Letters That Represent Them	Using picture cards and word cards from Online Resources, repeat the lesson until you have introduced all of the letters and sounds. Leave the more difficult sounds of *w* and *y* until the end. Try to help each child develop knowledge of a key word that will help him connect the letter and sound of the consonant. Use the Alphabet Linking Chart to help children remember a key word. In the next lessons, you will be working with letter-sound lessons again.	
34	LSR 3 ✓ page 321	Recognize Beginning Consonant Sounds and the Letters That Represent Them	Repeat the lesson, increasing the number of pictures to sort under certain consonant letters. If you have a group of children with low knowledge of letter-sound relationships, work with them in a small group at the pocket chart to repeat the matching. Work until each child can do it quickly.	
35	LSR 4 ✓ page 325	Recognize Beginning Consonant Sounds and the Letters That Represent Them	Play Lotto with a small group if needed. Continue repeating the lesson with matching pictures and consonants.	
36	LSR 5 ✓ page 329	Recognize Beginning Consonant Sounds and the Letters That Represent Them	Children may recognize letters and connect them with sounds, but the real goal is for them to do this when working on continuous print. Work with several more poems. Use *Sing a Song of Poetry* or *Words That Sing*. You can also use a shared reading book. Vary responses you ask from children. For example, make the sound and have children find the word, say it, and identify the first letter. Say the word and have children locate it and make the first sound. Read up to the word and pause, telling children to "get your mouth ready" to say the next word. Repeat some of these ideas with texts that are new to children.	

#	Lesson	Title	Teaching Suggestions for Extending Learning	Teacher Notes
			MIDDLE *(continued)*	
37	PA 13 ✓ page 157	Hear and Say the Ending Sound in a Word	Teach children a short poem that has rhyming words emphasizing strong ending sounds. Have children identify words that end with the same sound. In interactive writing, select words with easy-to-hear ending sounds, and have children identify the sound before writing the letter. On a finished piece, have them highlight words with the same ending sound.	
38	PA 14 ✓ page 161	Hear and Say the Same Ending Sound in Words	Repeat the lesson adding a third column and then a fourth column so that children have a more complex choice. Notice children who find sorting the sounds to be difficult, and have them do the sort in a small group. Play a line-up game: "I'm thinking of someone whose name ends like *top*."	
39	PA 15 ✓ page 165	Hear and Say the Same Ending Sound in Words	Identify children who have difficulty saying and matching the last sound in words. Bring them together in a small group. Separate the Lotto pictures into piles that have an even number of last sounds. Deal out half of the pictures, and have the children lay them out. Hold up a picture and say, "_____, do you have something that ends like _____?" If the child has a picture that matches, she takes the one you are holding and puts it on top. At the end, children say all of the names of pictures that have the same sound.	
40	PA 16 ✓ page 169	Change the Beginning Sound to Make a New Word	Play the game to line up or sit down. Say a word and ask children to change the first sound to make another word. Identify children who have trouble quickly changing the first sound, and bring them together in a small group. Use the picture cards from PA 16 to match words.	
41	PA 17 ✓ page 173	Hear and Say the Middle Sound in a Word With Three Phonemes	Convene a small group of children who have difficulty with the sort. Be sure that they can say the words to hear the short vowel sound in the middle. If needed, use Elkonin boxes (see page 38) to help them understand that there are three sounds in each of the words.	

Suggested Sequence for Phonics Lessons

#	Lesson	Title	Teaching Suggestions for Extending Learning	Teacher Notes
			MIDDLE *(continued)*	
42	PA 18 ✓ page 177	Hear and Say the Same Middle Sound in Words	Repeat the lesson using pictures representing the short *a* (*cat, van, mat, map, pan, jam*), short *i* (*fish, pig, pin, chick, dish, lid*), and short *o* (*pot, cot, spot, top, log*). Use a familiar poem like "Pease Porridge Hot" (see *Sing a Song of Poetry*). Invite children to say the poem and clap when they hear a short *o* sound. You may want to repeat the lesson one more time with a full sort of the five short vowel sounds.	
43	ELC 5 ✓ page 91	Connect a Name to Other Words	Make a duplicated set of high-frequency words that children know. (They may be from the word wall.) Give each child two words/names. Play a game by asking questions. Use the name chart. "If you have a word that ends with *y*, hold it up. If you have a word that ends like *Jeri*, hold it up." If some children continue to confuse first and last, work with them in a small group to establish the meaning of *last*. They draw a card with a name or word and quickly say and point to the last letter. Mix up the cards and do it again until children are pointing without hesitation.	
44	ELC 6 page 95	Understand First and Last in Written Language: Letters	Give each child a duplicated name chart with each name in a square. They can cut apart the names and work with a partner to sort them by first letter, and then by last letter. Ask children to share with the group what they learned about names–for example, "five people have names that end in *y*." Let them take home the names to sort. Fully establish the concept of first and last with a series of games. For example, have children stand in a row from left to right, and let others take turns identifying the first and last children. Repeat with objects or books.	
45	ELC 7 page 99	Understand First and Last in Written Language: Letters and Words	Use another well-known poem or a sentence from interactive writing to work with a small group of children who are confusing first and last. Give each child a copy and have them read it in a shared way. Have them highlight the first words in sentences and the first letters in some words. Ask them to point quickly to first words and first letters in words. Then work on a clean copy of the poem or sentence to highlight last words and last letters. Have children compare the two versions.	

#	Lesson	Title	Teaching Suggestions for Extending Learning	Teacher Notes
			MIDDLE *(continued)*	
46	ELC 8 page 103	Understand First and Last in Written Language: Words	Work with a small group of children who are not quick and automatic with first and last. Write their sentences from the Apply activity on a sentence strip for each child. Cut up the strips and have children reassemble them several times–remembering to start on the left. Use the words *first* and *last*. Then they can glue the pieces on a sheet of paper. You can repeat this activity using a cut-up word.	
47	LK 13 ✓ page 263	Form Letters with Writing Tools	In interactive writing, use the whiteboard to demonstrate making a letter that children want to use in a word. Say the verbal path while making it. Have children write the letter in the air and then on the floor in front of them, saying the verbal path. Choose a letter and have children make a whole page of them; they can then choose their "best" *b* (or other letter).	
48	LK 14 ✓ page 267	Form Letters with Writing Tools	This lesson begins more formal and systematic handwriting instruction. Notice that *h, l,* and *b* all begin in the same place, which makes it easy to use the verbal path. As suggested in this lesson, follow up by repeating the lesson with (1) *c, o, a, d, g, q;* (2) *b, h, t, l, j, k, l, p;* (3) *n, r, m, u;* (4) *v, x, w, y;* (5) *f, s;* (6) *e, z.* These groups of letters have some similarities. You probably can do two to three letters each day. Make a rainbow letter and use the verbal path. The handwriting lesson should take only about five minutes.	
49	LK 15 ✓ page 271	Make Connections Among Words by Noting the Position of a Letter	Extend the lesson by displaying charts of interactive writing the children have finished. You can also use *Words That Sing.* From the array of print, have them find words that begin with a selected letter (for example, *a*). Write the words on a chart in the first column (with *Aa* at the top). Have children put highlighter tape on selected words. Then repeat by finding words that end in *a*.	
50	LK 16 ✓ page 275	Categorize Letters by Features	Repeat the lesson, having children sort letters with circles and letters with tunnels (*a, d, b, u, n, m, o, q, h, g*). Then, sort letters with tails and letters without tails (*a, b, c, d, e, f, g, h, I, j, k, l, m, n, o, p*). Have a sorting tray in a center or at a place that children can visit to work with a partner. One child selects a group of letters and the other child tells how they are alike.	

#	Lesson	Title	Teaching Suggestions for Extending Learning	Teacher Notes
MIDDLE				

#	Lesson	Title	Teaching Suggestions for Extending Learning	Teacher Notes
			MIDDLE *(continued)*	
51	LK 17 ✓ page 279	**Categorize Letters by Features**	Keep the sorting tray available for independent work over a two-week period. Have children create a sort by placing two letters at the top of columns and then finding and adding to the columns other letters that have the same features. Children can then write the letters and share their sort at group share.	
52	HFW 2 ✓ page 381	**Recognize and Use High-Frequency Words with One, Two, or Three Letters**	In HFW 1 and HFW 2 children are learning how to learn a word by attending to every detail. They learn that the order of letters is important. You may want to repeat this lesson several times so that children understand the routine and can do it independently. Work towards knowing the 100 most frequent words (see Online Resources). For example, use the routine to learn *it, to, me, in, not.*	
53	HFW 3 ✓ page 385	**Recognize and Use High-Frequency Words With One, Two, or Three Letters**	Use the routine to learn *and, will, we, I, a, go, you, up, come, look.* You will find Lotto to be a very useful game. It encourages children to notice visual details in words. You may want to play Lotto with a small group to help them learn more words and also to get used to the routines of the game.	
54	WMV 1 ✓ page 407	**Recognize and Use Concept Words: Color Names**	You may want to carry this lesson over two days. Children may know the names of colors but not how to read and write the words; others may understand colors but label them in another language. A few children may not know the names of some colors (for example, *purple*). You can gather boxes of small objects that are clearly one of the primary colors. For example, use pens, small blocks, crayons, toys, ribbons, small pieces of paper, buttons, etc. Place the boxes at tables and have children work in groups of four to sort the objects by color. They will see that many different objects can be the same color. Then, they take turns naming the objects: "This is a red block." "This is a green frog."	*Start of WMV*
55	WMV 2 ✓ page 411	**Recognize and Use Concept Words: Color Names**	If children are still learning color names, you may want to take two days to do this lesson. It may be helpful to invite children to make a book of colors with sentences like *I like blue blueberries.* You can provide the sentence frame on the chart and they can fill in the color and write the name of the item, then illustrate the book. Children who are more advanced can add another line with another object. At group share, they can read their color books to a partner.	

#	Lesson	Title	Teaching Suggestions for Extending Learning	Teacher Notes
			MIDDLE *(continued)*	
56	WMV 3 page 415	Recognize and Use Concept Words: Number Names	Children are learning the definition of the phrase *how many*? They learn to count, and they learn that quantity has a number and a name. If children are learning all of this in math, then you may not need lessons on number names and concepts. But you can add number words to the word wall and work numbers into shared and interactive writing. Have children decide whether to write the number or the word. Read some counting books.	
57	WSA 2 ✓ page 459	Recognize and Read Known Words Quickly	Repeat the lesson using some shared reading books that children know. Have them quickly locate high-frequency words. Then use a new text that will be easy for them. Have them locate high-frequency words before they begin. Let them read a line or two without reading it to them first (but using the pointer to point to the words). Fill in words they don't know; then have individuals demonstrate reading the lines.	
58	WSA 3 ✓ page 463	Change the Beginning Sound or Sounds to Make and Solve a New Word	Lesson WSA 3 has children work with words in the absence of print so that they can learn to make a new word by changing the first sound. Once they know this, they can make new words by changing the first letters. Extend the principle with some simple substitutions that are connected to print. Say *me* and *he* and ask children to say the two words. They can describe how the first sound was changed. Write *he* and *me* on the board and ask them to look at the word. Repeat with *see, bee, tree*. If some children have difficulty with substitution, bring them together in a small group and have them work with magnetic letters to make the same examples.	
59	WSA 4 ✓ page 467	Change the Beginning Sound or Sounds to Make and Solve a New Word	Repeat the lesson using high-frequency words from the word wall or words that are common in children's oral vocabulary. Say two words and ask children to tell how you changed the first sound–for example, *day, say; hand, sand; sock, clock; he, me; more, shore, door; light, might, bright*.	

Suggested Sequence for Phonics Lessons

#	Lesson	Title	Teaching Suggestions for Extending Learning	Teacher Notes
			MIDDLE *(continued)*	
60	SP 1 ✓ page 347	Recognize and Use the CVC Pattern	Have the children explore the word wall to look for three-letter words with a vowel in the middle. If needed, repeat the lesson using *can, nap, mat, sit, pin, tip.*	Start of SP
61	SP 2 page 351	Recognize and Use Phonograms: *-an*	Identify children who have trouble seeing the pattern, and reteach the lesson in a small group. Give each child a copy of the list of *-an* words you made, and have them highlight the *-an* pattern in yellow. Then they can read the words. Play a game by saying a word and having them find it quickly.	
62	SP 3 page 355	Recognize and Use Phonograms: *-at*	Identify children who have trouble seeing the pattern, and reteach the lesson in a small group. Give each child a copy of the list of *-at* words you made, and have them highlight the *-at* pattern in yellow. Then they can read the words. Play a game by saying a word and having them find it quickly.	
63	SP 4 page 359	Recognize and Use Phonograms: *-ay*	If children understand the principle very well, repeat the lesson using *-ap -ad,* and *-am.*	

#	Lesson	Title	Teaching Suggestions for Extending Learning	Teacher Notes
			LATE IN THE YEAR	
64	PA 19 ✅ page 181	Hear and Divide Onsets and Rimes	Play several games until children can take apart onsets and rimes in a very flexible way. Have each child say his name, dividing the first part and the last part. Sit in a circle and have one child name an object in the room or say a word. Children put thumbs up if they can divide it and say the first part and the rest. The first child calls on someone, who then thinks of the next word. Bring some children together in a small group to play a quick Follow the Path game.	
65	PA 20 ✅ page 185	Blend Onsets with Rimes	Play several games until children can take apart onsets and rimes in a very flexible way. Have them line up one at a time by saying the child's name in onsets and rimes and having the child blend the sounds to say his whole name. Use the name chart as a game by saying the first part and having the children whose names fit it take turns saying the rime and then the whole name. Bring some children together in a small group to play a quick Go Fish game.	
66	PA 21 ✅ page 189	Hear and Say Two Sounds in a Word	Repeat the lesson adding more pictures with names that have two sounds–for example, *bow, knee, shoe, ape.* Repeat the lesson using high-frequency words that children know–for example, *it, at, go, in, he, she.*	
67	PA 22 ✅ page 193	Hear and Say Three Sounds in a Word	Repeat the lesson adding more pictures with names that have three sounds–for example, *dog, sheep, nut, boat, chick, ant, cat.* Repeat the lesson using high-frequency words that children know–for example, *and, dad, bike, run.* Explain that when you hear three sounds, there might be more letters. Convene a small group of children who have difficulty determining how many sounds are in a word. Use Elkonin boxes (see page 38) to help them develop a framework for a word spoken aloud. They can work with two or three boxes (see whiteboards).	

Suggested Sequence for Phonics Lessons

#	Lesson	Title	Teaching Suggestions for Extending Learning	Teacher Notes
LATE				
68	PA 23 ✓ page 197	Hear and Say Four or More Sounds in a Word in Sequence	Repeat the lesson mixing pictures with names that have two, three, four, or five sounds. Present them randomly and ask children to say them slowly with a partner and come up with the number of sounds they hear. Convene a small group of children who have difficulty determining how many sounds are in a word. Use Elkonin boxes (see page 38) to help them develop a framework for a word spoken aloud. They can work with two, three, or four boxes (see whiteboards). Have children say and talk about the number of sounds in words during interactive writing and notice that some words have more letters than sounds.	
69	PA 24 ✓ page 201	Blend Three or Four Sounds in a Word	Repeat the lesson using different picture cards–for example, *map, plant, hand, bug, sun, rake, globe, frog, flag, lunch*. Repeat with high-frequency words from the word wall, helping children notice that some words have more letters than sounds. Have children say a word and call on a classmate to show with fingers the number of sounds.	
70	PA 25 ✓ page 205	Delete the Beginning Sound of a Word	Repeat the lesson using high-frequency words from the word wall to practice deleting the first sound of a word. Then give pairs sets of picture cards again and tell them to lay them out so all can be seen. One child says a word without the first letter and the other tries to guess what it is, finds it, and says the whole word.	
71	PA 26 ✓ page 209	Delete the Beginning Sound of a Word	Repeat the lesson using high-frequency words from the word wall. Say the word to the children, and have them say it without the first letter. Then, have one child locate the word on the wall so that everyone can look at it. (They will notice some words with silent *e*.)	
72	LK 18 ✓ page 283	Form Letters with Writing Tools	In LK 18, you are demonstrating how to make letters using chart paper or an enlarged handwriting book. Each child will have a book with twenty-six pages and the appropriate letter written in the upper right-hand corner. In this way they can keep a record of their writing. Repeat Lesson LK 18 with groups of letters (two or three at a time) until children can form letters efficiently and correctly. Take only about five minutes a day to work on handwriting and use the verbal path.	

#	Lesson	Title	Teaching Suggestions for Extending Learning	Teacher Notes
			LATE *(continued)*	
73	LK 19 ⊘ page 287	Form Letters with Writing Tools	Continue demonstrating how to make letters and marking your "best" example. Have children practice in their own handwriting books. At group share you can have children share their "best" letter. This kind of evaluation will become routine. Go back to a shared reading alphabet book. As you read, trace over each letter and use the verbal path. Children make the letter in the air and on the floor in front of them. You can do this with a small group of children who need more practice. Have them make the letter with large movements on the chalkboard.	
74	LK 20 ⊘ page 291	Recognize Uppercase Letters and Lowercase Letters	Notice if children have difficulty sorting the letters and work with them in a small group. When doing shared reading or rereading a piece of interactive writing, have children quickly point to uppercase and lowercase letters. Using the Alphabet Linking Chart, point randomly to letters and have children clap every time you point to an uppercase letter.	
75	LK 21 ⊘ page 295	Distinguish the Differences Between Uppercase and Lowercase Forms of a Letter	Using the Alphabet Linking Chart, point randomly to letters, and have children clap every time you point to an uppercase letter. Repeat for lowercase letters.	
76	LK 22 page 299	Recognize That Letters Can Be Consonants or Vowels	In shared reading or a piece of interactive writing, ask children to identify the vowel or vowels in every word. Visit the Alphabet Linking Chart and have children highlight the vowels. Bring children who find this lesson difficult into a small group to repeat the sorting task. Lay out all the letters and have children take turns finding *a, e, i, o,* and *u.* Then mix up the letters and ask children to sort them quickly into consonants and vowels.	
77	LK 23 ⊘ page 303	Recognize the Order of the Alphabet	Go in order from *A* to *Z* to have children line up or sit down. Have them predict the next letter before you say it. Read some alphabet books and talk with children about the order of things in the books.	
78	LK 24 ⊘ page 307	Recognize the Order of the Alphabet	Children will not be expected to do complex alphabetization, but they can learn the order of the letters and be able to put them in order quickly. Give each child an alphabet strip that they can cut apart, mix up, and put back together in order. If needed, they can sing the alphabet song to check order.	

Suggested Sequence for Phonics Lessons

#	Lesson	Title	Teaching Suggestions for Extending Learning	Teacher Notes
			**LATE** *(continued)*	
79	LSR 6 ⊘ page 333	Recognize Beginning Consonant Sounds and the Letters That Represent Them	Lesson LSR 6 will probably take several days. You may want to work with the whole group on harder pages such as *w, x, y, z.* Others can be assigned to partners to produce them faster. Each day, reread what has been added to the *ABC* book. (You can always add more words and pictures later in the year.) Place the *ABC* book in the classroom library. As pointed out in the lesson, children may follow up by making their own books with one picture and word on a page.	
80	LSR 7 ⊘ page 337	Recognize Beginning Consonant Sounds and the Letters That Represent Them	You may need to carry this lesson over two days. The result will be a beautiful display. You can place these colorful letters around the wall. (Work with children on *ABC* order to place them.) Or you may place the letters on a bulletin board in several rows. Sometimes there is a place to line them up in the corridor. This is handy because you can play a game by having children stand next to *d* or *m.*	
81	LSR 8 ⊘ page 341	Recognize Ending Consonant Sounds and the Letters That Represent Them	You can work several days on ending sounds to help children be more flexible in using letters and sounds in flexible ways. In interactive writing, you can write the first part of the word and have children "finish" it by saying the word and listening for the ending sound. Repeat this lesson with other consonant sounds represented by the letters *f, l, n, p, r, s, t, w, x, z.*	
82	HFW 4 ⊘ page 389	Recognize and Use High-Frequency Words with Three or More Letters	Repeat the lesson so that children use the routine to practice new words from the word wall. Use high-frequency words rather than content words. Work toward the fifty most frequently used words in kindergarten (Online Resources).	
83	HFW 5 ⊘ page 393	Recognize and Use High-Frequency Words with Three or More Letters	Repeat the lesson so that children use the routine to practice new words from the word wall. Use high-frequency words rather than content words. Work toward the fifty most frequently used words in kindergarten (Online Resources).	
84	HFW 6 ⊘ page 397	Recognize and Use High-Frequency Words with Three or More Letters	Repeat the lesson so that children use the routine to practice new words from the word wall. Use high-frequency words rather than content words. Work toward the fifty most frequently used words in kindergarten (Online Resources).	

#	Lesson	Title	Teaching Suggestions for Extending Learning	Teacher Notes
			LATE *(continued)*	
85	HFW 7 ✓ page 401	Locate and Read High-Frequency Words in Continuous Text	Sometimes readers "know" a word in isolation yet fail to identify it when it is embedded in continuous print. You may want to repeat this lesson using other poems or shared reading books. Also, in shared and guided reading, you can have children quickly locate words. They should be able to locate known high-frequency words rapidly.	
86	WSA 5 ✓ page 471	Hear Sounds in Sequence	In interactive writing, have children say words slowly, working left to right across the words. Select words with three or four sounds that are new (or relatively new) to children. (They should write well-known high-frequency words quickly.) Notice children who have difficulty with hearing sounds in sequence. Convene them in a small group and use Elkonin boxes (see page 38) quickly. When children are working on their own writing independently, encourage them to say the words slowly and write letters representing sounds, left to right. When you are working beside them, you can fill in additional letters like silent *e*.	
87	WSA 6 ✓ page 475	Use Onsets and Rimes in Known Words to Read and Write Other Words with the Same Parts	Work further with the children to help them use known parts to read or write other words. Do some quick whiteboard activities in guided reading–for example, *me, he, be, bee; tree; the, then; and, stand, brand; go, no, slow, grow.* Work for flexibility. Give children magnetic letters, and have them make and change words–for example, *b, m, h, e, i, t, a, g, o.* They can work as partners with one child making a word and the other changing it.	
88	WSA 7 ✓ page 479	Use Onsets and Rimes in Known Words to Read and Write Other Words with the Same Parts	Repeat the lesson using a simple shared reading book that children have not seen before (two or three lines of print). Select several words in the poem that are related to words you have on the word wall. Use a small whiteboard to make connections and have children locate the word in the text–for example, *rain, train; down, town.* When hearing children read independently (or after a running record), ask, "Do you know a word like that?" Or show word connections as a teaching point after the child finishes reading a book.	

#	Lesson	Title	Teaching Suggestions for Extending Learning	Teacher Notes
			LATE *(continued)*	
89	WSA 8 ✓ page 483	Change the Ending Sound or Sounds to Make and Solve a New Word	Use magnetic letters as you work with children in guided reading groups. Or convene one or two small groups of children who need more work handling magnetic letters. Repeat WSA 8, but have children handle the letters. Extend by using other examples: *as, am, at; pig, pin, pit.*	
90	WSA 9 ✓ page 487	Change the Ending Sound or Sounds to Make and Solve a New Word	Repeat the lesson using other examples—for example, *hot, hop, hog; pig, pin, pit, pill, pip.* If children understand this principle really well, teach another lesson that moves flexibly between changing the beginning sound and changing the ending sound—for example, *see, tree, bee, beep, peep, creep*, etc.	
91	SP 5 page 363	Recognize and Use Phonograms with a VC*e* Pattern: *-ake*	Identify children who have trouble seeing the pattern and reteach the lesson in a small group. Give each child a copy of the list of *-ake* words you made and have them highlight the *-ake* pattern in yellow. Then they can read the words. Play a game by saying a word and having them find it quickly.	
92	SP 6 page 367	Recognize and Use Phonograms with a VC*e* Pattern: *-ine*	Identify children who have trouble seeing the pattern and reteach the lesson in a small group. Give each child a copy of the list of *-ine* words you made and have them highlight the *-ine* pattern in yellow. Then they can read the words. Play a game by saying a word and having them find it quickly.	
93	SP 7 ✓ page 371	Recognize Letter Patterns	Repeat the lesson using a set of words cards that can be sorted several ways: *the, they, three; is, in, it; go, no, so; make, take, tape, made.* Create a sorting tray with word cards that children can sort with a partner. They lay out the words, and one partner chooses two or more. The other partner guesses the common feature.	
94	WS 2 ✓ page 441	Understand the Concept of a Contraction	Repeat the lesson to be sure that children understand the concept of a contraction. Guide interactive writing so that contractions naturally occur. Use the whiteboard to help children connect the two words with the contraction. Point out contractions in guided reading. If children seem to understand the idea very well, work with *aren't, couldn't,* and *haven't.*	

#	Lesson	Title	Teaching Suggestions for Extending Learning	Teacher Notes
			LATE *(continued)*	
95	**WS 3** page 445	**Understand the Concept of Plural**	WS 3 focuses on the concept of *more than one*, which is usually implicitly understood and signaled by speakers of the language. You may have some children who understand it conceptually but don't know how to signal plural in English. Plurality is signaled in many different ways. Work in a small group to discuss plurals, maybe in reference to children's families, and use some shared writing. "I have one brother." "I have two brothers." "Katya has two grandmothers." Use fingers to indicate *1, 2,* and *3.* Children can draw pictures to represent more than one person.	
96	**WS 4** page 449	**Recognize and Use Plurals That Add -s**	Repeat the lesson to show plurals of the same words adding the magnet letter *s.* Make a word (either singular or plural) and ask children, "Does this word mean one or more than one?" Play Concentration with a small group to help them learn this routine and become more flexible with plurals that add *s*.	
97	**WMV 4** page 419	**Recognize and Use Concept Words: Number Names**	You can repeat this lesson to learn the numbers and names for *6–10*. Read books about counting. Teach them the rhyme "Buckle My Shoe," write it on a chart, and illustrate the big fat hen. Children can make their own number books from *1* to *10*, drawing the right number of animals or objects.	
98	**WMV 5** page 423	**Recognize and Use Concept Words: Days of the Week**	If children have learned the days of the week while working with the calendar, you may not want to use this lesson. But you can use it as a kind of culmination lesson that also helps children become quicker at recognizing the names of the days. You can extend this by having children work with a partner using two sets of names. They mix up the order and read them (not in sequence); have them work with the words until they can read them easily. They can then divide them, and individuals can lay them out in sequence. Finally, they can highlight the parts that are the same in all of the words.	

Suggested Sequence for Phonics Lessons

#	Lesson	Title	Teaching Suggestions for Extending Learning	Teacher Notes
			LATE *(continued)*	
99	WMV 6 page 427	Recognize and Use Concept Words: Days of the Week	Lesson WMV 6 is designed to help children bring the names of days of the week into their writing. You can extend this by having children make a book with seven pages telling something they like to do on each day. The application activity should help them engage independently in this task.	
100	WMV 7 ✓ page 431	Recognize Related Words	The concept that many words are related by meaning is important in early comprehension of texts. It helps readers predict new words and know what they mean. You can repeat this lesson with other categories of words (see the lesson). The charts children make of related words serve as resources for them when they do independent writing. Once they understand the concept, have children work with a partner to create a group of related words. They can draw pictures and/or write the words. At group share they can show their groups of words and others can guess the name of the big category.	

Early Literacy Concepts

Learning about literacy begins long before children enter school. Many children hear stories read aloud and try out writing for themselves; through such experiences, they learn some basic concepts about written language. Nearly all children begin to notice print in the environment and develop ideas about the purposes of print. The child's name, for example, is a very important word. Kindergartners and first graders are still acquiring some of these basic concepts, and they need to generalize and systematize their knowledge. In the classroom, they learn a great deal through experiences like shared and modeled reading and shared and interactive writing. Explicit teaching can help children learn much more about these early concepts, understand their importance, and develop ways of using them in reading and writing.

Connect to Assessment

See related (optional) ELC Assessment tasks in Online Resources.

- Assessment A: Writing a Name
- Assessment B: Locating a Name in a List
- Assessment C: Locating a Name in a Text
- Assessment D: Finding First and Last Letters
- Assessment E: Locating Words
- Assessment F: Locating Letters
- Assessment G: Matching Word by Word
- Assessment H: Individual Record
- Assessment I: Class Record (Names)
- Assessment J: Class Record (Locating Words)

Develop Your Professional Understanding

See *The Fountas & Pinnell Comprehensive Phonics, Spelling, and Word Study Guide*. 2017. Portsmouth, New Hampshire: Heinemann. Related pages: 2–12, 14–15.

See *The Fountas & Pinnell Literacy Continuum: A Tool for Assessment, Planning, and Teaching*. 2017. Portsmouth, New Hampshire: Heinemann. Related pages: 357–397.

See *Word Matters: Teaching Phonics and Spelling in the Reading/Writing Classroom* by G. S. Pinnell and I. C. Fountas. 1998. Portsmouth, New Hampshire: Heinemann. Related pages: 5, 8–10, 47–48, 67–69, 76–77, 88–89, 123, 141–142, 252, 254.

likes

ooples

Kallet

Heather
likes

riding
horses

Recognize Your Name

Plan

▶ Consider Your Children

This lesson is appropriate for children who are just beginning to learn about print. It will familiarize them with the letters that make up their names and will help them attend to sequence and orientation. The lesson engages children in learning the details of their own names and draws their attention to others' names. The lesson is also appropriate for children who already recognize or can write their names, because they will be learning the names of their friends as well.

Following this lesson, create a permanent name chart for daily reference in reading, writing, and word study activities. Copy the names of the children (grouped by first letter) on chart paper. You may wish to involve the children in circling each group of names that start with the same letter.

▶ Working with English Language Learners

For English language learners, recognizing their own names in print will provide a first and very personal entry into written English. Take care to pronounce each name accurately and to emphasize and point out its first letter. As you say the child's name, run your finger along the letters so that he can begin to notice the connections between letters and sounds. Give the children many opportunities to locate their names quickly on the name chart.

YOU WILL NEED

 Ready Resources
- ▶ Blank Pocket-Chart Cards

Online Resources
- ▶ ELC 1 Action Tags
- ▶ ELC 1 Blank Word Cards

Other Materials
- ▶ pocket chart or blank chart paper
- ▶ glue sticks
- ▶ magnetic letters
- ▶ manila envelope or sealable bags

UNDERSTAND THE PRINCIPLE

Beginning with their own names, children come to realize that a word is made up of distinct letters. They learn to notice some visual features of letters including the difference between uppercase and lowercase letters. Children begin also to connect visual features of letters to sounds in words.

EXPLAIN THE PRINCIPLE

A name is a word.

When you know the first letter in a name, it helps you find the name in print.

Comprehensive Phonics, Spelling, and Word Study Guide

Refer to: page **14**, row **6**

ACTIVITY: NAME CARDS

INSTRUCTIONAL PROCEDURE

SEE AND SAY

See page 36 for descriptions of Instructional Procedures.

EXPLAIN THE PRINCIPLE

A name is a word.

When you know the first letter in a name, it helps you find the name in print.

Comprehensive Phonics, Spelling, and Word Study Guide

Refer to: page **14**, row **6**

Teach

1. Explain to the children that they are going to work with their names.

2. Prepare cards with children's first names for the pocket chart. Print should be large enough for all children to see while seated on the rug. In alphabetical order, hold up each child's name, say it, and ask the children to repeat it. Then have each child put her name in the pocket chart as you point to the place.

3. *This is Avery's name. Avery starts with an A. Say Avery. • Say A for Avery. • Avery, please put your name on the chart.*

4. Repeat with each child in the class.

5. Read the complete name chart with the children.

ACTIVITY: NAME CARDS

INSTRUCTIONAL PROCEDURE
WORDS TO KNOW
See page 36 for descriptions of Instructional Procedures.

ACTION TAGS

glue

write

draw

make

check

switch

make

check

Apply

- Ask each child to take the pocket-chart card with his name on it, glue it onto a piece of paper, write the name underneath, and then draw a self-portrait. These pieces of paper can be stapled into a class book of names or placed in alphabetical order on a bulletin board. (You might also take a photograph of each child and make a class book with photographs or another name chart with photographs.)

- Prepare a sealable bag, manila envelope, or box for each child that contains his name on a blank word card and the magnetic letters to make his name. Children make their own names with magnetic letters using the card as a model. Then have them work with partners to switch names, make the names with magnetic letters, and check both names.

Share

- Ask the children to show their pictures and read their names. Then ask them to exchange names with a partner and show and read the partner's name.

- Remove the names from the chart and mix them up. Go quickly through the names again and have each child put his name in the chart. Then read the chart several different ways: backward, skip around, and so on.

Assess

- Notice how many letters children can produce when they write their names.

- Observe whether children use their names as a resource for interactive writing and independent writing.

- You may wish to use Early Literacy Concepts Assessment A, B, H, or I.

Connect Learning Across Contexts

Interactive Read-Aloud Read aloud alphabet books so children can practice letter recognition.

> [IRA] *Alphabet Under Construction* by Denise Fleming

> [IRA] *B Is for Bulldozer* by June Sobel

Shared Reading See "Bow-wow-wow" in *Words That Sing* (2019). If you don't have these poetry charts, enlarge the print of this poem or other poems such as "The Alphabet Song" or "Billy, Billy" in *Sing a Song of Poetry*, and have children practice letter recognition in names. You may also wish to use the following Shared Reading title from *Fountas & Pinnell Classroom*™ to look at more letters.

> [SR] *City ABCs* by Finnoula Louise

Interactive Writing Refer to the class name chart to show children how to make letters ["a *b* like the *b* in *Rebecca*"].

Independent Writing Have children write their names on their drawings and other writing. Remind children that they can use the letters they know from their names while writing stories.

Extend Learning

- Repeat the lesson, having children work with names of others in the class.

- Read the chart together. Then have individual children locate their names by thinking first about the beginning letter.

- Play a game: "I'm thinking of a boy whose name starts with *A*. He has a red shirt." Let children respond by going up and pointing to the name and reading it.

- After children can identify names by first letter, ask them to locate names by the next letter or the last letter: "I'm thinking of a girl whose name starts with *C*. The next letter is *a*."

- Make a class name chart on paper to display next to your easel so that it will be there for handy reference.

▶ Connect with Home

- Have the children take home their name cards and find and glue on the paper a picture of something that starts with the same beginning letter.

- Encourage children to invite caregivers to create a small name chart with names of family or friends. Provide blank word cards and a copy of the class name chart to use as a model for making a family name chart. Encourage children to read the chart several times a day.

Recognize Your Name

Plan

▶ Consider Your Children

Like ELC 1, this lesson is apt to be one of the children's first school experiences with print. A child's name is an important word because it has personal meaning. By noticing some visual aspects of print, children begin to learn to recognize their names, and this helps them learn the concept of a word. Children who already recognize their own names will find them quickly and may begin to notice other words within familiar texts. It will be important for children who do not recognize their own names to learn how to locate them within continuous text. Young children will enjoy chanting or singing the song.

▶ Working with English Language Learners

Initially some English language learners may not understand what is said in the classroom, and English in print will be difficult for them. Hearing and seeing their own names provides a way of entering the world of English language and literacy. As children begin to recognize their names they become oriented to print. Of course, showing that you value each child's name promotes a sense of community and inclusion. Be sure to pronounce children's names accurately and to say their names often. Help children say and find the names of other children in the class. By repeating chants and songs many times, you can encourage children to join in and add their own names.

UNDERSTAND THE PRINCIPLE

Beginning with their own names, children come to realize that a word is made up of distinct letters. They learn to notice some visual features of letters including the difference between uppercase and lowercase letters. Children begin also to connect visual features of letters to sounds in words. This principle sets the scene for noticing spelling patterns in words.

YOU WILL NEED

PWS Ready Resources
- ▶ ELC 2 Pocket-Chart Cards (long)

Online Resources
- ▶ ELC 2 Action Tags
- ▶ ELC 2 Song: Happy Birthday to You
- ▶ ELC 2 Rhyme: Good Morning
- ▶ ELC 2 Poem: Jack, Be Nimble

Other Materials
- ▶ pocket-chart cards (with children's names, from ELC 1)
- ▶ sentence strips with words to "Happy Birthday"

EXPLAIN THE PRINCIPLE

A name is a word.

When you know the first letter in a name, it helps you find the name in print.

A name starts with a capital letter. The other letters are lowercase.

 Comprehensive Phonics, Spelling, and Word Study Guide

Refer to: page **14**, row **6**

ACTIVITY: SONG

INSTRUCTIONAL PROCEDURE

SEE AND SAY

See page 36 for detailed descriptions of Instructional Procedures.

EXPLAIN THE PRINCIPLE

A name is a word.

When you know the first letter in a name, it helps you find the name in print.

A name starts with a capital letter. The other letters are lowercase.

Comprehensive Phonics, Spelling, and Word Study Guide

Refer to:
page **14**, row **6**

Teach

1. Tell children that they will learn to read their names as they sing and chant.

2. First, teach orally a song, such as "Happy Birthday to You," that can incorporate children's names.

3. After children know the song, introduce it in enlarged written form on a chart or on sentence strips. Read it in a shared way.

4. Select a card with a child's name, and ask the children to look at it carefully but not to say the name. Put the card in the appropriate position on the chart or sentence strip. Pointing to each word, say each word up to the name; then drop out and let children say the name. Afterward, ask children to talk about how they "read" the name.

5. Repeat this process with several cards. Afterwards, encourage children to talk about how they "read" the names.

6. Explain that today they are going to have their own copy of this song. They will read the song and write their name on the blank line.

Happy birthday to you.

Happy birthday to you.

Happy birthday, dear ___EMILY___ .

Happy birthday to you.

ELC 2 Song: Happy Birthday to You

ACTIVITY: SONG

INSTRUCTIONAL PROCEDURE

WORDS TO KNOW

See page 36 for detailed descriptions of Instructional Procedures.

ACTION TAGS

write

read

draw

Apply

Distribute photocopies of the song. Have children write their names in the blank. Then they can read the song to a partner. Later they may wish to add an illustration to the text and take the song home to read to family members.

Share

Ask the children what they have noticed about names. Responses like the following will let you in on their thinking:

"A name is for a person."

"A name has a capital letter at the beginning."

"Some of our names start the same."

"You can look at the first letter and the other letters to find a name."

Assess

- Check children's progress in recognizing their own names and the names of other children.

- Observe the children's progress in writing their names accurately and with fluency.

- You may wish to use Early Literacy Concepts Assessment A, B, C, H, or I.

Connect Learning Across Contexts

Interactive Read-Aloud Read aloud books that include names for children to practice name recognition.

> IRA *A, My Name Is Alice* by Jane Bayer

> IRA *The Doorbell Rang* by Pat Hutchins

Shared Reading See "Jack, Jack" in *Words That Sing* (2019). If you don't have these poetry charts, enlarge the print of this poem or other poems such as "Good Morning" or "Jack, Be Nimble" in *Sing a Song of Poetry*, and have children locate names. You may also wish to use the following Shared Reading title from *Fountas & Pinnell Classroom™* to locate and recognize other names.

> SR *Kate's Party* by Jane Simon

Interactive Writing Use the songs, nursery rhymes, and chants that include names as resources for identifying and writing new, interesting words.

Independent Writing Encourage children to put their names on their writing papers. You can also give children copies of familiar songs that feature names and have them put their names in the blanks and draw pictures.

Extend Learning

- Create a new name chart with storybook characters. Take the names of children's favorite storybook characters (for example, Goldilocks, Clifford, Chrysanthemum, Peter Rabbit, or Frances) and place them in the song or chant for shared reading.

- Place the first letter of a name on the chart and ask children to put in a name starting with that letter. Teach them how to check by comparing each word with the words on the class name chart.

- Repeat the lesson using chants such as "Pat-a-cake," and "Jack, Jack" (see *Sing a Song of Poetry*). In "Pat-a-cake," children insert an initial letter as well as a name; in "Jack, Jack," they insert the name four times.

▶ Connect with Home

Send home copies of "name" songs and chants with the child's name inserted (such as "Billy, Billy" or "Sally, Go 'Round" from *Sing a Song of Poetry*). Also send home blank versions, and encourage parents or caregivers to put other family members' names in the blanks and read the songs and chants with the child.

Match a Spoken Word with a Group of Letters

Plan

▶ Consider Your Children

Children need to learn to match one spoken word with one group of letters (defined by spaces before and after) in lines of print. This is best developed through shared reading and shared and interactive writing, but when children have the "feel" of it, you may wish to focus one or more lessons on word-by-word matching. These same teaching guidelines can be used in combination with interactive writing and with simple poems from shared reading.

▶ Working with English Language Learners

Matching one spoken word with one word in print is a challenge to all young children, especially those who may not fully understand word boundaries in English. Before you expect children to work on matching, be sure that they can say all of the words in a sentence and that they can understand its meaning. Using children's names is a good way to introduce known words so they can check accuracy as they point and read. Provide many opportunities for repetition of the task.

UNDERSTAND THE PRINCIPLE

Children need to understand that when they read, they match one spoken word with one group of printed letters. This information will be valuable as children read sentences in books, monitor their reading, and compose and write sentences.

YOU WILL NEED

PWS Ready Resources
- ▶ Blank Pocket-Chart Cards

Online Resources
- ▶ ELC 3 Action Tags
- ▶ ELC 3 Blank Book Page
- ▶ ELC 3 Blank Word Cards

Other Materials
- ▶ pocket chart
- ▶ photocopied strips of sentences with names of children in the class (from ELC 8)
- ▶ glue sticks

Generative Lesson
A generative lesson has a simple structure that you can use to present similar content or concepts. Use this lesson structure to teach children to locate a variety of spoken words in continuous text.

EXPLAIN THE PRINCIPLE
Say one word for each group of letters.

Comprehensive Phonics, Spelling, and Word Study Guide

Refer to: page **15**, row **10**

ACTIVITY: CUT-UP SENTENCES

INSTRUCTIONAL PROCEDURE

SEE AND SAY

See page 36 for detailed descriptions of Instructional Procedures.

EXPLAIN THE PRINCIPLE

Say one word for each group of letters.

Comprehensive Phonics, Spelling, and Word Study Guide

Refer to: page **15**, row **10**

Teach

1. Explain to the children that they can use words to make sentences.

2. Display a pocket chart that contains several children's names and some blank word cards.

3. Ask the children to look at the names on the pocket chart as you read them together. *Today we are going to write something about Caroline, Jamal, and Sara. We're going to write words on these blank cards. We'll make a sentence about each person.*

4. Generate ideas for the name Caroline, such as "Caroline likes to read" or "Caroline has a yellow shirt." Guide the spoken language so that the written sentence will be short enough to write on cards to be inserted into the pocket chart. Use the children's own language, making sure that they can say all of the words in the sentence.

5. Caroline *is the first word of our sentence.* Caroline . . . Children respond with the second word, for example, *likes.*

6. Say the second word aloud, write it on a card, and place the card right after *Caroline* (or invite a child to do it). Point out that you are leaving a space between the end of one word and the beginning of the next word. Invite children to read the second word together as you point. *Caroline likes* . . . Children respond with the third word.

7. Say the third word aloud, write it on a card, and place the card right after *likes*. Again point out the space you've left between the end of one word and the beginning of the next word. Invite children to read the third word together as you point. Continue until the sentence is written on cards. Place a period after the last word. Read it all together and ask children to check to see whether they have left spaces between words.

8. Repeat the process using one or two more children's names. Emphasize individual words and spacing, rereading each time you add a word. Help children see that each word is a group of letters that stands alone with space before and after it. Point out how the period means to come to a full stop. Finally, read all the sentences together as a unit.

**INSTRUCTIONAL
PROCEDURE**

SEE AND SAY

*See page 36 for detailed
descriptions of Instructional
Procedures.*

ACTION TAGS

cut

say

glue

draw

Apply

■ Distribute photocopied sentence strips for children to cut apart and then glue
back together into sentences that they illustrate. Encourage children to say
each word as they glue it onto the paper.

■ As an alternative, give each child a four-page blank book stapled along the 8½-
inch side. Ask children to draw a friend or family member on each page and
write a short sentence about this person, one word at a time, on blank word
cards (e.g., *Ben likes football*). Have them glue the cards in order at the bottom
of the page to make a sentence about the picture. (Their spelling will probably
be approximated.)

Share

Ask children to share the sentences they have put together or written.

Assess

■ Observe the children's writing and notice whether they are using spaces
between words.

■ Observe the children reading independently to see whether they are noticing
individual words and pointing word by word.

■ You may wish to use Early Literacy Concepts Assessment A, E, G, H, or J.

Connect Learning Across Contexts

Interactive Read-Aloud Read aloud books with large type in which children can clearly see the words and spaces. As you and the children explore these books, help them notice the words and spacing.

> IRA *The Bus for Us* by Suzanne Bloom
>
> IRA *Dog's Colorful Day* by Emma Dodd

Shared Reading See "Someone's Birthday" in *Words That Sing* (2019). If you don't have these poetry charts, enlarge the print of this poem or other poems such as "Jerry Hall" or "Go to Bed" in *Sing a Song of Poetry*, and show children how to read word-by-word. You may also wish to use the following Shared Reading title from *Fountas & Pinnell Classroom*™ to further point out spaces between words.

> SR *Smash! Crash!* by Catherine Friend

Interactive Writing Explicitly point out spaces; reread messages word by word.

Independent Writing Ask children to check their independent writing to be sure they are leaving spaces.

Extend Learning

- Prepare a pocket chart and cards with the names of children in the class and other words to combine for sentences. Ask children to put together sentences using a name card and other word cards. As they become more familiar with the messages (or more are added), they can vary the sentences they compose.

- Using shared or interactive writing, create a sentence about each child in the class and make a class big book with a page and drawing or photo for each child.

▶ Connect with Home

- Send the four-page books home for children to read to family members.

- Create sentence puzzles (three cut-up words) in envelopes for children to take home and glue on a sheet of paper. They can illustrate the sentence and read it to a family member.

Match a Spoken Word with a Group of Letters

Plan

▶ Consider Your Children

Early understanding about words is best developed through shared reading and shared and interactive writing. When children have the "feel" for what sentences are, focus a few very explicit lessons on this concept. At first, work with just one sentence at a time. The teaching suggestions in this lesson can be used in combination with interactive writing and with simple poems from shared reading.

▶ Working with English Language Learners

This lesson will give English language learners opportunities to compose and write sentences. Begin with very simple, short sentences and topics that children will easily understand. Using repetitive language will scaffold English language learners in their composition of sentences. Allow children to use structures you provide, varying only one or two words. Provide many opportunities to repeat sentences and reread them.

YOU WILL NEED

 Ready Resources
- ▶ Blank Pocket-Chart Cards (long)

Online Resources
- ▶ ELC 4 Action Tags

Other Materials
- ▶ blank chart paper
- ▶ pocket chart
- ▶ sheets for gluing sentences
- ▶ glue sticks

Generative Lesson
A generative lesson has a simple structure that you can use to present similar content or concepts. Use this lesson structure to teach a variety of spoken words in continuous text.

UNDERSTAND THE PRINCIPLE

Children need to understand that when they read, they match one spoken word with one group of printed letters. This information will be valuable as children read sentences in books, monitor their reading, and compose and write sentences.

EXPLAIN THE PRINCIPLE

Say one word for each group of letters.

 Comprehensive Phonics, Spelling, and Word Study Guide

Refer to: page **15**, row **10**

EARLY MIDDLE LATE

ACTIVITY: POCKET-CHART SENTENCES

INSTRUCTIONAL PROCEDURE

SAY AND WRITE

See page 36 for detailed descriptions of Instructional Procedures.

EXPLAIN THE PRINCIPLE

Say one word for each group of letters.

Comprehensive Phonics, Spelling, and Word Study Guide

Refer to:
page **15**, row **10**

Teach

1. Tell your children that they can use words to make sentences.

2. Ask the children to generate some ideas that you will write for them. Choose a simple topic that will allow you to shape the language. *Do you think it would be a good idea to think of things that you like to do in kindergarten? Then, if people visit our room, they can read about what you like to do.*

3. Have a discussion that will generate written sentences. Model language by saying some of the ideas in sentences suitable for the chart, but be sure that children generate the language you finally use.

4. Reach consensus on the first sentence. Write it word by word on a blank pocket-chart card and place it in the pocket chart. Reread the sentence a couple of times, telling children to watch how you are pointing to each word. Point out that you start reading on the left. Count the words. Point out the period at the end.

5. Use the first sentence as a model for one or two more. Write them yourself, but have the children come up to point out the spaces and show where to start reading. Reread the sentences word by word. This will probably be enough work for one day.

6. On the second day, have the lines of the message written on pocket-chart cards in the chart and read them.

7. Take out all but the first pocket-chart card. Cut the first sentence up into individual words. Place the words randomly at the bottom of the pocket chart.

8. Have the children help you put the sentence together one word at a time. *The first word is we. I'll put it in the pocket chart. What is the next word?* Children will have just reread the message, so most will probably remember the next word.

9. Model looking for the next word, *read*. Place the word in the pocket chart and reread the first two words. Continue putting together the simple sentence; then reread it. Move along at a good pace; don't let the lesson drag.

10. Replace the words randomly at the bottom of the pocket chart; then put the sentence together again quickly with the children's participation.

We | sing | songs | in | kindergarten.

ACTIVITY: CUT-UP SENTENCES

INSTRUCTIONAL PROCEDURE

FIND AND MATCH

See page 36 for detailed descriptions of Instructional Procedures.

ACTION TAGS

find

put

glue

draw

read

Apply

Provide cut-up versions of the sentences for the children to put together, glue on a sheet, and illustrate. In pairs, they can take turns pointing to the words and reading the sentences they make.

Share

Ask the children to share what they learned about how spaces before and after a word help you see the word. Have them go up to the chart to locate the spaces.

Assess

- Observe children in shared reading and notice whether they can read left to right and match word by word.
- Look at children's writing and notice whether they are using spaces.
- Conduct a quick test by asking individuals to point to the words as you read a couple of sentences.
- You may wish to use Early Literacy Concepts Assessment E, G, H, or J.

Connect Learning Across Contexts

Interactive Read-Aloud Read aloud books with large type in which children can clearly see the words and spaces. As you and the children explore these books, help them notice the words and spacing.

> IRA *Market Day* by Lois Ehlert

> IRA *Snowballs* by Lois Ehlert

Shared Reading See "Charlie over the Ocean" in *Words That Sing* (2019). If you don't have these poetry charts, enlarge the print of this poem or other poems such as "Good Morning" or "Apples, Peaches" in *Sing a Song of Poetry*, and point out the spaces. You may also wish to use the following Shared Reading title from *Fountas & Pinnell Classroom*™ and show children how to read word-by-word with a pointer.

> SR *The Dog Park* by Jackson Pace

Interactive Writing Explicitly point out spaces; reread messages word by word. Invite a child to use the pointer while others read.

Independent Writing Ask children to write their own stories about what they like to do in kindergarten and to draw a picture. Encourage them to leave spaces between words.

Extend Learning

Apply these teaching guidelines to texts from shared reading and interactive writing. Using simple sentences, make pocket-chart cards for children to cut up and put back together.

▶ Connect with Home

Send home copies of your series of sentences for children to read to their family members. Let children take their cut-up sentences home. Inform parents that children are not expected to read the words in isolation (as in word cards) but are to put them back together into a sentence, glue them on paper, illustrate the sentence, and read it with pointing.

Connect a Name to Other Words

Plan

▶ Consider Your Children

This lesson is best used after children can read most of the names of class members. In this lesson, you show children how to notice different aspects of words by asking them to sort names in a variety of ways. Depending on the group, you may want to show only one way of sorting on a given day. Children will also learn the routine of sorting.

▶ Working with English Language Learners

It will be especially important for English language learners to make connections among names and use them as resources for learning more about print. At the same time, in a multilingual classroom, many names may be different from those children have encountered in their homes and communities. Give children many opportunities to pronounce the names as you draw attention to the print. Emphasize the importance of saying individuals' names exactly as *they* say them (as much as you possibly can). There may be letter-sound relationships with names that do not fit regular English phonology; point out that these differences make people's names interesting and unique and that we can all learn different ways of saying names.

YOU WILL NEED

 Ready Resources
- ▶ Blank Pocket-Chart Cards

Online Resources
- ▶ ELC 5 Action Tags
- ▶ ELC 5 Three-Way Sorts
- ▶ ELC 5 Blank Word Cards

Other Materials
- ▶ pocket chart

Generative Lesson

A generative lesson has a simple structure that you can use to present similar content or concepts. Use this lesson structure to connect a variety of names and words.

UNDERSTAND THE PRINCIPLE

By closely examining their own and their classmates' names, children learn that words are made up of letters and that the order of letters is always the same. These concepts are important in recognizing words by sight (by letter patterns), beginning to recognize spelling patterns, and noticing relationships between letters and sounds. Sorting names helps children attend more closely to the specific features of names and make spelling-to-sound corrections.

EXPLAIN THE PRINCIPLE

A name is a word.

Connect your name with other words.

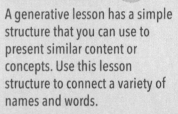

Comprehensive Phonics, Spelling, and Word Study Guide

Refer to: page **15**, row **11**

ACTIVITY: THREE-WAY NAME SORT

INSTRUCTIONAL PROCEDURE

SAY AND SORT

See page 36 for detailed descriptions of Instructional Procedures.

EXPLAIN THE PRINCIPLE

A name is a word.

Connect your name with other words.

Comprehensive Phonics, Spelling, and Word Study Guide

Refer to: page **15**, row **11**

Teach

1. Explain to the children that today they will be learning more about their names.

2. Write the children's names on pocket-chart cards. Put several cards in the pocket chart. Ask children to read the names in the pocket chart as you point.

3. Take all the names away except for one group (for example, the names that begin with M). *These names go together because they are alike in some way. How are they alike?* • *Yes, they have the same first letter. They all have an* M.

4. *Here is another name,* Donna. Put the name in the pocket chart. *Say* Donna. *Look at the first letter. Now look at this name,* Darien. *What do you notice about the names* Donna *and* Darien? • *Yes, they have the same first letter. Let's say them:* Donna, Darien. *What do you notice?* • *Yes, they sound alike at the beginning. They both have a* D. Put Darien's name card below *Donna* in the chart.

5. Continue showing names and have children decide whether they go with *Donna*. Place names that start with other letters in a third row that has a question mark at the top.

6. Demonstrate the three-way sorting process again using two more names that start with other letters. Place a question mark in the third column for names that don't start with these letters. *We have sorted our names by putting together the ones that have the same first sound or the same first letter. I'm going to put two names at the top of the chart,* Sunny *and* Robin. *Read them. As we look at the rest of the names, we'll decide whether they belong with* Sunny *or with* Robin. *If a name starts in a different way, we'll just put it over to the side under the question mark.*

7. If you feel the children are ready, repeat the three-way sorting process focusing on the last letter in the names. *Now let's sort the names by the last letter.* Place two or three children's names in the pocket chart and match names by last letter.

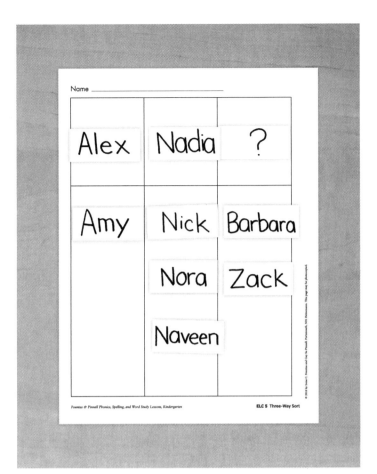

ACTIVITY: THREE-WAY NAME SORT (PAIRS)

INSTRUCTIONAL PROCEDURE

SAY AND SORT

See page 36 for detailed descriptions of Instructional Procedures.

ACTION TAGS

| sort |
| read |
| mix |
| sort |
| read |

Apply

- Have children, working with partners, use three-way sorts to sort the word cards by the first letter on the left. They can complete several sorts, using different pairs of names each time. As they finish each sort, have them take turns reading the list of names to each other.

- Ask them to mix up the cards and say and sort them by the last letter on the right. Again, they read the list of names to each other.

Share

Ask children to say their names and find someone in the room who has a name that starts the same. They can refer to the class name chart. (You may wish to have some picture cards of familiar objects in the pocket chart for children whose names won't have a match.)

Assess

- Notice the children's ability to sort names by first letters.
- Notice the children's ability to write the first letter of their names.
- Observe whether the children use first letters of names as resources in interactive and independent writing.
- Notice the children's ability to sort names by last letters.
- You may wish to use Early Literacy Concepts Assessment A, B, D, E, G, H, or I.

Connect Learning Across Contexts

Interactive Read-Aloud Read aloud books that have characters' names in the title.

> IRA *Big Al* by Andrew Clements

> IRA *Leo the Late Bloomer* by Robert Kraus

Shared Reading See "Jack, Jack" in *Words That Sing* (2019). If you don't have these poetry charts, enlarge the print of this poem or other poems such as "Sally, Go 'Round" in *Sing a Song of Poetry*, and substitute the children's names for the characters' names. You may also wish to use the following Shared Reading title from *Fountas & Pinnell Classroom*™ to locate and recognize other names.

> SR *Hand in Hand: Poems About Friends*

Shared or Interactive Writing Write stories with children's names in them: "Emily likes red. Justin likes blue. Emily wore her blue sweater."

Independent Writing Encourage children to write their names on their papers.

Extend Learning

When the children can sort names easily by the first letters, ask them to think of other ways of sorting names:

> by number of letters in the name;

> by names that have double letters and those that don't;

> by names that have the letter *a* (or any other vowel) and those that don't; or

> by girl and boy.

Place names in the pocket chart and invite children to sort them in a certain way. Ask other children to guess how they are sorted.

▶ Connect with Home

Make copies of the class name chart. Have children take the chart home, cut it apart into individual names, and sort them by first letter. Have them glue four names onto four sheets of paper and write a sentence about each of those classmates.

Understand First and Last in Written Language: Letters

Plan

▶ Consider Your Children

Be sure children have had experience with the class name chart and can read some of the names. If children are very inexperienced, focus only on the concept of "first"; save the concept of "last" for another lesson.

▶ Working with English Language Learners

English language learners' names will be known words and will provide an ideal way to learn the concept of first letter and last letter in a word. Be sure to be explicit in demonstrating the meaning of the words *first, last,* and *letter*. If you know these words in the children's own languages, you may want to use them to focus attention on the three concepts. Also, be ready to help children pronounce the names of their friends as they glue the letters of the names on paper. Have them "read" their charts of friends' names several times. You may wish to have children work in a small group to help them highlight first and last letters.

YOU WILL NEED

 Ready Resources
- ▶ Uppercase and Lowercase Letter Cards

Online Resources
- ▶ ELC 6 Action Tags

Other Materials
- ▶ class name chart (from ELC 1)
- ▶ highlighter tape or highlighter
- ▶ sheets of blank paper
- ▶ glue sticks

UNDERSTAND THE PRINCIPLE

A key concept in beginning reading is that *first* and *last* have particular meanings when applied to print. You will be using these words as you talk with children about the letters in words, the words in a sentence, and the parts of a page. The first letter of a word is the first graphic symbol on the left; the last letter is the symbol farthest to the right. To solve words, children need to learn to connect the temporal sequence of sounds with the symbols arranged spatially in print from left to right.

EXPLAIN THE PRINCIPLE

The first letter in a word is on the left.

The last letter in a word is on the right.

Comprehensive Phonics, Spelling, and Word Study Guide

Refer to: page **15**, row **9**

ACTIVITY: FIRST-LETTER HIGHLIGHT

INSTRUCTIONAL PROCEDURE

SEE AND SAY

See page 36 for detailed descriptions of Instructional Procedures.

EXPLAIN THE PRINCIPLE

The first letter in a word is on the left.

The last letter in a word is on the right.

Comprehensive Phonics, Spelling, and Word Study Guide

Refer to: page **15**, row **9**

Teach

1. Tell your children they are going to use their names to learn about first and last letters.

2. *This is Elizabeth's name. What is the* first *letter of Elizabeth's name?* • *It's an E. The first letter is on the left. It is at the beginning of the word.*

3. *What is the* last *letter of Elizabeth's name?* • *It's an h. The last letter is at the end of the word, on the right.* Remember that children may not understand the terms *left* and *right*. It will be necessary to point to the letters as you say them.

4. *I'm going to make the first letter of Elizabeth's name yellow. I'm going to make the last letter of Elizabeth's name orange.* Use highlighter tape or a highlighter. It is best not to circle letters because it obscures their features.

5. Repeat the process with several other names, each time asking children to identify the first and last letters.

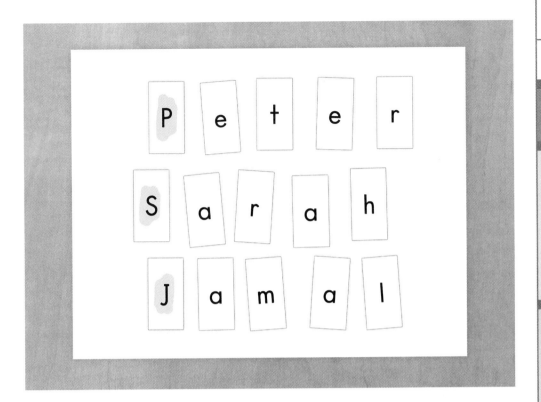

INSTRUCTIONAL PROCEDURE

WORDS TO KNOW

See page 36 for detailed descriptions of Instructional Procedures.

ACTION TAGS

say
glue
color

Apply

Have the children use letter cards to glue classmates' names on a sheet of paper, letter by letter, saying each one. Then ask them to use a yellow highlighter to color the first letter in each name.

Share

- Play a game: "I'm thinking of someone whose name begins with *T*." Children search the name chart for an answer. After your demonstration, children can say the prompt and call on someone to answer.

- Vary the game by asking for a name with a focus on the last letter.

- Make the game more challenging: "I'm thinking of someone whose name begins with *T* and ends with *y*." After your demonstration, children can say the prompt and call on someone to answer.

Assess

- Notice how many letters the children can produce when they write their own name and classmates' names.

- Observe whether the children use their names as a resource for interactive writing and independent writing.

- You may wish to use Early Literacy Concepts Assessment A, D, F, H, or I.

Connect Learning Across Contexts

Interactive Read-Aloud Read aloud books with names. Point out the first and last letters of the characters' names.

> [IRA] *Ruby the Copycat* by Peggy Rathman

> [IRA] *Miss Bindergarten Gets Ready for Kindergarten* by Joseph Slate

Shared Reading See "Elizabeth, Elspeth, Betsey, and Bess" in *Words That Sing* (2019). If you don't have these poetry charts, enlarge the print of this poem or other poems such as "Jack and Jill" in *Sing a Song of Poetry*, and have children locate names. You may also wish to use the following Shared Reading title from *Fountas & Pinnell Classroom*™ to locate and recognize other names.

> [SR] *Kate's Party* by Jane Simon

Interactive Writing When showing children how to write a word or having a child come to the easel to write, use the terms *first* and *last* to talk about letters.

Independent Writing Have children write their names on their drawings and in other writing. Remind children that they can use the letters in their names while writing other words. When you confer with them, use the terms *first* and *last* to talk about letters in words.

Extend Learning

Have children make five names of boys and girls in the class, using magnetic letters and the class name chart as a reference. You might use additional sets of words, such as color words, number words, or days of the week. With days of the week, children may notice that these seven words start with different letters, though each ends with *y*.

▶ Connect with Home

- Have children cut their names into individual letters; then ask them to take the letters home, reassemble them as their names, and identify the first and last letters.

- Caregivers can make and cut up names of family members for children to put together and glue on a sheet of paper.

- Have children collect a list of family members, friends, and storybook characters whose names have the same first or last letter.

Understand First and Last in Written Language: Letters and Words

Plan

▶ Consider Your Children

Use *Concepts About Print* (Clay 2000) or Early Literacy Concepts Assessment D to determine the extent to which children know the concept of *first* and *last* in relation to print. This assessment will help you decide how to focus the lesson. Choose a text appropriate for the children's present knowledge. When referring to uppercase and lowercase letters, use language common in your school (*capital* and *small letters*, for example). Focus on first/last letter or first/last word before combining the concepts. For children who are very inexperienced, work with only one concept in a lesson, building others in further lessons.

▶ Working with English Language Learners

Be sure to be explicit in demonstrating the meaning of the words *first, last, letter,* and *word*. If you know these words in the children's own languages, you may want to use them to focus attention on the four concepts. You may wish to have children work in a small group to help them highlight first and last letters.

YOU WILL NEED

PWS Ready Resources
▶ ELC 7 Pocket-Chart Cards (long)

Online Resources
▶ ELC 7 Action Tags

Other Materials
▶ class name chart (from ELC 1)
▶ highlighter tape or highlighter
▶ sheets of blank paper
▶ glue sticks

UNDERSTAND THE PRINCIPLE

A key concept in beginning reading is that *first* and *last* have particular meanings when applied to print. You will be using these words as you talk with children about the letters in words, the words in a sentence, and the parts of a page. The first letter of a word is the first graphic symbol on the left; the last letter is the symbol farthest to the right. To solve words, children need to learn to connect the temporal sequence of sounds with the symbols arranged spatially in print from left to right.

EXPLAIN THE PRINCIPLE

The first letter in a word is on the left.

The last letter in a word is on the right.

The first word in a sentence is on the left.

There are spaces between the words in a sentence.

The last word in a sentence is before the period or question mark or exclamation mark.

Comprehensive Phonics, Spelling, and Word Study Guide

Refer to: page **15**, row **9**

ACTIVITY: POCKET-CHART SENTENCES

INSTRUCTIONAL PROCEDURE

NOTICE PARTS

See page 36 for detailed descriptions of Instructional Procedures.

EXPLAIN THE PRINCIPLE

The first letter in a word is on the left.

The last letter in a word is on the right.

The first word in a sentence is on the left.

There are spaces between the words in a sentence.

The last word in a sentence is before the period or question mark or exclamation mark.

Comprehensive Phonics, Spelling, and Word Study Guide

Refer to: page **15**, row **9**

Teach

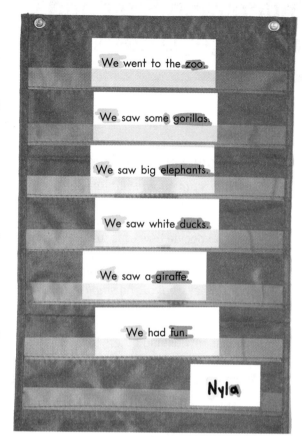

1. Write six sentences on six blank pocket-chart cards, such as those shown in the photo. Tell the children that they are going to learn more about *first* and *last*.

2. Display one child's name. *This is Nyla's name. What is the* first *letter of Nyla's name?* • *It's an N. The first letter is on the left. It is at the beginning of the word.*

3. *What is the* last *letter of Nyla's name?* • *It's an a. The last letter is at the end of the word, on the right.* Move your finger or a pointer left to right. Remember that children may not understand the terms *left* and *right*. It will be necessary to point to the letters as you say them.

4. *I'm going to make the first letter of Nyla's name yellow.* Use highlighter tape or a highlighter, or you can underline letters to add color. Circling the letters may obscure their features. *I'm going to make the last letter of Nyla's name orange.*

5. Repeat the process, focusing children's attention on a single word within a sentence. Point out that there is a space before the beginning of the word; then point out that there is a space after the end of the word.

6. Place a pocket-chart card showing a sentence in the chart. *This is a sentence. How many words does this sentence have?* • *There are five words in this sentence. Now think about what the first word of the sentence is. The first word of the sentence is* We. *The first word is on the left. Also, the first word of a sentence has a capital letter. Let's read it.* • *Now, what is the last word in this sentence?* • *The last word in the sentence is* zoo. *You can see a period at the end of the sentence.*

7. Have the children practice finding the first and last words in this sentence and in several others in the story. Use highlighter tape to identify the first and last words in sentences.

8. *We have been talking about first and last. What is the first letter in this word?* Indicate a word. • *What is the last letter?* • *In a sentence, we know that the first word is on the left, and the last word is right before the period. The first part of a story is at the top. The last part is at the bottom.*

9. Later you may wish to explain that sometimes the first word of a sentence appears in the middle of a printed line directly after a period.

10. Conclude by having the children quickly point out examples of first and last.

INSTRUCTIONAL PROCEDURE

NOTICE PARTS

See page 36 for detailed descriptions of Instructional Procedures.

ACTION TAGS

cut

mix

read

glue

Apply

Choose a familiar text such as one of the sentences from the Teach activity. Write the words on card stock or use a printed pocket-chart card from Online Resources. Have children use scissors to cut the card into individual words. Then they can put the words in order to recreate the sentences and glue the words on paper. Finally, have them take take turns reading the sentence to a partner and telling the first and last words of that sentence. If time allows, have children illustrate the sentences.

Share

Using a familiar text on a chart, play a game, "The first letter of the word I am thinking of is *m*. The last letter is *n*." The children then search the text for the answer. After your demonstration, the children can pose the questions and call on someone to answer.

Assess

- Notice whether the children are looking or pointing in the right place when you use the terms *first* and *last*.
- Have the children highlight the first/last letter in two or three words. Have them do the same with the first/last word in a sentence you give them. Work in a small group with children who still have difficulty with the concept.
- Notice the children's use of the words *first* and *last* in talking about their writing.
- You may wish to use Early Literacy Concepts Assessment A, D, F, or H.

Connect Learning Across Contexts

Interactive Read-Aloud Read aloud books that have large print so the children can notice the letters and words.

IRA *Top Cat* by Lois Ehlert

IRA *Feathers for Lunch* by Lois Ehlert

Shared Reading See "As I Was Going Along" in *Words That Sing* (2019). If you don't have these poetry charts, enlarge the print of this poem or other poems such as "Jack and Jill" or "Little Bo Peep" in *Sing a Song of Poetry*, and have children locate known words by predicting the first letter. Have them say the word, tell what letter it would begin with, and then highlight it with highlighter tape. You may also wish to use the following Shared Reading title from *Fountas & Pinnell Classroom*™ to have children point out the first and last words of a sentence.

SR *My Little Rooster* by Adam Habib

Interactive Writing When showing the children how to write a word or when a child comes to the easel to write, use the terms *first* and *last* to talk about words. Point out the last word of the sentence and ask the children what punctuation to use.

Independent Writing When you confer with children, use the terms *first* and *last*. Encourage the children to say their sentences out loud to evaluate whether they make sense. Encourage the children to use capital letters at the beginning of sentences and punctuation at the end.

Extend Learning

■ If you concentrated only on the concept of first for this lesson, do another lesson on the concept of last, or on both first and last.

■ If you concentrated only on letters in words, move on to talk about words in sentences.

▶ Connect with Home

Give the children copies of a text you used in the lesson. Ask them to highlight the first and last words in the sentences. Invite them to take the text home, read the sentences to their family members, and explain why the words are highlighted.

Understand First and Last in Written Language: Words

Plan

▶ Consider Your Children

For this lesson, provide only sentences that begin on the left side of the page, and avoid sentences with commas. Most books for very young readers have this kind of "friendlier" layout. The goal of this lesson is to firmly establish the concepts of *first* and *last* as they apply to written text. Because it will be helpful to generate and write sentences as quickly as possible, you will probably choose not to use interactive writing. All of the children may show that they understand the concepts and can demonstrate them during the lesson. However, if necessary, revisiting this lesson after children have more experience in shared reading will help them understand that a sentence may start in the middle (or even on the right side) of a line, after a period.

▶ Working with English Language Learners

Strive to demonstrate *first* and *last* by pointing, and make your directions as explicit as possible. If you know comparable words in a child's language, it is helpful to use them. Some English language learners may know the concept of "first word" but may not understand the English words in part or all of your question. This lesson involves children in composing and writing sentences. Be appreciative of their spelling approximations, remembering that they may have only partial control of English language syntax.

UNDERSTAND THE PRINCIPLE

Children need to know what you mean by first and last when you are teaching them about sounds, letters, and words. In relation to oral language, *first* and *last* refer to time of production. To solve words, children need to connect the temporal sequence of spoken sounds with the corresponding print symbols arranged spatially from left to right. The first word in a printed sentence is the one on the left side of the page or the one after a period or other mark of end punctuation. The first line of print on a page is usually the top line, and the last line of print on a page is usually the bottom line.

YOU WILL NEED

Online Resources
- ▶ ELC 8 Action Tags
- ▶ ELC 8 Blank Book Page

Other Materials
- ▶ chart paper and markers
- ▶ pointer

EXPLAIN THE PRINCIPLE

The first word in a sentence is on the left.

There are spaces between the words in a sentence.

The last word in a sentence is before the period or question mark or exclamation mark.

The first part of a page is at the top.

The last part of a page is at the bottom.

Comprehensive Phonics, Spelling, and Word Study Guide

Refer to: page **15**, row **9**

ACTIVITY: SENTENCES WITH COLOR WORDS

INSTRUCTIONAL PROCEDURE

SEE AND SAY

See page 36 for detailed descriptions of Instructional Procedures.

EXPLAIN THE PRINCIPLE

The first word in a sentence is on the left.

There are spaces between the words in a sentence.

The last word in a sentence is before the period or question mark or exclamation mark.

The first part of a page is at the top.

The last part of a page is at the bottom.

Comprehensive Phonics, Spelling, and Word Study Guide

Refer to: page **15**, row **9**

Teach

1. Explain that the children will write sentences with color words. (Feel free to generate sentences using other concept words that relate well to your curriculum and your children's interests.)

2. *Let's write something today about the children in our room, and let's use some words that name colors. Let's write about ourselves and what colors we like. I wrote a sentence about myself and the color I like. Let's read it together.* Read the sentence, using shared reading and pointing.

What color do you like?

Miss Yardley likes red.

Chamique likes blue.

Parker likes brown.

Tanya likes yellow.

Michael likes red.

Denine likes blue.

3. *The first word in my sentence is . . .* • *. . . that's right. In this story the first word in the sentence is on the left. It begins with a capital letter, doesn't it? That's because the first word in a sentence always begins with a capital letter.*

4. *Now let's find the last word in the sentence.* • From their experience in shared reading, many children will know how to find the last word. Confirm their choices. *The last word is right before the period, isn't it?*

5. *Now let's make a sentence about Chamique. Chamique, what color do you like?* • *Can we say,* Chamique likes blue? Write the sentence quickly. Ask children to point to the first word in the sentence and the last word in the sentence. You might draw a patch of the color at the end of the sentence to provide a support for reading.

6. Repeat the process for other names. (It is not always necessary to write a sentence for every child in the room, because you will write other stories using other names.) You will end up with a chart similar to the one pictured.

7. When the text is finished for the day, point out the first part of the page—the first line—at the top. Then point out the last part of the page at the bottom. Help children understand that when you look at a message in print, you can point to the first or last word in a sentence, and you can point to the first or last part of a page.

ACTIVITY: FOUR SENTENCES

INSTRUCTIONAL PROCEDURE

SAY AND WRITE

See page 36 for detailed descriptions of Instructional Procedures.

ACTION TAGS

write
draw
read

Apply

Place the text from the Teach activity on the wall. Then ask the children to say and then write four sentences, one on each page of a four-page blank book. Invite them to say and write something about themselves and three friends or family members—what each person likes or what each person is wearing. Have children draw a picture to illustrate each sentence. They should make their own attempts at spelling but can use the group text as a resource if they wish. When the children are finished, they can read their writing to a partner.

Share

■ Have the children read their stories and show their pictures. For some of the writing that is shared, ask the group to identify the first word and the last word in a sentence.

■ Read the group story again together.

Assess

■ Notice whether the children know what you mean when you refer to the first word and the last word in a sentence.

■ Ask individual children to point to the first word and the last word in a line of print.

■ You may wish to use Early Literacy Concepts Assessment C, E, F, H, I, or J.

Connect Learning Across Contexts

Interactive Read-Aloud Read aloud books that repeat a word at the beginning or end of multiple sentences. After you have read the text several times, children can approximate reading for themselves and locate the repeated words.

IRA *I Like Me!* by Nancy Carlson

IRA *From Head to Toe* by Eric Carle

Shared Reading See "Gray Squirrel" in *Words That Sing* (2019). If you don't have these poetry charts, enlarge the print of this poem or other poems such as "Color Song" or "Roses Are Red" in *Sing a Song of Poetry*, and have children locate particular color words. You may also wish to use the following Shared Reading title from *Fountas & Pinnell Classroom*™.

SR *Slip and Slide* by Amanda Yskamp

Shared or Interactive Writing Use the terms *first* and *last* when referring to a text while constructing the message.

Independent Writing Use the terms *first* and *last* when talking with children about the texts that they are writing.

Extend Learning

- Write a sentence about each child in the room on a separate sheet of paper for children to illustrate; then staple the sheets together to make a class book.
- Cut the class text for this lesson into sentence strips and glue the sentences onto separate pages to make an illustrated book.

▶ Connect with Home

Have children take home the stapled book they created and read it to their family members.

Phonological Awareness

Phonological awareness refers to both explicit and implicit knowledge of the sounds in language. It includes the ability to identify and make rhymes, hear syllables in words, hear the parts of words (onsets and rimes), and hear individual sounds in words. *Phonemic awareness* is one kind of phonological awareness. It refers to the ability to identify, isolate, and manipulate the individual sounds (phonemes) in words.

Phonological awareness can be taught orally. When it is taught in connection with letters, it is called *phonics*. Phonics instruction refers to teaching children to connect sounds and letters in words. While very early experiences focus on hearing and saying sounds in the absence of letters, most of the time you will want to teach children to hear sounds in connection with letters. Many of the lessons in this section begin with teaching orally but move toward connecting the sounds to letters in later lessons.

Principles related to letter-sound relationships, or phonics, are included in the letter-sound relationships category of this book.

Connect to Assessment

See related (optional) PA Assessment tasks in Online Resources.

- Assessment A: Hearing Rhymes
- Assessment B: Hearing Syllables
- Assessment C: Identifying Sounds in Words
- Assessment D: Segmenting a Word into Sounds
- Assessment E: Identifying Beginning Consonant Sounds
- Assessment F: Identifying Ending Consonant Sounds
- Assessment G: Blending Sounds to Make Words
- Assessment H: Blending Word Parts
- Assessment I: Removing Sounds from Words
- Assessment J: Segmenting Word Parts
- Assessment K: Individual Record

Develop Your Professional Understanding

See *The Fountas & Pinnell Comprehensive Phonics, Spelling, and Word Study Guide*. Related pages: 2–12, 17–20.

See *The Fountas & Pinnell Literacy Continuum: A Tool for Assessment, Planning, and Teaching*. 2017. Portsmouth, New Hampshire: Heinemann. Related pages: 357–397.

See *Word Matters: Teaching Phonics and Spelling in the Reading/Writing Classroom* by G. S. Pinnell and I. C. Fountas. 1998. Portsmouth, New Hampshire: Heinemann. Related pages: 5, 63–64, 76–77, 82, 90–91, 95, 98–99, 137.

Hear and Say Rhyming Words

Plan

▶ Consider Your Children

This lesson will be more successful if children learn the song as an oral activity first so they can feel the rhythm of the song and enjoy it. This foundation will make the print more meaningful. Having strong familiarity with the song will allow children to focus on the rhyming words and enjoy the variations.

▶ Working with English Language Learners

Some children may be hearing these rhymes for the first time. Show pairs of pictures that represent words that rhyme (for example, *sheep, jeep* or *frog, log*), pointing to the pictures as you name them. Have children say the rhymes so that they can feel the movement of their mouths as they pronounce the words. As you sing the song with children, use rhythm in an enjoyable way, so that they can remember it.

YOU WILL NEED

PWS **Ready Resources**
- ▶ PA 1 Pocket-Chart Word Cards
- ▶ PA 1 Pocket-Chart Picture Cards
- ▶ PA 1 Pocket-Chart Cards (long)
- ▶ Blank Pocket-Chart Cards

Online Resources
- ▶ PA 1 Action Tags
- ▶ PA 1 Did You Ever See Sheet

Other Materials
- ▶ pocket chart or other chart with words of "Did You Ever See"
- ▶ pointer
- ▶ highlighter tape or highlighter

✓ Generative Lesson

A generative lesson has a simple structure that you can use to present similar content or concepts. Use this lesson structure to teach children to listen for and identify a variety of ending parts or rhymes.

UNDERSTAND THE PRINCIPLE

Hearing and singing songs can help children become more aware of the sounds of language, including rhyming words. Internalized rhymes and songs are powerful exemplars that help children recognize when parts of words sound the same.

EXPLAIN THE PRINCIPLE

Some words have parts at the end that sound the same. They rhyme.

Listen for the rhymes in poems and songs.

Say words and listen for how they rhyme.

Comprehensive Phonics, Spelling, and Word Study Guide

Refer to: page **18**, row **1**

ACTIVITY: "DID YOU EVER SEE" RHYMES

INSTRUCTIONAL PROCEDURE

HEAR AND SAY

See page 36 for detailed descriptions of Instructional Procedures.

EXPLAIN THE PRINCIPLE

Some words have parts at the end that sound the same. They rhyme.

Listen for the rhymes in poems and songs.

Say words and listen for how they rhyme.

Comprehensive Phonics, Spelling, and Word Study Guide

Refer to: page **18**, row **1**

Teach

1. Tell the children that they will be learning a song that will give them some practice with rhyming words.

2. Children may have previously learned to sing "If You're Happy and You Know It." If so, they will know the tune; if not, teach them the tune.

3. Introduce the "Did You Ever See" song, telling the children it has the same tune. Teach this song by playfully singing it with the children, using the words *sheep* and *jeep* in the blanks.

4. Then invite the children to think about the words *sheep* and *jeep*. Say each word, and help children recognize that these two words have end parts that sound the same. They rhyme.

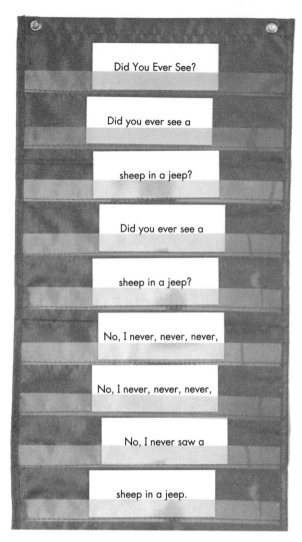

5. After children have learned the basic song, have them sing it several times, using one or two pairs of words from the pocket-chart word cards. Then invite children to suggest their own pairs of rhyming words to use in the blanks. The idea is to enjoy all kinds of rhymes, so you can allow some nonsense words while children catch on to the idea.

6. Place the chart on the wall, insert the word cards in the blanks, and invite children to point and read. Provide highlighter tape to call attention to the rhymes.

7. Vary the ways in which the children can enjoy this song:

    Have half the group sing the question and the other half sing the answer.

    Say the words of the song, snapping your fingers when you come to the rhyming words to reinforce them. Invite children to do the same.

    Point to the written text as you and the children sing. Drop out on the second rhyming word, and let the children sing it by themselves.

INSTRUCTIONAL PROCEDURE

HEAR AND SAY

See page 36 for detailed descriptions of Instructional Procedures.

ACTION TAGS

write
draw
read

Apply

Create books with "Did you ever see" on the front cover and the sentence "Did you ever see a _____ in a _____?" on the bottom of the inside page. Ask children to fill in the blanks with their own words in approximated spelling and to illustrate the page. Then have them read their books to a partner.

Share

■ Have the children sing the song together again and identify the rhyming words.

■ Invite the children to share one page from their books.

Assess

■ Observe how easily the children can identify words that rhyme.

■ Notice if the children are able to match pictures with rhyming names.

■ You may wish to use Phonological Assessment A or K.

Connect Learning Across Contexts

Interactive Read-Aloud Read aloud books with rhyming words.

> IRA *Mary Wore Her Red Dress* by Merle Peek

> IRA *Over on the Farm* by Marianne Berkes

Shared Reading See "Dance a Merry Jig" in *Words That Sing* (2019). If you don't have these poetry charts, enlarge the print of this poem or other poems such as "A-hunting We Will Go" in *Sing a Song of Poetry,* and have children use highlighter tape to find rhyming words. You may also wish to use the following Shared Reading title from *Fountas & Pinnell Classroom™.*

> SR *Wiggles: Poems to Make You Wiggle Your Fingers and Toes*

Interactive Writing If the writing activity includes rhyming words, point them out and ask children to say them. Then mark with highlighter tape.

Independent Writing Encourage children to think of pairs of rhyming words to write and illustrate.

Extend Learning

■ Have the children select pocket-chart picture cards of rhyming words to create variations of the song in the pocket chart.

■ Change the answer in the chart to the following:

> Yes, I saw a _____ on a _____.

> Yes, I saw a _____ on a _____.

> Yes, I saw a _____ that was sitting/standing/playing on a _____.

> Yes, I saw a _____ on a _____.

■ Once children have learned alternate "yes" and "no" versions, they can think about whether you could *really* see a frog on a log or not, and they can select either the "yes" or the "no" version.

▶ Connect with Home

■ After children have learned the "Did You Ever See" song, have them take home a copy to read to their family members. Communicate to family members that enjoying songs like this helps children learn phonics, even if they are not yet ready to read the words in isolation. Family members and caregivers can have fun making up new variations of the song.

■ You may also send home a blank "Did You Ever See" book for the children to make with family members.

Hear and Say Rhyming Words

Plan

▶ Consider Your Children

This early lesson will help to build children's knowledge of traditional rhymes. Use the teaching guidelines and variations with appropriate poems and songs; *Words That Sing* (2019) and *Sing a Song of Poetry* include many examples. Engage children in a great deal of shared reading of rhymes and poems before identifying or working with the rhyming words. If the children know a rhyme and have enjoyed it many times, they will have an internal sense of the rhythm and sound that will make this explicit lesson easier and more meaningful.

▶ Working with English Language Learners

Many English language learners will be hearing traditional English nursery rhymes for the first time and may need more repetitions to become fluent with them. If possible, use illustrations to help children understand the rhyming words you are using (for example, *quick* and *candlestick*). Select rhymes from *Sing a Song of Poetry* that you think English language learners will enjoy. You may also ask children to share traditional rhymes that they say at home in their native language.

UNDERSTAND THE PRINCIPLE

Enjoying rhymes leads children to pay close attention to how language sounds. They learn to hear similarities and differences. Eventually they hear individual speech sounds and are able to connect those sounds to letter symbols.

YOU WILL NEED

PWS Ready Resources
- ▶ PA 2 Pocket-Chart Cards (long)

Online Resources
- ▶ PA 2 Action Tags
- ▶ PA 2 Poem: Jack, Be Nimble

Other Materials
- ▶ pocket chart or other chart with words of "Jack, Be Nimble"
- ▶ pointer
- ▶ highlighter tape or highlighter
- ▶ glue sticks
- ▶ drawing supplies
- ▶ poetry notebooks

Generative Lesson

A generative lesson has a simple structure that you can use to present similar content or concepts. Use this lesson structure to teach children to listen for and identify a variety of ending parts or rhymes.

EXPLAIN THE PRINCIPLE

Some words have parts at the end that sound the same. They rhyme.

Listen for the rhymes in poems and songs.

Say words and listen for how they rhyme.

Comprehensive Phonics, Spelling, and Word Study Guide

Refer to:
page **18**, row **1**

ACTIVITY: RHYMING POEM

INSTRUCTIONAL PROCEDURE

HEAR AND SAY

See page 36 for detailed descriptions of Instructional Procedures.

EXPLAIN THE PRINCIPLE

Some words have parts at the end that sound the same. They rhyme.

Listen for the rhymes in poems and songs.

Say words and listen for how they rhyme.

Comprehensive Phonics, Spelling, and Word Study Guide

Refer to: page **18**, row **1**

Teach

1. Tell the children that they will be learning a rhyme that will give them more practice with rhyming words.

2. Introduce "Jack, Be Nimble" by reading it aloud to the children without showing the print; the chart can be introduced later. Emphasize enjoyment of the language, the rhythm, and the rhyme.

3. Then invite the children to think about the words *quick* and *candlestick*. Say each word, and help children recognize that these two words have end parts that sound the same. They rhyme. Discuss the rhyming words *fox* and *box* in the same way.

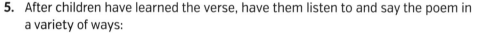

4. Say the rhyme, one line at a time, having children repeat after you. After doing this several times, invite children to say the verse with you. Repeat it a few times so that the children become very familiar with it.

5. After children have learned the verse, have them listen to and say the poem in a variety of ways:

   Have half of the group say the first line, the other half say the second line, and so on throughout the poem.

   Divide the children into groups, having each group say one line of the poem.

   Say the verse, clapping when you come to the rhyming words. Invite children to do the same.

   Say the verse, snapping your fingers when you come to the rhyming words.

   Say the verse in a normal voice, but whisper when you come to the rhyming words.

   Start saying the poem in a loud voice, and get softer as you get to the end. End in a whisper.

   Whisper the whole verse.

   Say the poem together, but designate one child to say the rhyming words. Have everyone else stop while this child reads the rhyming words independently.

   Read the poem while pointing briefly to each of the written words on the chart.

   Have children locate the words that rhyme and put highlighter tape over them or underline them.

Jack, be nimble,
Jack, be quick,
Jack, jump over
The candlestick.

Fontas & Pinnell Phonics, Spelling, and Word Study Lessons, Kindergarten   PA 2 Poem: Jack, Be Nimble, a

ACTIVITY: RHYMING POEM

INSTRUCTIONAL PROCEDURE

HEAR AND SAY

See page 36 for detailed descriptions of Instructional Procedures.

ACTION TAGS

| glue |
| draw |
| read |

Apply

Give the children a copy of "Jack, Be Nimble" to glue on a blank page of their poetry notebooks and illustrate. Have the children read the poem to a partner. Have them continue to add poems to the notebook throughout the year.

Share

Have the children repeat the poem together, clapping when they say the rhyming words.

Assess

- Notice how easily children identify words that rhyme.
- As a general assessment, say two or three words and have the children provide a rhyming word for each.
- You may wish to use Phonological Awareness Assessment A or K.

Connect Learning Across Contexts

Interactive Read-Aloud Read aloud books that emphasize rhyme and rhythm.

IRA *Over on the Farm* by Christopher Gunson

IRA *It's Raining, It's Pouring* by Kin Eagle

Shared Reading See "Every Morning at Eight O'Clock" in *Words That Sing* (2019). If you don't have these poetry charts, enlarge the print of this poem or other poems such "Jack, Jack" in *Sing a Song of Poetry,* and have children use highlighter tape to find rhyming words. Give children individual copies to illustrate and add to their poetry notebooks. You may also wish to use the following Shared Reading title from *Fountas & Pinnell Classroom*™.

SR *The Itsy Bitsy Spider* adapted by Helen Lorraine

Interactive Writing If the writing activity includes rhyming words, point them out and ask children to say them. Then mark them with highlighter tape. You might wish to use different colors for different rhymes.

Independent Writing Encourage each child to write his name and one word—it may be a nonsense word—that rhymes with the name.

Extend Learning

■ Repeat the lesson with other nursery rhymes and poems such as "Jack and Jill" or "Hickory, Dickory, Dock!" from *Sing a Song of Poetry*.

■ Print a copy of a poem from this lesson in very large print and glue it on a large piece of cardboard. Put this "poem card," along with similar ones, in a box labeled Poetry. Have children choose and read these previously learned poems. Provide colored highlighter tape for them to place on rhyming words.

▶ Connect with Home

■ After children have learned a poem (or a verse of a poem), have them take home a copy to read to family members.

■ In addition, encourage caregivers to read poems and books with rhymes and to sing songs with rhymes.

Hear and Connect Rhyming Words

Plan

▶ Consider Your Children

Introduce this activity after children have participated in a great deal of shared reading of poems from *Sing a Song of Poetry*, *Grade K* or other sources. If rhyming is a new concept for children, begin with only two or three pairs of rhymes. Because this is an oral activity, it's important not to use printed words with the pictures.

▶ Working with English Language Learners

Children who are not familiar with English phonology may need many experiences to be able to hear rhymes and understand that the similar-sounding parts are at the ends of words. To identify rhymes, use poems that they already know through shared reading and have practiced many times. Be sure that children can say and understand the meaning of all of the picture cards that you use; set aside those that are too far from their experience or that you cannot explain.

YOU WILL NEED

PWS Ready Resources
- ▶ PA 3 Pocket-Chart Picture Cards

Online Resources
- ▶ PA 3 Action Tags
- ▶ PA 3 Picture Cards
- ▶ PA 3 Two-Way Sorts

Other Materials
- ▶ pocket chart

Generative Lesson
A generative lesson has a simple structure that you can use to present similar content or concepts. Use this lesson structure to teach children to hear and connect a variety of words that rhyme.

UNDERSTAND THE PRINCIPLE

Hearing and connecting words that rhyme, or sound the same at the end, helps children understand that words are made up of sounds. Working with rhymes encourages them to distinguish individual sounds and to begin thinking about how sounds and letters are related. Later this knowledge will help children break words apart to solve them.

EXPLAIN THE PRINCIPLE

Listen for and connect words that rhyme.

Comprehensive Phonics, Spelling, and Word Study Guide

Refer to: page **18**, row **2**

ACTIVITY: TWO-WAY PICTURE SORT

INSTRUCTIONAL PROCEDURE

HEAR AND SAY

See page 36 for detailed descriptions of Instructional Procedures.

EXPLAIN THE PRINCIPLE

Listen for and connect words that rhyme.

Comprehensive Phonics, Spelling, and Word Study Guide

Refer to: page **18**, row **02**

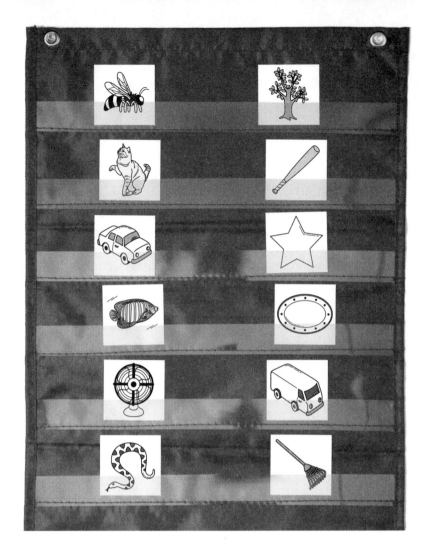

Teach

1. Tell children that they are going to do more work with rhyming words.

2. Using the pocket-chart picture cards, line up two easy rhyming words at the top of a pocket chart. Have children name these pictures. *Some words sound the same at the end. Listen to these two words:* bee, tree. Point to the pictures as you say the words. *Now say those words with me.* • *These two words have parts at the end that sound the same, don't they? When the last part of the words sound the same at the end, they* rhyme.

3. Guide children to talk about how the words have parts at the end that sound the same. Then demonstrate matching another pair of pictures, having children name the pictures with you: *cat, bat.*

4. Line up pictures of the *car, fish, fan,* and *snake* in a column on the left of the pocket chart. Then ask one child to find the picture of the word that rhymes with *car* and say both words aloud to check that they have parts at the end that sound the same. Ask the class to judge whether or not the words rhyme.

5. Proceed through the rest of the pictures, matching pairs and saying the rhyming words aloud each time. Have children match pictures for the rhyming words *car* and *star, fish* and *dish, fan* and *van,* and *snake* and *rake.*

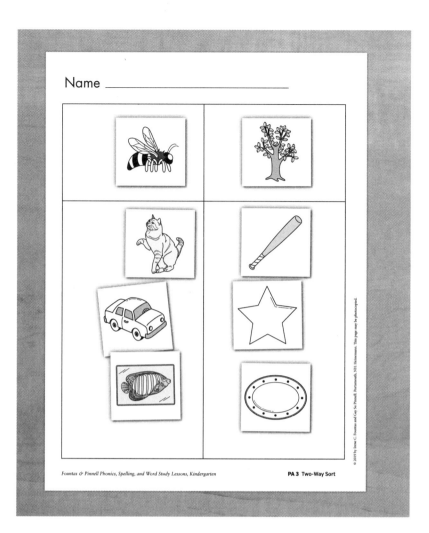

Name _____

Fountas & Pinnell Phonics, Spelling, and Word Study Lessons, Kindergarten

© 2019 by Irene C. Fountas and Gay Su Pinnell. Portsmouth, NH: Heinemann. This page may be photocopied.

PA 3 Two-Way Sort

ACTIVITY: TWO-WAY PICTURE SORT

INSTRUCTIONAL PROCEDURE

SAY AND SORT

See page 36 for detailed descriptions of Instructional Procedures.

ACTION TAGS

cut
say
match
glue

Apply

Have sheets of picture cards for children to cut, say, match, and glue on a two-way sort.

Share

Have children share pairs of pictures of rhyming words by naming the pictures aloud. Afterward you may want to read a poem together and identify two words that rhyme.

Assess

- Observe the children's ability to recognize and match pairs of rhyming words.
- Notice the children's spontaneous recognition of rhymes in shared reading.
- You may wish to use Phonological Awareness Assessment A or K.

Phonological Awareness: Hear and Connect Rhyming Words

Connect Learning Across Contexts

Interactive Read-Aloud Read aloud books and poems that have fun with rhyme.

🔲 *The Doorbell Rang* by Pat Hutchins

🔲 *Baa Baa Black Sheep* by Iza Trapani

Shared Reading See "High and Low" in *Words That Sing* (2019). If you don't have these poetry charts, enlarge the print of this poem or other poems such as "Pease Porridge Hot" in *Sing a Song of Poetry,* and have children use highlighter tape to find rhyming words. You may also wish to use the following Shared Reading title from *Fountas & Pinnell Classroom*™.

🔲 *Hand in Hand: Poems About Friends*

Interactive Writing Create a two-line rhyming poem, and point out rhyming words in the interactive writing.

Independent Writing When children are saying words slowly to hear sounds, encourage them to make connections to other words that have parts at the end that sound the same.

Extend Learning

- Repeat this lesson with the following pairs of pictures of rhyming words: *bear, chair; mouse, house; dog, log; shell, bell; bib, crib; pen, hen; shirt, skirt; crown, clown; socks, box; moon, spoon.*

- After children have read simple poems many times in shared reading, have them glue copies of the poems on paper, illustrate the poems, and place the sheets in their poetry folders. On some poems, they can highlight rhyming words.

▶ Connect with Home

Give children sheets of picture cards (Online Resources) to cut apart and match again at home. Invite family members to play these rhyming games:

Say two words and have the child repeat them. Have the child clap only if the two words rhyme.

Say three or more words. If all of the words rhyme, the child stands; if all of the words do not rhyme, the child sits.

Hear and Generate Rhyming Words

Plan

▶ Consider Your Children

This activity will be effective after your children have listened to many rhyming books and poems for pleasure and have some understanding of rhyme. The routine established in the game Concentration will be useful in practicing hearing rhyme as well as many other literacy concepts.

▶ Working with English Language Learners

Be sure that English language learners understand the procedures of the game Concentration; you may want to work with a small group, playing the game for a short time with each child in turn. In the game, you will use the same picture cards over and over, helping English language learners to develop a repertoire of words that they can say and use in different ways. When you read books aloud, stop and call attention to rhymes that children know so that they begin to understand that they will meet the same words in other contexts.

YOU WILL NEED

Online Resources
- ▶ PA 4 Action Tags
- ▶ PA 4 Picture Cards
- ▶ PA 4 Deck Card Template
- ▶ PA 4 Directions for Concentration

Generative Lesson

A generative lesson has a simple structure that you can use to present similar content or concepts. You can use this lesson structure to teach children to make a variety of other rhymes.

UNDERSTAND THE PRINCIPLE

When children recognize words that rhyme, they are making connections between words that have end parts that sound the same. This information helps them take words apart to solve them and will help them understand letter-sound relationships.

EXPLAIN THE PRINCIPLE

Make rhymes by playing with words and thinking of words that sound the same at the end.

Comprehensive Phonics, Spelling, and Word Study Guide

Refer to: page **18**, row **3**

ACTIVITY: OTHER RHYMING WORDS

INSTRUCTIONAL PROCEDURE

HEAR AND SAY

See page 36 for detailed descriptions of Instructional Procedures.

EXPLAIN THE PRINCIPLE

Make rhymes by playing with words and thinking of words that sound the same at the end.

Comprehensive Phonics, Spelling, and Word Study Guide

Refer to: page **18**, row **3**

Elizabeth, Elizabeth
what do you see?

I see Javon looking at me.

Teach

1. Tell the children that they are going to listen to some rhymes and make some rhymes of their own.

2. Read a variety of rhyming stories. Some examples are *Better Not Get Wet, Jesse Bear* by Nancy White Carlstrom; *"Fire! Fire!" Said Mrs. McGuire* by Bill Martin Jr.; *Brown Bear, Brown Bear, What Do You See?* by Bill Martin Jr.; and the classic *The Cat in the Hat* by Dr. Seuss.

3. As you read, emphasize the rhythm and rhyme so the children will anticipate words and listen actively. Invite them to join in on the rhyming parts as they become more familiar with the story.

4. As you reread the story, stop after a pair of rhyming words and ask the children to identify the words that rhyme, or sound the same at the end.

5. Reread the story and invite the children to elaborate on the text. They can think of another word that would rhyme ("Change the *tire*," said Mrs. McGuire) or think of two different rhyming words ("Come here *quick*," said Mrs. *Flick*). They can search for words that rhyme with names of children in the class ("Up the *hill*," said *Bill*), or they can put classmates' names into the existing rhyme ("*Elizabeth, Elizabeth,* what do you see? I see *Javon* looking at me").

6. Write the variations that children create on enlarged print charts. Place them on the walls so that children can "read around the room."

**ACTIVITY:
CONCENTRATION**

**INSTRUCTIONAL
PROCEDURE**

FIND AND MATCH

*See page 36 for detailed
descriptions of Instructional
Procedures.*

ACTION TAGS

say

match

Apply

Have the children play the game Concentration with a partner using the picture
cards of rhyming words. You may also wish to customize picture cards using
Gamemaker in Online Resources. Use the directions for Concentration as needed.

Share

As they hear familiar rhyming stories, have children clap when they hear the
rhyming words and/or identify them afterward. Ask the children to share rhymes
they have discovered in stories.

Assess

- Notice the children's ability to recognize rhymes in texts.
- As a quick assessment, say three to five words and have the children provide a
  rhyming word for each.
- You may wish to use Phonological Awareness Assessment A or K.

Connect Learning Across Contexts

Interactive Read-Aloud Read aloud books with rhyming stories to build up a large repertoire of rhymes that children can predict.

> IRA *When It Starts to Snow* by Phillis Gershator

> IRA *Sleepy Bears* by Mem Fox

Shared Reading See "Red, White, and Blue" in *Words That Sing* (2019). If you don't have these poetry charts, enlarge the print of this poem or other poems such as "Five Little Ducks" in *Sing a Song of Poetry,* and have children use highlighter tape to find rhyming words. You may also wish to use the following Shared Reading title from *Fountas & Pinnell Classroom*™.

> SR *My Little Rooster* adapted by Adam Habib

Interactive Writing Create a four-line rhyming poem, and point out rhyming words in the interactive writing.

Independent Writing When children are writing independently and want to write a tricky word, help them think of another word they know that ends the same. Help the children say a word slowly to hear its sounds, and encourage them to make connections to one or more words that rhyme with the word.

Extend Learning

- Read other rhyming texts aloud and bring rhymes to children's attention. On a subsequent rereading, stop briefly before the second word in a pair of rhyming words and ask the children to predict what it will be.

- Have children play the game several times with other pictures of rhyming words.

▶ Connect with Home

- Create a book of rhymes using the names of the children in the class. Model the text on books such as *Brown Bear, Brown Bear, What Do You See?* or *"Fire! Fire!" Said Mrs. McGuire* or any other simple rhyming text (see *Sing a Song of Poetry*).

- Send a photocopy home with children to read to family members. Invite family members to play rhyming games in places like the car or the kitchen. The caregiver might name an object such as a tree, and the child gives a rhyming word, such as *knee*.

Plan

▶ Consider Your Children

This activity is best used after the children have participated in shared reading of poems and have listened to many rhyming books and poems for pleasure. Having internalized the concept of rhyme, they will be ready to expand their knowledge. Generating rhymes is an application of the concept of rhyme, and children's ability to generate rhymes represents rhyme awareness, which is one important aspect of phonological awareness.

▶ Working with English Language Learners

Be sure that English language learners know and can repeat one or two rhymes that are meaningful and enjoyable to them. You might wish to go over some rhymes with them just before you play the tossing game so that they have responses ready. Consider giving a little more "wait and think" time to children who are just learning rhymes in English. Accept responses that repeat those just made by other children, or quickly make suggestions—for example, "Would *cake* be a good thing to take on the trip?" As children's understanding and repertoire of rhymes grows, you can challenge them more.

YOU WILL NEED

Online Resources
- ▶ PA 5 Action Tags
- ▶ PA 5 Picture Cards
- ▶ PA 5 Lotto and Bingo Game Boards
- ▶ PA 5 Directions to Lotto and Bingo

Other Materials
- ▶ beanbag or ball
- ▶ plastic chips or other markers
- ▶ highlighter tape

Generative Lesson ✔

A generative lesson has a simple structure that you can use to present similar content or concepts. You can use this lesson structure to teach children a variety of rhyming words.

UNDERSTAND THE PRINCIPLE

When children recognize words that rhyme, they are making connections between words that have end parts that sound the same. This information helps them take words apart to solve them and will help them understand letter-sound relationships. When children are aware of the sounds of oral language, they can begin to connect those sounds to letter patterns.

EXPLAIN THE PRINCIPLE

Make rhymes by playing with words and thinking of words that sound the same at the end.

Comprehensive Phonics, Spelling, and Word Study Guide

Refer to: page **18**, row **3**

EARLY MIDDLE LATE

**ACTIVITY:
BEANBAG TOSS**

**INSTRUCTIONAL
PROCEDURE**

HEAR AND SAY

*See page 36 for detailed
descriptions of Instructional
Procedures.*

EXPLAIN THE PRINCIPLE

*Make rhymes by playing with
words and thinking of words
that sound the same at the end.*

 Comprehensive
Phonics, Spelling,
and Word Study
Guide

Refer to:
Page **18**, row **3**

Teach

1. Tell the children that they are going to listen to some rhymes and make some rhymes of their own.

2. *We're going to play a game with rhymes. I'll start a story, then you can help me by thinking of rhymes. "There once was a group of magic bunnies who decided to pack their spaceship with lots of good things to take with them to a new planet. They packed some* hats, mats, *and* cats." *What do you notice about the things they packed?* [Children may respond that the three words rhyme.]

3. *The bunnies think of one thing, and everything else they pack has a name that rhymes with the first word. Let's try another one. This time I will start, then I'll throw this beanbag to someone, and that person will think of the next thing, the next rhyming word.* Repeat the introduction, ending with "they packed some cats. . . ."

4. Throw the beanbag to a child, who thinks of an object with a name that rhymes. Then ask that child to throw the beanbag to another child, who will try to think of another rhyme.

5. When any child with the beanbag cannot come up with a rhyme, he can toss it back to you; you start another rhyme. Some examples are *cakes, rakes, snakes; bears, chairs, pears; goats, boats, coats; fishes, dishes, wishes; dogs, logs, hogs; trees, bees, keys; cans, vans, fans; jars, bars, cars; clowns, crowns, towns.*

6. Children will learn to play this game quickly and enjoy the rhymes. Keep it easy at first so that the game moves along quickly.

Name: _____

Fountas & Pinnell Phonics, Spelling, and Word Study Lessons, Kindergarten   **PA 5** Lotto and Bingo Game Board

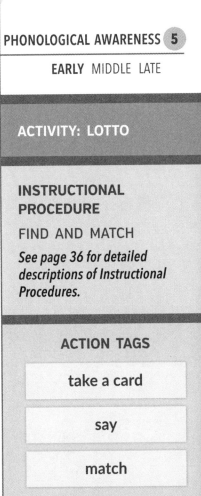

© 2018 by Irene C. Fountas and Gay Su Pinnell. Portsmouth, NH: Heinemann. This page may be photocopied.

ACTIVITY: LOTTO

INSTRUCTIONAL PROCEDURE

FIND AND MATCH

See page 36 for detailed descriptions of Instructional Procedures.

ACTION TAGS

take a card

say

match

Apply

Have the children play Lotto at a table with pictures of rhyming words. Give each player a Lotto game board (there are six unique versions for six players). You also may wish to customize gameboards using Gamemaker in Online Resources. Place the picture cards and the plastic chips or markers in the middle of the table. Players take turns taking a card and naming the picture on the card. All players search their game boards for pictures of words that rhyme with the word on the card. They put a chip or marker on any space that has a rhyming word. The first player to cover the entire board is the winner. The game continues until the other players fill their cards.

Share

Invite each child to share a pair of rhyming words from the game they played.

Assess

- Notice the children's ability to recognize and generate rhymes.
- Observe the children's spontaneous recognition of rhymes in interactive read-alouds or shared reading.
- You may wish to use Phonological Awareness Assessment A or K.

Connect Learning Across Contexts

Interactive Read-Aloud Read aloud books that draw attention to rhymes.

IRA *Sleepy Bears* by Mem Fox

IRA *The Doorbell Rang* by Pat Hutchins

Shared Reading See "Stretching Fun" in *Words That Sing* (2019). If you don't have these poetry charts, enlarge the print of this poem or other poems such as "Stop, Look, and Listen" in *Sing a Song of Poetry,* and have children use highlighter tape to mark rhyming words. You may also wish to use the following Shared Reading title from *Fountas & Pinnell Classroom™.*

SR *Jump and Hop: Poems to Make You Move*

Interactive Writing When the writing you are doing contains rhyming words, invite children to notice the parts of the words that rhyme. Create a verse in interactive writing. Have children suggest rhyming words. Reread and match rhyming words with highlighter tape or highlighter.

Independent Writing Encourage children to write some of the rhyming words they have found. When children write independently they can use end parts of words they know to write new words.

Extend Learning

Repeat the lesson with a variety of other rhymes. Use other themes like packing for a trip to the beach or the park.

▶ Connect with Home

■ In a meeting or a newsletter, share this rhyming game with family members so that they can play it with their children. Invite caregivers to have children cut out magazine pictures that represent pairs of rhyming words–*house* and *mouse, pan* and *man*–and glue the pictures on a sheet.

■ Family members might also play a game called "let's go shopping" using a paper bag and magazine or newspaper pictures of food and other objects. The caregiver cuts out the pictures and spreads them on the table facedown. The child turns over a picture and says its name and a rhyming word–*meat* and *feet* or *fish* and *dish*, for example. Then the child can put the picture in the bag. At the end, the child takes out all the objects and names them, and the caregiver says a rhyming word for each.

Hear, Say, and Clap Syllables

Plan

▶ Consider Your Children

In this lesson, the children begin to work on distinguishing the parts in a word that they can hear, a valuable skill that they will use repeatedly over the next few years. You will not use printed words with the pictures; at this point, the exercise is only for hearing syllables.

▶ Working with English Language Learners

English language learners will need to know the name of each picture before they can hear the syllables in each word. Go over the pictures several times until you are sure they know the words and can say them. Accept some approximations in English pronunciation but help them use an appropriate number of syllables. Don't use words that children find too difficult to say or that are beyond their present understanding or experience. Observe and/or work with them the first time they do the application activity to make sure they understand the task.

YOU WILL NEED

PWS Ready Resources
▸ PA 6 Pocket-Chart Picture Cards

Online Resources
▸ PA 6 Action Tags
▸ PA 6 Picture Cards
▸ PA 6 Two-Way Sorts

Other Materials
▸ pocket chart
▸ flag

Generative Lesson

A generative lesson has a simple structure that you can use to present similar content or concepts. You can use this lesson structure to teach children to hear, say, and clap words with a different number of syllables.

UNDERSTAND THE PRINCIPLE

Hearing and saying the syllables in words helps children learn how to break them down into parts that can be represented with letters and letter clusters. It helps children relate the oral language they know to written language.

EXPLAIN THE PRINCIPLE

Words can have one or more parts.

Listen for, say, and clap the parts in a word.

Comprehensive Phonics, Spelling, and Word Study Guide

Refer to:
page **19**, row **6**

**ACTIVITY: THREE-WAY
PICTURE SORT**

**INSTRUCTIONAL
PROCEDURE**

HEAR AND SAY

*See page 36 for detailed
descriptions of Instructional
Procedures.*

EXPLAIN THE PRINCIPLE

*Words can have one or more
parts.*

*Listen for, say, and clap the parts
in a word.*

Comprehensive
Phonics, Spelling,
and Word Study
Guide

Refer to:
page **19**, row **6**

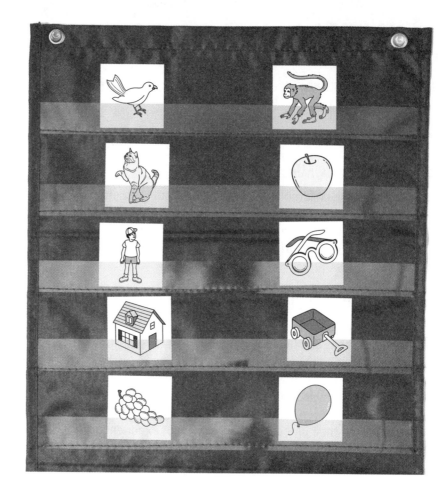

Teach

1. Tell the children that today they are going to learn about hearing the parts in words. Explain that words can have one or more parts.

2. Show the pocket-chart picture cards of the two key words (*bird* and *monkey*). Have the children say the name of each picture and clap as they say each syllable. For each word, ask, "How many parts do you hear in this word?" Demonstrate several times if necessary until they can say and clap the parts of each word accurately.

3. Place the two pictures along the top of the pocket chart. (You may want to use a red line to set apart this top row.) Explain that these pictures stand for words and that each word has a different number of parts. The bird stands for words with one part (such as *bird*), and the monkey stands for words with two parts (such as *mon/key*).

4. Go through the rest of the cards with the children. Each time, ask the children to say and clap the parts of the word. Have them decide whether the word belongs with *bird* or *monkey,* according to how many parts it has. When finished, you will have sorted all the pictures.

5. Quickly demonstrate the task of sorting the smaller picture cards on a tabletop using two-way sorts. Children place the same two pictures (bird and monkey) at the top of the sheet. Then they say the name of each picture and place it under the corresponding picture according to the number of parts it has.

Fountas & Pinnell Phonics, Spelling, and Word Study Lessons, Kindergarten

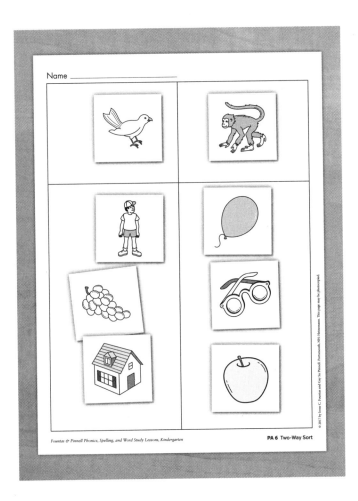

Name _____

Fountas & Pinnell Phonics, Spelling, and Word Study Lessons, Kindergarten

PA 6 Two-Way Sort

© 2017 by Irene C. Fountas and Gay Su Pinnell. Portsmouth, NH: Heinemann. This page may be photocopied.

Apply

Have the children work in pairs to sort picture cards. First have them place the pictures of the two key words (*bird* and *monkey*) at the top of each column of a two-way sort. Then have them say and sort the rest of the pictures. First, one partner says the name of each picture, sorts the pictures according to the number of parts in the word, and reads the completed list. Then they mix up the cards, and the other partner repeats the activity. You may choose to have several sets of the picture cards copied on different colors of paper so that the each child can practice with a partner using a particular set of cards.

Share

Have the children demonstrate saying and clapping the parts of a few one- and two-syllable words of their choice.

Assess

- Observe the children's ability to say and clap the syllables in words.
- Notice whether children recognize and use syllables when writing.
- You may wish to use Phonological Awareness Assessment B or K.

Phonological Awareness: Hear, Say, and Clap Syllables

Connect Learning Across Contexts

Interactive Read-Aloud When you find an interesting two-syllable word in a book you are reading aloud, ask children to say and clap its parts.

> IRA *Flower Garden* by Eve Bunting

> IRA *Does a Kangaroo Have a Mother, Too?* by Eric Carle

Shared Reading When reading poetry together, point out two-syllable words and have children say and clap the parts. See "Dormy, Dormy, Dormouse" in *Words That Sing* (2019). If you don't have these poetry charts, enlarge the print of this poem or other poems such as "Bouncing Ball" in *Sing a Song of Poetry*, and have children use their finger, highlighter tape, or a flag to identify words with a certain number of syllables. (A flag is a T-shaped tool that can be made with a tongue depressor and cardstock–and that is placed under words on a chart to show their location.) You may also wish to use the following Shared Reading title from *Fountas & Pinnell Classroom*™.

> SR *Fly Away* by Alina Kirk

Interactive Writing Say and clap the parts of words before writing the words. Write each word one part at a time (for example, *flow/er*). Show children how they can use their knowledge to represent the different parts of long words (*oc/to/pus*).

Independent Writing Encourage children to clap the parts in words they want to write and to listen for the parts in words that they can represent with letters.

Extend Learning

■ Repeat the lesson with pictures representing other words (you can find additional cards in *Ready Resources* or you can customize cards using Gamemaker in Online Resources): for example, *book, dog, bus; turtle, balloon, carrot, toothbrush, football, hammer, pencil, pumpkin.*

■ You may want to clap the parts of some three-syllable words: for example, *hamburger, violin, skeleton, newspaper.*

▶ Connect with Home

■ Explain to caregivers how to emphasize syllables by saying words and clapping each part. Then they can practice listening for, saying, and clapping word parts at home with children.

■ They can also have children cut out magazine pictures representing words with one and two syllables. Children can glue these pictures on pieces of paper that are divided into two columns, one column for each category.

Hear, Say, and Clap Syllables

Plan

▶ Consider Your Children

This lesson will help to build a foundation for children's attention to the sounds and syllables in words as they read a chant. If necessary, help children grow more familiar and comfortable with shared reading so that they readily join in when you invite them.

▶ Working with English Language Learners

This lesson requires children to remember a repetitive chant. Go over the chant many times so that children are able to say it smoothly and quickly. You may wish to gather photos or drawings of the food words you will use, making sure that children understand the meaning of each English word. To enrich the lesson, ask English language learners what other favorite foods they would put in the blank. If you do not have pictures of the foods they suggest, they may be able to provide drawings.

YOU WILL NEED

PWS Ready Resources
- ▶ PA 7 Sentence Strips
- ▶ PA 7 Pocket-Chart Cards

Online Resources
- ▶ PA 7 Action Tags
- ▶ PA 7 Book Page
- ▶ PA 7 Blank Book Page

Other Materials
- ▶ pocket chart
- ▶ pointer

UNDERSTAND THE PRINCIPLE

Hearing and saying the syllables in words helps children learn how to break them down into parts that can be represented with letters and letter clusters. It helps children relate the oral language they know to written language. Hearing and saying the syllables in words helps children understand word-by-word matching when reading continuous text. Even though a word may have more than one part, you point to it only once when you say it and read it.

EXPLAIN THE PRINCIPLE

Words can have one or more parts.

Listen for, say, and clap the parts in a word.

Comprehensive Phonics, Spelling, and Word Study Guide

Refer to: page **19**, row **6**

ACTIVITY: FOOD CHANT

INSTRUCTIONAL PROCEDURE

HEAR AND SAY

See page 36 for detailed descriptions of Instructional Procedures.

EXPLAIN THE PRINCIPLE

Words can have one or more parts.

Listen for, say, and clap the parts in a word.

Comprehensive Phonics, Spelling, and Word Study Guide

Refer to: page **19**, row **6**

| I love pizza |
| Yum, yum, yum |
| I love pizza |
| In my tum. |

Teach

1. Explain to the children that today they are going to learn a chant that will help them think about words with one or more parts.

2. *You have been learning to clap the parts in a word to help you hear how many parts are in the word. In this chant, you will be clapping the parts in some food words.*

3. Introduce the chant orally, and repeat it enough times so that children know the name of the food and can join in comfortably.

4. When the children say the chant, have them clap the two parts of the word *pizza* while saying it. *When you say* piz/za, *you can hear two parts.*

5. Demonstrate clapping syllables with several other food words until clapping becomes an integral part of the chant. *Let's clap as we say 'I love* ap/ples' *together. Clap quickly two times while saying the word* apples.

6. Once children know the chant, have them vary it using other food words. Display the rhyme on sentence strips in a pocket chart, or prewrite it on chart paper with blanks. Use the food words on the word cards (you may want to add simple drawings) and/or quickly write children's suggestions on cards.

7. Point to the words while children read the chant. *When you read, you point to each word. Look at the word* apples. *Listen to me say it:* ap/ples. *How many parts does it have?* [Demonstrate clapping–children respond.] *This word has two parts, so when you read, you keep your finger (or the pointer) under it while you say both parts.*

8. Demonstrate and repeat this process with different food words. Continue shared reading of the chant, as you point to the words and the children clap the syllables of the food words. Discuss how you keep your pointer or finger under each word as you say all of its parts.

ACTIVITY:
FOUR-PAGE BOOK

INSTRUCTIONAL
PROCEDURE

NOTICE PARTS

See page 36 for detailed descriptions of Instructional Procedures.

ACTION TAGS

write
draw
read
clap

Apply

Give each child a two-page stapled book using preprinted book pages or blank book pages with the handwritten text: *I love* _____. Ask children to write their own favorite foods in the blanks, draw it, and then read the book to a partner, clapping the syllables of food words when they come to them. If they write the word, accept approximated spelling. The purpose of this activity is to choose words and to listen to identify if a word has one or more syllables.

Share

Read through the chant again and have children talk about what they learned about words. You may hear comments like:

"*Tacos* has two parts."

"*Apples* has two parts."

"*Cookies* has two syllables."

If a term like *ice cream* comes up, explain that *ice cream* is made up of two separate words. Have children clap the single part in each word. Suggested language: "Let's say the first word, *ice*. Now let's clap once to show that this word has only one part. Now let's say the second word, *cream*. Let's clap once to show that this word has only one part. You can point to each word when you read, like this."

Assess

- Perform a quick individual assessment by asking children to clap the syllables in a series of words: for example, *horse* and *pony*.
- Notice how children are representing syllables in their writing. Notice their use of vowels, which indicates increasing sophistication.
- You may wish to use Phonological Awareness Assessment B or K.

Connect Learning Across Contexts

Interactive Read-Aloud Read aloud books that have rhythms that children will enjoy. Clap the syllables of some of the longer words after the first read.

IRA *One Duck Stuck* by Phyllis Root

IRA *When It Starts to Snow* by Phillis Gershator

Shared Reading See "Little Ball" in *Words That Sing* (2019). If you don't have these poetry charts, enlarge the print of this poem or other poems such as "Ladybug! Ladybug!" or "I'm Dusty Bill" in *Sing a Song of Poetry,* and have children clap the syllables in words to help hear how words can have one or more parts. You may also wish to use the following Shared Reading title from *Fountas & Pinnell Classroom*™.

SR *The Orange Butterfly: A Story in Pictures* by Margie Sigman

Interactive Writing Clap as a way to break words into syllables for writing group charts.

Independent Writing Prompt children to clap as a way to break words into syllables for writing independently.

Extend Learning

You may want to display the chant on several pocket charts around the room. Place food words along the bottom of the chart, and have children choose three different food words and read the chant three times, pointing under each word as they say it. Children will need to distinguish between words by noticing the first letter or some other visual feature. They will also need to match word by word while reading continuous text.

▶ Connect with Home

- Have the children read their two-page books to family members.

- You might wish to have each child take home a sheet containing five or six pictures that represent words having to do with animals, clothing, or food. Have children practice saying word and clapping their syllables with caregivers.

Hear, Say, and Clap Syllables

Plan

▶ Consider Your Children

If clapping syllables is new to children, begin with one- and two-syllable words only. Clapping syllables will be a new concept for many of the children early in the year. This technique will be very useful as they learn to take words apart, but it may take some practice to coordinate saying and clapping the words. Be sure that they can listen to you say the word and then repeat it after you. The contrast of words with one part and two parts will help them understand the concept you are demonstrating.

▶ Working with English Language Learners

Be sure to use English words the children can understand or learn easily from the pictures. Articulate the words slowly and carefully, and provide many opportunities for children to repeat the words and clap them. Invite children to say and clap their first and last names as well as some words in their own languages. For example, *cat* is *gato* in Spanish, and *gato* could be placed in the two-syllable column.

YOU WILL NEED

PWS Ready Resources
 ▸ PA 8 Pocket-Chart Picture Cards

Online Resources
 ▸ PA 8 Action Tags
 ▸ PA 8 Picture Cards
 ▸ PA 8 Two-Way Sorts

Other Materials
 ▸ pocket chart
 ▸ glue sticks

Generative Lesson
A generative lesson has a simple structure that you can use to present similar content or concepts. You can use this lesson structure to teach children to hear, say, and clap words with a different number of syllables.

UNDERSTAND THE PRINCIPLE

Hearing the syllables in words helps children learn how to break words into parts that can be represented with letters and letter clusters. It also helps children learn how to match their oral language to the written language as they begin to read.

EXPLAIN THE PRINCIPLE

Words can have one or more parts.

Listen for, say, and clap the parts in a word.

Comprehensive Phonics, Spelling, and Word Study Guide

Refer to:
page **19**, row **6**

ACTIVITY: PICTURE SORT

INSTRUCTIONAL PROCEDURE

SAY AND SORT

See page 36 for detailed descriptions of Instructional Procedures.

EXPLAIN THE PRINCIPLE

Words can have one or more parts.

Listen for, say, and clap the parts in a word.

Comprehensive Phonics, Spelling, and Word Study Guide

Refer to: page **19**, row **6**

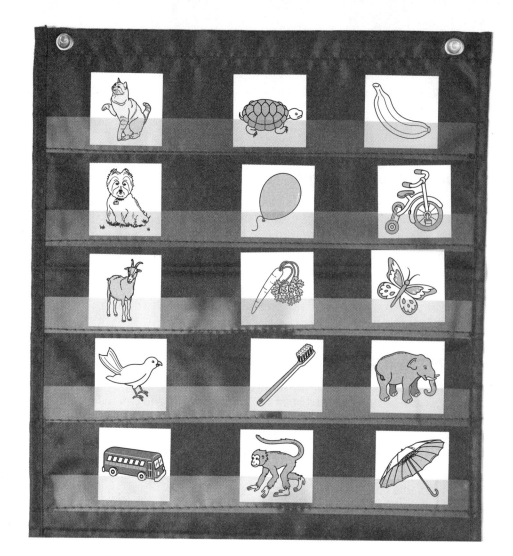

Teach

1. Tell the children they are going to clap the parts of words.

2. Begin by showing the picture representing the first one-syllable word. Ask children to say and clap the word. *When you say words, you can clap the parts you hear.* Demonstrate with *cat. How many parts do you hear in* cat? *You hear one part and you clap once.*

3. Say and clap the rest of the one-syllable words.

4. *Some words have two parts that you can hear.* Demonstrate with *turtle. You hear two syllables and you clap two times.*

5. Continue through the rest of the two- and three-syllable words.

6. Saying and clapping the words may be enough for one lesson. If you feel the children can continue, move to the next part of the lesson.

7. Display a pocket chart with three columns.

8. Go through the pictures again. This time, have children tell you where to place the picture under 1, 2, or 3, according to the number of syllables. Say and clap words as many times as needed for children to hear the syllables.

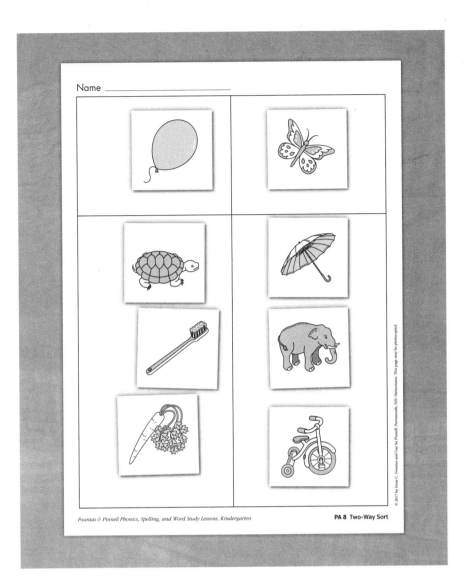

Name _____

Fountas & Pinnell Phonics, Spelling, and Word Study Lessons, Kindergarten

PA 8 Two-Way Sort

© 2017 by Irene C. Fountas and Gay Su Pinnell. Portsmouth, NH: Heinemann. This page may be photocopied.

INSTRUCTIONAL PROCEDURE

SAY AND SORT

See page 36 for detailed descriptions of Instructional Procedures.

ACTION TAGS

say
sort
glue
read

Apply

Have the children use two-way sorts to say and sort pictures representing two- and three-syllable words. Alternatively, give them two-column sorts and pictures to say, sort, and glue. They should read their final lists to a partner.

Share

As a review, have children choose a word of their own and clap the syllables. You may want to give them a category: for example, food, clothes, animals.

Assess

- Observe the children's ability to say and clap the syllables in words.
- Notice whether children recognize and use syllables when writing.
- You may wish to use Phonological Awareness Assessment B or K.

Phonological Awareness: Hear, Say, and Clap Syllables

Connect Learning Across Contexts

Interactive Read-Aloud When you find an interesting two- or three-syllable word in a book you are reading aloud, ask children to say and clap it.

> IRA *A Visitor for Bear* by Bonnie Becker

> IRA *When Sophie Gets Angry* by Molly Bang

Shared Reading See "Puppies and Kittens" in *Words That Sing* (2019). If you don't have these poetry charts, enlarge the print of this poem or other poems such as "Little Jack Horner" or "Open, Shut Them" in *Sing a Song of Poetry*, and point out two- and three-syllable words and have children say and clap them. You might have them use highlighter tape to mark rhyming words. You may also wish to use the following Shared Reading title from *Fountas & Pinnell Classroom*™.

> SR *Ten Big Elephants* by Susan F. Rank

Interactive Writing Say and clap some words when writing them, or revisit the text to clap words.

Independent Writing Encourage children to say and clap words to identify the parts so that they can hear the sounds and connect them to letters as they write.

Extend Learning

- Repeat the lesson with other words: for example, *book, bus, top, house, grapes; lemon, wagon, football, flower, hammer, pencil, pumpkin, water; dinosaur, icicle, kangaroo, tornado, strawberry.*

- You may want to clap four-syllable words (*alligator, caterpillar, escalator, motorcycle, pepperoni, watermelon*) as an oral activity.

▶ Connect with Home

Show family members how to say and clap syllables with children. The caregiver might say a word and have the child beat a pan with a wooden spoon or clap the number of syllables he or she can hear in the word. They can clap words in the supermarket or in the kitchen while cooking. Suggest starting with the names of family and friends.

Blend Syllables

Plan

▶ Consider Your Children

This lesson is most successful after children have learned how to write their names and have participated in interactive writing. They should know how to count the parts in words by clapping syllables. In this lesson, children take a more analytic look at syllables by identifying and blending them. You will be saying syllables in words, pausing very briefly after each, which requires children to think about the whole word and its parts. If children find this task confusing, say the word more smoothly, emphasizing the syllables rather than dividing them. The important thing is for them to grasp the concept of breaks within words.

▶ Working with English Language Learners

Saying words and clapping syllables will help children give more attention to the parts of words and set the scene for taking words apart. Be sure that the children can say the words with some accuracy. Eliminate words that are more difficult to pronounce or understand. If you can, include some words in their own language (e.g., *gato*); the principle of clapping syllables is the same. Demonstrate the game of Lotto, taking enough time to ensure that children understand that they must listen to a word and count its syllables to know whether to place a card on a 1 or a 2 on the game board. Of course, you must be sure that children know the names of all of pictures on the cards.

YOU WILL NEED

Online Resources
- ▶ PA 9 Action Tags
- ▶ PA 9 Lotto and Bingo Game Boards
- ▶ PA 9 Picture Cards
- ▶ PA 9 Blank Book Page
- ▶ PA 9 Directions for Lotto and Bingo

Other Materials
- ▶ masking card
- ▶ flag

Generative Lesson

A generative lesson has a simple structure that you can use to present similar content or concepts. You can use this lesson structure to teach children to blend the syllables in a variety of words.

UNDERSTAND THE PRINCIPLE

Blending individual sounds to form a word requires children to put together discrete elements. Children need to recognize each syllable as a separate entity before they can blend two syllables. This process helps children think analytically about the fact that a word can have one or more parts.

EXPLAIN THE PRINCIPLE

Blend the parts in a word.

Comprehensive Phonics, Spelling, and Word Study Guide

Refer to: page **19**, row **7**

ACTIVITY: SYLLABLE GUESSING GAME

INSTRUCTIONAL PROCEDURE

HEAR AND SAY

See page 36 for detailed descriptions of Instructional Procedures.

EXPLAIN THE PRINCIPLE

Blend the parts in a word.

Comprehensive Phonics, Spelling, and Word Study Guide

Refer to: page **19**, row **7**

Teach

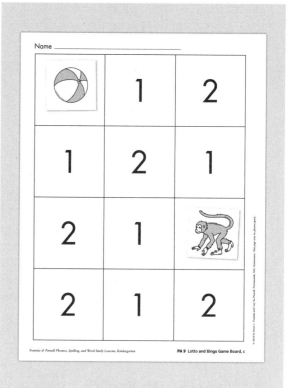

1. Explain to the children that today they will be thinking about the parts, or syllables, in words.

2. *You are really good at learning and clapping the parts in a word. Let's try some.* Demonstrate with words such as *go, tree, sandwich,* and *water.* Let children think of some words one- and two-syllable words to clap.

3. *Today, we are going to play a game with the parts in words. I'm going to say a word slowly. I'll wait a little between the first part and the second part. After I say the first part, you try to think what the word is, but don't say it out loud. Here is the first word:* mon/ster. *Are you thinking of the word? It has two parts. Do you hear each part?* Mon/ster.

4. Try several more words, separating the syllables and asking children to say the whole word. Some examples are *hap/py, pa/per, pen/cil, pret/zel,* and *sand/box.* To avoid confusion, say each word with only a very brief pause between the syllables.

5. *Now I'm going to say a word, and I want you to say each part of the word like I do.* Use some of the same words you used earlier; have children practice making each syllable distinct with their voices.

6. *Today you are going to play Lotto. In this game, you have game boards with numbers on them–1 and 2.* Show them a Lotto game board and use a picture card of a two-syllable word to model taking a card, saying the part or parts of the name of the picture, and covering a square with the correct numeral. *If a word has more than one part, say the first part, and then say the last part. Then say the two parts together, blending them. Then the next person takes a turn.* Demonstrate again with a one-syllable word. Also explain that "free" cards can be used to cover any empty square on the game board. *When you have covered all the squares, you have won the game.*

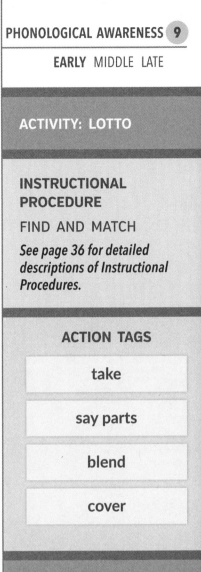

ACTIVITY: LOTTO

INSTRUCTIONAL PROCEDURE

FIND AND MATCH

See page 36 for detailed descriptions of Instructional Procedures.

ACTION TAGS

take

say parts

blend

cover

Apply

Have children play Lotto using the game boards and picture cards. They take a card, say the parts, blend them, and cover the number. You also may wish to customize gameboards using Gamemaker in Online Resources.

Share

Ask the children to clap the syllables in a few words they used in the game.

Assess

■ Give the children five words, and notice whether they are able to hear and clap one and two syllables.

■ Notice whether children refer to and use their work with syllables when they attempt to write words with two or more syllables.

■ You may wish to use Phonological Awareness Assessment B or K.

Connect Learning Across Contexts

Interactive Read-Aloud Read aloud books that include multisyllabic words.

[IRA] *The Feelings Book* by Todd Parr

[IRA] *The Ugly Vegetables* by Grace Lin

Shared Reading See "Higglety, Pigglety, Pop!" in *Words That Sing* (2019). If you don't have these poetry charts, enlarge the print of this poem or other poems such as "Apple Harvest" or "Ring Around the Rosie" in *Sing a Song of Poetry*, and point out two-syllable words and have children say and clap them. You might have them use highlighter tape to mark rhyming words. You may also wish to use the following Shared Reading title from *Fountas & Pinnell Classroom*™ to clap more syllables.

[SR] *The Sleeping Giant* by Barbara Gannet

Interactive Writing Have children clap the syllables in words in order to think about how to write the parts in group interactive writing.

Independent Writing Encourage children to say the word and break it down into parts by clapping as they say each syllable. Then they can listen for the sounds in each part.

Extend Learning

Repeat the Lotto game with different words, perhaps adding words that are likely unfamiliar to children to increase the challenge. You also may wish to customize gameboards using Gamemaker in Online Resources.

▶ **Connect with Home**

- Give children photocopies of the Lotto game boards and picture cards so that they can play the game at home with family members.

- You may give children blank four-page books to take home in which they can glue picture cards representing two-syllable words. Have them glue a picture on each page and then "read" the book by saying the name of the picture and saying the syllables in the word.

Hear and Say the Same Beginning Sound in Words

Plan

▶ Consider Your Children

This lesson works best after children have worked with their names and have done some interactive writing. In this lesson, they learn an important procedure for matching beginning sounds. Children will be matching and sorting in many different ways in a wide variety of lessons.

▶ Working with English Language Learners

Saying the names of pictures to hear and connect the same beginning sound in words will help children take on the phonology of English. Saying words slowly with emphasis on the beginning sound will make words more accessible to children than they are when children are listening to the rapid succession of sounds in normal speech. (But this is not intended to be so slow that children cannot understand the word.) Be sure that children know, understand, and can say the name of the picture that represents each word before they match the pictures. Work with a small group to play the matching game so that they understand the task. Provide support for several repetitions of the task.

YOU WILL NEED

PWS Ready Resources
- ▶ PA 10 Pocket-Chart Picture Cards

Online Resources
- ▶ PA 10 Action Tags
- ▶ PA 10 Picture Cards
- ▶ PA 10 Sorts

Other Materials
- ▶ pocket chart

Generative Lesson

A generative lesson has a simple structure that you can use to present similar content or concepts. You can use this lesson structure to teach children to hear and say the same beginning sounds in a variety of words.

UNDERSTAND THE PRINCIPLE

With the ability to identify the beginning sound in a word, children can begin to make connections between words that have the same beginning sound. It is important for them to say each word slowly and to listen for the sound in a particular location within both words.

EXPLAIN THE PRINCIPLE

Some words sound the same at the beginning.

Connect words that sound the same at the beginning.

Comprehensive Phonics, Spelling, and Word Study Guide

Refer to: page **19**, row **17**

ACTIVITY: TWO-WAY PICTURE SORT

INSTRUCTIONAL PROCEDURE

SAY AND SORT

See page 36 for detailed descriptions of Instructional Procedures.

EXPLAIN THE PRINCIPLE

Some words sound the same at the beginning.

Connect words that sound the same at the beginning.

Comprehensive Phonics, Spelling, and Word Study Guide

Refer to: page **19**, row **17**

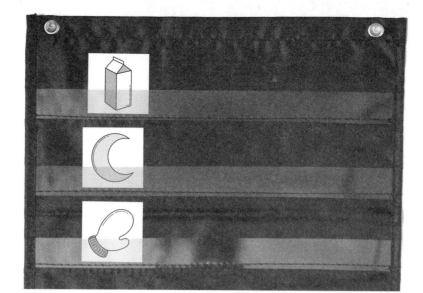

Teach

1. Explain to the children that they are going to learn more about beginning sounds in words.

2. Place a pocket-chart picture card for *moon* at the top of the pocket chart. Have ready picture cards representing words that begin with /m/ and others that have contrasting beginning sounds: *milk, moon, mitten, mouse, mop, monkey, cow, camel, cat, duck, dog, goat, gum, bell, house.*

3. Have children say the word *moon* slowly and think about the sound at the beginning of the word. *Look at my mouth and listen as I say a word.* Say *moon* slowly. *What sound do you hear at the beginning of the word? • It's /m/. When you say the word* moon, *you can hear the /m/ sound at the beginning. Say this word,* milk. *• Does it have an /m/ sound at the beginning? • Say* moon, milk. *• You can hear the same sound at the beginning of both words. Because those beginning sounds match, I'll place the picture of* milk *under the picture of* moon.

4. Go through two more words that begin with /m/ (*mitten, mouse*), each time having children say the word and think about how it has the same beginning sound as the word *moon*. Each time, place the picture under the moon.

5. Then show the picture of the duck and have the children say *duck. Does the word* duck *have the beginning sound /m/? • The word* duck *and the word* moon *have different beginning sounds.* Explain that you will not put the duck in the pocket chart because the words do not sound the same at the beginning. Place the pictures not placed in the chart in a pile on the table.

6. *We are going to play a game to decide which words have an /m/ sound at the beginning, like the word* moon *does. First say* moon, *listen to the beginning sound, then say the name of the other picture, like this.* Demonstrate. *If both words have the same beginning sound, put the card under the moon. If the words don't have the same beginning sound, I will put the card on the table.* Demonstrate with the stack of picture cards, inviting children to join in. *You can say both words to see if they have the same beginning sound.*

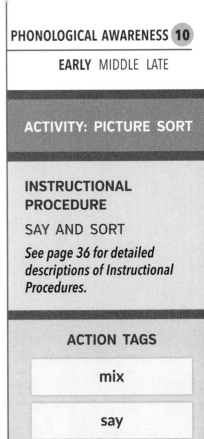

ACTIVITY: PICTURE SORT

INSTRUCTIONAL PROCEDURE

SAY AND SORT

See page 36 for detailed descriptions of Instructional Procedures.

ACTION TAGS

mix

say

sort

Apply

Have children repeat the Teach activity using a simple sorting sheet. First they mix up all of the picture cards. As they look at each picture, show them how to first say *moon* and then the name of the picture. Using the two-way sort, they place the pictures that begin like *moon* under the moon and those that do not begin like *moon* in a pile on the table. It doesn't matter that children may have varied labels in mind for some pictures (e.g., *rat, mouse*). The purpose of the activity is to say the words and think about the beginning sounds.

Share

Have children bring their papers to a circle discussion and say the names of the pictures they have sorted. Show the pocket chart with pictures accurately matched under moon and others to the side, and ask children to talk about what they notice. Statements like these reveal what children are noticing as they hear sounds in words:

"*Mouse* starts with an *m* sound, like *moon* and *milk* and *mitten.*"

"*House* is the only word that starts with an *h* sound."

"*Duck* and *dog* have the same beginning sound."

Assess

- Observe whether the children can match picture cards according to beginning sound.

- In interactive writing, notice whether children can come up with examples of other words with the same beginning sound as the word they want to write.

- You may wish to use Phonological Awareness Assessment E or K.

Phonological Awareness: Hear and Say the Same Beginning Sound in Words

Connect Learning Across Contexts

Interactive Read-Aloud Read aloud books that draw children's attention to the beginning sounds in words.

IRA *B Is for Bulldozer* by June Sobel

IRA *A, My Name is Alice* by Jane Bayer

Shared Reading See "I Measure Myself" in *Words That Sing* (2019). If you don't have these poetry charts, enlarge the print of this poem or other poems such as "Apples, Peaches" or "Five Fat Pumpkins" in *Sing a Song of Poetry*, and bring children's attention to two successive words that begin with the same sound (like *peaches* and *pears*). Have them say both words and think about the beginning sound. You may also wish to refer to the following Shared Reading title from *Fountas & Pinnell Classroom*™.

SR *One Summer Day: A Story in Pictures* by Susan A. Layne

Interactive Writing Have children say a word slowly and think about what letter might stand for this sound. Connect the word to picture cards you have used or to children's names to decide whether the word in question begins with the same sound as another word.

Independent Writing Encourage children to say the words they want to write and think what letter might stand for the beginning sound.

Extend Learning

Repeat the lesson with words that have other beginning consonant sounds.

▶ Connect with Home

■ Reproduce and cut apart a collection of picture cards of words with different beginning consonant sounds. Send home these cards and a piece of paper with one picture (for example, *bear*) placed at the top above a large circle. Children can select and glue into the circle pictures of things whose names begin with /b/. Show them how to say the name of the first picture along with the name of each picture in the circle.

■ Encourage family members to play silly alliterative sentence games like *Mary makes many muffins* and *Peter packs pickles.*

Hear and Say the Same Beginning Sound in Words

Plan

▶ Consider Your Children

This lesson works best after children have worked with their names and have participated in interactive writing. In this lesson, they practice an important procedure for matching beginning sounds. Children will be matching and sorting in many different ways in a wide variety of lessons.

▶ Working with English Language Learners

Be sure that your English language learners know the names of each picture used in the Apply activity, and give them many opportunities to say these words. Remember that children may only approximate English pronunciation, so be alert to when they are using phonology from their own languages. You may want to work with English language learners in small groups to be sure that they understand how to sort the picture cards into the correct categories.

YOU WILL NEED

PWS Ready Resources
- ▶ Alphabet Linking Chart
- ▶ PA 11 Pocket-Chart Picture Cards

Online Resources
- ▶ PA 11 Action Tags
- ▶ PA 11 Picture Cards
- ▶ PA 11 Three-Way Sorts
- ▶ PA 11 Three-Column Sorts

Other Materials
- ▶ pocket chart

Generative Lesson
A generative lesson has a simple structure that you can use to present similar content or concepts. You can use this lesson structure to teach children how to hear and say other beginning consonant sounds in a variety of words.

UNDERSTAND THE PRINCIPLE

With the ability to identify the beginning sound in a word, children can begin to make connections between words that have the same beginning sound. It is important for them to say each word slowly and to listen for the sound in a particular location within both words. Successfully identifying the beginning sound in words will lead to children's ability to connect sounds to the letters that represent them.

EXPLAIN THE PRINCIPLE

Some words sound the same at the beginning.

Connect words that sound the same at the beginning.

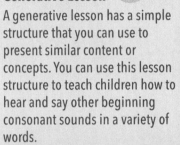 Comprehensive Phonics, Spelling, and Word Study Guide

Refer to: page **19**, row **17**

ACTIVITY: THREE-WAY PICTURE SORT

INSTRUCTIONAL PROCEDURE

SAY AND SORT

See page 36 for detailed descriptions of Instructional Procedures.

EXPLAIN THE PRINCIPLE

Some words sound the same at the beginning.

Connect words that sound the same at the beginning.

Comprehensive Phonics, Spelling, and Word Study Guide

Refer to: page **19**, row **17**

Teach

1. Explain to children that they are going to learn more about beginning sounds in words.

2. Show the pocket-chart picture card for *bear.* Have children say the word *bear* slowly and think about the sound at the beginning of the word. *What sound do you hear at the beginning of the word* bear? • *It's* b (or isolate the phoneme /b/). *When you say the word* bear, *you can hear the* b *sound at the beginning.* Show the card for *boot. Say this word,* boot. • *Does it have a* b *sound at the beginning?* • *Say* bear, boot. • *You can hear the same sound at the beginning of both words. Because those beginning sounds match, the picture of* boot *can be placed under the picture of* bear. Ask a child to place the picture of *boot* under the picture of *bear.*

3. Go through additional pictures of words that begin with /b/ (*box, bat, bird*), as well as pictures of other words that do not begin with /b/ (*heart, monkey*), each time having children say the two words and think about whether they sound the same at the beginning. Each time, place the picture of a word beginning with /b/ under the picture of *bear,* or place the picture of a word not beginning with /b/ on the table.

4. Repeat the same activity with words that begin with /h/ (*hat, horse, heart, hook, hand*) and then with words that begin with /m/ (*moon, mitten, mouse, mask, monkey*).

5. Keep the pictures of the bear, the hat, and the moon along the top of the pocket chart, and remove the other pictures. Explain that the picture of the bear stands for words that begin with /b/, the hat stands for words that begin with /h/, and the moon stands for words that begin with /m/.

6. Mix up the rest of the cards, then pick up one card at a time. Invite children to say the word, hear the beginning sound of the word, and decide whether the picture should go under the bear, the hat, or the moon. Encourage children to say the two words (e.g., *bear, bird*) to check that the new word is placed in the correct column.

7. After children have sorted all of the cards, have children name all of the pictures in each column with the same beginning sound.

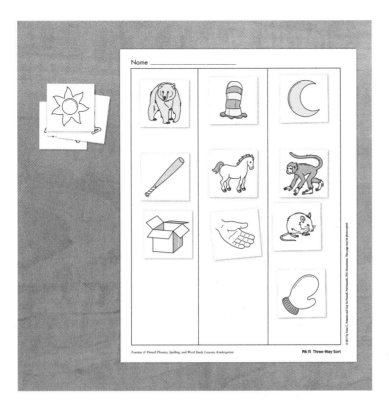

ACTIVITY: THREE-WAY PICTURE SORT

INSTRUCTIONAL PROCEDURE

SAY AND SORT

See page 36 for detailed descriptions of Instructional Procedures.

ACTION TAGS

say

put

read

Apply

Give the children a pile of picture cards. Invite them to place the pictures that stand for the words *bear*, *hat*, and *moon* at the top of the three columns of a three-way sort. Then have children take each remaining card, say the name of the picture, and place the picture in the correct column according to its beginning sound. Ask children to read their completed columns of picture cards to a partner. Children can use a three-column sort if they need to extend the columns.

Share

Show the categorized words in the pocket chart at circle time. Ask children to discuss what they noticed about the beginning sounds of words. Demonstrate by making some comments yourself. Comments such as these reveal children's thinking about sounds in words:

"*Bear* and *bird* start the same."

"*Hat* and *mitten* have different sounds at the beginning."

"*Hat* has an *h* sound at the beginning."

"If it's *mouse*, it starts like *moon*, but if it's *rat*, it doesn't."

Assess

- Notice whether the children can match picture cards according to beginning sound.

- You may wish to use Phonological Awareness Assessment E or K.

Phonological Awareness: Hear and Say the Same Beginning Sound in Words

Connect Learning Across Contexts

Interactive Read-Aloud Read aloud books that emphasize the sounds at the beginning of words.

   IRA *Alphabet Under Construction* by Denise Fleming

   IRA *Wemberly Worried* by Kevin Henkes

Shared Reading See "Five Fingers on Each Hand" in *Words That Sing* (2019). If you don't have these poetry charts, enlarge the print of this poem or other poems such as "Little Tommy Tucker" in *Sing a Song of Poetry*, and point out two or more words that appear in the same line of a poem and that have the same sound at the beginning. You may also wish to use the following Shared Reading title from *Fountas & Pinnell Classroom™*.

   SR *The Old Lady Who Swallowed a Fly* adapted by Vivian Malone

Interactive Writing Ask children to say a word before writing it. Then have them isolate the first sound and predict what letter might represent that sound. As you start to write the word, invite the children to see if that letter does appear at the beginning of the word.

Independent Writing Encourage children to say a word and think about the beginning sound before writing it.

Extend Learning

■ Repeat the lesson, matching other beginning sounds using words from the Alphabet Linking Chart. You might start with names (e.g., *goat, jar*) that have a beginning consonant sound before moving on to names (e.g., *apple, egg*) that have a beginning vowel sound.

■ After children become very proficient, show the three pictures to be placed at the tops of the columns. Then give directions without going through the entire set. That will leave some challenges for them to work out independently and discuss during sharing time.

▶ Connect with Home

■ Give each child a sheet of paper with a picture of a bear, a hat, or a moon on it. Ask her to find objects at home that have a name with the same beginning sound as the name of the picture.

■ Alternatively, give each child an envelope with one of the pictures glued on the outside. In the envelope, they can place pictures of things (or actual small objects) that have names with the same beginning sound as the name shown on the envelope.

Hear and Say the Same Beginning Sound in Words

Plan

▶ Consider Your Children

This lesson introduces a type of quick game that can be played anytime during the school day. When children have to line up for an activity, for example, you can have them do so by playing a game that calls their attention to sounds in words. These games help children realize that the print on the classroom walls is a resource for reading and writing. To successfully play the game, children need to hear and say a word, identify and isolate the beginning sound of the word, and connect that sound to other words—a complex task.

▶ Working with English Language Learners

This lesson helps you build language play into classroom activities. Be sure that you prepare English language learners with some key examples so that they can respond to the game (e.g., coming up with a *coat* to take to *California*). Allow more "wait and think" time for children who need it, and accept responses that repeat the answer of children before them. This repetition will help English language learners expand their vocabularies.

YOU WILL NEED

Online Resources
▶ PA 12 Action Tags
▶ PA 12 Trip Sentences

Other Materials
▶ chart paper

Generative Lesson
A generative lesson has a simple structure that you can use to present similar content or concepts. You can use this lesson structure with other words to teach children how to hear, say, and connect other beginning sounds.

UNDERSTAND THE PRINCIPLE

With the ability to identify the beginning sound in a word, children can begin to make connections between words that have the same beginning sound. It is important for them to say each word slowly and to listen for the sound in a particular location within both words. Successfully identifying the beginning sound in words will lead to children's ability to connect sounds to the letters that represent them. Once children have learned that there is a relationship between the first sound in a word and the first letter or letters in a word, they can use this information to self-monitor as they read continuous text and write words.

EXPLAIN THE PRINCIPLE

Some words sound the same at the beginning.

Connect words that sound the same at the beginning.

Comprehensive Phonics, Spelling, and Word Study Guide

Refer to:
page **19**, row **17**

ACTIVITY: TRIP GAME

INSTRUCTIONAL PROCEDURE

HEAR AND SAY

See page 36 for detailed descriptions of Instructional Procedures.

EXPLAIN THE PRINCIPLE

Some words sound the same at the beginning.

Connect words that sound the same at the beginning.

Comprehensive Phonics, Spelling, and Word Study Guide

Refer to: page **19**, row **17**

Teach

1. Tell the children that they are going to learn a word game.

2. *Let's pretend we're going on a trip. You know, when you go on a trip, you have to pack. You have to take something with you. On this trip, we're going to California. Say* California. • *What is the first sound in the word* California? • *Yes, it's a* k *sound* [isolate the phoneme], *so everyone needs to take something that starts with the* k *sound. Like this: I'm going to California, and I'm taking a* coat. *Say those words,* California, coat. *What else could I take?* • Words do not have to share the same first letter, just the beginning /k/; a word such as *kite* is also correct.

3. As you write on a piece of chart paper, have children say the words "I'm going to California, and I'm taking _____." Invite them to fill in more examples. Some possibilities are a *car, candy,* a *can,* a *cat,* a *kite,* a *key,* a *clock,* a *cake,* and *cookies.* Children might use other children's names, as well: for example, "I'm going to California and I'm taking Carlos."

4. Have children look around the room for ideas (on a chart or a word wall, for example). Point out that not *every* /k/ word will work. If a child says, for example, "I'm going to California and I'm taking *climb,*" explain that he did good thinking about the beginning sound. Then help him come up with a /k/ word that makes sense in the sentence.

5. Have children practice finding /k/ words in the room. They can point to or go to the word or object while saying, "I'm going to California and I'm taking a *coat.*" This variation will help children become more aware of how to use print resources.

6. Line up chairs as if they were seats on a bus, and have one child at a time say, "I'm going to California and I'm taking _____." After successfully generating a /k/ example, the child can get on the "bus."

7. At first, accept any /k/ word children generate. After children know the game, make it more challenging by requiring a *different* word from the one before or from any words that have been used so far. If a child cannot generate an appropriate word, you can also say, *Would you like to take a [word]?* The child can say yes and use that word in the sentence.

8. Repeat using other locations and sounds: for example, *I'm going to the store and I'm going to get a sweater/a sandwich/soup; I'm going to the beach and I'm taking a ball/Bob/a basket/a banana.*

I'm going to California
and I'm taking _____.

I'm going to _the bech_ and I'm taking _Beth_ .

ACTIVITY: ILLUSTRATED TRIP SENTENCES

INSTRUCTIONAL PROCEDURE

SAY AND WRITE

See page 36 for detailed descriptions of Instructional Procedures.

ACTION TAGS

say
write
draw
read

Apply

Have children choose a place they are going: for example, store, market, beach. Write their chosen destination word in the first space on PA 12 Trip Sentence, make copies of the sentence, and distribute them. Have children say the destination word and fill in the empty space with another word that has the same beginning sound and makes sense in the sentence (for example, *I'm going to the beach and I'm taking Beth*). Then invite children to illustrate the sentence. You might give children three or four pages, have them say and draw other items, and read their pages to a partner.

Share

Have children bring their illustrated trip pages to a circle discussion and say what words they illustrated. Display these pages in the room.

Assess

- Observe whether children can generate appropriate examples for the trip game.
- During interactive writing, check whether the children can come up with examples of words that have the same beginning sound as the one they want to write.
- You may wish to use Phonological Awareness Assessment E or K.

Phonological Awareness: Hear and Say the Same Beginning Sound in Words

Connect Learning Across Contexts

Interactive Read-Aloud Read aloud books that draw attention to sounds in words.

> IRA *Creak! Said the Bed* by Phyllis Root

> IRA *Max Found Two Sticks* by Brian Pinkney

Shared Reading See "Windshield Wiper" in *Words That Sing* (2019). If you don't have these poetry charts, enlarge the print of this poem or other poems such as "Little Miss Muffet" in *Sing a Song of Poetry*, and have children locate and say words that begin with the same sound. You may also wish to use the following Shared Reading title from *Fountas & Pinnell Classroom*™.

> SR *Stripes* by Catherine Friend

Interactive Writing Have children say a word slowly and think about how to start writing it. Connect the word to picture cards you have used (or a classroom word chart) to help them think about whether it starts like another word.

Independent Writing Encourage children to say the words they want to write and to think about how to start them in writing.

Extend Learning

Play the trip game with other beginning sounds. Select places that are familiar to children and that will engage their attention: for example, the desert, the zoo, the subway, the seashore, the mountains, a train, a bus, a plane, the market. Have children play the game as they line up to go to the gym or cafeteria.

▶ Connect with Home

Encourage family members to play the trip game with their children at home or on family outings. Suggest several clear examples as starters: for example, "I'm going to the park" or "I'm going to the lake."

Hear and Say the Ending Sound in a Word

Plan

▶ Consider Your Children

This activity will be effective for children who have had a great deal of experience saying and hearing sounds in words, matching words for ending sounds, and associating letters and sounds in their names. Be sure that children know what you mean when you talk about the last sound in a word. This lesson presents a word play activity that can be used at any time during the school day; if you have a minute or two of downtime between activities, you can make a game of one or two quick questions.

▶ Working with English Language Learners

In this lesson, children will be using picture cards as they say the name of the picture slowly and notice the last sound in the word. Articulation will be important, and some words may be difficult for English language learners. First, be sure that all children know and can say the English name of each picture. Check their articulation and note their ability to clearly pronounce the last sound of each word. Eliminate picture cards that are too difficult. It is important that the children understand the concept of attending to the last sound. Also be sure they understand what you mean by the words *first* and *last*.

YOU WILL NEED

PWS Ready Resources
▶ PA 13 Pocket-Chart Picture Cards

Online Resources
▶ PA 13 Action Tags
▶ PA 13 Picture Cards

Other Materials
▶ pocket chart

Generative Lesson
A generative lesson has a simple structure that you can use to present similar content or concepts. You can use this lesson structure to teach children to hear and say the ending sounds in a variety of words.

UNDERSTAND THE PRINCIPLE

As children become more aware of the sounds in words, they learn to isolate and identify the last sound in a word when they hear it. The ability to hear this last sound provides a foundation for connecting other sounds and letters beyond the first letter. This knowledge helps readers begin to decode words and monitor their reading of continuous text.

EXPLAIN THE PRINCIPLE

Say a word to hear the last sound.

Listen for the last sound in a word.

Comprehensive Phonics, Spelling, and Word Study Guide

Refer to: page **19**, row **16**

**ACTIVITY:
PICTURE CARDS**

**INSTRUCTIONAL
PROCEDURE**

HEAR AND SAY

*See page 36 for detailed
descriptions of Instructional
Procedures.*

EXPLAIN THE PRINCIPLE

*Say a word to hear the last
sound.*

*Listen for the last sound in a
word.*

Comprehensive
Phonics, Spelling,
and Word Study
Guide

Refer to:
page **19**, row **16**

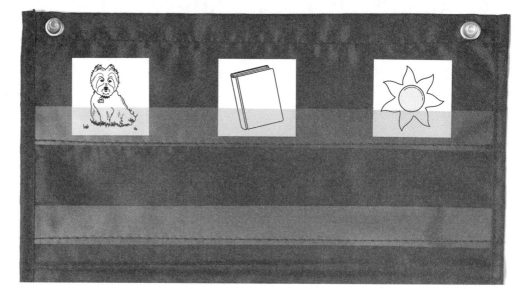

Teach

1. Explain to the children that today they will be learning how to listen for the last sound in a word that they say.

2. Display the pocket-chart picture cards for *dog, book,* and *sun. When you say a word, you can hear the first sound, right?* • Invite children to say the word *dog* together with you, then say the word slowly, but don't distort it, emphasizing the first letter. *You can hear the first sound of* dog, *can't you?* • *The first sound of the word* dog *is* /d/.

3. *We've learned to say just the first sound of* dog [demonstrate]. *You try it.* • *Now I'm going to say just the last sound of* dog–/g/ [demonstrate]. *That's the last sound you hear at the end of the word. You say it like this:* dog, /g/.

4. *Let's try another one. Say* sun. • *What is the first sound?* • *What is the last sound?* • *Let's try one more, just thinking about the last sound. Say* book. • *Say the last sound of* book.

5. Continue to demonstrate with two or three more examples [*hat, flag, bear*], focusing on just the last sound, and invite children to offer additional examples.

6. For a variation, take some of the names of children in your class and say them, isolating the ending sound.

ACTIVITY: PICTURE CARDS (PARTNERS)

INSTRUCTIONAL PROCEDURE

HEAR AND SAY

See page 36 for detailed descriptions of Instructional Procedures.

ACTION TAGS

take card

say word

say last sound

Apply

Children have a pile of about twenty picture cards to use with a partner. They take turns drawing a card, saying the name of the picture, and then saying the last sound in the word.

Share

Encourage the children to come up with a variety of words in a category, such as school or home, and then to say each word and its last sound.

Assess

■ Notice whether the children can clearly say the last sound in a word and if they can identify the last sound in a word. A quick check of just two or three examples will tell you whether they understand the concept.

■ You may wish to use Phonological Awareness Assessment K.

Phonological Awareness: Hear and Say the Ending Sound in a Word

Connect Learning Across Contexts

Interactive Read-Aloud Read aloud books that offer examples of the repetition of final sounds.

> IRA *One Duck Stuck* by Phyllis Root

> IRA *When It Starts to Snow* by Phillis Gershator

Shared Reading See "Five Little Snowmen" in *Words That Sing* (2019). If you don't have these poetry charts, enlarge the print of this poem or other poems such as "Ladybug! Ladybug!" in *Sing a Song of Poetry,* which offer flexible play with last sounds in words. You may also wish to use the following Shared Reading title from *Fountas & Pinnell Classroom*™.

> SR *A Bear and His Honey* by Fannie Morris

Interactive Writing Have children say a word slowly and think about how to start it. After representing the first sound with a letter, write the rest of the word up to the final sound. Ask children to say the word again and think about the last sound. When they say the sound, you can respond: *We use the letter* (write and name it) *to stand for that sound.*

Independent Writing Encourage children to say a word they want to write and think about how to start it. Encourage them to repeat the word and try to represent additional sounds in the word with letters. For some words, you may also show them how to listen for the last sound and write the letter that represents that sound.

Extend Learning

When children can easily come up with the last sound of a word, use picture cards of some simple examples to show them how to connect the last sound of a word with the last letter of a word.

▶ Connect with Home

Ask family members to listen for the last sound in a series of words with children. Provide examples or categories to use, such as colors (e.g., *red*–/d/), animals (e.g., *mouse*–/s/), or food (e.g., *bread*–/d/). Emphasize that the activity should be quick and fun; the purpose of the activity is to make children curious about words and to help them enjoy manipulating sounds.

Hear and Say the Same Ending Sound in Words

Plan

▶ **Consider Your Children**

If children have been accustomed to listening for beginning sounds, you can then provide clear demonstrations to help them attend to last sounds. Use a variety of words, including some two-syllable words, so children learn to be flexible in how they listen for the last sound. Because of dialect and individual differences, some children may not say the last sounds in exactly the same way you do. For this activity, demonstrate standard articulation and have children practice it. Finally, remember that children are listening for the last sound they hear, independent of letters. It doesn't matter here that *kite* has an *e* at the end; the last sound in *kite* is /t/.

▶ **Working with English Language Learners**

You may need to work in a small group to make sure English language learners can hear the last sound and can clearly articulate the words and say the last sound. Children will be expected to use picture cards to categorize words by last sound, so they will need to hear the similarity in the final phonemes. Provide more examples as needed, and be sure that children say the words themselves rather than just listening to you say them. Begin with a limited set of picture cards; have children say each word and place each picture card in the correct category. Be sure that the children know and can say the names of the words they will be using and that they understand the words *first* and *last* in English.

YOU WILL NEED

PWS Ready Resources
▶ PA 14 Pocket-Chart Picture Cards

Online Resources
▶ PA 14 Action Tags
▶ PA 14 Two-Way Sorts
▶ PA 14 Picture Cards
▶ PA 14 Two-Column Sorts

Other Materials
▶ pocket chart

Generative Lesson ✓

A generative lesson has a simple structure that you can use to present similar content or concepts. You can use this lesson structure to teach children to hear and say the same ending sounds in a variety of words.

UNDERSTAND THE PRINCIPLE

With the ability to identify the ending sound in a word, children can begin to make connections between words that have the same ending sound. It is important for them to say each word slowly and to listen for the sound in a particular location within both words. Successfully identifying the ending sound in words will lead to children's ability to connect sounds to the letters that represent them.

EXPLAIN THE PRINCIPLE

Some words sound the same at the end.

Connect words that sound the same at the end.

Comprehensive Phonics, Spelling, and Word Study Guide

Refer to: page **19**, row **18**

EARLY **MIDDLE** LATE

ACTIVITY: TWO-WAY PICTURE SORT

INSTRUCTIONAL PROCEDURE

SAY AND SORT

See page 36 for detailed descriptions of Instructional Procedures.

EXPLAIN THE PRINCIPLE

Some words sound the same at the end.

Connect words that sound the same at the end.

Comprehensive Phonics, Spelling, and Word Study Guide

Refer to: page **19**, row **18**

Teach

1. Explain to the children that they are going to learn more about ending sounds.

2. Place the picture card for the word *cat* in the pocket chart. *Say the word* cat *slowly.* • *What sound do you hear at the end of the word?* • *It's the* t *sound. When you say the word, you can hear the sound at the end.* Show the picture card for the word *basket. Now slowly say the word* basket. Emphasize the last sound when you pronounce it. • *Does this word have the same ending sound as the word* cat? • *Say* cat, basket. • *You can hear the same* t *sound at the end, right? So I'm going to place the picture of the basket under the picture of the cat.*

3. Go through other words that end with /t/ (*kite, coat, goat, net, hat*), as well as pictures of other words that do not end with /t/ (*cake, dress*). Each time, have the children say the word *cat* and the second word and think about whether the two words sound the same at the end. Each time, place the picture of a word ending with /t/ under the picture of *cat*, or place the picture of a word not ending with /t/ on the table.

4. Repeat the process with *moon* and other words that end with /n/ (*spoon, fan, sun, bone, lion, ten, nine*).

5. Leave the picture cards for *cat* and *moon* on the top of the pocket chart. Mix up the other picture cards, then go through them one at a time. Invite the children to say the word and decide whether the picture should go under the cat or the moon.

6. Encourage them to check their categories by saying *cat, basket,* and so on, accentuating the last sound.

7. When finished, you will have categorized all of the picture cards into two columns.

8. Check that children have correctly sorted the cards by having them name all of the pictures in each column.

ACTIVITY: TWO-WAY PICTURE SORT (PARTNERS)

INSTRUCTIONAL PROCEDURE

SAY AND SORT

See page 36 for detailed descriptions of Instructional Procedures.

ACTION TAGS

take
say
sort

Apply

Have children work with a partner to complete a two-way sort using a pile of picture cards. First, they place the pictures for *cat* and *moon* at the top of the sort. The first child takes a picture card, says the word, and places the card in the correct column or sets it aside on the table if its ending sound is neither /t/ nor /n/. He reads the completed columns of pictures as a final check and then mixes up the cards for his partner to take a turn. Two-column sorts can be used to extend the columns, if needed.

Share

Display the categorized words in the pocket chart. Ask children to discuss what they noticed about the ending sounds of words. Demonstrate by making some comments yourself. You may hear comments like these, which reveal children's thinking about sounds in words:

"*Cat* and *net* end the same."

"*Nine* sounds like *moon* at the end but like *net* at the beginning."

"*Nine* sounds like /n/ at the end, but there's an *e*."

Assess

- Notice whether the children can match words that sound the same at the end.
- When you have worked with ending sounds for a while, you can ask all the children to try to write three to five words. Check their approximations to see if they are representing ending sounds.
- You may wish to use Phonological Awareness Assessment F or K.

Phonological Awareness: Hear and Say the Same Ending Sound in Words

Connect Learning Across Contexts

Interactive Read-Aloud Read aloud books that emphasize ending sounds.

> IRA *It's Raining, It's Pouring* by Kin Eagle

> IRA *Over on the Farm* by Marianne Berkes

Shared Reading See "Grandpa Grig" in *Words That Sing* (2019). If you don't have these poetry charts, enlarge the print of this poem or other poems such as "The Mockingbird" in *Sing a Song of Poetry,* and cover the last letter of some words using a masking card. When you approach such a word, invite the children to predict the last sound. You may also wish to use the following Shared Reading title from *Fountas & Pinnell Classroom*™.

> SR *Giggles: Poems to Make You Laugh*

Interactive Writing Ask children to say the word and predict the first letter before writing it. Write the word up to the last letter and ask them to say the word again and predict the last letter.

Independent Writing Encourage children to say the word and think about the ending sound before writing the letter that represents it.

Extend Learning

Repeat the lesson with different pictures to practice matching other ending sounds. Gradually increase the range of sounds children can work with at one time.

▶ Connect with Home

- Give each child a paper with a picture of some object on it; the name of the object should have a distinct ending sound. Ask children to find pictures of other objects with names that have the same ending sound as the one represented in the picture you provided.

- Alternatively, give each child an envelope with the picture glued on the outside. In the envelopes children can place three pictures or small objects representing words that have the same ending sound. Then they can bring the envelopes to school to share.

Hear and Say the Same Ending Sound in Words

Plan

▶ Consider Your Children

This lesson is best used after children have had some experience matching pictures for ending sounds. Lotto is similar to Bingo, except that in Lotto, players cover every square, so there is more work to do. In this game, children match the last sounds of the words represented by the pictures. They say both words to show that they match. Remember that a picture may have more than one correct name (e.g., *hat* or *cap*); the purpose of the activity is to match ending sounds.

▶ Working with English Language Learners

You will be using this lesson after English language learners have already learned the names of quite a few pictures. You may be expanding their repertoire in this lesson, so be sure that you go over the names of the pictures and have them say the words several times. Also, provide a clear demonstration of Lotto, acting out the directions as needed. The first time the children play the game, either observe and coach them or play with them so that you are sure they understand how to play.

YOU WILL NEED

PWS Ready Resources
- ▶ PA 15 Pocket-Chart Picture Cards

Online Resources
- ▶ PA 15 Action Tags
- ▶ PA 15 Lotto and Bingo Game Boards
- ▶ PA 15 Picture Cards
- ▶ PA 15 Directions for Lotto and Bingo

Other Materials
- ▶ pocket chart

Generative Lesson

A generative lesson has a simple structure that you can use to present similar content or concepts. You can use this lesson structure to teach children how to listen for and connect two words with the same ending consonant sound.

UNDERSTAND THE PRINCIPLE

With the ability to identify the ending sound in a word, children can begin to make connections between words that have the same ending sound. It is important for them to say each word slowly and to listen for the sound in a particular location within both words. Successfully identifying the ending sound in words will lead to children's ability to connect sounds to the letters that represent them.

EXPLAIN THE PRINCIPLE

Some words sound the same at the end.

Connect words that sound the same at the end.

Comprehensive Phonics, Spelling, and Word Study Guide

Refer to: page **19**, row **18**

ACTIVITY: PICTURE CARD MATCH

INSTRUCTIONAL PROCEDURE

FIND AND MATCH

See page 36 for detailed descriptions of Instructional Procedures.

EXPLAIN THE PRINCIPLE

Some words sound the same at the end.

Connect words that sound the same at the end.

Comprehensive Phonics, Spelling, and Word Study Guide

Refer to: page **19**, row **18**

Teach

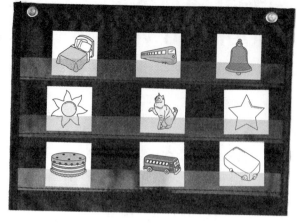

1. Tell the children that today they are going to learn to play a game to practice ending sounds in words.

2. Using a pocket chart, place the picture cards for *bed, train, bell, sun, cat, star, cake, bus,* and *soap* in three rows. Set aside the remaining pocket-chart picture cards for *sled, fan, tub, ball, moon, leaf, net, pear, duck, glass,* and *cup* in a pile for later use.

3. *Some words sound the same at the end, like* sit *and* get *or* mom *and* dream. *Today we are going to play Lotto. In this game, you match words that sound the same at the end. Let's try it with the pictures you see in the pocket chart. Let's say the name of each picture, and let's listen for the last sound of each word.* Have children say the name of each picture and repeat the last sound of each word. Some children may identify the last sound by letter.

4. *I'm going to take a picture card from this stack and see if I can match it to a picture on the pocket chart.*

5. Hold up the picture that stands for the word *cup. I can see that this is a picture of a cup. Now I'm going to see if there is a picture of another word that sounds the same as the end of* cup. *Can anyone see a picture of a word that has the same ending sound as* cup?

6. Model checking *cup* and *soap* by saying both words. Have children say both words to check whether they sound have the same sound at the end. Place the picture card of the cup over the picture card of the soap.

7. Draw cards one at a time, showing how to check for a match by saying both words and listening for the same ending sound. Place any cards that do not have a match to the side.

8. Continue until all the pictures on the chart have been matched. *I've covered all the pictures on the chart. That's what you need to do to win Lotto. Remember to say both words to check that both words have the same sound at the end.*

9. Ask children to discuss what they have to do to fill the Lotto game board. Then demonstrate the game on the floor with three or four children in a circle. Show them how to take turns drawing cards from a pile and matching them to the pictures on their game boards. The first child to cover all of the boxes on her board wins the game.

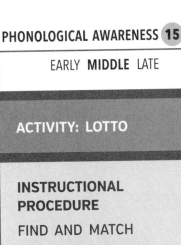

ACTIVITY: LOTTO

INSTRUCTIONAL PROCEDURE

FIND AND MATCH

See page 36 for detailed descriptions of Instructional Procedures.

ACTION TAGS

take

say

match

cover

Apply

Children practice matching ending sounds in words by playing Lotto in groups of three or four. If you provide enough Lotto game boards and picture cards, several games can be played at once.

Share

Ask children to remember and share some of the words with matching ending sounds they found while they played Lotto. You may get comments such as, "If it's a rat, it ends like *net*, but if it's a mouse, it ends like *bus*." Welcome these comments, because they are evidence that children are becoming more flexible with phonemic awareness.

Assess

■ Notice whether the children are able to hear ending sounds of words during interactive and independent writing.

■ Place a few picture cards in a pocket chart. Then, holding up other picture cards one at a time, ask individual children to name the picture and match it to a card in the pocket chart according to the ending sound. This will give you an idea which ending sounds children are hearing and connecting.

■ You may wish to use Phonological Awareness Assessment F or K.

Connect Learning Across Contexts

Interactive Read-Aloud Read aloud stories that include words that end alike.

IRA *One Duck Stuck* by Phyllis Root

IRA *The Eeensy-Weensy Spider* by Mary Ann Hoberman and Nadine Bernard Westcott

Talk about the fact that rhyming words (for example, *duck* and *stuck*) have the same sound at the end, whereas not all words that have the same ending sound rhyme (*rake* and *bike*, for example). All four words end with /k/, but in *duck* and *stuck* the preceding vowel sound is the same.

Shared Reading See "Two, Four, Six, Eight" in *Words That Sing* (2019). If you don't have these poetry charts, enlarge the print of this poem or other poems such as "Go to Bed Early" in *Sing a Song of Poetry*, and draw children's attention to words that sound the same at the end. Invite them to use highlighter tape to point out these words in the text. You may also wish to use the following Shared Reading title from *Fountas & Pinnell Classroom*™.

SR *Wiggles: Poems to Make You Wiggle Your Fingers and Toes*

Interactive Writing When children are thinking about how to write a word, have them say it slowly and connect it to a name or other word that ends with the same sound.

Independent Writing Encourage children to say words slowly when they are writing. They may be representing the beginning sound with a letter already, but by saying the word again they can represent more sounds, including the ending sound.

Extend Learning

Vary the sounds and expand the repertoire of sounds when playing Lotto. Gradually increase the complexity of the game and/or take away the easy-to-match sounds. You also may wish to customize gameboards using Gamemaker in Online Resources.

▶ Connect with Home

Give children photocopies of three or four Lotto game boards and an envelope of picture cards so they can play Lotto at home with family members.

Change the Beginning Sound to Make a New Word

Plan

▶ Consider Your Children

This lesson will be helpful to children if they have had experience saying and hearing sounds in words, as well as matching initial sounds of words. You may have noticed children spontaneously making connections between words or using words or parts of words they know to make new words. This lesson introduces a game involving word play that can be used at any time during the school day.

▶ Working with English Language Learners

English language learners must develop the ability to hear individual sounds and to connect words that sound alike. Learning to play this phoneme manipulation game will help them make connections and develop tools for spelling words. They may learn the concept of substituting a different phoneme for the first sound but have trouble recognizing whether they are making actual English words or not (since many English words are meaningless to them). Help children make this exercise concrete by providing as many comprehensible examples as possible. Play the game often, repeating the same examples so that children develop a repertoire.

YOU WILL NEED

Ready Resources
- ▶ PA 16 Pocket-Chart Picture Cards

Online Resources
- ▶ PA 16 Action Tags
- ▶ PA 16 Picture Cards

Generative Lesson

A generative lesson has a simple structure that you can use to present similar content or concepts. You can use this lesson structure to teach children to use known word parts to make a variety of words.

UNDERSTAND THE PRINCIPLE

As children become more aware of individual sounds in words, they learn to isolate and identify the first sound they hear. This ability helps them connect initial sounds with letters, a skill that helps readers begin to decode words and monitor their reading of continuous text.

EXPLAIN THE PRINCIPLE

Change the first sound in a word to make a new word.

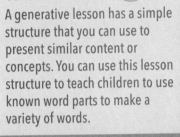

Comprehensive Phonics, Spelling, and Word Study Guide

Refer to: page **20**, row **21**

16 PHONOLOGICAL AWARENESS

EARLY **MIDDLE** LATE

ACTIVITY: NEW WORD GAME

INSTRUCTIONAL PROCEDURE

HEAR AND SAY

See page 36 for detailed descriptions of Instructional Procedures.

Teach

1. Tell children that they will play a word game in which they will change the sound at the beginning of a word.

2. *Say the word* ran. • *What is the first sound?* • *The first sound in the word* ran *is /r/. Now say the word* can. • *What is the first sound?* • *The first sound in the word* can *is /k/. What did you notice?* • *You can change the first sound in a word to make a new word.*

3. Repeat with the words *land* and *sand. Say* land. • *What is the first sound in the word* land? • *The first sound is /l/. Change the first sound to /s/. What's the new word?* • */s/-and. The new word is* sand.

4. Continue the game using several more word pairs from the list below. Use the same language each time so that children know exactly what it means to change the first sound: *Say* not. • *What is the first sound?* • *The first sound is /n/. Change the first sound to /h/. What's the new word?*

go, no	hide, ride	day, way	jump, bump
pack, sack	mice, rice	sat, mat	sale, tale
bank, sank	best, nest	sock, rock	mail, sail
my, by	bed, red	hip, lip	rain, pain
tap, cap	heat, seat	bit, fit	bake, make
pink, link	pay, say	can, man	ball, fall
king, wing	late, gate		

5. To prepare children for the Apply activity, model playing this game using picture cards. Display the pocket-chart picture card of a cat. *Cat. Make a new word by changing the first sound in* cat. Invite several children to respond with new words. Repeat using pictures of a boy, a pan, and a bell.

EXPLAIN THE PRINCIPLE

Change the first sound in a word to make a new word.

Comprehensive Phonics, Spelling, and Word Study Guide

Refer to: page **20**, row **21**

ACTIVITY: PICTURE CARD GAME (PARTNERS)

INSTRUCTIONAL PROCEDURE

NOTICE PARTS

See page 36 for detailed descriptions of Instructional Procedures.

ACTION TAGS

take

say

change

Apply

Have pairs of children use the picture cards to play the game. Partners take turns choosing a picture (e.g., a dog), saying the word the picture represents, and then changing the first sound to make new words, possibly including nonsense words: for example, *fog, log, sog, zog*. You can help children think about whether the new words are real or made up, but the manipulation of beginning sounds is the primary goal.

Share

Hold up picture cards at random and have various partners share the new words that they made.

Assess

- Observe whether children can create words by replacing the initial sound with a different sound. A quick check of just two or three examples will tell you whether they understand the concept.

- Notice whether children consistently contribute appropriate examples during the game.

Connect Learning Across Contexts

Interactive Read-Aloud Read aloud books that include rhymes.

IRA *The Doorbell Rang* by Pat Hutchins

IRA *Over on the Farm* by Marianne Berkes

Shared Reading See "Higglety, Pigglety, Pop!" in *Words That Sing* (2019). If you don't have these poetry charts, enlarge the print of this poem or other poems as "Make a Pancake" or "My Dog, Rags" in *Sing a Song of Poetry*, and examine rhyming words to reinforce the concept that changing the first sound of a word can create a new word. You may also wish to use the following Shared Reading title from *Fountas & Pinnell Classroom™*.

SR *The Big Race: An Aesop Fable* retold by David Edwin

Shared or Interactive Writing As appropriate examples arise, use the whiteboard to demonstrate making new words by changing the beginning sound and corresponding letter or letters.

Independent Writing Encourage children to use known words to spell words they want to write by changing the first sound and thinking what letter stands for the new sound.

Extend Learning

Play the word game by changing the first sound in the names of children in your class. Invite them to continue the game using names of their family members.

▶ Connect with Home

During a meeting or in a newsletter, teach parents and caregivers to play a game with their children in which they change the initial sound of one-syllable words. They can say a word and ask the child to change the first sound to make a new word–*mop, hop; rake, bake;* and so on. Emphasize that the activity should be enjoyable and create curiosity about and power over words.

Hear and Say the Middle Sound in a Word with Three Phonemes

Plan

▶ Consider Your Children

This lesson is best taught after children have worked with their names and taken part in interactive writing using a variety of words. They should understand the concept of a word and be able to hear consonants at the beginning and end of words. In this lesson, children will learn an important routine for matching vowel sounds in the middle of words. Use one-syllable words with short vowel sounds. If children are very inexperienced in hearing sounds in the middle of words, you will want to practice for several days. In this lesson, they listen for short vowel sounds only.

▶ Working with English Language Learners

English language learners will be successful in this exercise if they know, understand, and can say the names of the pictures on the cards and have had previous experience identifying the first and last sounds of words. They will need to learn to listen for the middle vowel sound, so they may need many demonstrations. Play the matching game with them the first time so that you will be sure they are saying the word slowly and matching by middle sound.

YOU WILL NEED

 Ready Resources
- ▶ **PA 17** Pocket-Chart Picture Cards

Online Resources
- ▶ **PA 17** Action Tags
- ▶ **PA 17** Three-Way Sorts
- ▶ **PA 17** Three-Column Sorts
- ▶ **PA 17** Picture Cards

Other Materials
- ▶ pocket chart

Generative Lesson
A generative lesson has a simple structure that you can use to present similar content or concepts. You can use this lesson structure to teach children to hear the middle sound in a variety of words.

UNDERSTAND THE PRINCIPLE

Children need to hear and say medial sounds in words to develop a beginning understanding of the structure of words. First listening to the sounds without looking at the letters will lead children to attend more carefully to all parts of words, so that later they will begin to compare words and make letter-sound connections.

EXPLAIN THE PRINCIPLE

Listen for and say the sound in the middle of a word.

 Comprehensive Phonics, Spelling, and Word Study Guide

Refer to: page **20**, row **23**

ACTIVITY:
POCKET-CHART CARDS

INSTRUCTIONAL
PROCEDURE

HEAR AND SAY

See page 36 for detailed descriptions of Instructional Procedures.

EXPLAIN THE PRINCIPLE

Listen for and say the sound in the middle of a word.

Comprehensive
Phonics, Spelling,
and Word Study
Guide

Refer to:
page **20**, row **23**

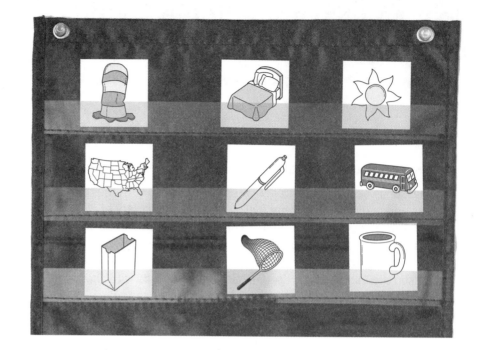

Teach

1. Tell the children that they are going to listen for the sounds in the middle of words.

2. *You have been thinking hard about the sound at the beginning of a word and the sound at the end of a word. Today we are going to think about the sound in the middle of a word. Say the word* hat. • *What sound do you hear at the beginning of* hat? • *That's right,* /h/. *What sound do you hear at the end of* hat? *That's right,* /t/.

3. *Now say the word* hat *and think about the sound in the middle.* After children give the short *a* sound, place the pocket-chart card for *hat* in the pocket chart.

4. Show the pocket-chart card with the picture for *map* on it. *The word* map *has an* /ă/ *in the middle just like the word* hat *did. Why don't you say each of those words.* • *Can you hear the* /ă/ *in the middle of* hat *and in the middle of* map? • Place the card for *map* in the pocket chart under the picture for *hat*. *I have another picture here. Let's say the name of the thing in this picture and see if it sounds like* hat *in the middle.* Bag—*it has that* /ă/ *in the middle, doesn't it?* • *Say it with me.* Say *bag* along with the children, slightly exaggerating the middle sound without segmenting the word. Place the card in the pocket chart under the others with the same middle sound.

5. Repeat the process using *bed* and *sun* as key words, matching the pictures of *pen* and *net* to the picture of *bed*, and matching *bus* and *mug* to the picture of *sun*.

6. *Today you are going to sort picture cards by thinking about the middle sound in the words shown on the cards.*

Name _____

Fountas & Pinnell Phonics, Spelling, and Word Study Lessons, Kindergarten   **PA 17 Three-Way Sort**

ACTIVITY: THREE-WAY PICTURE SORT

INSTRUCTIONAL PROCEDURE

SAY AND SORT

See page 36 for detailed descriptions of Instructional Procedures.

ACTION TAGS

say
sort

Apply

Using the three-way sorts and the loose picture cards, children sort the cards into the three columns according to the short vowel sound they hear in the middle of the word represented by each picture. Remind children to say aloud the word shown on the picture card and the word shown in the picture at the top of one of the columns on the three-way sort to check that the words are a good match.

Share

Using the class name chart if relevant, have children find pairs of names that have the same short vowel sound in the middle: for example, Jen/Jess, Matt/Pat, Kim/Bill, Ted/Ken, Tom/Jon. You may also ask some children to share the middle-sound matches they made in the sorting activity. Ask the other children to give a thumbs up if they agree with the matches.

Assess

- Observe whether the children can identify the cards representing words with a short *a* sound, a short *e* sound, or a short *u* sound.
- Notice whether the children make good attempts at writing short vowels during interactive writing.
- You may wish to use Phonological Awareness Assessment C or K.

Phonological Awareness: Hear and Say the Middle Sound in a Word with Three Phonemes

Connect Learning Across Contexts

Interactive Read-Aloud Read aloud books that include many words with short vowel sounds.

> IRA *Red Is a Dragon: A Book of Colors* by Roseanne Thong
>
> IRA *My Steps* by Sally Derby

Shared Reading See "Lucy Locket" in *Words That Sing* (2019). If you don't have these poetry charts, enlarge the print of this poem or other poems such as "Downy Duck" and "Hot Cross Buns" in *Sing a Song of Poetry.* Have the children use highlighter tape to identify words in the text that have a certain short vowel sound in the middle. You may also wish to use the following Shared Reading title from *Fountas & Pinnell Classroom*™.

> SR *Fly Away* by Alina Kirk

Interactive Writing Have children say a word slowly to hear all of its sounds, and ask children to think about how to write the letters that stand for those sounds.

Independent Writing Encourage children to say each word they want to write and think about how to write the vowel sound they hear in the middle.

Extend Learning

- Repeat the lesson adding pictures of three-phoneme words with short vowels *o* and *i.*

- Have children make a book with five stapled pages (one for each short vowel) on which they glue pictures of objects whose names contain the appropriate middle sound. They can read their books by saying the names of the pictures on each page.

▶ Connect with Home

Have children take home a number of picture cards from the lesson and say the names aloud to a family member.

Hear and Say the Same Middle Sound in Words

Plan

▶ Consider Your Children

For this lesson, choose common, one-syllable words that follow a consonant-vowel-consonant (CVC) pattern. Children should be able to hear consonants at the beginning and end of words. As children learn to identify and match middle vowel sounds, you can expect some variation in the way they pronounce vowel sounds because of individual differences and dialect differences. When matching pictures, all children may not have the same word in mind, but their own word choices will work. The goal is for them to think about, say, and match the middle sounds.

▶ Working with English Language Learners

Children will categorize picture cards by saying the word represented by the picture and listening for a matching vowel sound in the middle. These sounds may be difficult for some English language learners to hear. Provide more opportunities for children to practice saying the words and hearing the middle sounds of short *a* and *o*. Be sure that children understand the words *beginning*, *middle*, and *end;* demonstrate the meanings for children. Also, make sure they understand the meaning of *sort*; again, demonstrating the entire application activity and supporting them while they do it will be beneficial. Point out the action tags and demonstrate each action.

YOU WILL NEED

 Ready Resources
- ▶ **PA 18** Pocket-Chart Picture Cards

Online Resources
- ▶ **PA 18** Action Tags
- ▶ **PA 18** Two-Way Sorts
- ▶ **PA 18** Picture Cards

Other Materials
- ▶ pocket chart

Generative Lesson

A generative lesson has a simple structure that you can use to present similar content or concepts. You can use this lesson structure to teach children to hear and say the same middle sounds in a variety of words.

UNDERSTAND THE PRINCIPLE

The ability to hear and say medial sounds in words helps children develop their understanding of the structure of words. Isolating the vowel sounds within words can be challenging. Early practice attending to individual vowel sounds in the absence of letters helps children listen more carefully to all parts of words, forming a foundation for comparing words and connecting letters and sounds.

EXPLAIN THE PRINCIPLE

Some words sound the same in the middle.

Connect words that sound the same in the middle.

 Comprehensive Phonics, Spelling, and Word Study Guide

Refer to: page **20**, row **24**

ACTIVITY: TWO-WAY PICTURE SORT

INSTRUCTIONAL PROCEDURE

HEAR AND SAY

See page 36 for detailed descriptions of Instructional Procedures.

EXPLAIN THE PRINCIPLE

Some words sound the same in the middle.

Connect words that sound the same in the middle.

Comprehensive Phonics, Spelling, and Word Study Guide

Refer to: page **20**, row **24**

Teach

1. Explain to the children that they are going to listen carefully to the middle sound in words.

2. Place a picture of a cat in the pocket chart, and have children say the word *cat* with you.

3. *When you say the word* cat, *you can hear a middle sound. Say the word slowly, /k/ /a/ /t/. What sound do you hear? The sound /a/ is the middle sound in the word* cat.

4. Place a picture of a pig beside the cat in the pocket chart, and have children say the word *pig* with you. Repeat the teaching as you model hearing the middle sound, */p/ /i/ /g/. What sound do you hear? The sound /i/ is the middle sound in the word* pig.

5. Tell children that they are going to sort pictures that stand for words with the middle sound /a/ or /i/. *I'll hold up a picture. You say the name of the picture and the middle sound. If the middle sound is /a/, I'll place the picture under the cat. If the middle sound is /i/, I'll place the picture under the pig. If the middle sound is different from /a/ and /i/, I'll place the picture on the table.*

6. Guide children to name and sort the pictures of a van, a bug, a lid, a dish, a bed, and a mat. If needed, slightly exaggerate the middle sound of each word, but keep the words smooth rather than segmenting them.

Name _____

Fountas & Pinnell Phonics, Spelling, and Word Study Lessons, Kindergarten   **PA 18** Two-Way Sort

ACTIVITY: TWO-WAY PICTURE SORT

INSTRUCTIONAL PROCEDURE

SAY AND SORT

See page 36 for detailed descriptions of Instructional Procedures.

ACTION TAGS

take

say

sort

Apply

■ Have children do a two-way picture sort with a partner. For key words, have children place pictures of a cat and a pig at the top of each column of a two-way sort. *If the middle sound in a word is /a/, place the picture under the cat. If the middle sound is /i/, place the picture under the pig. If it has a different sound, put it in a pile on the table.* Have partners take turns drawing a card, saying the name of the picture and the middle sound, and then placing the picture in the correct column.

■ Children can extend this activity by drawing another picture that stands for a word with either the /a/ or /i/ sound in the middle and adding it to the correct column.

Share

When children finish the sort, have them take turns saying the words in each column. Invite them to give other words that fit each category.

Assess

■ Check whether children can identify the cards that represent words with the sound /a/ or /i/ in the middle.

■ Notice whether children can name other words that have the sound /a/ or /i/ in the middle.

■ You may wish to use Phonological Awareness Assessment C or K.

Phonological Awareness: Hear and Say the Same Middle Sound in Words

Connect Learning Across Contexts

Interactive Read-Aloud Read aloud books that invite play with the sounds in words.

> IRA *Creak! Said the Bed* by Phyllis Root

> IRA *Charlie Parker Played Be Bop* by Chris Raschka

Shared Reading See "Diddlety, Diddlety, Dumpty!" in *Words That Sing* (2019). If you don't have these poetry charts, enlarge the print of this poem or other poems such as "Cross Patch" and "Hickory, Dickory, Dock!" in *Sing a Song of Poetry*. Have the children use highlighter tape to mark the words in the text that have the same sound in the middle. You may also wish to use the following Shared Reading title from *Fountas & Pinnell Classroom*™.

> SR *Scream for Ice Cream* by Keisha Johnson

Interactive Writing Have children say a word slowly, identify the middle sound, and think how to write the corresponding letter or letters.

Independent Writing Encourage children to say the words they want to write and to think how to write the vowel in the middle. Do not expect complete, conventional spelling of vowel sounds, but encourage children to make attempts. You will find that children will often use a vowel in the vowel position in a word even if it is not the right vowel: for example, *peg* for *pig*.

Extend Learning

Repeat the lesson with picture cards of common words having vowels /e/, /o/, and /u/ as medial sounds. Example key words are *net, dog,* and *sun.*

▶ Connect with Home

Give children copies of a two-column sort with key pictures (for example, a cat and a pig) already in place and a sheet of applicable picture cards. Children can cut and sort the pictures with family members.

Hear and Divide Onsets and Rimes

Plan

▶ Consider Your Children

This lesson focuses on onsets and rimes in one-syllable words only. Children do not need to know the words *onset* and *rime* to understand the concept; however, be sure that they understand how the concepts of *first* and *last* apply to oral language. Dividing onsets and rimes is an oral task in which you say the first part and the last part of a word. Ultimately, children need to hear and say a word and automatically divide it into first and last parts.

▶ Working with English Language Learners

The task in the Follow the Path game is to say the word that represents the picture, then say the word in a divided, or segmented, way (*onset* plus *rime*). To perform this task, your English language learners will need to know the names of the pictures and understand the articulation process. Provide as many examples as necessary when you are teaching children to divide words into onsets and rimes.

YOU WILL NEED

PWS **Ready Resources**
- ▶ PA 19 Pocket-Chart Picture Cards

Online Resources
- ▶ PA 19 Action Tags
- ▶ PA 19 Follow the Path Game Boards
- ▶ PA 19 Directions for Follow the Path

Other Materials
- ▶ dice
- ▶ game pieces or other markers

Generative Lesson ✓

A generative lesson has a simple structure that you can use to present similar content or concepts. You can use this lesson structure to teach children to hear and divide the first and last parts of a variety of words.

UNDERSTAND THE PRINCIPLE

In a syllable, an *onset* is the part that comes before the vowel. An onset may be a consonant, a consonant cluster, or a consonant digraph. In a syllable, a *rime* is the ending part containing the letters that represent the vowel sound and the consonant letters that follow. Children's ability to hear the onset and rime in a one-syllable word is a first step toward word analysis by letter and sound. It is also good preparation for their thinking about individual phonemes.

EXPLAIN THE PRINCIPLE

Listen for and say the first and last parts of a word.

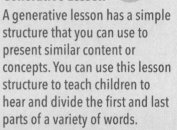

Comprehensive Phonics, Spelling, and Word Study Guide

Refer to:
page **19**, row **10**

**ACTIVITY:
PICTURE CARDS**

**INSTRUCTIONAL
PROCEDURE**

HEAR AND SAY

*See page 36 for detailed
descriptions of Instructional
Procedures.*

EXPLAIN THE PRINCIPLE

*Listen for and say the first and
last parts of a word.*

Comprehensive
Phonics, Spelling,
and Word Study
Guide

Refer to:
page **19**, row **10**

Teach

1. Tell the children they are going to learn about parts of words.

2. *When you say and listen to a word, you can think about the first and last
   parts. I'll say a word:* make. *Now I'll say the first part by itself:* m. *Now I'll say
   the last part:* ake. *There are two parts in the word* make.

3. *Let's try another one. This word is* take. *Say the first part.* • *That's right,* t. *Now
   say the second part of the word* t-ake. • *That's right,* ake. *There are two parts
   in the word* take. *Now I'll say the another word, and let's see if you can hear a
   first part and a second part:* r-ed.

4. Have the children try several other examples: *n-est, r-ing, st-ick, gr-een.*

5. Now present a series of picture cards. For each card, say the name of the
   picture (e.g., *saw, tub, bow, gum, cow, shell, pen, fox, star, hose, rope, train*).
   Then have children say the first sound and second sound in the word. Then
   say the whole word in unison.

6. Tell children that they will be playing a game called Follow the Path.

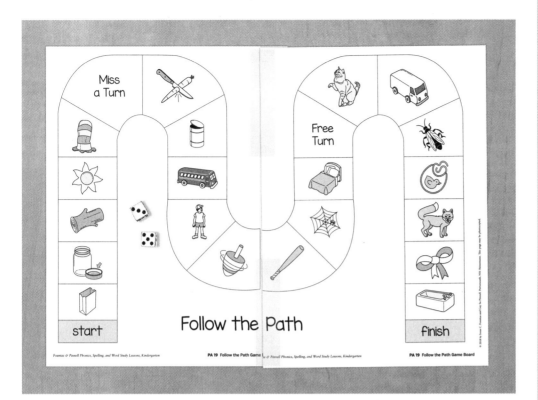

INSTRUCTIONAL PROCEDURE

HEAR AND SAY

See page 36 for detailed descriptions of Instructional Procedures.

ACTION TAGS

say word

say first part

say last part

Apply

Have children play Follow the Path. Show the game board and game pieces. Then explain that a player tosses a die to determine the number of spaces to move a game piece forward. When the player lands on a space, she says the word that represents the picture in that space. Then she says the first part and the last part of the word. Then another player takes his turn.

Share

Encourage children to discuss their thinking about the first part and the last part of words by sharing some words they encountered during the game of Follow the Path. Demonstrate and encourage comments like these:

"The first part of *bag* and *bed* sounds the same."

"The last part of *bat* and *cat* sounds the same."

Assess

- Say a word, and ask children to say the first part and the last part of the word. Repeat with four or five other words.

- Notice whether the children are using their awareness of the first part of words to figure out new words as they read and write.

- You may wish to use Phonological Awareness Assessment H, J, or K.

Connect Learning Across Contexts

Interactive Read-Aloud Read aloud books that have many one-syllable words. After reading, choose two or three words to divide into onset and rime.

> IRA *Two Homes* by Claire Masurel

> IRA *I Know a Lady* by Charlotte Zolotow

Shared Reading See "Jack, Jack" in *Words That Sing* (2019). If you don't have these poetry charts, enlarge the print of this poem or other poems such as "Hickory, Dickory, Dock!" in *Sing a Song of Poetry*, and invite children to say the first part and the last part of two or three one-syllable words from the poem. Using a masking card, cover the last part of a word prior to another reading. Invite children to read the first part of the word and predict the last part. Uncover the word to confirm children's predictions. You may also wish to use the following Shared Reading title from *Fountas & Pinnell Classroom*™ to gain more practice with syllables.

> SR *By the Light of the Moon* by Maggie Bridger

Interactive Writing Have the children say a one-syllable word and think about the first part and the last part as they write the word. If children understand vowels, point out that the last part of the word contains the vowel and the letters after it.

Independent Writing Encourage the children to say one-syllable words they want to write and to think about the letters they need for the first part and the last part.

Extend Learning

- Play Follow the Path with other pictures or picture cards on the path. You may wish to customize gameboards using Gamemaker in Online Resources.

- Blend onsets and rimes using names of objects in the classroom.

▶ Connect with Home

- Encourage parents to play a word game with their children in which they identify the first part and the last part of one-syllable words. Provide several examples, such as *tr-unk*, *c-ar*, and *d-oor*. Emphasize that the activity should be quick and fun; the purpose of the game is to make children curious about words and get them to enjoy manipulating sounds.

- Send a Follow the Path game and directions home with children to play with family members.

Blend Onsets with Rimes

Plan

▶ Consider Your Children

This lesson focuses on onsets and rimes in one-syllable words only. Children do not need to know the words *onset* and *rime* to understand the concept; however, be sure that they understand how the concepts of *first* and *last* apply to oral language. Blending onsets and rimes is an oral task in which you use your voice to put the first part and the last part of a word together.

▶ Working with English Language Learners

The phonology of English may be difficult for children who are just beginning to speak it; however, they are fast learners who are very flexible in learning new sounds. Say the names of the objects in pictures and have children repeat them. Discard those pictures that are not within the children's experience. Use real objects, or act out the meaning of other items as needed. Give learners many opportunities to say the names of the objects in the pictures before playing the game.

YOU WILL NEED

PWS Ready Resources
- ▶ PA 20 Pocket-Chart Picture Cards

Online Resources
- ▶ PA 20 Action Tags
- ▶ PA 20 Game Cards
- ▶ PA 20 Directions for Go Fish

Other Materials
- ▶ pocket chart or easel

Generative Lesson

A generative lesson has a simple structure that you can use to present similar content or concepts. You can use this lesson structure to teach children to blend the first and last parts in a variety of words.

UNDERSTAND THE PRINCIPLE

In a syllable, an *onset* is the part that comes before the vowel. An onset may be a consonant, a consonant cluster, or a consonant digraph. In a syllable, a *rime* is the ending part containing the letters that represent the vowel sound and the consonant letters that follow. Children's ability to divide the onset and rime in a one-syllable word is a first step toward word analysis by letter and sound. Their ability to blend the onset and rime furthers their understanding of how sounds go together in words.

EXPLAIN THE PRINCIPLE

Blend the parts of a word.

Comprehensive Phonics, Spelling, and Word Study Guide

Refer to: page **19**, row **11**

**ACTIVITY:
PICTURE CARDS**

**INSTRUCTIONAL
PROCEDURE**

HEAR AND SAY

*See page 36 for detailed
descriptions of Instructional
Procedures.*

EXPLAIN THE PRINCIPLE

Blend the parts of a word.

**Comprehensive
Phonics, Spelling,
and Word Study
Guide**

Refer to:
page **19**, row **11**

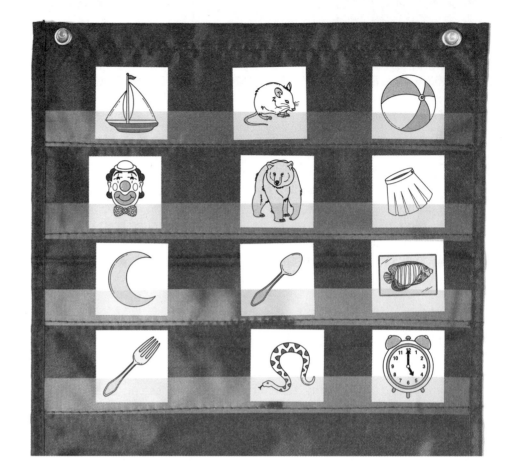

Teach

1. Tell the children they will play a word game.

2. *I'm going to say the first part of a word, and then I'll say the last part:* d-ay. *Do you hear two parts?* • *I can blend the parts together to make a word:* d-ay, day. *Do you hear how the two parts of the word go together?* • *Now I'll say the two parts of another word, but I won't say them together. You say the first part and the last part of the word together:* st-ay.

3. Repeat using several more words, each time saying the two parts and then having children say the whole word: *w-ay, way; b-ay, bay; p-ay, pay; pl-ay, play*. Give children feedback on their responses. You may need to say the parts more than once.

4. Place a collection of picture cards in the pocket chart or on the easel. Use pictures of a variety of words, such as *boat, clown, moon, fork, mouse, bear, spoon, snake, ball, skirt, fish,* and *clock. I'm going to say the first part of a word and the last part of a word. When you say the first part and the last part together, it will be the name of one of the pictures. Tell me which word it is.* B-oat.

5. Have children take turns saying the first and last parts of words for others to guess.

6. Tell children that they will be playing a game called Go Fish. In preparation for the activity, create a deck of between forty and forty-eight game cards that includes twenty to twenty-four pairs of pictures. You may also wish to customize game cards using Gamemaker in Online Resources.

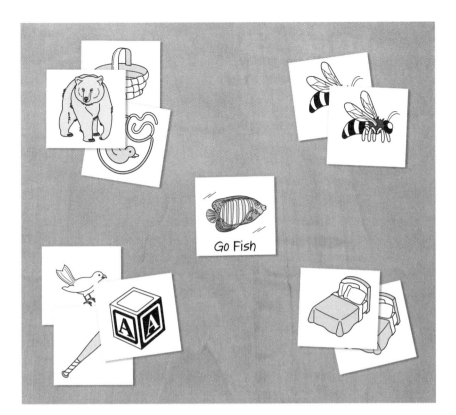

INSTRUCTIONAL PROCEDURE

HEAR AND SAY

See page 36 for detailed descriptions of Instructional Procedures.

ACTION TAGS

player 1

ask

take card

player 2

match

say the word, give the card

say "Go fish"

Apply

Have children play Go Fish with a partner or in groups of three or four. Model how to play Go Fish by bringing two children to the front of the group. Deal each child five cards, and put the rest of the cards in a draw pile. Partners alternate turns. The first player asks the second player for a particular picture by saying the word in segmented form: "Do you have *c-at?*" If the second player has a card with a picture of a cat, he responds by blending the word parts to say *cat* and giving the card to the first player. The first player now has a match and puts the two cards down on the table. If–when asked at the beginning of the turn–the second player does not have the card requested, he says, "Go fish," and the first player takes a card from the draw pile. The winner is the first player with no cards left.

Share

Ask children what they learned from playing the game. Briefly play the oral onset and rime game (see Teach steps 2 and 3) again with a few different words.

Assess

- Notice whether children can identify and blend onsets and rimes. A quick check of just two or three examples will tell you whether they understand the concept.
- Do a quick assessment in the form of a line-up game. Present words in segmented form and ask children to blend the parts.
- You may wish to use Phonological Awareness Assessment H or K.

Connect Learning Across Contexts

Interactive Read-Aloud After reading aloud books like those mentioned below, reread the books and draw children's attention to the last word of each line. Segment the onset and rime in each word, and invite children to blend the onset and rime.

   IRA *Cat's Colors* by Jane Cabrera

   IRA *Building a House* by Byron Barton

Shared Reading See "Come and Listen" in *Words That Sing* (2019). If you don't have these poetry charts, enlarge the print of this poem or other poems such as "Baby Seeds" in *Sing a Song of Poetry*. Say a word from the text in segmented form and ask the children to say the same word in blended form. Then invite the children to locate the word. You may also wish to use the following Shared Reading title from *Fountas & Pinnell Classroom*™ to locate more onsets and rimes in words.

   SR *Pitter Patter* by Miriam David

Interactive Writing Have children say a word and think about the first and last parts as they write it. If children are familiar with the concept of vowels, you may wish to point out that the last part of each segmented word starts with a vowel.

Independent Writing Encourage children to say the words they want to write and think about the letters they need to represent the sound or sounds in the first part of the word and the sound or sounds in the last part of each word.

Extend Learning

- Repeat the lesson if children are not using the concept in their own writing and reading. Explicitly show them how to think about the first part and the last part of a word they want to write. Then model saying the first and last parts in blended form.

- Play line-up games with several words, saying each onset and rime and having children blend them.

- Create another deck of cards for the Go Fish game using pictures of other words.

- Add the printed word to each game card and repeat the lesson. Though the children may not be able to read the words on the card, they will be exposed to the print along with the picture.

▶ Connect with Home

Explain to family members how to play the oral game described in Teach steps 2 and 3. They can play the game with children in the supermarket or in the car. Emphasize that the activity should be quick and fun; the purpose of the game is to make children curious about words.

Hear and Say Two Sounds in a Word

Plan

▶ Consider Your Children

Children already have the ability to say words quickly in their daily use of oral language, and they may be curious about what can happen when they slow down their pronunciation of words. This lesson provides explicit demonstrations to help children listen carefully in order to recognize and isolate discrete sounds in spoken words. This skill will have immediate value if children are engaging in interactive writing, during which the clear, slow enunciation of words is modeled and elicited for the authentic purpose of spelling words accurately. As children attempt to apply this understanding by writing or telling letters for sounds they hear, confirm any accurate letter-sound pairings.

▶ Working with English Language Learners

Saying words slowly will make the phonology of English words more available to English language learners. Be sure to enunciate clearly and provide many demonstrations with words. Accept children's approximations as they pronounce words, as certain sounds may be difficult for them to say with accuracy. Internally, they will probably be making their own connections with idiosyncratic pronunciations of words.

YOU WILL NEED

 Ready Resources
▶ **PA 21** Pocket-Chart Picture Cards

Online Resources
▶ **PA 21** Action Tags
▶ **PA 21** Picture Cards

Other Materials
▶ scissors

Generative Lesson

A generative lesson has a simple structure that you can use to present similar content or concepts. You can use this lesson structure to teach children to hear and say two sounds in a variety of words.

UNDERSTAND THE PRINCIPLE

Children need to recognize that words contain a sequence of sounds. Developing the ability to isolate individual sounds in words leads children eventually to understand the alphabetic principle—that is, letters in written words represent the sounds in spoken words.

EXPLAIN THE PRINCIPLE

Say a word slowly.

Listen for each sound in a word.

 Comprehensive Phonics, Spelling, and Word Study Guide

Refer to:
page **19**, row **12**

ACTIVITY: FINGER AND SOUND MATCH

INSTRUCTIONAL PROCEDURE

HEAR AND SAY

See page 36 for detailed descriptions of Instructional Procedures.

EXPLAIN THE PRINCIPLE

Say a word slowly.

Listen for each sound in a word.

Comprehensive Phonics, Spelling, and Word Study Guide

Refer to: page **19**, row **12**

Teach

1. Tell the children that they are going to listen for the sounds in words. Explain that each word they hear in this lesson will have two sounds.

2. Hold up a picture of a bee and ask children to identify it. *You can hear each sound in this word by saying it slowly: /b/ /ē/. The first sound you hear is /b/.* Put a finger in the air as you say the /b/ sound. *What sound do you hear next? The next sound you hear is /ē/.* Put a second finger in the air as you say the sound of long *e*. *Say the word slowly with me: /b/ /ē/.* Put one and then two fingers in the air as children say each sound.

3. Repeat the teaching using pictures of an egg, a tie, and a key as you continue to model hearing each sound in a word.

4. Reinforce the principle as you review the four words. *By saying a word slowly, you can hear each sound in the word. When you said the words* bee, egg, tie, *and* key *slowly, you heard two sounds in each word.*

Apply

Have children cut apart pictures to use with a partner. One child says each word slowly, and the partner puts a finger up in the air as he hears each sound in each word. Then, the children can mix up the pictures and reverse roles.

Share

Have pairs of children repeat the activity with two or three words, and invite others in the class to join in putting fingers in the air.

Assess

- Notice children's ability to say a word slowly.
- Observe whether children are able to produce each sound in a word clearly and distinctly.
- Note sounds that are hard for certain children to hear or say.
- You may wish to use Phonological Awareness Assessment C, D, or K.

ACTIVITY: FINGER AND SOUND MATCH

INSTRUCTIONAL PROCEDURE

HEAR AND SAY

See page 36 for detailed descriptions of Instructional Procedures.

ACTION TAGS

cut

say

listen

put finger up

Phonological Awareness: Hear and Say Two Sounds in a Word

Connect Learning Across Contexts

Interactive Read-Aloud Read aloud books that draw children's attention to the sounds of words. Occasionally point out a word that has two sounds and have children say the word slowly to hear each sound.

IRA *Baa Baa Black Sheep* by Iza Trapani

IRA *Flower Garden* by Eve Bunting

Shared Reading See "Five Little Froggies" in *Words That Sing* (2019). If you don't have these poetry charts, enlarge the print of this poem or other poems such as "Jerry Hall" in *Sing a Song of Poetry*, and have children listen for individual sounds in words such as *he, is, so, eat,* and *all.* You may also wish to have children listen for individual sounds in words in the following Shared Reading title from *Fountas & Pinnell Classroom™*.

SR *By the Light of the Moon* by Maggie Bridger

Interactive Writing When solving a word, ask children to say it slowly and think about the letter or letters that stand for each sound they hear. Children may suggest many of the letters while you fill in the rest to achieve standard spelling.

Independent Writing Encourage the children to say slowly the new words they are attempting to spell (e.g., *see, two, my*), representing as many letters as they can.

Extend Learning

Say more words with two sounds, such as *say, me, zoo, eat,* and *day*. Have children say each word slowly, snapping their fingers as they say each sound in unison.

▶ Connect with Home

Give children additional copies of the picture cards used in the lesson: *knee, pie,* and *saw*. Explain to caregivers that children should say each word slowly in order to hear each sound. As children say a word, caregivers should have children raise one finger for each sound they hear. Caregivers can then ask, "What is the first sound you hear in this word? What is the second sound you hear?"

Hear and Say Three Sounds in a Word

Plan

▶ Consider Your Children

This activity is best used after the children have had a great deal of experience saying and hearing sounds in words, matching the initial sounds of words, and associating sounds and letters. Be sure that the children know what *first* and *last* mean in relation to a word. When you emphasize and/or isolate beginning or ending sounds slightly, it helps children identify them more easily, but do not let children become dependent on your pronunciation. Move quickly to simply saying the whole word smoothly. Also, remember that children need to say the words themselves. As you work with children in reading, they will learn a great deal more about the sequence of sounds in words. It is not necessary for the children to be completely successful in this activity before they begin to read and write stories.

▶ Working with English Language Learners

Saying words slowly will make the phonology of English words more available to English language learners. Be sure to enunciate clearly and provide many demonstrations with words. Accept children's approximations as they pronounce words, as certain sounds may be difficult for them to say with accuracy. Internally, they will probably be making their own connections with idiosyncratic pronunciations of words.

YOU WILL NEED

PWS Ready Resources
- ▶ PA 22 Pocket-Chart Picture Cards

Online Resources
- ▶ PA 22 Action Tags
- ▶ PA 22 Picture Cards

Generative Lesson

A generative lesson has a simple structure that you can use to present similar content or concepts. You can use this lesson structure to teach children to hear and say three sounds in a variety of words.

UNDERSTAND THE PRINCIPLE

As children become more aware of the sounds in words, they learn to isolate and identify the sounds in sequence. The better children can hear sounds, the easier it will be for them to connect sounds and letters within words.

EXPLAIN THE PRINCIPLE

Say a word slowly.

Listen for each sound in a word.

Comprehensive Phonics, Spelling, and Word Study Guide

Refer to: page **19**, row **14**

ACTIVITY: FINGER AND SOUND MATCH

INSTRUCTIONAL PROCEDURE

HEAR AND SAY

See page 36 for detailed descriptions of Instructional Procedures.

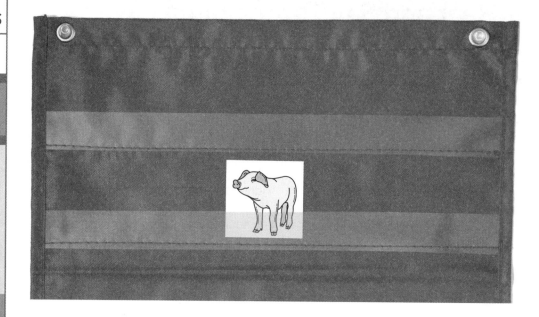

Teach

1. Explain to the children that today they will listen for the first sound, the last sound, and the middle sound in a word. Explain that each word they hear in this lesson will have three sounds.

2. *When you say a word, you can hear the first sound, can't you?* Hold up a picture of a pig and ask children to identify it. *You can hear each sound in this word by saying it slowly: /p/ /i/ /g/.* Put a finger in the air as you say the /p/ sound.

3. *What sound do you hear next? The next sound you hear is /i/.* Put a second finger in the air as you say /i/. Repeat for the third sound, /g/.

4. *Say the word slowly with me: /p/ /i/ /g/.* Put one and then two and then three fingers in the air as children say each sound.

5. Present two or three more examples, or hold up picture cards and invite children to sound out the words they represent: *man, net, lock.* Some children may come up with the name of the letter; accept either the letter name or the sound in isolation.

6. Reinforce the principle as you review the four words. *By saying a word slowly, you can hear each sound in the word. When you said the words* pig, man, net, and lock *slowly, you heard three sounds in each word.*

EXPLAIN THE PRINCIPLE

Say a word slowly.

Listen for each sound in a word.

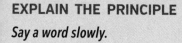
Comprehensive Phonics, Spelling, and Word Study Guide

Refer to: page **19**, row **14**

Apply

Have children cut apart pictures to use with a partner. One child says each word slowly, and the partner puts a finger up in the air as she hears each sound in each word. Then, the children can mix up the pictures and reverse roles.

Share

Have partners take turns pointing to the picture of a word as the other child says the three sounds in the word.

Assess

- Notice children's ability to say a word slowly.
- Observe whether children are able to produce each sound in a word clearly and distinctly.
- Note sounds that are hard for certain children to hear or say.
- You may wish to use Phonological Awareness Assessment C, D, or K.

ACTIVITY: FINGER AND SOUND MATCH

INSTRUCTIONAL PROCEDURE

HERE AND SAY

See page 36 for detailed descriptions of Instructional Procedures.

ACTION TAGS

cut

say

listen

put finger up

Connect Learning Across Contexts

Interactive Read-Aloud Read aloud books containing words that sound alike at the beginning and/or the end.

IRA *Rattletrap Car* by Phyllis Root

IRA *One Duck Stuck* by Phyllis Root

Shared Reading See "If I Were a Bird" in *Words That Sing* (2019). If you don't have these poetry charts, enlarge the print of this poem or other poems such as "The Cat" in *Sing a Song of Poetry*, and have children listen for individual sounds in words such as *cat, sat, side, fire, pig, Jack, took, his, and, bit* and *jig*. You may also wish to use the following Shared Reading title from *Fountas & Pinnell Classroom*™.

SR *The Right Tools* by Ingrid Jacobsen

Interactive Writing When solving a word, ask children to say it slowly and think about the letter or letters that stand for each sound they hear. Children may suggest many of the letters while you fill in the rest to achieve standard spelling.

Independent Writing Encourage children to say slowly the new words they are attempting to spell (e.g., *hat, ten, dog*), representing as many letters as they can.

Extend Learning

Say more words with three sounds, such as *mop, pen, dice, tail, bus,* and *block*. Have children say each word slowly, snapping their fingers as they say each sound in unison.

▶ Connect with Home

Give children additional copies of the picture cards used in the lesson: *map, man,* and *bear*. Explain to caregivers that children should say each word slowly in order to hear each sound. As children say a word, caregivers should have children raise one finger for each sound they hear. Caregivers can then ask, "What is the first sound you hear in this word? What is the second sound you hear? What is the last sound you hear in this word?"

Hear and Say Four or More Sounds in a Word in Sequence

Plan

▶ Consider Your Children

Children already have the ability to say words quickly in their regular use of oral language, and they may be curious about what can happen when they slow down their pronunciation. This lesson provides explicit demonstrations to help children listen carefully in order to recognize and isolate discrete sounds in spoken words. This skill will have immediate value if children are engaging in interactive writing, during which the clear, slow enunciation of words is modeled and elicited for the authentic purpose of spelling words accurately. As children attempt to apply this understanding by writing or telling letters for sounds they hear, confirm any accurate letter-sound pairings.

▶ Working with English Language Learners

This lesson will help English language learners attend to the sequence of sounds in English words. They will hear words slowly and clearly articulated in contrast to encountering them within rapid speech. You may need to include more demonstrations and to complete the application task with children to be sure that they can hear and say each sound. Observing them will help you identify sounds that are problematic for children.

YOU WILL NEED

PWS **Ready Resources**
▶ PA 23 Pocket-Chart Picture Cards

Online Resources
▶ PA 23 Action Tags
▶ PA 23 Picture Cards

Generative Lesson
A generative lesson has a simple structure that you can use to present similar content or concepts. You can use this lesson structure to teach children to hear and say four or more sounds in sequence in a variety of words.

UNDERSTAND THE PRINCIPLE

The ability to isolate and identify the individual sounds in words helps children understand the alphabetic principle–that twenty-six letters, in a variety of combinations, represent all of the sounds in the English language. Hearing the component sounds of a word in sequence makes it possible for children to think analytically about words and lays a foundation for writing letters in words with accuracy.

EXPLAIN THE PRINCIPLE

Say a word slowly.

Listen for each sound in a word.

Comprehensive Phonics, Spelling, and Word Study Guide

Refer to:
page **20**, row **25**

ACTIVITY: FINGER AND SOUND MATCH

INSTRUCTIONAL PROCEDURE

HEAR AND SAY

See page 36 for detailed descriptions of Instructional Procedures.

EXPLAIN THE PRINCIPLE

Say a word slowly.

Listen for each sound in a word.

Comprehensive Phonics, Spelling, and Word Study Guide

Refer to: page **20**, row **25**

Teach

1. Explain to the children that they are going to listen for the order of sounds in words.

2. Show a picture of a glass and ask children to identify it. *I can hear each sound in this word by saying it slowly: /g/ /l/ /ă/ /s/. The first sound I hear is /g/.* Put one finger in the air as you say the first sound. *The second sound I hear is /l/.* Keep the first finger in the air, and put a second finger in the air as you say the second sound. Continue with the remaining two sounds. *When I said the word* glass *slowly, I could hear the four sounds in order.*

3. *Let's do one together.* Show a picture of a snake and ask children to identify it. *Let's say the word slowly together: /s/ /n/ /ā/ /k/. What is the first sound you hear?* • Put one finger in the air as you say the first sound. *What is the second sound you hear?* • Keep the first finger in the air, and put a second finger in the air as you say the second sound. Continue to guide children to hear and say the remaining sounds.

4. *Are you ready to think about a word with five sounds?* Show a picture of a plant in the pocket chart, and repeat the procedure to guide children to hear and say each sound in order, /p/ /l/ /ă/ /n/ /t/.

5. Have children continue to practice hearing and saying sounds in order using the words *fruit* (four sounds) and *zebra* (five sounds).

6. Reinforce the teaching as you review the words represented by the pictures. *By saying a word slowly, you can hear each sound in a word in order.*

Apply

Have partners take turns showing a picture card, slowly saying the word that the picture represents, and putting fingers in the air as they hear each sound. Check a child's understanding by asking: *What sounds do you hear in this word?*

Share

Have partners categorize the picture cards into two groups, words with four sounds (e.g., *clock, slide, vest, socks*) and words with five sounds (e.g., *grapes, stamp, branch*). Then have partners take turns selecting a word at random and saying each sound in order.

Assess

- Notice children's ability to say a word slowly.
- Observe whether children are able to produce each sound in a word distinctly and in the correct order.
- Note sounds that are hard for certain children to hear or say.
- You may wish to use Phonological Awareness Assessment C, D, or K.

ACTIVITY: FINGER AND SOUND MATCH

INSTRUCTIONAL PROCEDURE

HEAR AND SAY

See page 36 for detailed descriptions of Instructional Procedures.

ACTION TAGS

show
say
listen
put finger up

Phonological Awareness: Hear and Say Four or More Sounds in a Word in Sequence

Connect Learning Across Contexts

Interactive Read-Aloud Read aloud books that foster children's attention to the sounds in words.

> IRA *Creak! Said the Bed* by Phyllis Root

> IRA *Two Homes* by Claire Masurel

Shared Reading See "Grandpa Grig" in *Words That Sing* (2019). If you don't have these poetry charts, enlarge the print of this poem or other poems such as "The Lost Shoe" in *Sing a Song of Poetry,* and, using a masking card, cover some words that have four or five sounds. Invite children to say the word slowly. As they say each sound, slide the masking card to establish and reinforce letter-sound relationships. You may also wish to use the following Shared Reading title from *Fountas & Pinnell Classroom*™ to look at more sounds in words.

> SR *Smash! Crash!* by Catherine Friend

Interactive Writing When solving a word, ask children to say it slowly and think about the letter or letters that stand for each sound they hear. Children may suggest many of the letters while you fill in the rest to achieve standard spelling.

Independent Writing When children are attempting to spell a new word, encourage them to say the word slowly and then represent as many letters as they can.

Extend Learning

After a few weeks, repeat the lesson with more words containing four or more sounds that children have been attempting to spell or have encountered in their reading. This lesson can be very quick.

▶ Connect with Home

Have children take home the picture cards used in the lesson: grapes, clock, stamp, slide, vest, socks, and branch. Explain to caregivers that children should say each word slowly in order to hear each sound. As children say a word, caregivers should have children raise one finger for each sound they hear. Caregivers can then ask, "What is the first sound you hear in this word? What is the second sound you hear?" and so on.

Blend Three or Four Sounds in a Word

Plan

▶ Consider Your Children

Blending phonemes is a complex task. Use this lesson after children have experienced shared reading, know the concept of a word, are able to say words slowly, and can hear and identify beginning, end, and middle sounds. Children should also have experience hearing and blending syllables as well as onsets and rimes. In this lesson you demonstrate close attention to sounds in words by pausing after each. This means a slight *schwa* or "uh" sound after some consonants, which distorts the word as a whole. For most children, this segmentation accelerates learning because it makes individual sounds so explicit. However, if children are struggling with the task, go back to *slightly* blending the sounds so children clearly understand the word and the task.

▶ Working with English Language Learners

Involve English language learners in this activity only after they have considerable experience hearing and manipulating sounds in words. Be sure that the examples you select are words that children know, understand, and can say; moreover, they should be able to identify the first and last sounds in each word. Preview the names of any pictures with which children are unfamiliar.

YOU WILL NEED

 Ready Resources
- ▶ PA 24 Pocket-Chart Picture Cards

Online Resources
- ▶ PA 24 Action Tags
- ▶ PA 24 Lotto and Bingo Game Boards
- ▶ PA 24 Directions for Lotto and Bingo

Other Materials
- ▶ pocket chart
- ▶ coins or other markers

Generative Lesson

A generative lesson has a simple structure that you can use to present similar content or concepts. You can use this lesson structure to teach children to blend three or four sounds in a variety of words.

UNDERSTAND THE PRINCIPLE

Blending individual sounds to form a word requires children to recognize discreet sounds in words and then put them together to say the word smoothly. Blending sounds acquaints children with the structure of words and forms the basis for decoding words. This important skill can be challenging for young children; keep teaching brief and make practice game-like.

EXPLAIN THE PRINCIPLE

Blend the sounds to say a word.

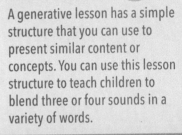

Comprehensive Phonics, Spelling, and Word Study Guide

Refer to: page **20**, row **26**

ACTIVITY: GUESSING GAME WITH PICTURE CARDS

INSTRUCTIONAL PROCEDURE

HEAR AND SAY

See page 36 for detailed descriptions of Instructional Procedures.

EXPLAIN THE PRINCIPLE

Blend the sounds to say a word.

Comprehensive Phonics, Spelling, and Word Study Guide

Refer to: page **20**, row **26**

Teach

1. Tell your children they are going to play a game in which they put sounds together to guess words.

2. *Today we're going to play a guessing game. I'm going to put three pictures in the pocket chart. I'm going to say the name of one of the pictures slowly so that you can hear each sound in the word. You put the sounds together, or blend the sounds, to guess the word.*

3. Place pictures of a bat, a cup, and a bed in the pocket chart. *Let's do one together. I'm thinking of a /b/ /ĕ/ /d/. What word am I thinking of?* ● *Yes, you blended the sounds /b/ /ĕ/ /d/ to make the word* bed. Continue by saying the words *bat* and *cup* slowly and asking children to guess each word.

4. Repeat the procedure with the following sets of picture cards: *cat, fan, fox*; *skate, milk, hand*; and *gift, nest, glass*.

5. Reinforce the principle as you review some of the words. *You have blended sounds together to say a lot of words.*

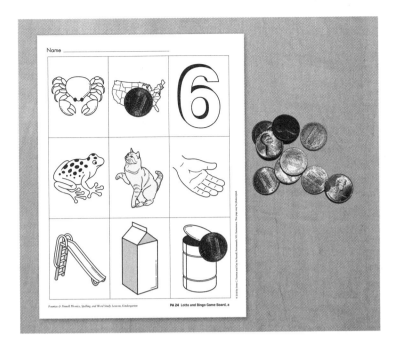

ACTIVITY: LOTTO (SMALL GROUPS)

INSTRUCTIONAL PROCEDURE

HEAR AND SAY

See page 36 for detailed descriptions of Instructional Procedures.

ACTION TAGS

listen

say

put

Apply

- Have children play Lotto in groups of three or four. Distribute Lotto game boards so that each child in a group receives a different game board. Place coins or other markers in the center of each group.

- Explain how to play the game. *I'm going to say a word slowly so that you can hear each sound. You blend the sounds to say the word. If you have a picture that shows that word on your card, put a coin on the picture. We'll keep going until someone in each group has covered all the pictures on his card.*

- Say the following words, sound by sound. Allow time for children to blend each word and search for the corresponding picture on their cards before you say the next word.

duck	cat	can
frog	dog	slide
map	fish	fan
pan	hand	crab
globe	milk	six

- If you'd rather, you can copy enough game boards to allow children to sit on the floor in groups of four. Once children learn the game, they can play it independently with a leader using picture cards. You also may wish to customize gameboards using Gamemaker in Online Resources.

Share

Invite each child to share one word from his or her Lotto game board. The child says the word slowly and other children raise their hands to say the word at a natural speed.

Assess

- Notice whether children can blend words with three sounds smoothly.
- Notice whether children can blend words with four sounds smoothly.
- You may wish to use Phonological Awareness Assessment G, H, or K.

Connect Learning Across Contexts

Interactive Read-Aloud Read aloud books that emphasize the sounds in words.

IRA *Rattletrap Car* by Phyllis Root

IRA *Charlie Parker Played Be Bop* by Chris Raschka

Shared Reading See "There Was an Old Woman" in *Words That Sing* (2019). If you don't have these poetry charts, enlarge the print of this poem or other poems such as "To Market, to Market" in *Sing a Song of Poetry,* and guide children in blending words with three and four sounds. You may also wish to use the following Shared Reading title from *Fountas & Pinnell Classroom*™ to look at sounds in words.

SR *The Big Race: An Aesop Fable* retold by David Edwin

Interactive Writing After children have written a new word, guide them to blend the sounds to confirm that they have written the word correctly.

Independent Writing Encourage children to reread their writing and to take the time to blend the sounds in less common words to confirm that each word is spelled correctly.

Extend Learning

Repeat the Teach activity with sets of picture cards that show words that begin with the same sounds, such as *scarf, skirt,* and *skate,* or that end with the same sounds, such as *man, pan,* and *can,* challenging children to attend to different parts of words when blending.

▶ Connect with Home

Have children share their Lotto game boards with family members by saying the sounds of each picture name slowly and then saying the whole word naturally.

Delete the Beginning Sound of a Word

Plan

▶ Consider Your Children

Deleting phonemes requires children to have a clear sense of the sequence of sounds in words. Children should be able to identify and isolate beginning, ending, and middle sounds before being asked to manipulate sounds in this way. The ability to delete a sound mentally is evidence that children can segment and manipulate a range of sounds, a foundation for building and taking apart words. Making phoneme deletion into a quick game that you can play during line-up or at other times throughout the day will help children gain control over letters and sounds in words. If children clearly understand the principle, you will not want to spend much time on it.

▶ Working with English Language Learners

For children who are just learning the English sound system and words, deleting sounds is likely to be quite difficult. You may want to delay using this lesson until your English language learners are very comfortable using English orally. Say words very clearly and listen carefully as children attempt to pronounce them. Accept their approximations, and skip words that seem too difficult. You will want to start with only a few very simple examples and make the activity quick and lively.

YOU WILL NEED

PWS Ready Resources
▶ **PA 25** Pocket-Chart Picture Cards

Online Resources
▶ **PA 25** Action Tags
▶ **PA 25** Picture Cards

Other Materials
▶ **pocket chart**

Generative Lesson
A generative lesson has a simple structure that you can use to present similar content or concepts. You can use this lesson structure to teach children how to remove the beginning sound from a variety of words.

UNDERSTAND THE PRINCIPLE

As children become more aware of the sounds in words, they learn to isolate and say individual sounds and identify their sequence within a word. Deleting sounds indicates a great deal of control of the phonology of English.

EXPLAIN THE PRINCIPLE

Say a word without the first sound.

Comprehensive Phonics, Spelling, and Word Study Guide

Refer to:
page **20**, row **27**

ACTIVITY: BEGINNING-SOUND DELETION

INSTRUCTIONAL PROCEDURE

NOTICE PARTS

See page 36 for detailed descriptions of Instructional Procedures.

Teach

1. Tell the children they are going to practice saying words without the first sound.

2. *When you say a word, you can hear the first sound, can't you?* Place the card with the picture of a pig in the pocket chart. *Say* pig. • *What's the first sound in this word?* • *The first sound in the word* pig *is /p/.*

3. *Now I'm going to say the word* pig *without the first sound: -ig. Let's do one together.* Place the card with the picture of a cat in the pocket chart. *Say* cat. • *The first sound is. . . .* • *Now say* cat *without the /k/.* • *Yes, the word* cat *without the first sound is -at.*

4. Continue to practice the concept using *bat* and *duck*, then repeat the process with two or three more examples offered by children.

5. For additional practice, have children say the names of classmates without the first sound (*Mike, -ike; Jan, -an*).

EXPLAIN THE PRINCIPLE

Say a word without the first sound.

Comprehensive Phonics, Spelling, and Word Study Guide

Refer to: page **20**, row **27**

ACTIVITY: DECK OF PICTURE CARDS (PAIRS)

INSTRUCTIONAL PROCEDURE

NOTICE PARTS

See page 36 for detailed descriptions of Instructional Procedures.

ACTION TAGS

take

say

take away

Apply

Distribute a set of picture cards to each pair of children. Have partners take turns taking a card, saying the word represented by the picture, and then saying the word without the first sound.

Share

Encourage children to make up additional examples and to demonstrate deleting the first sound in a word.

Assess

- Notice whether the children can hear, say, and delete the first sounds of words. A quick check of just two or three examples will tell you whether they understand the concept.
- Check whether children can generate appropriate examples during the Teach and Share activities.
- You may wish to use Phonological Awareness Assessment I or K.

Phonological Awareness: Delete the Beginning Sound of a Word

Connect Learning Across Contexts

Interactive Read-Aloud Read aloud books that contain words that start with the same sound.

> IRA *Wemberly Worried* by Kevin Henkes

> IRA *A, My Name is Alice* by Jane Bayer

Shared Reading See "Willaby, Wallaby, Woo" in *Words That Sing* (2019). If you don't have these poetry charts, enlarge the print of this poem or other poems such as "Hickory, Dickory, Dock!" in *Sing a Song of Poetry.* Delete some initial sounds and read for fun: for example, *ickory, ickory, ock! The ouse an up the lock.* You may also wish to use the following Shared Reading title from *Fountas & Pinnell Classroom*™ to look at more sounds in words.

> SR *The Itsy Bitsy Spider* adapted by Helen Lorraine

Interactive Writing Have children say a word slowly and think about what the first sound is. While children don't need to delete the first sound, the activities in this lesson will increase their awareness of the sequence of phonemes in words, making individual sounds easier to isolate and hear.

Independent Writing Encourage children to say the words they want to write and to think about the beginning sound. Then demonstrate how to say the words again to identify more letters.

Extend Learning

Display picture cards that represent different categories, such as a picture of a cat for "animals," a picture of a hat for "things you wear," and a picture of baseball bat for "sports." Have children take turns choosing a category, thinking of a word that fits that category, and then saying the word without the first sound. For example, "I'm thinking of a word that is a sport. It's *-occer.*" Other children guess the missing sound and say the whole world.

▶ Connect with Home

In a newsletter or during a meeting, encourage family members to play word games that involve taking away the first sound (for example, *cat, -at*). Suggest that while driving in the car or going for a walk, families play a version of I Spy. A family member says "I see a *-ouse;*" the child says *house;* and then they switch roles. Emphasize that the activity should be quick and fun, with the goal of making children curious about words and encouraging them to manipulate sounds and play with language.

Delete the Beginning Sound of a Word

Plan

▶ Consider Your Children

Use this lesson after children have had a great deal of experience saying and hearing sounds in words, matching the initial sounds of words, and associating letters and sounds. When children grasp the concept of a word and are noticing and identifying sequences of sounds, it will be easier for them to take on the complex task of deleting sounds. This operation is also an outcome of much experience in writing, in which children take words apart to spell them. If children can easily perform the task of deleting initial phonemes, you do not need to spend much time on these kinds of activities.

▶ Working with English Language Learners

Phoneme manipulation may be especially difficult for English language learners and could confuse them. You may choose not to use this activity if children are very inexperienced in English and have not worked a great deal with English letters and sounds. Use only examples that focus on words children know, understand, and can say. Say words clearly when you demonstrate. Accept variations in children's pronunciation. Make the deletion of sounds into a game rather than a test, and value approximation.

YOU WILL NEED

PWS Ready Resources
▶ **PA 26** Pocket-Chart Picture Cards

Online Resources
▶ **PA 26** Action Tags
▶ **PA 26** Picture Cards

Other Materials
▶ pocket chart

Generative Lesson ✓

A generative lesson has a simple structure that you can use to present similar content or concepts. You can use this lesson structure to teach children how to delete the beginning sound from a variety of words.

UNDERSTAND THE PRINCIPLE

As children become more aware of the sounds in words, they learn to isolate and say individual sounds and identify their sequence within a word. Deleting sounds indicates a great deal of control of the phonology of English. Manipulating words by removing one of the sounds helps make the knowledge of phonemes more explicit and the application of that knowledge more flexible.

EXPLAIN THE PRINCIPLE

Say a word without the first sound.

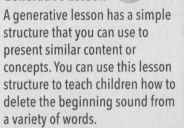

Comprehensive Phonics, Spelling, and Word Study Guide

Refer to: page **20**, row **27**

EARLY MIDDLE **LATE**

ACTIVITY: BEGINNING-SOUND GAME

INSTRUCTIONAL PROCEDURE

HEAR AND SAY

See page 36 for detailed descriptions of Instructional Procedures.

EXPLAIN THE PRINCIPLE

Say a word without the first sound.

Comprehensive Phonics, Spelling, and Word Study Guide

Refer to: page **20**, row **27**

Teach

1. Say *horse, orse. What did I do?* • *I took away the first sound.* Tell the children they are going to play a word game in which they take away the first sound in words.

2. *When you say a word, you can hear the first sound, can't you? Say* horse. • *What's the first sound in this word?* • *That's right. The first sound in the word* horse *is /h/. Now I'm going to say the word* horse *without the first sound:* -orse.

3. *Let's try another one. Say* cat. • *The first sound is . . .* • *Now say* cat *without the /k/.* • *Yes, the word* cat *without the first sound is* at.

4. *Sometimes when you take away the first sound in a word, you have a made-up word, such as* -orse. *Sometimes you are left with a real word, such as* at. *Today we're going to play a game in which you will take away the first sound in a word to make a new real word.*

5. Play the game using several of the following word pairs. Say the first word and ask children to take away the first sound, resulting in them saying the second word.

shy–eye	fold–old	rice–ice	cow–ow
tall–all	neat–eat	farm–arm	pat–at
make–ache	sink–ink	cold–old	heart–art
shout–out	mat–at	hair–air	bus–us
mice–ice	hill–ill	feel–eel	bend–end

6. Continue to play the game using two or three more examples offered by children.

ACTIVITY: BEGINNING-SOUND GAME

INSTRUCTIONAL PROCEDURE

HEAR AND SAY

See page 36 for detailed descriptions of Instructional Procedures.

ACTION TAGS

take

say

take away

say

Apply

Distribute a set of picture cards to each pair of children. In turn, have partners take a card, say the word represented by the picture, and then say the word without the first sound.

Share

Encourage children to make up additional examples and to demonstrate deleting the first sound in a word.

Assess

- Notice whether the children can say, hear, and delete the first sounds of words. A quick check of just two or three examples will tell you whether they understand the concept.
- Check whether children can generate appropriate examples during the Teach and Share activities.
- You may wish to use Phonological Awareness Assessment I or K.

Connect Learning Across Contexts

Interactive-Read Aloud Read aloud books that feature word play, such as:

IRA *Miss Bindergarten Gets Ready for Kindergarten* by Joseph Slate

IRA *Max Found Two Sticks* by Brian Pinkney

Shared Reading See "Hickory, Dickory, Dore!" in *Words That Sing* (2019). If you don't have these poetry charts, enlarge the print of this poem or other poems such as "Higglety, Pigglety Pop!" in *Sing a Song of Poetry,* which features word play. You may also wish to use the following Shared Reading title from *Fountas & Pinnell Classroom™,* which plays with the words *scream* and *ice cream.*

SR *Scream for Ice Cream* by Keisha Johnson

Interactive Writing Have children say a word slowly and think how to start it. After generating the sound, write the first letter. (You don't need to delete the first sound in this activity.)

Independent Writing Encourage children to say the words they want to write and think how to start them; then demonstrate how to say the words again, sound-by-sound as needed, to represent more letters.

Extend Learning

Have children make up simple riddles that include a clue that is missing the beginning sound. For example, "This is something that I wear. I have a red one on today. It is my *-irt*." The child that guesses the answer can then make up the next riddle.

▶ Connect with Home

In a newsletter or during a meeting, encourage family members to play word games that involve taking away the first sound (for example, *cat, at*). Suggest that they choose a category, such as animals or food, and then take turns naming words that fit the category but without the first sound, for example, *-og* (*dog*) or *-anana* (*banana*). Emphasize that the activity should be quick and fun, with the goal of making children curious about words and encouraging them to manipulate sounds.

Letter Knowledge

Letter knowledge refers to what children need to learn about the graphic characters that correspond with the sounds of language. English is an alphabetic system. A finite set of twenty-six letters, two forms of each, is related to all of the sounds of the English language (approximately forty-four phonemes). The sounds vary with factors such as dialect, articulation, and other speech idiosyncrasies. Children will also encounter alternative forms of some letters–for example, g, g; a, a; y, *y*–and will eventually learn to recognize letters in cursive writing. Children need to learn the names and purposes of letters. But identifying and naming them is not easy because, when first encountered, letters look very much alike. Children need to learn distinctive features of each letter form. When children can identify letters by noticing the very small differences that make them unique, they can then associate letters and letter clusters with phonemes and parts of words. Knowing the letter names is useful information that helps children talk about letters and understand what others say about them. As writers, children need to be able to use efficient directional movements when making letters.

Connect to Assessment

See related (optional) LK Assessment tasks in Online Resources.

- Assessment A: Reading the Alphabet
- Assessment B: Writing the Alphabet
- Assessment C: Connecting Uppercase and Lowercase Letter Forms
- Assessment D: Individual Record (Alphabet Recognition)
- Assessment E: Class Record (Alphabet Writing)
- Assessment F: Class Record (Uppercase and Lowercase Letters)

Develop Your Professional Understanding

See *The Fountas & Pinnell Comprehensive Phonics, Spelling, and Word Study Guide*. Related pages: 2–12, 22–23.

See *The Fountas & Pinnell Literacy Continuum: A Tool for Assessment, Planning, and Teaching*. 2017. Portsmouth, New Hampshire: Heinemann. Related pages: 357–397.

See *Word Matters: Teaching Phonics and Spelling in the Reading/Writing Classroom* by G. S. Pinnell and I. C. Fountas. 1998. Portsmouth, New Hampshire: Heinemann. Related pages: 7–8, 46–47, 47–48, 69–72, 87–88, 90–93, 123, 138–139, 141–142, 143–147, 252–254.

Understand That Words Are Formed with Letters

Plan

▶ Consider Your Children

This lesson helps children learn about letters by focusing their attention on the particular letters that are likely to be the most familiar to them. You can begin working with the name puzzle once you have introduced the class name chart (see ELC 1) and children have had some experience locating their names and noticing the letters in their names.

▶ Working with English Language Learners

This lesson will help English language learners make personal connections to written language. It will also help them understand the terms *letter*, *word*, and *name*. Be sure each child can say his name clearly. Demonstrate the task several times with small groups so that children understand how to look closely at the model and build the name in exactly the same way. Use the term *letter* while pointing to the individual graphic signs. Say the letters of each child's name and have the child repeat the letter names. Work with the puzzles each day until the children can put their names together easily and say the letters.

YOU WILL NEED

Online Resources
- ▶ LK 1 Action Tags
- ▶ LK 1 Directions for Name Puzzle and Folder

Other Materials
- ▶ file crate or basket for name puzzle folder storage
- ▶ chopsticks or other small pointers
- ▶ name puzzles for each child
- ▶ name puzzle folders for each child

Generative Lesson ✓

A generative lesson has a simple structure that you can use to present similar content or concepts. You can use this lesson structure to focus children's attention on less familiar letters, as well.

UNDERSTAND THE PRINCIPLE

A word is made with one or more letters. A name is a word and is made with letters. Saying and looking at the letters in their names helps children notice the orientation and distinguishing features of each letter, and it helps them understand that the order of letters in a word is always the same. These concepts are important in recognizing words on sight (by letter patterns) and in beginning to recognize spelling patterns.

EXPLAIN THE PRINCIPLE

Put letters together to make a word.

Your name is a word.

Put letters together to make your name.

Say the letters in your name.

Comprehensive Phonics, Spelling, and Word Study Guide

Refer to: page **23**, row **9**

ACTIVITY: NAME PUZZLE

INSTRUCTIONAL PROCEDURE

FIND AND MATCH

See page 36 for detailed descriptions of Instructional Procedures.

EXPLAIN THE PRINCIPLE

Put letters together to make a word.

Your name is a word.

Put letters together to make your name.

Say the letters in your name.

Comprehensive Phonics, Spelling, and Word Study Guide

Refer to: page **23**, row **9**

Teach

1. Use the directions for the name puzzle and folder to prepare materials for this activity.

2. Tell the children that today they are going to put together their name puzzles. Arrange children in a circle so they can place their folders open flat on the floor in front of them, where you will be able to observe their work.

3. *I'm going to show you how to put together your name puzzle. Take out the letters that are in the envelope inside your folder. Open your folder and lay it flat in front of you. Be sure you can see your name. Use the letter pieces to make your name. Put down the first letter first; then put down the next letter. Make sure the letters are right side up. Make sure all of the letters match.*

4. Demonstrate using one child's folder and puzzle pieces. Emphasize that each letter must look the same as the corresponding letter written on the folder. Also point out that each later must face the same way as the corresponding letter on the folder.

5. Using a pointer, point to each letter, demonstrating how to check letter by letter. Say the letters and point to each one as you go: *E–E, m–m, i–i, l–l, y–y.*

6. Show how to mix up the letters so children can form the name again.

7. Be sure all the children have formed their names at least once.

8. Demonstrate how to put the name puzzle away: put all the pieces back in the envelope and put the folder in a crate or basket with the name on the folder facing up.

Apply

Children put together their names, mix up the letters, and make the names again three times.

Share

Have the children sit in a circle with their name puzzles in front of them. Ask them to take turns saying the letters of their names while they point to each letter with a chopstick or other small pointer. Say the letters with any child who cannot yet do so independently. Be sure each child gets a turn. Then have children talk about what they notice about their names. Model the process first:

"I have a *b* in my name."

"I have four letters in my name."

"My name starts with a capital *B*."

If children perform this task easily, ask them to work with a partner. Partners can tell what they have noticed about the letters in each other's names.

Assess

- Notice whether the children are able to put together their names, letter by letter, from left to right.
- Notice whether the letters are right side up (correct orientation).
- Check whether the children are able to say the letters of their names accurately.

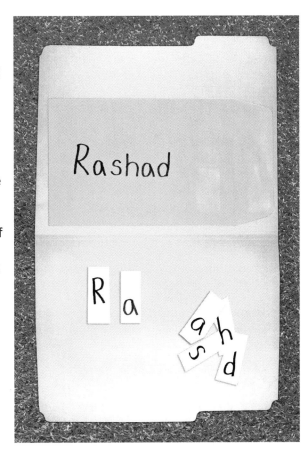

ACTIVITY: NAME PUZZLE

INSTRUCTIONAL PROCEDURE

FIND AND MATCH

See page 36 for detailed descriptions of Instructional Procedures.

ACTION TAGS

mix
find
put
check

Connect Learning Across Contexts

Interactive Read-Aloud Read aloud books that have characters' names in the titles.

> **IRA** *Mary Wore Her Red Dress and Henry Wore His Green Sneakers* by Merle Peek

> **IRA** *Ruby the Copycat* by Peggy Rathman

Shared Reading See "Lucy Locket" in *Words That Sing* (2019). If you don't have these poetry charts, enlarge the print of this poem or other poems such as "Tommy Snooks" in *Sing a Song of Poetry,* and invite children to identify some of the names with highlighter tape. You may also wish to use the following Shared Reading title from *Fountas & Pinnell Classroom*™ to locate more names.

> **SR** *Kate's Party* by Jane Simon

Shared or Interactive Writing Write sentences with children's names in them: "Emily likes red." "Justin wore a blue shirt."

Independent Writing Encourage the children to use their names as resources when writing words. Encourage them to write their names on their papers.

Extend Learning

- When children are able to put the letters of their names together while checking against the model, have them put the letters together, left to right, without using the model, and then check against the model.

- Have children use uppercase and lowercase letter cards to form their names. Ask them to glue the names on a piece of paper and draw a self-portrait.

- When children can make their names easily, ask them to make a partner's name and check it.

- When children can put together and say the letters in their first names easily, add their surnames to the puzzle.

- When all the children can say all the letters in their names, invite them to say the consonants or the vowels or to clap the syllables. Have children make their names using various types of letters (letter tiles, magnetic letters, foam letters, plastic letters, or sandpaper letters).

▶ Connect with Home

When children know to put together the name puzzle, let them take it home to show family members. Ask family members to help children form their names using magnetic letters or copies of the uppercase and lowercase letter cards.

Recognize the Distinctive Features of Letter Forms

Plan

▶ Consider Your Children

This will be a very early lesson. Notice how many letters of the alphabet children can name and locate quickly on a chart and in a text that has continuous print. Children who are unfamiliar with letters in general will need a great deal of letter exploration such as the activity in this lesson. This lesson will help very inexperienced children learn how to look for the distinctive features of letters. It will also help children understand the purposes of print.

▶ Working with English Language Learners

Observing children explore is a way for you to discover the thinking that English language learners are bringing to their work with the letters of the alphabet. Even though you will be guiding them to notice the distinguishing features of letters, it will be helpful to know the connections they are making on their own, perhaps to their native languages or aspects of their cultures. Encourage them to talk about what they notice about various letters.

YOU WILL NEED

Online Resources
- ▶ LK 2 Action Tags

Other Materials
- ▶ magnetic letters
- ▶ magnetic surface

Generative Lesson ✓
A generative lesson has a simple structure that you can use to present similar content or concepts. You can use this lesson structure to teach children the distinctive features of a variety of letter forms.

UNDERSTAND THE PRINCIPLE

The characteristics that make a letter different from every other letter–its distinctive features–are often quite small. For examples, the length of the "stick" distinguishes *n* from *h*. Children must be able to make these distinctions before they can match letters with the sounds they represent. Children's names are a valuable learning resource. By examining their names, children learn to notice specific features of letters, and they learn about the consistency of letter order in words. They notice that letters are formed in different ways, with straight or curved lines. They realize that directionality is important in making letters and in putting letters together to make words. They also learn how to notice first and last letters, letter clusters, and word length.

EXPLAIN THE PRINCIPLE

Each letter looks different.

Some letters have long straight lines. Some letters have short straight lines.

Some letters have curves [e.g., circles, tails].

Comprehensive Phonics, Spelling, and Word Study Guide

Refer to: page **22**, row **1**

ACTIVITY: MAGNETIC-LETTER PLAY

INSTRUCTIONAL PROCEDURE

NOTICE PARTS

See page 36 for detailed descriptions of Instructional Procedures.

EXPLAIN THE PRINCIPLE

Each letter looks different.

Some letters have long straight lines. Some letters have short straight lines.

Some letters have curves [e.g., circles, tails].

Comprehensive Phonics, Spelling, and Word Study Guide

Refer to: page **22**, row **1**

Teach

1. Explain to children that they are going to use colored plastic letters to learn about letters.

2. Place a variety of letters on a magnetic board or magnetic cookie sheet and ask the children what they notice about them. They may offer comments such as "They are all different colors," "Some letters look the same," and "Some are big and some are little."

3. *When you look at a letter, and when you hold a letter in your hand, you begin to notice things about it. You may notice what shape the letter is.* Show children a lowercase *h*. *What do you notice about the shape of this letter?* • *It has a long straight line. It also has one tunnel.* Show a lowercase *m*. *How about this letter? Does it have the same shape?* • *It does have a short straight line. But it also has two tunnels, doesn't it? Do you see how these two letters look different from each other?* • *In fact, each letter in the alphabet is different from all of the other letters.*

4. Show children that letters can be put together to make a word. Make some of the children's names and some simple words. *Have you seen this word before?* • Say the word aloud as you point to it. *When I put these letters together like this, I made the word . . .* Point to one of the names. *This is another word. This is somebody's name. Do you see how the letters go together to make this name?* • *This is the name . . .*

5. Explain to children that today they will spend time playing with letters—looking at them, touching them, putting them in groups, matching them. Invite children to make words, either real ones or words they make up. *As you play with the letters, see if they have straight lines or curves.*

6. Remind children to keep the letters on the table and to put them back in the container when they are finished.

ACTIVITY: MAGNETIC-LETTER PLAY

INSTRUCTIONAL PROCEDURE

NOTICE PARTS

See page 36 for detailed descriptions of Instructional Procedures.

ACTION TAGS

look

touch

play

match

put

Apply

Have children spend a minimum of fifteen minutes exploring letters and making words. Encourage them to notice–and use their fingers to touch–features such as short straight lines, curves, and long straight lines. You may choose to display a few word cards for children to refer to as models of how letters can be grouped into words.

Share

In the group meeting, invite the children to talk about what they've discovered. If they haven't noticed, explain that the twenty-six letters have uppercase and lowercase forms and that some lowercase letters look like their uppercase forms.

Assess

■ Observe the children working with letters. Be aware of how they are using them and what they notice about them.

■ Ask children to find specific letters or to make their names.

Letter Knowledge: Recognize the Distinctive Features of Letter Forms

221

Connect Learning Across Contexts

Interactive Read-Aloud Read aloud a variety of alphabet books about letters.

IRA *Alphabet Under Construction* by Denise Fleming

IRA *ABC I Like Me* by Nancy Carlson

Shared Reading See "Diddlety, Diddlety, Dumpty!" in *Words That Sing* (2019). If you don't have these poetry charts, enlarge the print of this poem or other poems such as "The Alphabet Song" in *Sing a Song of Poetry*. Have children use highlighter tape to locate letters. You may also wish to use the following Shared Reading title from *Fountas & Pinnell Classroom*™ to look at more letters with the children.

SR *City ABCs* by Finnoula Louise

Interactive Writing Guide a child's hand as he contributes letters to the writing, or hold up a model magnetic letter for the child to copy. Use descriptive language from the Verbal Path for the Formation of Letters (see *Ready Resources*) as the child writes.

Independent Writing Reinforce children's correct letter formation as they write stories. Remind them about long "sticks," etc., as needed.

Extend Learning

Repeat the lesson, each time helping the children notice more about letters.

▶ Connect with Home

If children do not have a set of magnetic letters at home, send copies of letter cards home with them. Also, you may wish to provide copies of 25 Ways to Use Magnetic Letters at Home (see *Ready Resources*) for a variety of activities family members can do at home using letters.

Recognize the Distinctive Features of Letter Forms

Plan

▶ Consider Your Children

Use this lesson with children who are just beginning to learn to write and read their names. If they are able to recognize some letters in their names but do not have full control of the specific features of individual letters, this lesson will be helpful. If all children can quickly, accurately, and automatically write their first names and say the letters in them, you may want to include surnames or not use this lesson.

▶ Working with English Language Learners

Children enjoy working with their names, and every time you recognize a child's name, his or her presence in your class will be affirmed. Noticing the features of the letters in their names will be a first step for children in distinguishing the letters from each other. Be sure that you know how to pronounce the children's names correctly, and work with them to say their own names clearly along with the names of their classmates.

YOU WILL NEED

PWS Ready Resources
- ▶ Blank Pocket-Chart Cards
- ▶ Verbal Path for the Formation of Letters

Online Resources
- ▶ LK 3 Action Tags

Other Materials
- ▶ whiteboard or magnetic drawing board
- ▶ large name card
- ▶ children's name cards (from ELC 1)
- ▶ large sheets of paper
- ▶ gluesticks
- ▶ colored glitter
- ▶ colored markers

Generative Lesson ✓

A generative lesson has a simple structure that you can use to present similar content or concepts. You can use this lesson structure to teach children the distinctive features of letter forms with a variety of letters.

UNDERSTAND THE PRINCIPLE

The characteristics that make a letter different from every other letter–its distinctive features–are often quite small. For examples, the length of the "stick" distinguishes *n* from *h*. Children must be able to make these distinctions before they can match letters with the sounds they represent. Children's names are a valuable learning resource. By examining their names, children learn to notice specific features of letters, and they learn about the consistency of letter order in words. They notice that letters are formed in different ways, with straight or curved lines. They realize that directionality is important in making letters and in putting letters together to make words. They also learn how to notice first and last letters, letter clusters, and word length.

EXPLAIN THE PRINCIPLE

Each letter looks different.

Some letters have long straight lines. Some letters have short straight lines.

Some letters have curves [e.g., circles, tails].

Comprehensive Phonics, Spelling, and Word Study Guide

Refer to: page **22**, row 1

ACTIVITY: LETTER FEATURES

INSTRUCTIONAL PROCEDURE

NOTICE PARTS

See page 36 for detailed descriptions of Instructional Procedures.

EXPLAIN THE PRINCIPLE

Each letter looks different.

Some letters have long straight lines. Some letters have short straight lines.

Some letters have curves [e.g., circles, tails].

Comprehensive Phonics, Spelling, and Word Study Guide

Refer to: page **22**, row **1**

Teach

1. Tell the children you are going to show them how to notice the parts of letters in a name.

2. Write your name or a child's name in large letters on a whiteboard or magnetic drawing board.

3. As you do so, use language describing letter formation. Refer to the Verbal Path for the Formation of Letters. Point out features such as circles, slants, tunnels, long sticks, and short sticks.

4. *You are going to do the same thing with the letters of your name on your name card.* Using the large letters of the name on the whiteboard or magnetic drawing board, show children how to use a finger to trace over the letters in a name. *After you have traced your name and noticed all of the letters, take your name card and put glue onto the shape of the letters. Then I will put glitter on the letters of your name.* Alternatively, write children's names in pencil and let them choose marker colors to carefully trace over the name.

ACTIVITY: COLOR
ON LINES

**INSTRUCTIONAL
PROCEDURE**

NOTICE PARTS

*See page 36 for detailed
descriptions of Instructional
Procedures.*

ACTION TAGS

trace

glue

draw

Apply

Give children their name cards. Have them outline each letter in their names with glue. Then you can add colored glitter to the letters of their names. Then have children glue the name card on the bottom half of a larger sheet of paper, and draw self-portraits on the top half of their papers.

Share

- Display the class glitter names on the bulletin board.
- Ask children to share what they noticed about the letters in their names.
- Read the names together with the children.
- Point to a "star" name and ask children to quickly locate with their eyes the same name on the name chart.

Assess

- Have each child write her name independently and observe how many letters she can represent.
- Have each child locate her name several times within continuous text as well as on the name chart. Notice how quickly children find their names.
- You may wish to use Letter Knowledge Assessment D.

Connect Learning Across Contexts

Interactive Read-Aloud Read aloud alphabet books or books featuring names. Ask the children what they notice about some of the letters.

IRA *Miss Bindergarten Gets Ready for Kindergarten* by Joseph Slate

IRA *A, My Name Is Alice* by Jane Bayer

Shared Reading See "Window Watching" in *Words That Sing* (2019). If you don't have these poetry charts, enlarge the print of this poem or other poems such as "Two Little Houses" in *Sing a Song of Poetry,* and have children use highlighter tape to point out a letter with a particular feature: e.g., a circle, slant, tunnel, long stick, short stick. You may also wish to use the following Shared Reading title from *Fountas & Pinnell Classroom*™ to look at more names and letters.

SR *Miss Mary Mack* Retold by Susannah Franco

Interactive Writing As children form letters, use the Verbal Path for the Formation of Letters to guide them with language that supports the correct formation.

Independent Writing Prompt children to use correct, efficient letter formation when writing. You might wish to post an enlarged version of the letter formation charts (see *Ready Resources*) in the classroom for reference.

Extend Learning

Repeat the lesson with last names and the appropriate titles: for example, *Mr. Sonora, Miss Rivera.*

▶ Connect with Home

Encourage family members to have children make their name several times with magnetic letters or letter cards.

Recognize Letters and State Their Names

Plan

▶ Consider Your Children

This lesson establishes a procedure for sorting letters and will be helpful to children who have not noticed the features or shapes of letters and who do not know many letter names. We suggest this sequence: *b, m, r, s, t, g, n, p, c, h, f, d, l, k, j, w, y, z, v, x, q*. Work with two or three letters at a time that are dissimilar in shape and in letter sound.

▶ Working with English Language Learners

It will be important for English language learners to learn the names of the letters so that they can understand classroom instruction. They may need several demonstrations of letters and names. You may want to work with a small set of letters at the beginning–for example, having children find every *b* in a set of four different letters. Begin with letters that are very different from each other. Have children say the name of the letter each time they find it.

YOU WILL NEED

PWS Ready Resources
▶ Lowercase Letter Cards

Online Resources
▶ LK 4 Action Tags
▶ LK 4 Two-Way Sorts

Other Materials
▶ whiteboard
▶ marker
▶ magnetic letters *b, r, m,* and others
▶ magnetic surface
▶ containers of plastic letters

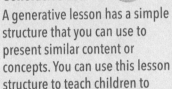

Generative Lesson

A generative lesson has a simple structure that you can use to present similar content or concepts. You can use this lesson structure to teach children to recognize and state a variety of letter names.

UNDERSTAND THE PRINCIPLE

The ability to recognize and name letters is an important tool for beginning readers and writers. Although the names of letters do not necessarily match the sound they represent, they are part of the language of the classroom. Knowing letter names and shapes should become quick and automatic.

EXPLAIN THE PRINCIPLE

Look at the shape of a letter and say its name.

Comprehensive Phonics, Spelling, and Word Study Guide

Refer to: page **22**, row **2**

ACTIVITY: LETTER MATCH

INSTRUCTIONAL PROCEDURE

SAY AND SORT

See page 36 for detailed descriptions of Instructional Procedures.

EXPLAIN THE PRINCIPLE

Look at the shape of a letter and say its name.

Comprehensive Phonics, Spelling, and Word Study Guide

Refer to: page **22**, row **2**

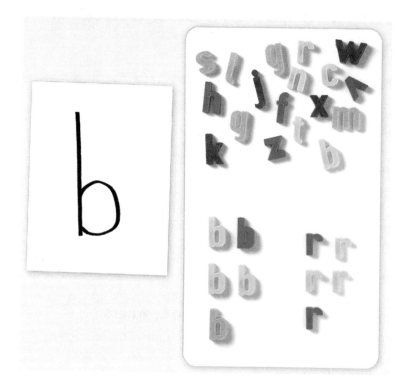

Teach

1. Tell the children they are going to learn more about the shapes and names of letters.

2. Be sure that all children can see the whiteboard and the magnetic surface clearly. Place some *b*'s and *r*'s on the magnetic surface along with several other letters. Children will be discriminating between letters, so limit the selection of letters for them as appropriate.

3. *I'm going to make a letter.* Make a *b* on the whiteboard, being sure that the line is thick and black. *This is a* b. *Say* b. • *Whisper* b. • *To make* b, *pull down, half up, and around.* Repeat the motions. *This is a* b. *Who can find a* b *on the alphabet chart?* • *Who can find a* b *on the name chart?*

4. *Now I'm going to find a* b *among the magnetic letters you see here.* Demonstrate finding a *b* among the letters on the magnetic surface and pulling it down. Place the *b* clearly away from the others.

5. Ask several children to come up and find additional examples of the letter *b* and group them with the first one. Help as needed so that the process moves quickly.

6. Say the name of the letter each time it is placed with the group. Also, show children how to "check" the group by pointing to each *b*, looking closely, and naming the letter.

7. Repeat using the letter *m* or *r*.

8. Demonstrate the sorting activity. Show the children that they will look at the pile of letters and find all the *b*'s first. Then they will find the *r*'s. Show them how to place the *b*'s on the left side of the two-way sort and the *r*'s on the right side.

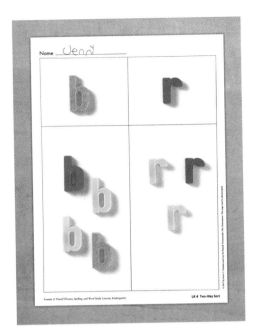

INSTRUCTIONAL PROCEDURE

SAY AND SORT

See page 36 for detailed descriptions of Instructional Procedures.

ACTION TAGS

find
sort

Apply

- Give each child a two-way sort and provide a container of *b*'s, *r*'s, and other letters. Children find *b*'s and place them in the left column, and they find *r*'s and place them in the right column. Other letters are not used.

- Encourage children to say the letter names and look closely at the letters as they sort them.

Share

Have children discuss what they have noticed about the letters *b* and *r*. Demonstrate and encourage comments like these:

"*b* is a tall letter."

"*r* has a little curl on it."

"I have a *b* in my name."

"*r* is shorter."

Assess

- Observe whether the children can find letters quickly and can match and check them.

- Observe whether the children can say the name of the letter quickly.

- Give a quick test using letter cards that are not in alphabetical order. Ask children to say quickly the name of the letter.

- You may wish to use Letter Knowledge Assessment A or D.

Connect Learning Across Contexts

Interactive Read-Aloud Read aloud alphabet books.

 *ABC I Like Me* by Nancy Carlson

On Market Street by Arthur Lobel and Anita Lobel

Shared Reading See "Wee Willie Winkie" in *Words That Sing* (2019). If you don't have these poetry charts, enlarge the print of this poem or other poems such as "Time to Pick Up" or "Tommy Snooks" in *Sing a Song of Poetry,* and name letters and have children use highlighter tape to locate them. You may also wish to use the following Shared Reading title from *Fountas & Pinnell Classroom*™.

City ABCs by Finnoula Louise

Interactive Writing Use the names of letters to help children locate the letter needed in a piece of writing. Make connections with the Alphabet Linking Chart and the class name chart.

Independent Writing Point out letters by name when conferring with children about their writing.

Extend Learning

■ Repeat this lesson with different letters, two or three at a time. Follow the sequence for lowercase letters from the Consider Your Children section.

■ After children are comfortable with finding and grouping specific letters, you can increase the challenge by providing a larger group of distracting letters. Prompt children to work quickly and to check their groupings.

▶ Connect with Home

Encourage family members to have a set of magnetic letters or letter cards for the child's use at home. Send home a list of ways children can sort the letters. You may also ask children to search the large print of newspapers or magazines for several examples of a particular letter, cut them out, and glue them on a sheet.

Recognize the Distinctive Features of Letter Forms

Plan

▶ Consider Your Children

The procedures described here may be used many times for different lowercase and uppercase letters. Begin with lowercase letters, which are useful because children encounter them so much more frequently when reading and writing. Work on letters that most children know or nearly know. Once children grasp the principle, the lessons will be quite short; the children will have developed a system for learning the verbal path and physical movements to make a letter. It may not be necessary to go over every letter in such detail. Children should have good control of efficient movements before they are asked to attend to variables such as size or lines. Kindergartners require plenty of room to make letters; unlined paper allows them free motion and allows them to look only at the letters–not letters and lines.

▶ Working with English Language Learners

This lesson will be helpful to English language learners even if they know only a few letters. Be sure that children say the verbal description of the letter as they write it or trace it in sand or other material. You may want to start with a common letter for the whole group or bring children together in a small group to work with the letters they know. They can also look through magazines, newspapers, or any other collections of large print to find examples of the same letter.

UNDERSTAND THE PRINCIPLE

The characteristics that make a letter different from every other letter–its distinctive features–are often quite small. For examples, the length of the "stick" distinguishes *n* from *h*. Children must be able to make these distinctions before they can match letters with the sounds they represent. Learning efficient movements for making letters helps children keep the features of each letter in visual memory and associate that letter with its name.

YOU WILL NEED

PWS Ready Resources
- ▶ Verbal Path for the Formation of Letters
- ▶ Alphabet Linking Chart

Online Resources
- ▶ LK 5 Action Tags

Other Materials
- ▶ easel and blank chart paper, whiteboard, or magnetic drawing board
- ▶ marker
- ▶ class name chart (from ELC 1)
- ▶ sand/salt in tray or box
- ▶ copies of large lowercase *g* (or another selected letter) on 8 ½ x 11 paper
- ▶ tissue paper cut into small squares or circles
- ▶ glue

Generative Lesson

A generative lesson has a simple structure that you can use to present similar content or concepts. You can use this lesson structure to teach children the distinctive features of a variety of letter forms.

EXPLAIN THE PRINCIPLE

Each letter looks different.

Some letters have long straight lines. Some letters have short straight lines.

Some letters have curves [e.g., circles, tails].

Comprehensive Phonics, Spelling, and Word Study Guide

Refer to: page **22**, row **1**

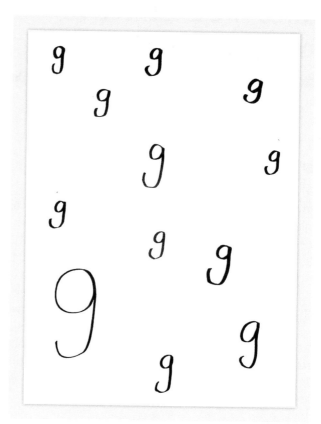

ACTIVITY: LETTER FORMATION

INSTRUCTIONAL PROCEDURE

NOTICE PARTS

See page 36 for detailed descriptions of Instructional Procedures.

EXPLAIN THE PRINCIPLE

Each letter looks different.

Some letters have long straight lines. Some letters have short straight lines.

Some letters have curves [e.g., circles, tails].

Comprehensive Phonics, Spelling, and Word Study Guide

Refer to: page **22**, row **1**

Teach

1. Start by making a letter on the chart paper (or other display medium). Say the name of the letter and demonstrate how it is formed, using the simple, clear language provided in the Verbal Path for the Formation of Letters. *I'm going to make a* g. *To make a lowercase* g, *you pull back, around, up, down, and curve back.* Make the letter slowly as you describe the movement.

2. Make the letter again, inviting the children to describe the verbal path with you as you write.

3. Make the letter using several other writing media (magnetic drawing board, crayons, colored markers), each time describing the verbal path. Move along quickly. *I am going to make a* g *on the chart.* Have the children describe the movements with you as you demonstrate. *I'm going to make a big* g. Make a large version of the lowercase letter. *I'm going to make a smaller* g. Make a smaller version of the lowercase g. *Who can find* g *on the alphabet chart?* ● *Who can find* g *on the name chart?* ● *Now I'll make* g *in the salt tray.* Place the tray on the floor and let children stand to look at it.

4. Demonstrate *g* one more time using a different medium.

5. *Today, you get to make* g *with tissue paper.* Show children a finished product of a letter *g* made out of tissue paper. Demonstrate how to crumple small squares of tissue paper around the bottom of a pencil, dip it in glue, and arrange the paper in the form of the letter *g*.

ACTIVITY: THREE-DIMENSIONAL LETTERS

INSTRUCTIONAL PROCEDURE

NOTICE PARTS

See page 36 for detailed descriptions of Instructional Procedures.

ACTION TAGS

fold
glue
put

Apply

Give each child a sheet of paper with a large lowercase *g* on it. Have children make a three-dimensional letter by folding and gluing tissue paper to the outline. They can use several colors of tissue if you like.

Share

Have children hold up the letter *g*, say the letter name, and describe the verbal path of the letter. Ask them what they want to remember about the letter *g*. Look for comments that tell you what the children are noticing about the distinctive features of letters:

"A *g* has a tail."

"A *g* looks kind of like a *q*."

"I have a *g* in my name."

Assess

■ Select a familiar text from *Sing a Song of Poetry*. Have individual children point to or circle a specific letter in the text. Assess a selection of up to five different letters with each child.

■ Make a note of letters you want to revisit with particular children or with the whole group.

■ You may wish to use Letter Knowledge Assessment D.

Letter Knowledge: Recognize the Distinctive Features of Letter Forms

Connect Learning Across Contexts

Interactive Read-Aloud Read aloud alphabet books.

IRA *B Is for Bulldozer* by June Sobel

IRA *A, My Name Is Alice* by Jane Bayer

Shared Reading See "This Is the Way We Wash Our Face" in *Words That Sing* (2019). If you don't have these poetry charts, enlarge the print of this poem or other poems such as "The Alphabet Song" or "Great *A*" in *Sing a Song of Poetry*, and have children use a highlighter to point out a particular letter in the text. You may also wish to use the following Shared Reading title from *Fountas & Pinnell Classroom*™ to point out more letters.

SR *Country ABCs* by Finnoula Louise

Interactive Writing Describe the verbal path while forming a difficult letter on the small whiteboard so the child will have a model. When a child is forming a letter in front of other children, use language to describe her motions.

Independent Writing Encourage children to use efficient motions when forming letters and to describe the motions as they make them.

Extend Learning

- Repeat the lesson with other letters, varying the media. Children might make the letter out of modeling clay; glue together beans, macaroni, or buttons in the shape of the letter; write the letter on a piece of paper in different sizes and colors; use a letter stamp to make the letter; or draw three things whose names begin with that letter.

- Have children make their first names by gluing tissue paper or buttons together in the shapes of the letters.

- Have children "paint" letters on schoolyard cement with water, or write letters on the cement with colored chalk.

▶ Connect with Home

Have children take home the letters they make. Give caregivers copies of the Verbal Path for the Formation of Letters and ask them to have children explain to them how to make the letters.

Recognize Letters and State Their Names

Plan

▶ Consider Your Children

This lesson establishes procedures for "reading" the Alphabet Linking Chart and using it as a tool. It is especially helpful to children who have not noticed the features or shapes of letters and who do not know many letter names. It will help all children learn how to use the chart as a tool as they do their own writing.

▶ Working with English Language Learners

The Alphabet Linking Chart is a tool that will be very helpful to English language learners. Many repetitions of reading this chart will help children internalize the names of the letters of the alphabet and connect them with the letters' shapes. Varying the task will help English language learners become automatic with the letter names, which will help them understand and respond to classroom instruction.

YOU WILL NEED

 Ready Resources
- ▶ Alphabet Linking Chart

Online Resources
- ▶ LK 6 Action Tags
- ▶ LK 6 Alphabet Linking Charts

Other Materials
- ▶ pointer

 Generative Lesson

A generative lesson has a simple structure that you can use to present similar content or concepts. You can use this lesson structure to teach children to recognize and state a variety of letter names.

UNDERSTAND THE PRINCIPLE

The ability to recognize and name letters is an important tool for beginning readers and writers. Although the names of letters do not necessarily match the sound they represent, they are part of the language of the classroom. Knowing letter names and shapes should become quick and automatic.

EXPLAIN THE PRINCIPLE

Look at the shape of a letter and say its name.

 Comprehensive Phonics, Spelling, and Word Study Guide

Refer to: page **22**, row **2**

**ACTIVITY: ALPHABET
LINKING CHART**

**INSTRUCTIONAL
PROCEDURE**

SEE AND SAY

*See page 36 for detailed
descriptions of Instructional
Procedures.*

EXPLAIN THE PRINCIPLE

*Look at the shape of a letter and
say its name.*

Comprehensive
Phonics, Spelling,
and Word Study
Guide

Refer to:
page **22**, row **2**

Teach

1. Explain to children that you will work together to learn more about the names of letters.

2. *Today we are going to learn some ways to read the Alphabet Linking Chart. This chart is important because it helps you remember the names of the letters and how they look. You can practice reading the Alphabet Linking Chart to help you remember the names and shapes of letters.*

3. Read the chart letter by letter, using a thin pointer. Be sure that the pointer (or your arm) does not obscure children's view of the letters. Say the letters out loud: *a, b, c, d*, etc. *That's one way to read the chart. Let's do it together.* Repeat with the children.

4. *Now let's read it another way. This time I am going to skip every other letter: a, c, e, g, etc.* Have children join you. This task will be much more difficult for them, so you may need to move slowly. They will have to look at the letters carefully. If children find this task challenging, repeat reading every other letter a couple of times. Save steps 5 and 6 for another lesson.

5. *Now I'm going to show you another way. This time I am going to read the letters and say the names of the pictures: a–apple, b–bear, etc.* Have the children join you.

6. *Let's try one more way. This time I am going to read just the words under the pictures: apple, bear, cat, dog, egg, etc.* Have the children join you.

7. *We'll be learning lots of ways to read this chart. Today, each of you will be getting a small copy of this chart. Take your pointing finger or a chopstick and read the chart two different ways. Then bring your chart to sharing time.* Demonstrate the process with a partner.

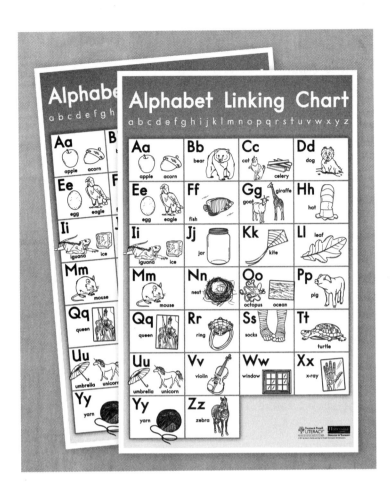

INSTRUCTIONAL PROCEDURE

SEE AND SAY

See page 36 for detailed descriptions of Instructional Procedures.

ACTION TAGS

read

color

Apply

Children work with a partner. They take turns reading the chart in different ways. One variation of the activity is to have the first child read the chart in one way. The second child reads it in the same way and then in a different way, which the first child repeats. Then they color their charts.

Share

Have children demonstrate different ways of reading the chart.

Assess

- Notice whether the children can find letters quickly on the Alphabet Linking Chart.
- Check whether the children can say the names of letters quickly.
- Observe whether the children use the Alphabet Linking Chart as a resource during interactive or independent writing.
- Point randomly to letters on the chart, asking children to say the names of the letters and the names of the pictures.
- Using a shuffled pile of lowercase letter cards, individually test children, noting the letter names they know and the ones they need to learn.
- You may wish to use Letter Knowledge Assessment A or D.

Letter Knowledge: Recognize Letters and State Their Names

Connect Learning Across Contexts

Interactive Read-Aloud Read aloud a variety of alphabet books.

 IRA *Alphabet Under Construction* by Denise Fleming

IRA *On Market Street* by Arthur and Anita Lobel

Shared Reading See "Willaby, Wallaby, Woo" in *Words That Sing* (2019). If you don't have these poetry charts, enlarge the print of this poem or other poems such as "Apples, Peaches" or "The Beach" in *Sing a Song of Poetry*. Name a letter of the alphabet, and have children use highlighter tape to locate the letter in the text. You may also wish to use the following Shared Reading title from *Fountas & Pinnell Classroom*™ to locate more letters.

SR *Country ABCs* by Finnoula Louise

Interactive Writing Help children locate a letter needed in a piece of writing by saying the name of the letter. Make connections with the Alphabet Linking Chart and with the class name chart.

Independent Writing Point out letters by name when conferring with children about their writing.

Extend Learning

As children learn more about letters, teach them different ways to read the Alphabet Linking Chart:

Read every other box, starting sometimes with *a* and sometimes with *b*.

Start in the middle or end of the chart and read back to the beginning.

Read only the letters.

Say the names of the pictures.

Read only the words under the pictures.

Read only the consonants or vowels.

Read down the columns.

▶ Connect with Home

Give children a copy of the Alphabet Linking Chart to read at home. Suggest that family members sing it as an alphabet song, read the lowercase letters, read the words (*apple-bear-cat-dog*), start with the last box, read only the vowels or consonants, or use some other variation.

Recognize Letters and State Their Names

Plan

▶ Consider Your Children

Use this lesson after children have learned a few letters. This lesson will not be necessary for children who already know and can identify lowercase letters, but you may want to use the poem for enjoyment or to develop other strategies, such as word-by-word matching.

▶ Working with English Language Learners

This lesson brings the alphabet together for English language learners and helps them understand it as a finite set of letters. You may want to work with the poem over several days, being sure children understand the meaning, before you ask them to name and locate letters. Once they have learned the poem, it will become an important resource for noticing, locating, and naming letters. Help English language learners to make connections between this poem and the Alphabet Linking Chart. Provide opportunities for individual children or small groups to read all of the alphabet charts in the room, as well as the poem. English letter names may be unfamiliar to children who have talked about letters in another language. Play some extra games with English language learners to help them quickly locate letters in the poem or on the chart as you say the name of the letter.

YOU WILL NEED

PWS Ready Resources
  ▶ Alphabet Strips

Online Resources
  ▶ LK 7 Action Tags

Other Materials
  ▶ chart with poem
  ▶ pointer
  ▶ letter tiles or magnetic letters
  ▶ cups for letters

Generative Lesson ✔

A generative lesson has a simple structure that you can use to present similar content or concepts. You can use this lesson structure to teach children to recognize and state a variety of letter names.

UNDERSTAND THE PRINCIPLE

The ability to recognize and name letters is an important tool for beginning readers and writers. Although the names of letters do not necessarily match the sound they represent, they are part of the language of the classroom. Knowing letter names and shapes should become quick and automatic. Knowing how to look at print is basic to making letter-sound connections.

EXPLAIN THE PRINCIPLE

Look at the shape of a letter and say its name.

Comprehensive Phonics, Spelling, and Word Study Guide

Refer to: page 22, row 2

ACTIVITY: POEM

INSTRUCTIONAL PROCEDURE

SEE AND SAY

See page 36 for detailed descriptions of Instructional Procedures.

EXPLAIN THE PRINCIPLE

Look at the shape of a letter and say its name.

Comprehensive Phonics, Spelling, and Word Study Guide

Refer to: page **22**, row **2**

Room 4

a   b   c   d   e

Room 4 is the place to be.

f   g   h   i   j

We will work and we will play.

k   l   m   n   o

Together we will learn and grow.

p   q   r   s   t

I'll help you and you'll help me.

u   v   w   x   y

So give a wave and just say "Hi."

z   z   z   z   z

Room 4 is the place to be!

Teach

1. Display the poem you have written on chart paper. Tell the children you are going to teach them more about letters.

2. Read the title and then read the poem.

3. Ask children what they notice in the poem: e.g., letters they know, the alphabet.

4. Guide children to notice lots of different letters. Point out that each has a name.

5. Point as you reread the poem.

6. Reread the poem with the children joining in.

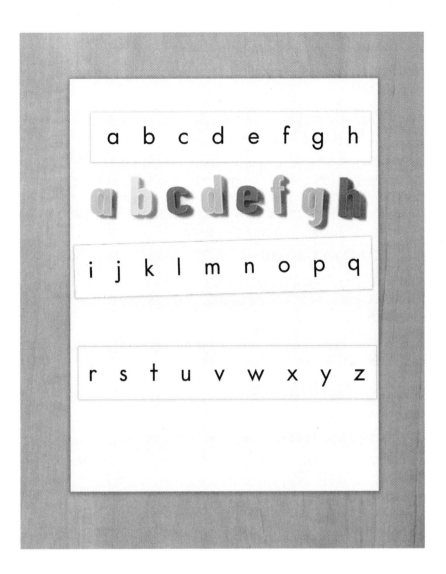

INSTRUCTIONAL PROCEDURE

FIND AND MATCH

See page 36 for detailed descriptions of Instructional Procedures.

ACTION TAGS

take
match
say
check

Apply

Have pairs of children work on a flat surface. Tell them to take letter tiles or magnetic letters from a cup and place them under the Alphabet Sheets to match each letter, saying the name of the letter as they match it. After their partner checks their work, they mix up the letters and reverse roles.

Share

Ask children to locate letters that match one or more letters in their names.

Assess

- Note how quickly children are able to match letters. Note the letters for which most children know the names.

- Give quick letter-recognition tests to inventory children's letter-name knowledge at different times during the year.

- You may wish to use Letter Knowledge Assessment A or D.

Connect Learning Across Contexts

Interactive Read-Aloud Read aloud several alphabet books that reinforce the names of letters.

> [IRA] *ABC Like Me* by Nancy Carlson

> [IRA] *B Is for Bulldozer* by June Sobel

Shared Reading See "Hickory, Dickory, Dare!" in *Words That Sing* (2019). If you don't have these poetry charts, enlarge the print of this poem or other poems such as "The Alphabet Song" in *Sing a Song of Poetry,* and have children sing the song while you point to the text. You may also wish to use the following Shared Reading title from *Fountas & Pinnell Classroom™.*

> [SR] *City ABCs* by Finnoula Louise

Interactive Writing Display the class list and read the names, pointing out the first lowercase letter of each. Place bright highlighter tape on the lowercase letters of each name.

Independent Writing When children are attempting to write a letter and need support, show them a magnetic letter as an example.

Extend Learning

- Have children point out lowercase letters in the poem.
- Have children match lowercase magnetic letters to an uppercase Alphabet Sheets.
- Have children match uppercase magnetic letters to a lowercase Alphabet Sheets.

▶ Connect with Home

Encourage caregivers to sing "The Alphabet Song" with their children, to read alphabet books, and to help their children notice the lowercase letters on boxes in the supermarket and on street signs.

Recognize Letters and State Their Names

Plan

▶ Consider Your Children

Use this lesson when the children are very familiar with the letters in their own names, as well as with the order of those letters. This lesson requires children to think about letter order in their names as they consider individual letters, so the task is challenging.

▶ Working with English Language Learners

English language learners may need to work in small groups with you as they attempt to play alphabet soup for the first time. Provide many opportunities for them to repeat the language they need to use, simplifying it if necessary.

YOU WILL NEED

Online Resources
- ▶ LK 8 Action Tags

Other Materials
- ▶ *Alphabet Soup* by Kate Banks
- ▶ packets or envelopes of individual handwritten letters that make up each child's name
- ▶ small bowls
- ▶ stirring utensils

Generative Lesson

A generative lesson has a simple structure that you can use to present similar content or concepts. You can use this lesson structure to teach children to recognize and recall a variety of letter names.

UNDERSTAND THE PRINCIPLE

The ability to recognize and name letters is an important tool for beginning readers and writers. Although the names of letters do not necessarily match the sound they represent, they are part of the language of the classroom. Knowing letter names and shapes should become quick and automatic. In this lesson, children give close attention to letter features and letter names as they work with their own names. They also explore the idea that in a word (in this case, a name), the letters are always in a particular order.

EXPLAIN THE PRINCIPLE

Look at the shape of a letter and say its name.

Comprehensive Phonics, Spelling, and Word Study Guide

Refer to: page **22**, row **2**

ACTIVITY:
ALPHABET SOUP

**INSTRUCTIONAL
PROCEDURE**

SEE AND SAY

*See page 36 for detailed
descriptions of Instructional
Procedures.*

EXPLAIN THE PRINCIPLE

*Look at the shape of a letter and
say its name.*

Comprehensive
Phonics, Spelling,
and Word Study
Guide

Refer to:
page **22**, row **2**

Teach

1. Prepare packets or
   envelopes of individual
   handwritten letters that
   make up each child's
   name for this activity.

2. Read the book *Alphabet
   Soup* by Kate Banks. If it is
   unavailable to you, give a
   summary of the story: *As
   he eats a bowl of soup
   with noodles in the shapes
   of letters, a boy imagines
   himself on an adventure.
   To overcome a series of difficulties, the boy dips his spoon into his soup and
   uses letters to make the words of the things he needs. The words the boy
   makes are* sword, boat, net, rope, tree, cage, house, *and* bed. *The purpose of
   the story is to get children interested in letters and their associations.*

3. *You know that we have letters in our names, and there are letters in alphabet
   soup, too! Today we are going to make alphabet soup with our names.* Ask for
   a pair of volunteers to come up to the front of the group with their name
   packets.

4. Have a small bowl available. Ask for two volunteers. Ask the two children to
   dump their names into the bowl. Then stir the letters and invite both children
   to help.

5. *Jamal is going to go first. Jamal, take one letter out of our bowl of alphabet
   soup.* Child demonstrates. *Jamal, does that letter belong in your name?* Jamal
   responds, "Yes."

6. *Jamal is going to say the name of a food that begins with this letter, which is in
   his name. Jamal, say this: "I have a lowercase* a *and it goes in my name,* Jamal.
   A *is for* apple." The child demonstrates.

7. *This letter is in Jamal's name, so he gets to keep it. If it doesn't belong in his
   name—for example, if it is a* y—*he'll put it back in the soup bowl. Then Tony will
   take a turn.*

8. Continue demonstrating until the bowl is empty and the children have all the
   letters in their names. *So Jamal and Tony have all of the letters in their names.
   They are going to put their names together, read them, and then check each
   other's names.* Children can check the names with the class name chart.

9. *Today you learned that you can recognize the letters in your names even if
   they are mixed into your alphabet soup. You also learned that you can think of
   food that begins like the letters of your names.* Explain that the children will
   play the alphabet soup game in pairs.

**ACTIVITY:
ALPHABET SOUP**

INSTRUCTIONAL PROCEDURE

SEE AND SAY

See page 36 for detailed descriptions of Instructional Procedures.

ACTION TAGS

mix
take
say letter name
say food
make name

Apply

Children pair up and play alphabet soup. Using bowls and utensils for stirring, they mix the letters. Then one child takes a letter and says its name. If the letter is in that child's name, she gives the name of a food that starts with the letter. The partners take turns until they have picked all of the letters. Then they make their names and check each other's work.

Share

Have children talk about what they learned about their names. Also ask them to share some of the foods they thought of in connection with their names. Demonstrate and look for comments such as these:

"My name has two s's."

"My name starts with uppercase *M*."

"*Peppers* and *Pedro* start with the same letter."

Assess

- Notice whether the children can recognize the letters of their names and put them together in the correct order.
- Observe whether letter recognition is becoming quick and automatic.
- During writing time, conduct a quick check by asking children to name the letters in their names.
- You may wish to use Letter Knowledge Assessment A or D.

Connect Learning Across Contexts

Interactive Read-Aloud Read aloud books that connect children's names with sounds of letters.

> IRA *Lola at the Library* by Anna McQuinn
>
> IRA *Wemberly Worried* by Kevin Henkes

Shared Reading See "Lucy Locket" in *Words That Sing* (2019). If you don't have these poetry charts, enlarge the print of this poem or other poems such as "Bingo" or "The Alphabet Song" in *Sing a Song of Poetry,* to learn and reinforce letter-name knowledge. You may also wish to use the following Shared Reading title from *Fountas & Pinnell Classroom*™.

> SR *Miss Mary Mack* by Susannah Franco

Interactive Writing Take the opportunity to have children name letters within the context of creating a text. Consider making an Alphabet Soup book or mural, with each child drawing a picture of a food that begins like his or her name and the group creating a label for that food with a shared pencil or marker.

Independent Writing Provide each child with a template of a bowl. Have children draw food items that start like each letter in their names and label the foods. They can use approximated spelling.

Extend Learning

- To make the task easier, have children name the letter but not a food that begins with it.
- Children can play the game again with a different partner.
- Children can play the game with last-name packets.
- Children can play the game with four players, increasing the challenge. They can also make one another's names.

▶ Connect with Home

Have children take home some letter cards with which to make their names and the names of their family members. Have them teach a family member how to play alphabet soup. Encourage them to play the game several times with different family members.

Understand That Words Are Formed with Letters

Plan

▶ Consider Your Children

This lesson works best when a number of children can read their own names and some of the names of other children. Think about whether children are beginning to understand the concept of "first" as it applies to the letters in words and whether they have familiarity with the letters in their names. This lesson will help them generalize their knowledge about names and notice letters in names. It will also help them to connect first letters and sounds.

▶ Working with English Language Learners

Help English language learners say the names of all the children in the classroom. Provide as many repetitions as needed, but accept approximations in phonology. This lesson will provide personal connections and examples that will help children connect letters and sounds. It is important that you pronounce the children's names in the way that they pronounce them.

YOU WILL NEED

PWS Ready Resources
- ▶ Alphabet Strips
- ▶ Blank Pocket-Chart Cards
- ▶ Pocket-Chart Letter Cards

Online Resources
- ▶ LK 9 Action Tags
- ▶ LK 9 Blank Word Cards

Other Materials
- ▶ pocket chart

UNDERSTAND THE PRINCIPLE

A word is made with one or more letters. A name is made with letters. Saying and looking at the letters in their names helps children notice the orientation and distinguishing features of each letter. These details help children begin to recognize words and spelling patterns on sight. Children begin to make connections between names and to generalize knowledge of first letters. They also learn aspects of word structure such as number of letters and ending letters.

EXPLAIN THE PRINCIPLE

Put letters together to make a word.

Your name is a word.

Put letters together to make your name.

Say the letters in your name.

Comprehensive
Phonics, Spelling,
and Word Study
Guide

Refer to:
page **23**, row **9**

ACTIVITY: NAME COUNT

INSTRUCTIONAL PROCEDURE

SAY AND SORT

See page 36 for detailed descriptions of Instructional Procedures.

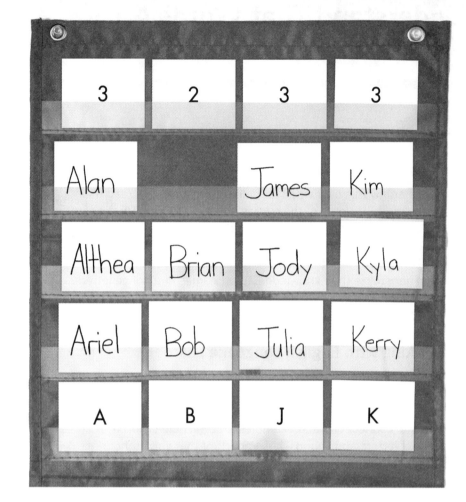

EXPLAIN THE PRINCIPLE

Put letters together to make a word.

Your name is a word.

Put letters together to make your name.

Say the letters in your name.

Comprehensive Phonics, Spelling, and Word Study Guide

Refer to:
page **23**, row **9**

Teach

1. Tell the children that they can learn a lot about letters from their names.

2. Use the pocket-chart cards to make a name card for each child and letter cards for first letters of all children's names. Show children the name cards one at a time. Ask them to read the name of the person on the card and to identify the first letter.

3. *Today we are going to see how many of you have the same first letter in your names. Whose name is this?* Hold up the card for *Ariel.* ● *What is the first letter?* ● *That's right, an* A. *I'm going to put this name right above the* A *on our pocket chart. Whose name is this?* Hold up a name that begins with another letter.

4. Continue showing the names and asking children to categorize them on the pocket chart. Place them above the previous cards, building a graph.

5. Then count the number of children in each letter category. Using additional pocket-chart cards, place the number above the column for each letter.

6. Prepare for the Apply activity by writing children's names on the page of blank word cards and reproducing the page so each child can have a copy.

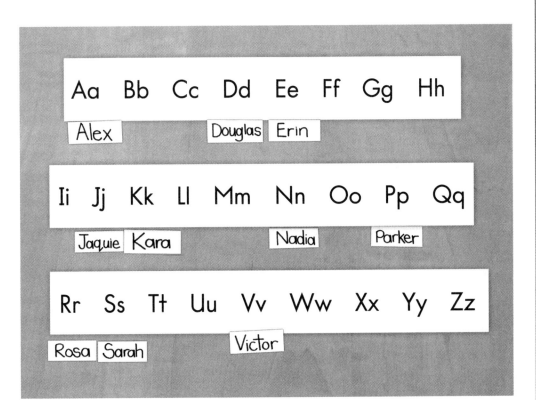

INSTRUCTIONAL PROCEDURE

SAY AND SORT

See page 36 for detailed descriptions of Instructional Procedures.

ACTION TAGS

cut
say
sort

Apply

Distribute a sheet of name cards to each child and have children cut out the names. Place each child's alphabet strips on a tabletop. Have children say each name and place it under the appropriate first letter along the alphabet strips.

Share

Invite children to discuss what they have noticed about their own names and the names of their classmates. Elicit comments such as these:

"*Ariel* and *Alan* start with the same letter."

"Two people have names that start with *R*."

"Four people have names that start with *M*."

"*Jody* and *James* start with the same letter."

Assess

■ Observe children's ability to remember the first letters of their names and the first letters of the names of others.

■ Notice children's use of their own names and the names of classmates as resources for writing words.

■ Observe children's ability to make connections to names during interactive writing.

Connect Learning Across Contexts

Interactive Read-Aloud Read aloud books that contain alliteration. Point out that the words sound the same at the beginning because they start with the same letter–like *Jody*, *James*, and *John*.

   [IRA] *A, My Name Is Alice* by Jane Bayer

   [IRA] *Cat's Colors* by Jane Cabrera

Shared Reading See "Puppies and Kittens" in *Words That Sing* (2019). If you don't have these poetry charts, enlarge the print of this poem or other poems such as "Peas" in *Sing a Song of Poetry,* and have children use highlighter tape to find names that begin with certain letters [*I'm thinking of a word in the text that begins like Peter*]. You may also wish to use the following Shared Reading title from *Fountas & Pinnell Classroom*™.

   [SR] *Kate's Party* by Jane Simon

Interactive Writing Make connections to first letters of names on the class name chart when writing words.

Independent Writing Encourage children to use the class name chart as a resource for their writing: for example, how to start a word.

Extend Learning

- Repeat the lesson with the children's last names.
- Repeat the lesson, this time counting the number of letters in names and sorting them that way.

▶ Connect with Home

Have children sort the names of their classmates and family members at home. In addition, encourage family members to cut up children's names into letter squares to make puzzles they can put together. Suggest that they count the letters and say the letter names when they are finished.

Recognize the Sequence of Letters in a Word

Plan

▶ Consider Your Children

Use this lesson after children have worked with their own names and are beginning to realize that it is important to place the letters in the same order every time they build or write a word. You may want to shorten this lesson or complete the activities over several days.

▶ Working with English Language Learners

Be sure that English language learners have plenty of experience learning the song "Bingo" before they do the puzzle. Be sure that they understand that Bingo is a dog and that this song is all about his name. Once they know what the word *Bingo* looks like, you may want to have children work in a small group, taking turns pointing to the letters as they sing the part of the song that spells the name. Then work several times with children so that they understand how to omit letters. Using a name card, demonstrate how children are to put together their own names three times.

YOU WILL NEED

PWS Ready Resources
- ▶ Blank Pocket-Chart Cards

Online Resources
- ▶ LK 10 Action Tags
- ▶ LK 10 Name Cards
- ▶ LK 10 Song: There Was a Child in Kindergarten

Other Materials
- ▶ double-sided tape
- ▶ chart paper with words to "Bingo"
- ▶ envelope for each child

Generative Lesson

A generative lesson has a simple structure that you can use to present similar content or concepts. You can use this lesson structure to teach children the sequence of letters in a variety of words.

UNDERSTAND THE PRINCIPLE

Children need to learn that an individual word is constant—that is, it is always spelled the same way, with letters in the same order. The first letter of a word is on the left, and the rest of the letters in the word follow in a specific sequence. It may be big or small or in different colors, but it always has the same letters in the same order, left to right.

EXPLAIN THE PRINCIPLE

The letters in a word are always in the same order.

The first letter is on the left.

Find and name the first letter in a word.

Find and name all of the letters in a word in order.

Comprehensive Phonics, Spelling, and Word Study Guide

Refer to: page **23**, row **11**

ACTIVITY: "BINGO" SONG

INSTRUCTIONAL PROCEDURE

SEE AND SAY

See page 36 for detailed descriptions of Instructional Procedures.

EXPLAIN THE PRINCIPLE

The letters in a word are always in the same order.

The first letter is on the left.

Find and name the first letter in a word.

Find and name all of the letters in a word in order.

Comprehensive Phonics, Spelling, and Word Study Guide

Refer to: page **23**, row **11**

Teach

1. In preparation for the lesson, create a Bingo name puzzle using five pocket-chart cards, each with one letter of the name *Bingo* written on it. Each card should have double-sided tape on the back. Also have ready a name card for each child.

2. Show the chart paper with the words to the song "Bingo."

3. Introduce the song, pointing to each word as you sing it. Choose volunteers to point to the letters as you sing *B-i-n-g-o.*

> BINGO
> There was a farmer
> Had a dog
> And Bingo
> Was his name-o
> B-i-n-g-o
> B-i-n-g-o
> B-i-n-g-o
> And Bingo
> Was his name-o

4. Ask the children questions about the song: *What is the name of this dog? • How do you know? • Show me his name. • Where is the first letter of his name? • What is the first letter of his name? • What is the next letter in his name? •* Continue through the remaining letters. *Let's spell his whole name together:* B-i-n-g-o. *The letters in Bingo's name are always in the same order.*

5. Sing the complete song in the traditional way. Then continue singing the song, but substitute claps for the letters on subsequent verses, beginning with *B* and omitting each additional letter until you are clapping for all the letters.

6. Display a Bingo name puzzle.

7. Sing the song again, but when you omit the letters of the dog's name, use a slight pause instead of a clap. As you omit each additional letter, have a volunteer remove that letter from the puzzle.

8. Display the letters of the Bingo name puzzle out of order. Have children fix the letters and spell the name. Sing the song one more time.

9. Hold up a child's name card and have the child put it on the third line of the chart paper in place of the name Bingo. Have a volunteer find and say the first letter in the name. Have another volunteer say the rest of the letters in the name.

10. Introduce the words "There was a child . . ." to the tune of Bingo: *There was a child in kindergarten, And [name] was the name-o.*

11. Point to the the child's name card, and invite the children to sing the song using the child's name. Repeat for a few more children.

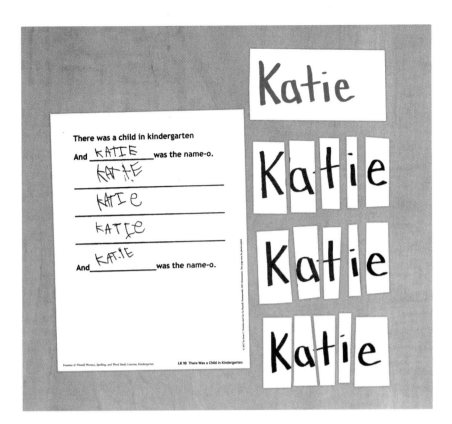

ACTIVITY: CUT-UP NAME CARDS

INSTRUCTIONAL PROCEDURE

FIND AND MATCH

See page 36 for detailed descriptions of Instructional Procedures.

ACTION TAGS

cut

match

write

Apply

- Give each child an envelope containing four name cards–three printed in black, and one printed in a color. The name card in color remains in one piece and serves as a model. Have children cut apart the other three cards by letter. Each child puts together his name three times, matching the letters with the letters on the whole card.

- Then have children write their names in the five blank spaces on the "There Was a Child in Kindergarten" Sheet.

Share

Sing the song a final time with a surprise name (e.g., a character from a storybook: Clifford, Goldilocks, Arthur).

Assess

- Notice how children begin to put together the letters in their names.

- Observe whether they are learning the printed names of other children in the class and can recognize them by the first letter.

- Notice whether children are writing their names with the letters in the correct order.

- You may wish to use Letter Knowledge Assessment D.

Letter Knowledge: Recognize the Sequence of Letters in a Word

Connect Learning Across Contexts

Interactive Read-Aloud Read aloud books about names. Invite children to think about the first letter and the rest of the letters in each name.

> IRA *Miss Bindergarten Gets Ready for Kindergarten* by Joseph Slate

> IRA *A, My Name Is Alice* by Jane Bayer

Shared Reading See "Elizabeth, Elspeth, Betsey, and Bess" in *Words That Sing* [2019]. If you don't have these poetry charts, enlarge the print of this poem or other poems such as "Mary, Mary, Quite Contrary" in *Sing a Song of Poetry,* and have children use highlighter tape to find names. Let them insert their own names into one rendition of the song. You may also wish to refer to the following Shared Reading title from *Fountas & Pinnell Classroom*™ to look at more names.

> SR *Mondo* by Quentin Ripple

Interactive Writing Relate words you are trying to write to names. Also note that words are always spelled the same. The letters are in the same order, from left to right. Connect words you are trying to write to the names of the children on the class name chart.

Independent Writing When children are trying to write new words, suggest that they refer to words they know, such as the names on the class name chart.

Extend Learning

- Repeat the lesson with names of friends or family or with names of characters that children have met in books: for example, Hansel, Gretel, Jack, Jill.
- Have each child find someone else whose name has the same first letter.
- Make a class big book with one page for each child. Have children draw a picture of themselves and then glue the letters of their names beneath the drawings. Use the class big book for shared reading.

▶ Connect with Home

Have children take home the envelope with their name cards so that they can put together their names at home. Also give children a copy of the "Bingo" song and invite them to sing it with family members at home.

Recognize Letters and State Their Names

Plan

▶ Consider Your Children

This lesson establishes a system for working with letter minibooks. Teach it after children are accustomed to using pencils and paper and can follow a few simple directions. Children should have some beginning understanding of how to use the class name chart and the Alphabet Linking Chart as tools. Also, they should have had some practice writing their names. Plan to introduce two or three minibooks a week over a period of eight to twelve weeks. We suggest this sequence for consonants: *b, m, r, s, t, g, n, p, c, h, f, d, l, k, j, w, y, z, v, x, q.* We suggest introducing vowels in their regular order: *a, e, i, o, u.* With some groups of children, you can introduce more than one book in a lesson.

▶ Working with English Language Learners

Letter minibooks are an important tool for English language learners. Have children use the minibooks at school until you are sure they know how to use them, store them, and care for them. These books will have pictures and names of objects, so they will help children acquire a repertoire of nouns. For each minibook, go through the pictures carefully; have children say the words that name the pictures and then read the book several times. Have them locate the first letter of each word, say the letter, and read the word.

YOU WILL NEED

PWS Ready Resources
- ▶ Alphabet Linking Chart

Online Resources
- ▶ LK 11 Action Tags
- ▶ LK 11 Letter Minibook

Other Materials
- ▶ *Mm* book model
- ▶ small storage boxes (e.g., small tissue boxes with top cut open or cereal boxes cut in half) labeled with children's names
- ▶ writing materials and crayons
- ▶ glue sticks
- ▶ name chart

Generative Lesson ✓

A generative lesson has a simple structure that you can use to present similar content or concepts. You can use this lesson structure to teach children to recognize and state a variety of letter names.

UNDERSTAND THE PRINCIPLE

The ability to recognize and name letters is an important tool for beginning readers and writers. Although the names of letters do not necessarily match the sound they represent, they are part of the language of the classroom. Knowing letter names and shapes should become quick and automatic. These skills help them understand teachers' and caregivers' language about letters. Using letter minibooks lets children practice letter names and helps them build a repertoire of words they are able to connect with beginning letters.

EXPLAIN THE PRINCIPLE

Look at the shape of a letter and say its name.

Comprehensive Phonics, Spelling, and Word Study Guide

Refer to: page **22**, row **2**

11 LETTER KNOWLEDGE

EARLY **MIDDLE** LATE

ACTIVITY: LETTER MINIBOOKS

INSTRUCTIONAL PROCEDURE

SEE AND SAY

See page 36 for detailed descriptions of Instructional Procedures.

EXPLAIN THE PRINCIPLE

Look at the shape of a letter and say its name.

Comprehensive Phonics, Spelling, and Word Study Guide

Refer to: page **22**, row **2**

Teach

1. Create a letter *Mm* minibook for each child. Refer to the letter minibook template for folding and cutting instructions.

2. Show the children a boxed set of letter books and tell them they will each be getting their own box and set of books. *Today you are going to get a letter book, and I am going to show you what to do with it.* Show the *Mm* book. *This book is about the letter . . .*

3. *The letter m. This book has two ms on the front. This is the uppercase M, and this is the lowercase m.* Point to the uppercase and lowercase letters. *I am going to write my name on the front cover.* Demonstrate.

4. Show the second page of the book and point to the letter. *On this page, it says m at the top, and here is a picture of a mouse. Here is the word* mouse, *which has an m at the beginning.*

5. *On this page, I read the letter m, at the top. Then I say the name of the picture,* mouse. *Then I read the word* mouse, *and the first time I read the book, I'm going to trace over the letter m.* Demonstrate the same process on the page for *mop.*

6. *On the last page, I see the m at the top and I get to choose (or draw) a picture to go with m.* Children can use picture cards, or you may guide them to draw something. Demonstrate gluing in a picture. Don't write the label, as children will perform this task independently.

7. *Now I'm going to show you how to read your book.* Go through the book reading the letter, saying the name of the picture, and then reading the name of the picture.

8. *Today you are going to work on your own Mm book. You are going to write your name on the line on the first page. On the next page, you will read the letter m, say the name of the picture, and trace the m on the name of the picture. Do the same on page 3. On the last page, you will trace the m, glue or draw a picture that begins with m, and write the word below the picture. Then you will point to the letters as you reread your whole letter book.*

ACTIVITY: LETTER Mm MINIBOOKS

INSTRUCTIONAL PROCEDURE

SEE AND SAY

See page 36 for detailed descriptions of Instructional Procedures.

ACTION TAGS

write name
read
trace
draw
read
color

Apply

Have children make and read *Mm* books. You can circulate and help them perform the different steps. After making the books, children can color the pictures. Once children have learned how to make their first minibook, they can repeat the same steps on their own with other letters.

Share

Have each child tell another child the name of the picture glued in or drawn. Show them how to read their books to a partner, taking turns pointing and reading. Have children make connections to the class name chart by noticing names that include the letter *m*. Also, make connections to the Alphabet Linking Chart.

Assess

- Observe whether the children can locate letters by name.
- Observe whether the children can name letters correctly.
- Give a quick letter-naming test with uppercase and lowercase letter cards or a letter chart (or use the letter minibooks); don't present the letters in alphabetical order.
- You may wish to use Letter Knowledge Assessment A or D.

Connect Learning Across Contexts

Interactive Read-Aloud Read aloud alphabet books.

　[IRA] *B Is for Bulldozer* by June Sobel

　[IRA] *On Market Street* by Arthur and Anita Lobel

Shared Reading See "My Head" in *Words That Sing* (2019). If you don't have these poetry charts, enlarge the print of this poem or other poems such as "Bouncing Ball" or "Cackle, Cackle, Mother Goose" in *Sing a Song of Poetry.* Name some letters and have children use highlighter tape to locate them in the text. You may also wish to use the following Shared Reading title from *Fountas & Pinnell Classroom*™.

　[SR] *City ABCs* by Finnoula Louise

Interactive Writing Use letter names to help children identify a letter needed in a piece of writing. Make connections with the Alphabet Linking Chart and the class name chart.

Independent Writing Pull out a particular letter minibook to help a child associate a sound he wants to write with the correct letter.

Extend Learning

- Repeat this lesson with different letter books (maybe two or three letters at a time).

- Repeat the instructions for making a minibook until children understand them and can perform the steps independently. (Post simple directions with pictures if needed.) Then work quickly on each successive letter, saying its name and linking it to the Alphabet Linking Chart, the class name chart, and any other print in the room.

- Children can select their letter minibooks from a tray and work with them independently.

- Have children read all the books in their letter boxes, or have a small group read their books to partners.

▶ Connect with Home

After children have practiced the routines for eleven or twelve books, you can send the storage boxes home, and children can then take the books home as they make them. Encourage family members to keep the box in a special place and to make sure the books are always stored there. Have children read each book to a family member.

Recognize Letters and State Their Names

Plan

▶ Consider Your Children

This lesson will be effective for children who know the first letters of their names but do not have automatic recall and recognition of them. Using letter-sound knowledge efficiently in reading and writing requires rapid automatic processing of print. This lesson will provide the necessary practice.

▶ Working with English Language Learners

Go over the marching song as many times as necessary to help English language learners remember it and enjoy it. Names will be an important resource for English language learners. Children will like working with their own names and those of classmates. Go over names several times to be sure that everyone can easily say everyone else's name.

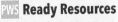

YOU WILL NEED

PWS Ready Resources
- ▶ **LK 12** Uppercase Letter Cards

Online Resources
- ▶ **LK 12** Action Tags
- ▶ **LK 12** Blank Word Cards
- ▶ **LK 12** Three-Way Sorts

Other Materials
- ▶ chart paper displaying words to "Friends' March"
- ▶ pocket chart
- ▶ double-sided tape
- ▶ glue
- ▶ envelopes for extra names

Generative Lesson ✓

A generative lesson has a simple structure that you can use to present similar content or concepts. You can use this lesson structure to teach children to recognize a variety of letters.

UNDERSTAND THE PRINCIPLE

The ability to recognize and name letters is an important tool for beginning readers and writers. Although the names of letters do not necessarily match the sound they represent, they are part of the language of the classroom. Knowing letter names and shapes should become quick and automatic. By studying their own names, children can learn that it is important to notice the first letter and think about its name and sound. They will also be able to use the letters and sounds of their names to make connections to other words.

EXPLAIN THE PRINCIPLE

Look at the shape of a letter and say its name.

Comprehensive Phonics, Spelling, and Word Study Guide

Refer to: page **22**, row **2**

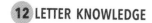

ACTIVITY: FRIENDS' MARCH SONG

INSTRUCTIONAL PROCEDURE

SAY AND SORT

See page 36 for detailed descriptions of Instructional Procedures.

EXPLAIN THE PRINCIPLE

Look at the shape of a letter and say its name.

Comprehensive Phonics, Spelling, and Word Study Guide

Refer to: page **22**, row **2**

Teach

1. Explain to the children that they are going to sing a song that will help them learn names of letters.

2. Have children practice sitting down in response to hearing the first letters of their names. *Today we are going to learn a song and a game that are about the first letter of your name.* Refer to the class name chart. *Let's practice. Everyone stand up. Now, if your name begins with C, sit down.*

3. Quickly review selected letters to refresh children's memory of the first letters of their names. Emphasize that it is important to sit down immediately when they hear the name of the first letter of their names.

4. Teach children to sing "Friends' March" (sung to the tune of "When Johnny Comes Marching Home"). At this point, make this an oral activity; don't worry about shared reading from the chart. Once children are familiar with the song, you can use the chart for shared reading, inserting self-adhesive pocket-chart cards with first letters of the children's names (use double-sided tape). Children can also use this chart for independent reading later.

5. Have children march around in a circle and sing. Each time you change letters, hold up a letter card so they will know what is coming next. When a child hears the first letter of his name, he quickly sits down in the middle of the circle but keeps singing. (Don't let the circle get smaller; children should keep marching around the perimeter until everyone is sitting down.)

6. Place a pocket-chart letter card for each letter used in the song at the top of a pocket chart. (Large classes may require two pocket charts.) Also use the pocket-chart cards to create a name card for each child in the class.

7. Have children read and sort the names under the appropriate first letter.

> **Friends' March**
> My friends are marching
> Round and round,
> Hurrah, hurrah.
> My friends are marching
> Round and round,
> Hurrah, hurrah.
> My friends are marching
> Round and round,
> Names beginning with
> Sit down.
> And we'll march around
> Until we all sit down.

260

Apply

Use the blank word cards to create a sheet of class names, and distribute a copy to each child. Give each child a three-way sort on which you have written three letters, one at the top of each column. Have children cut apart each name, say the name, and glue it under the appropriate letter. (Have children save the extra names in an envelope, and repeat the activity later using other letters.)

Share

Have children say their own names and identify the first letter. You may also have children point to a child whose name begins with *C*, *M*, and so on.

Assess

- Observe the children's ability to quickly remember the first letter of their names.
- Notice the children's use of their names and the names of classmates as resources for writing words.
- Observe the children's ability to make connections to names during independent and interactive writing.
- You may wish to use Letter Knowledge Assessment A or D.

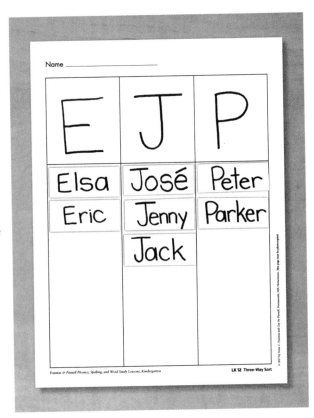

ACTIVITY: THREE-WAY LETTER SORT

INSTRUCTIONAL PROCEDURE

SAY AND SORT

See page 36 for detailed descriptions of Instructional Procedures.

ACTION TAGS

cut
sort
glue

Letter Knowledge: Recognize Letters and State Their Names

Connect Learning Across Contexts

Interactive Read-Aloud Read aloud books that have a character's name in the title. Discuss where that name would go on the chart if that character were in your class.

> IRA *Jessica* by Kevin Henkes

> IRA *Alicia's Happy Day* by Meg Starr

Shared Reading See "Here Is a House" in *Words That Sing* (2019). If you don't have these poetry charts, enlarge the print of this poem or other poems such as "Here Are My Eyes" in *Sing a Song of Poetry,* and point to and read the song several more times until the children can recognize letters quickly. You may also wish to use the following Shared Reading title from *Fountas & Pinnell Classroom™.*

> SR *Country ABCs* by Finnoula Louise

Interactive Writing Use children's names and first letters as connections to words you are writing. Children can offer names of family members as examples of names that start with certain letters if there is not an example on the class name chart.

Independent Writing Encourage children to use the class name chart as a resource for their writing: for example, for how to start a word.

Extend Learning

- Repeat the lesson with children's last names.
- Sing the song and change the verse to names *ending* with particular letters.

▶ Connect with Home

Encourage children to teach the "Friends' March" song to their family members and perhaps use it as an activity at a family event. You may also have children collect names of family members in a simple "family name book" (one name per page). Children can draw pictures of family members.

Form Letters with Writing Tools

Plan

▶ Consider Your Children

This lesson, in which children learn how to form the letters in their names efficiently, is best used after children have worked with the class name chart and name puzzles. Children should also be able to recognize and locate their names. Through writing their names, they will learn to attend more closely to detail. You may wish to punch a hole in the corner of their name cards and keep them on a ring for easy reference.

▶ Working with English Language Learners

Children are highly motivated to write their names, and this is a good place to start when teaching them to say the motions need to form letters. Do not assume that English language learners will understand your directions for making letters. You may want to work with children in small groups so that you can demonstrate the task several times. Then observe them to be sure they are using the dots or dashes to trace each letter, saying the steps, and making the letters correctly.

YOU WILL NEED

Ready Resources
- ▶ Blank Pocket-Chart Cards
- ▶ Verbal Path for the Formation of Letters
- ▶ Letter Formation Charts

Online Resources
- ▶ LK 13 Action Tags
- ▶ LK 13 Name Cards

Other Materials
- ▶ magnetic letters
- ▶ dry-erase markers
- ▶ lined paper

Generative Lesson
A generative lesson has a simple structure that you can use to present similar content or concepts. You can use this lesson structure to teach children how to form a variety of letters.

UNDERSTAND THE PRINCIPLE

Young children need to learn to form letters with efficient and consistent motions. Using consistent motions while saying aloud the steps to make individual letters improves children's memory of letters and words and develops children's writing fluency.

EXPLAIN THE PRINCIPLE

Make the shape of a letter.

Say the steps you use to make a letter.

Check to see if a letter looks right.

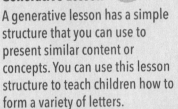

Comprehensive Phonics, Spelling, and Word Study Guide

Refer to: page **23**, row **14**

ACTIVITY: TRACED LETTERS

INSTRUCTIONAL PROCEDURE

SAY AND WRITE

See page 36 for detailed descriptions of Instructional Procedures.

EXPLAIN THE PRINCIPLE

Make the shape of a letter.

Say the steps you use to make a letter.

Check to see if a letter looks right.

Comprehensive Phonics, Spelling, and Word Study Guide

Refer to: page **23**, row **14**

Teach

1. Have ready some pocket-chart cards for you and each of the children. Write each child's name on one side; place dotted outlines of the letters in the name on the other side.

2. Tell the children they are going to learn more about writing the letters in their names. Post the Letter Formation Charts for reference.

3. *You will each have a name card.* Show the side of a name card that has one child's name written clearly. *Here is Atory's name.* Point out the uppercase letter at the beginning and the lowercase letters in the rest of the name. Emphasize how the letters are placed right next to each other in a special order.

4. *You are going to look at your name on your name card. Then you will make your name with magnetic letters. Will the first letter of your name be on the left or on the right? • The first letter will be on the left. Then you will add each letter, moving from the left to right. It is important to get the letters in the correct order.*

5. Explain that you are now going to trace the letters of Atory's name. Show the other side of the card, and, first with your finger and then with a dry-erase marker, trace each letter, using the arrows in the Letter Formation Charts as a guide. *Do you see how you make the shape of each letter? You can say the steps you use to make each letter.* As you write, use the language in the Verbal Path for Formation of Letters to describe the motions.

6. *After you make your name with magnetic letters, and after you have traced the letters of your name, you can write the letters in your name. As you write the letters, you can say the steps you use to make them.*

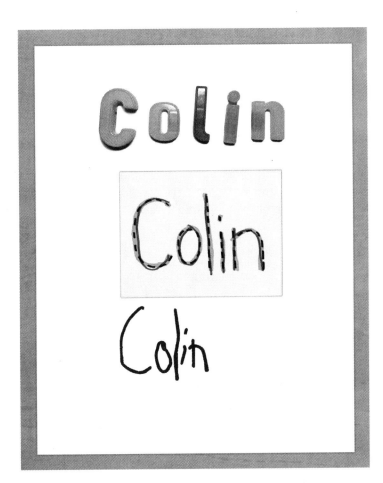

INSTRUCTIONAL PROCEDURE

SAY AND WRITE

See page 36 for detailed descriptions of Instructional Procedures.

ACTION TAGS

make
trace (with finger)
trace (with marker)
write

Apply

Have children use magnetic letters to make their names, using the fully written side of the name card as a model. Then have them trace the dotted outlines of the letters on the other side of the card, first with a finger and then with a dry-erase marker, referring to the Letter Formation Chart as a guide. Finally, have them use lined paper to write their names. Encourage children to say the steps they use to make each letter.

Share

Invite the children to bring their name cards to show at the group meeting.

Assess

- Observe whether children are forming letters efficiently and correctly.
- Notice whether children are attempting to say the steps they use to make each letter.
- Have the children write the alphabet so you have evidence of their letter formation.
- You may wish to use Letter Knowledge Assessment B or E.

13 LETTER KNOWLEDGE

EARLY **MIDDLE** LATE

Connect Learning Across Contexts

Interactive Read-Aloud Read aloud books about letters and/or names.

IRA *Mary Wore Her Red Dress and Henry Wore His Green Sneakers* by Merle Peek

IRA *Jessica* by Kevin Henkes

Shared Reading See "Elizabeth, Elspeth, Betsey, and Bess" in *Words That Sing* (2019). If you don't have these poetry charts, enlarge the print of this poem or other poems such as "Johnny Taps with One Hammer" and "Rain, Rain, Go Away" in *Sing a Song of Poetry,* and incorporate the children's names into the text. You may also wish to use the following Shared Reading title from *Fountas & Pinnell Classroom*™.

SR *Molly's Leash* by Susan Scott

Interactive Writing As children contribute letters, guide their formation using the Letter Formation Charts.

Independent Writing As children write, reinforce correct letter formation. Tape the Letter Formation Charts in clear view.

Extend Learning

- Repeat the lesson for more practice.
- Have children write the names of their peers.
- Repeat the lesson with last names.
- Repeat the lesson, having the children write their names with other writing tools—markers, paintbrushes, crayons.

▶ Connect with Home

Photocopy the children's dotted-outline names for them to take home and trace with their family members.

266

Fountas & Pinnell Phonics, Spelling, and Word Study Lessons, Kindergarten

Form Letters with Writing Tools

Plan

▶ Consider Your Children

The procedures described in this lesson may be used many times for different lowercase and uppercase letters. Begin with the lowercase letters; they are more useful for children, and children also encounter them more frequently in the texts they read. Work on letters that most children know or nearly know. Use children's names as a resource to make connections to letters. Start with unlined paper; children should have good control of efficient movements before they are asked to attend to variables such as size and lines. Once children have developed systems for learning a verbal path, lessons can be quite short.

▶ Working with English Language Learners

Be sure that English language learners hear and say the verbal directions enough times to know what they mean. As they do more handwriting and think about and say the motions, they will take on new letters faster. At a meeting for caregivers, demonstrate making some letters while saying the steps of letter formation so that caregivers know the reason children are using the verbal path and what it means.

YOU WILL NEED

PWS Ready Resources
- ▶ Verbal Path for the Formation of Letters
- ▶ Letters Made in Similar Ways
- ▶ Letter Formation Charts

Online Resources
- ▶ LK 14 Action Tags

Other Materials
- ▶ magnetic drawing board, whiteboard and dry-erase marker, or chart paper on easel
- ▶ sand or salt in a box or tray
- ▶ sandpaper letters
- ▶ newsprint paper
- ▶ crayons

✓ Generative Lesson

A generative lesson has a simple structure that you can use to present similar content or concepts. You can use this lesson structure to teach children to form a variety of letters.

UNDERSTAND THE PRINCIPLE

Young children need to learn to form letters with efficient and consistent motions. Using consistent motions while saying aloud the steps to make individual letters improves children's memory of letters and words and develops children's writing fluency. An additional benefit is the growing legibility of their handwriting.

EXPLAIN THE PRINCIPLE

Make the shape of a letter.

Say the steps you use to make a letter.

Check to see if a letter looks right.

Comprehensive Phonics, Spelling, and Word Study Guide

Refer to:
page **23**, row **14**

ACTIVITY: VERBAL PATH

INSTRUCTIONAL PROCEDURE

SAY AND WRITE

See page 36 for detailed descriptions of Instructional Procedures.

EXPLAIN THE PRINCIPLE

Make the shape of a letter.

Say the steps you use to make a letter.

Check to see if a letter looks right.

Comprehensive Phonics, Spelling, and Word Study Guide

Refer to:
page **23**, row **14**

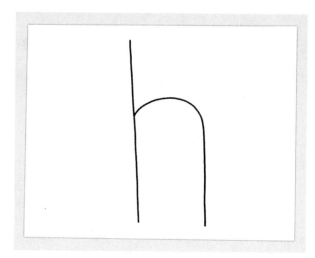

Teach

1. Explain to the children that they are going to learn more about how to make good letters.

2. Say the name of a letter. Then, using a magnetic drawing board or chart paper, demonstrate how it is formed using the simple, clear language in the Verbal Path for the Formation of Letters: *I'm going to make an* h. *To make a lowercase* h, *you pull down, up, over, and down.* Make the letter slowly as you describe the movement.

3. Make the letter again, inviting the children to say the verbal path with you as you write.

4. Invite the children to talk through the movements as you make the letter in the air a few times and then on the floor in front of them.

5. Over time, work with a group of letters that start in the same place—*h, l,* and *b,* for example. Refer to Letters Made in Similar Ways.

Apply

- On large pieces of newsprint, make "rainbow letters" with the group. Write a letter in pencil and place dots and arrows on it with black marker. Then each child, in turn, while saying the motions, traces the letter on the newsprint using a different-color crayon. At the end, you will have a large letter written in a number of different colors. One child can take it home–perhaps someone whose name contains the letter.

- Have children make a selection of letters, talking through the motions as they do so. You may wish to demonstrate one or more ways children can make letters: for example, trace sandpaper letters; trace letters on laminated Letter Formation Charts with a dry-erase marker; write the letter in salt or sand in a flat tray or box; write the letter on paper with a crayon.

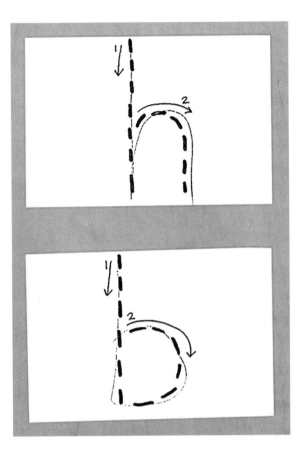

ACTIVITY: RAINBOW LETTERS

INSTRUCTIONAL PROCEDURE

SAY AND WRITE

See page 36 for detailed descriptions of Instructional Procedures.

ACTION TAGS

trace
write

Share

Ask what children noticed about the letters they made today. Look for comments such as these:

"They are all tall letters."

"You pull down to make them all."

"The *b* is different because it has a circle."

"The *h* is different because it has a tunnel."

These comments will tell you what the children are noticing about the distinctive features of letters.

Assess

- Observe the children as they write to see whether their letter formation is getting more efficient.

- Evaluate the children's written products to determine whether their handwriting is becoming more legible.

- Make an inventory of children's ability to write letters by asking them to write a series of letters that you dictate. This task will tell you which letters need continued detailed attention.

- You may wish to use Letter Knowledge Assessment B or E.

Letter Knowledge: Form Letters with Writing Tools

Connect Learning Across Contexts

Interactive Read-Aloud Read aloud alphabet books that emphasize sounds as well as names.

> IRA *A, My Name Is Alice* by Jane Bayer

> IRA *The Bus for Us* by Suzanne Bloom

Shared Reading See "A Little Doggie" in *Words That Sing* (2019). If you don't have these poetry charts, enlarge the print of this poem or other poems such as "Roses Are Red" in *Sing a Song of Poetry,* and have children use highlighter tape to find letters in the text that you make in the air while stating the verbal path. You may also wish to use the following Shared Reading title from *Fountas & Pinnell Classroom*™.

> SR *Molly's Leash* by Susan Scott

Shared or Interactive Writing Say the motions while writing a difficult letter on the whiteboard. When a child is writing a letter at the easel, say the motions as the child writes.

Independent Writing Encourage children to use efficient motions when writing and to say the motions (the verbal path) if that helps them.

Extend Learning

■ Repeat the lesson with other lowercase letters:

  c, o, a, d, g, q

  b, h, t, i, j, k, l, p

  n, r, m, u

  v, x, w, y

  f, s

  e, z

■ Repeat the lesson with uppercase letters that children are making in an inefficient way or finding difficult. It will usually not be necessary to repeat this lesson for every letter (or you may do more letters in one lesson).

▶ Connect with Home

Let caregivers know that you teach handwriting in special lessons. Explain your reasons for using words to describe the motions for forming letters, and give them a copy of the Letter Formation Charts and the Verbal Path for the Formation of Letters so that they can use them at home. Caution caregivers not to expect perfect handwriting right away, and explain that you do not correct handwriting when children are concentrating on what they want to write (independent writing).

Make Connections Among Words by Noting the Position of a Letter

Plan

▶ Consider Your Children

This lesson works best when most children can read their own names, some of the names of other children, and a dozen or more high-frequency words or words from the word wall. They should be noticing details of words and making connections between names and other words.

▶ Working with English Language Learners

The English language learners in your classroom may have richly diverse names. Have all children work to pronounce correctly the names of all of their classmates. You can get family members to help you. As children work to identify recurring letters, encourage them to refer to the Alphabet Linking Chart as needed. It may be helpful to review the uppercase and lowercase forms of each letter, especially those with very different shapes, such as *Hh* and *Qq*.

UNDERSTAND THE PRINCIPLE

By noticing recurring letters and studying the position of letters in words, children become more aware of features, patterns, similarities, and differences among words. They begin to learn that an awareness of letter position helps them accurately blend the sounds that the letters stand for into complete words. By making connections among words, they begin to generalize knowledge of beginning letters, ending letters, and middle letters.

YOU WILL NEED

PWS Ready Resources
- ▶ LK 15 Pocket-Chart Word Cards
- ▶ Blank Pocket-Chart Cards
- ▶ Uppercase Letter Cards
- ▶ Lowercase Letter Cards

Online Resources
- ▶ LK 15 Action Tags
- ▶ LK 15 Word Cards

Other Materials
- ▶ pocket chart

Generative Lesson

A generative lesson has a simple structure that you can use to present similar content or concepts. You can use this lesson structure to teach children to make connections between words by noticing letter placement in a variety of words.

EXPLAIN THE PRINCIPLE

Find words that begin with the same letter.

Find words that end with the same letter.

Comprehensive Phonics, Spelling, and Word Study Guide

Refer to:
page **23**, row **13**

ACTIVITY:
WORD-CARD SORT

INSTRUCTIONAL PROCEDURE

FIND AND MATCH

See page 36 for detailed descriptions of Instructional Procedures.

EXPLAIN THE PRINCIPLE

Find words that begin with the same letter.

Find words that end with the same letter.

Comprehensive Phonics, Spelling, and Word Study Guide

Refer to: page **23**, row **13**

Teach

1. Tell your children that they will be learning to find words that have the same letter.

2. On the left side of a pocket chart, display ten to twenty words that children are learning. You may wish to choose a combination of high-frequency words, words currently on the word wall, and children's names. Have children read aloud the words with you.

3. Select a letter that is found at the beginning of two or more words and display the corresponding uppercase letter card and lowercase letter card near the top right of the pocket chart, e.g., the letters *T* and *t*. *You can find words that begin with the same letter. The letter may be uppercase or lowercase. Which words on our chart begin with the letter* t? ● As children identify words, move the word cards below the uppercase letter card and lowercase letter card. Point to the letter *t* in each word as you reinforce the principle. *Yes, the words* to, Tia, top, *and* the *all begin with the letter* t.

4. Continue the process, selecting letters that are found at the end of two or more words. As you sort, give children time to notice details about letter placement in various words.

5. Conclude by reinforcing the principle. *This morning you found words that begin with the same letter and end with the same letter.*

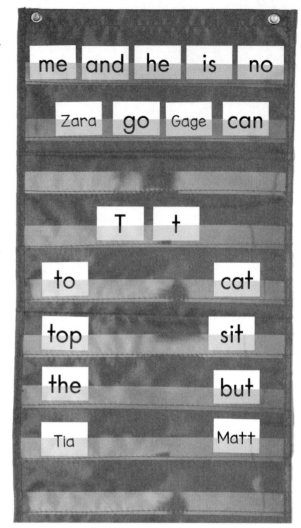

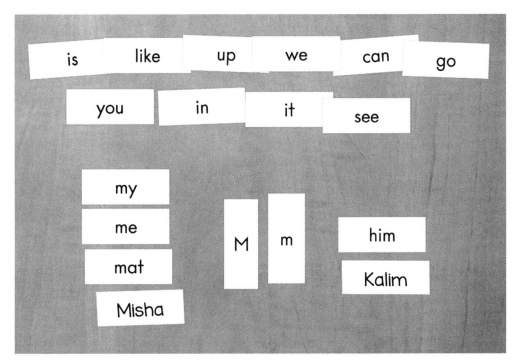

INSTRUCTIONAL PROCEDURE

FIND AND MATCH

See page 36 for detailed descriptions of Instructional Procedures.

ACTION TAGS

read

find

sort

Apply

■ Distribute a set of cards for words such as *my, me, Misha, mat, him,* and *Kalim,* and a selection of particular uppercase letter cards and lowercase letter cards to partners. Tell children that their set contains the words used during the lesson but also new words. Ask partners to read through their word cards together.

■ *Work with your partner to find words that have the same letter at the beginning and at the end.* Demonstrate placing a letter card at the top of a table and sorting words with that letter. Encourage partners to sort words by several different letters and in all positions.

Share

Ask partners to share one of their word sorts with the class.

Assess

■ Ask individual children to find all of the words in a set of word cards with a particular letter at the beginning, at the end, or in the middle.

■ Notice whether children can identify recurring letters in words that are in shared reading texts.

Connect Learning Across Contexts

Interactive Read-Aloud Read aloud books that feature alliteration or other word play with letters.

> IRA *Wemberly Worried* by Kevin Henkes
>
> IRA *Cat's Colors* by Jane Cabrera

Shared Reading See "Hickory, Dickory, Dare!" in *Words That Sing* (2019). If you don't have these poetry charts, enlarge the print of this poem or other poems such as "A Tisket, a Tasket" or "Here Is a Bunny" in *Sing a Song of Poetry,* and have children use highlighter tape to find words with the same letter in various locations. You may also wish to use the following Shared Reading title from *Fountas & Pinnell Classroom*™.

> SR *Coco Steps Out* by Lionel Page

Interactive Writing As you write with children, guide them to notice words that have the same letter at the beginning, at the end, or in the middle.

Independent Writing Remind children that the word wall is organized by the beginning letter of words. Demonstrate how to use a beginning letter to find a word on the word wall, and encourage children to use the word wall as a resource while writing.

Extend Learning

Have children hunt for words with the same letter while walking as a class to other locations in the school. For example, have children look for words that begin with the letter *l* while walking to the cafeteria. Before leaving the classroom, brainstorm words that children might see, such as *lunch, library,* and *line.*

▶ Connect with Home

Send home a set of word cards and encourage family members to play "I Spy" by laying out the word cards and then taking turns saying a letter in a certain position, for example, "I spy a word with the letter *d* at the end."

Categorize Letters by Features

Plan

▶ Consider Your Children

When children have developed some idea of the purposes of print (through shared reading and interactive writing) and have worked with their names enough to recognize them visually, you will want them to examine letter features more closely. After children understand how to look for certain letter features (e.g., long straight lines or curves), they can group letters that have these features; the sorting activity will help them solidify their recognition of such differences. It will benefit all children to repeat this lesson as needed.

▶ Working with English Language Learners

This lesson will help English language learners notice the distinctive features of letters and learn a way to talk about them. You want them to internalize language that will help them notice and locate letters. Be sure that the letters you use are consistent in form without a great deal of variation. You may need to work with a small group and take it slow, not looking at more than two features at a time.

UNDERSTAND THE PRINCIPLE

Children need help learning how to look at print. Looking at print involves noticing the distinctive features of a letter, as well as understanding what makes a letter different from every other letter. When children can identify letters by noticing the very small differences that make them unique, they can then associate letters and letter clusters with phonemes and parts of words.

YOU WILL NEED

PWS Ready Resources
- ▶ Lowercase Letter Cards

Online Resources
- ▶ LK 16 Action Tags
- ▶ LK 16 Two-Way Sorts

Other Materials
- ▶ magnetic easel or other magnetic surface
- ▶ magnetic letters (*l, d, h, a, m, n, k, b, r, i, u, p, q*) mixed together in a container

Generative Lesson

A generative lesson has a simple structure that you can use to present similar content or concepts. You can use this lesson structure to teach children to sort a variety of letters by their features.

EXPLAIN THE PRINCIPLE

Some letters have parts that look the same.

Some letters have long straight lines [e.g., d, p].

Some letters have short straight lines [e.g., i, n].

Some letters have curves [e.g., e, c].

Some letters have dots [e.g., i, j].

Some letters have tunnels [e.g., h, n].

Comprehensive Phonics, Spelling, and Word Study Guide

Refer to: page **22**, row **5**

ACTIVITY: LETTER FEATURES

INSTRUCTIONAL PROCEDURE

SAY AND SORT

See page 36 for detailed descriptions of Instructional Procedures.

EXPLAIN THE PRINCIPLE

Some letters have parts that look the same.

Some letters have long straight lines [e.g., d, p].

Some letters have short straight lines [e.g., i, n].

Some letters have curves [e.g., e, c].

Some letters have dots [e.g., i, j].

Some letters have tunnels [e.g., h, n].

Comprehensive Phonics, Spelling, and Word Study Guide

Refer to: page **22**, row **5**

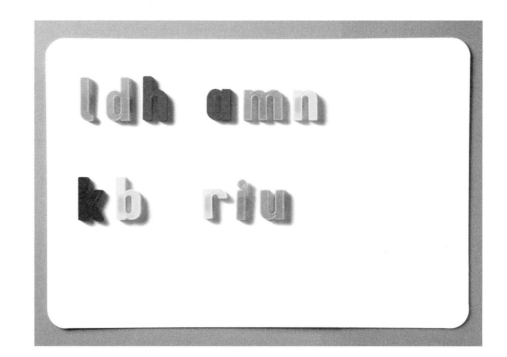

Teach

1. Explain to the children that they are going to learn about letters by looking closely at them.

2. Using a magnetic easel or other magnetic surface, show children the magnetic letters.

3. *Every letter looks different from every other letter. For instance, some letters have long straight lines, and some letters have short straight lines. Here is a lowercase letter with a long straight line.* Show *h. Here is a lowercase letter with a short straight line.* Show *n. Do you see the difference?*

4. Introduce the rest of the lowercase letters: *l, d, a, m, k, b, r, i, u, p, q.* Ask children to say which group is appropriate for each letter to be placed in–the group of letters with long straight lines, or the group of letters with short straight lines.

5. If you are using a white magnetic easel, draw a circle around each category.

6. Show children how to sort letters into two categories, those with long straight lines and those with short straight lines, using the two-way sort. Model how to use the two-way sort by using an enlarged version of it drawn on the board or on chart paper.

7. You can revisit this lesson one or more times and invite children to categorize selected letters by other features such as curves, dots, or tunnels.

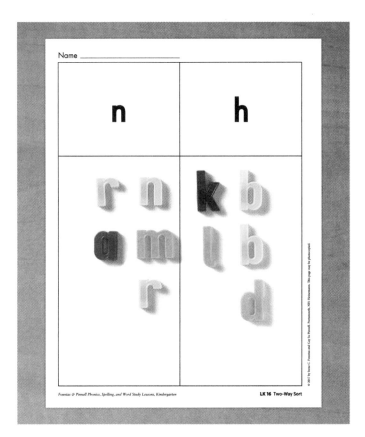

INSTRUCTIONAL PROCEDURE

SAY AND SORT

See page 36 for detailed descriptions of Instructional Procedures.

ACTION TAGS

take
say
sort
check

Apply

Give pairs of children a two-way sort with the letter *n* at the top of the left column and the letter *h* at the top of the right column. Point out that the letter *n* has a short straight line and that the letter *h* has a long straight line. Have partners use magnetic letters or lowercase letter cards to say and sort the letters *l, d, a, m, k, b, r, i, u, p,* and *q*. Partners can check each other's work.

Share

Invite the children to discuss what they noticed about the letters they have sorted. They may mention long lines and short lines along with features such as curves, dots, and tunnels.

Assess

- Notice children's ability to sort letters by common feature.
- Examine children's writing to note the quality of the letter features that appear in their handwriting.

Connect Learning Across Contexts

Interactive Read-Aloud Read aloud alphabet books that single out letters and use alliteration to tell a story.

> IRA *On Market Street* by Arthur and Anita Lobel

> IRA *Miss Bindergarten Gets Ready for Kindergarten* by Joseph Slate

Shared Reading See "If I Were a Bird" in *Words That Sing* (2019). If you don't have these poetry charts, enlarge the print of this poem or other poems such as "Little Tommy Tucker" or "Peas" in *Sing a Song of Poetry,* and have children use highlighter tape to find letters (within words) that have long straight lines, short straight lines, curves, dots, and tunnels. You may also wish to use the following Shared Reading title from *Fountas & Pinnell Classroom*™ to look at more letters.

> SR *Slip and Slide* by Amanda Yskamp

Interactive Writing When children are making letters, help them notice the letters' distinguishing features.

Independent Writing When holding conferences with children, guide them to say "long straight line," "short straight line," "curve," "dot," and "tunnel" when making letters until they make them correctly without thinking.

Extend Learning

- Have children sort lowercase letter cards into those with long straight lines and those with short straight lines and glue them on a two-way sort.

- Have children sort letters in a variety of other ways:

    Letters with circles and letters with tunnels: *a, d, b, u, n, m, o, q, h, g.*

    Letters with tails and letters without tails: *a, b, c, d, e, f, g, h, i, j, k, l, m, n, o, p, q, r, s, t, u, v, w, x, y, z.*

    Letters with crossed lines and letters without crossed lines: *t, f, v, a, m, o, c, l, r, s.*

    Letters with dots and letters without dots: *i, j, f, t, g, x, p, s, m.*

    Letters with only straight lines and letters with only curves: *c, o, k, s, t, w, x, y, z, i.*

    Letters with straight lines, letters with curves, and letters with both straight lines and curves. (Children will use a three-way sort with all letters of the alphabet.)

▶ Connect with Home

Send home copies of a full set of lowercase letter cards and ask children to sort them by long straight lines and short straight lines, curves, dots, tunnels, and so on.

Categorize Letters by Features

Plan

▶ Consider Your Children

This lesson works best when children are familiar with the features of letters and understand the concept of sorting. They need many opportunities to distinguish letter features in order to be able to recognize letters in context. Once children can distinguish these features quickly, letter sorting should be phased out.

▶ Working with English Language Learners

In this lesson, you will be asking children to sort letters that have similar features. Encourage English language learners to explore letters and find connections between them. Observe or work with only a few children at a time so that you get information about what they are attending to and so that you can encourage them when they make connections. Use (and ask children to repeat) specific language that describes the features of letters.

UNDERSTAND THE PRINCIPLE

Children need help learning how to look at print. Looking at print involves noticing the distinctive features of a letter, as well as understanding what makes a letter different from every other letter. When children can identify letters by noticing the very small differences that make them unique, they can then associate letters and letter clusters with phonemes and parts of words.

YOU WILL NEED

PWS Ready Resources
- ▶ Lowercase Letter Cards

Online Resources
- ▶ LK 17 Action Tags
- ▶ LK 17 Two-Way Sorts
- ▶ LK 17 Three-Way Sorts

Other Materials
- ▶ magnetic easel or other magnetic surface
- ▶ magnetic letters

Generative Lesson
A generative lesson has a simple structure that you can use to present similar content or concepts. You can use this lesson structure to teach children to sort a variety of letters by their features.

EXPLAIN THE PRINCIPLE

Some letters have parts that look the same.

Some letters have long straight lines [e.g., d, p].

Some letters have short straight lines [e.g., i, n].

Some letters have curves [e.g., e, c].

Some letters have dots [e.g., i, j].

Some letters have tunnels [e.g., h, n].

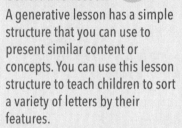

Comprehensive Phonics, Spelling, and Word Study Guide

Refer to: page **22**, row **5**

ACTIVITY: LETTER FEATURES

INSTRUCTIONAL PROCEDURE

SAY AND SORT

See page 36 for detailed descriptions of Instructional Procedures.

EXPLAIN THE PRINCIPLE

Some letters have parts that look the same.

Some letters have long straight lines [e.g., d, p].

Some letters have short straight lines [e.g., i, n].

Some letters have curves [e.g., e, c].

Some letters have dots [e.g., i, j].

Some letters have tunnels [e.g., h, n].

Comprehensive Phonics, Spelling, and Word Study Guide

Refer to: page **22**, row **5**

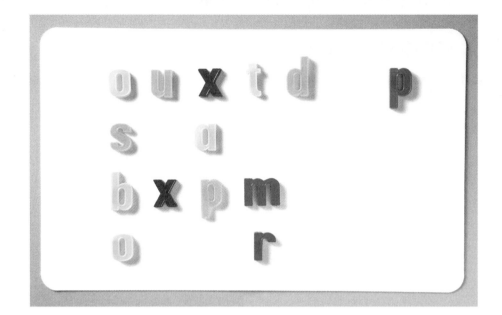

Teach

1. Explain to the children that they are going to learn about letters by looking closely at them.

2. Using a magnetic easel or other magnetic surface, show children the magnetic letters *a, b, d, o, p, r, s, t, u, x*.

3. Place one letter to the right side of the easel. Ask children to tell you what they notice about the letter you've moved. For example, if you place the *p* to the right, children may say it has a curve or a long straight line.

4. Invite children to find another letter that has the same feature. Focusing on only one feature at a time, have them find other letters with curves or other letters with long straight lines.

5. Have children take turns coming up to the easel to find a letter that fits the feature category and move it to the right—for example, if the category is letters with curves, children may move *p, g, o, b*, and *a* to the right side.

6. Move all the letters back to the left and repeat the process using another feature (e.g., letters with short straight lines).

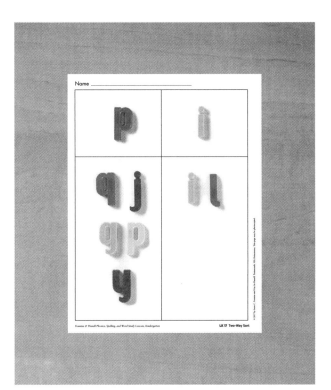

Fountas & Pinnell Phonics, Spelling, and Word Study Lessons, Kindergarten

LK 17 Two-Way Sort

ACTIVITY: TWO-WAY LETTER SORT (PAIRS OR SMALL GROUPS)

INSTRUCTIONAL PROCEDURE

SAY AND SORT

See page 36 for detailed descriptions of Instructional Procedures.

ACTION TAGS

put

find

say

sort

Apply

Give containers of mixed magnetic letters or lowercase letter cards to small groups or pairs of children. Have each child put a letter at the top of each column of a two-way sort. Then have them find other letters that have a similar feature, say the name of each one, and place it in the correct column. Each child should repeat the process with three letters, using a three-way sort. Observe children's sorting so that you can guide and reinforce what they are noticing. A key element of this lesson is encouraging children to pay attend to and explore the features of letters–that is, what makes the letter *a* an *a* or the letter *g* a *g*.

Share

Display a group of letters and invite children to tell what is the same about them. Then give each child a magnetic letter. Draw a circle on the magnetic easel or whiteboard. Place the letter *d* in the circle. Explain that *d* has a long straight line. Ask each child to take a turn placing her letter inside the circle if it has a long straight line and outside the circle if it does not. (Children may attend to a different feature–an *a* is also similar to the *d* in that it has a circle. Tell them they are correct in that it is similar, but get them to focus on the category under discussion.) Continue until all children have placed their letters inside or outside the circle.

Assess

- Notice children's growing ability to attach names to letters according to their distinctive features.

- Observe the speed with which children sort letters because it is an indication of their ability to pick up on print information. If they are sorting slowly, seeing the differences may be difficult for them.

Letter Knowledge: Categorize Letters by Features

Connect Learning Across Contexts

Interactive Read-Aloud Read aloud a variety of alphabet books.

> IRA *ABC I Like Me* by Nancy Carlson

> IRA *Alphabet Under Construction* by Denise Fleming

Shared Reading See "Gray Squirrel" in *Words That Sing* (2019). If you don't have these poetry charts, enlarge the print of this poem or other poems such as "Cobbler, Cobbler" in *Sing a Song of Poetry,* and have children use highlighter tape to find pairs of different letters and say why they are alike. You may also wish to use the following Shared Reading title from *Fountas & Pinnell Classroom*™.

> SR *City ABCs* by Finnoula Louise

Interactive Writing When helping children make letters, use terms like long straight line, short straight line, curve, dot, and tunnel to help children notice the distinctive features of each letter.

Independent Writing In conferences, use terms like long straight line, short straight line, curve, dot, and tunnel to remind children of the distinctive features of each letter.

Extend Learning

- Select other letters to place at the top of columns for sorting into categories: *x, s, i, m, o.*
- Conduct sorting exercises with different letters and distinctive features.

▶ Connect with Home

Encourage family members to use magnetic letters with children at home. You may wish to send home copies of 25 Ways to Use Magnetic Letters at Home (see *Ready Resources*). Explain how valuable it is for children to handle letters as they learn about letters and words.

Form Letters with Writing Tools

Plan

▶ Consider Your Children

This lesson establishes the procedures for using a handwriting book. The activity is best introduced after children are accustomed to using writing materials (paper, markers, pencils), can work independently and follow simple directions for several minutes, and are using mostly conventional letters in their approximated writing. Don't wait too long to show children how to write letters because you don't want them to establish inefficient habits. You will want to work with one or more letters at a time, choosing letters that begin the same way. (See Letters Made in Similar Ways.)

▶ Working with English Language Learners

Be sure to demonstrate the task as many times as necessary to be certain children know how to use efficient motions to make letters and how to say the words that will help them. Focus on only one or two letters at first. If you are storing handwriting books in colored boxes, be sure that English language learners know their colors. Demonstrate–and have children practice– taking out the books, getting writing materials, writing a page of letters, and putting the books away. These procedures will be used over and over.

UNDERSTAND THE PRINCIPLE

Young children need to learn to form letters with efficient and consistent motions. Using consistent motions while saying aloud the steps to make individual letters improves children's memory of letters and words and develops children's writing fluency. An additional benefit is the growing legibility of their handwriting. Handwriting lessons take only a few minutes a day, are easy to manage, and are a way to help children practice regularly. Frequent practice will help children become more efficient and fluent at handwriting.

YOU WILL NEED

PWS Ready Resources
- ▶ Letters Made in Similar Ways

Online Resources
- ▶ LK 18 Action Tags

Other Materials
- ▶ chart paper
- ▶ pencil
- ▶ large handwriting book for demonstration
- ▶ handwriting book for each child
- ▶ baskets or boxes for storing handwriting books
- ▶ newsprint paper
- ▶ crayons or markers

Generative Lesson

A generative lesson has a simple structure that you can use to present similar content or concepts. You can use this lesson structure to teach children to form a variety of letters.

EXPLAIN THE PRINCIPLE

Make the shape of a letter.

Say the steps you use to make a letter.

Check to see if a letter looks right.

Comprehensive Phonics, Spelling, and Word Study Guide

Refer to: page **23**, row **14**

ACTIVITY: RAINBOW LETTER AND HANDWRITING BOOK

INSTRUCTIONAL PROCEDURE

SAY AND WRITE

See page 36 for detailed descriptions of Instructional Procedures.

EXPLAIN THE PRINCIPLE

Make the shape of a letter.

Say the steps you use to make a letter.

Check to see if a letter looks right.

Comprehensive Phonics, Spelling, and Word Study Guide

Refer to: page **23**, row **14**

Teach

1. In preparation for the lesson, have individual handwriting books for the children–and for yourself–already prepared. Standard composition books cut in half across the width work well. Write the letter at the beginning of a line on a page.

2. Tell the children today they are going to learn more about writing letters.

3. *Today we're going to practice forming lowercase* b *by making a rainbow letter. Watch while I make a big one with a pencil. Pull down, up, and around.* Make the b–on newsprint–about twenty-four inches tall. Have children practice making the *b* in the air and remind them of the steps. Then have each child trace over the *b* with a colored crayon or marker while describing the motions. At the end of the day, let one child take the "rainbow" *b* home.

4. Show children a handwriting book. *Today we are going to start our handwriting books. You will each have your own book. This is my handwriting book that I will use to show you what to write. On the front, it says "My Handwriting Book," and here is my name.*

5. *We'll keep our handwriting books in these boxes.* Point out the boxes of handwriting books. *I'm going to give each of you a book with your name carefully written on the cover. It also has a colored dot that matches the color of your box. When you put your book back, look at the colored dot to help you remember the color of your box. Each time when you finish your book, you will need to put it back in the right box. How many of you remember your color? Look at the dot if you forget.*

6. Show children the handwriting book. *I'm going to show you how to write letters on each page of this book. Every time you use your handwriting book, you will be writing a page of letters or words. You will use this book to practice good writing.*

7. Show the children what you want them to do in their handwriting books. Explain that they will see a letter at the beginning of the line and they will make the letter carefully several times to fill the row. Remind them to say the steps they use to make the letter as they write it.

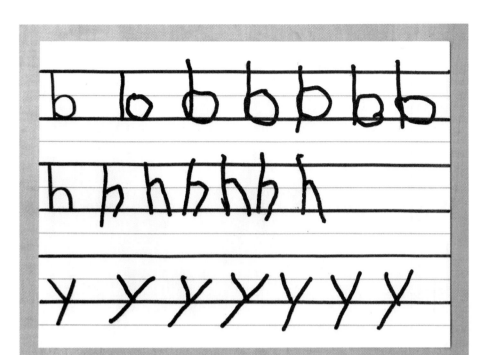

**ACTIVITY:
HANDWRITING BOOKS**

**INSTRUCTIONAL
PROCEDURE**

SAY AND WRITE

*See page 36 for detailed
descriptions of Instructional
Procedures.*

ACTION TAGS

write
check

Apply

Children take their handwriting books and practice lines of the letter or letters you modeled, creating a page of letters like the one you started.

Share

Have children demonstrate saying the motions to make *b*. Have them show a partner the best letter they made in each line. Have several children demonstrate finding their handwriting books in the colored boxes and putting them away.

Assess

- Evaluate the children's writing to determine other handwriting lessons they need.
- Observe the children while they are writing to determine whether they are using efficient movements to write letters and to decide which letters to focus on in handwriting lessons.
- You may wish to use Letter Knowledge Assessment B or E.

Connect Learning Across Contexts

Interactive Read-Aloud Read aloud alphabet books that emphasize noticing letters.

[IRA] *A, My Name Is Alice* by Jane Bayer

[IRA] *Miss Bindergarten Gets Ready for Kindergarten* by Joseph Slate

Shared Reading See "Diddlety, Diddlety, Dumpty!" in *Words That Sing* (2019). If you don't have these poetry charts, enlarge the print of this poem or other poems such as "Make a Pancake" or "Jumping Joan" in *Sing a Song of Poetry,* and have children use highlighter tape to locate recently practiced letters. You may also wish to refer to the following Shared Reading title from *Fountas & Pinnell Classroom*™ to point out more letters.

[SR] *Country ABCs* by Finnoula Louise

Shared or Interactive Writing Describe the motions from the Verbal Path for the Formation of Letters when you are modeling a letter on the whiteboard or when a child is writing a letter at the easel. Have children check the letter and its formation after it is written. Have children locate a "really good" *b* or "your best" *b* (or any letter) after a piece is written.

Independent Writing Encourage children to say the motions while writing letters that are difficult for them. Encourage them by pointing to really good examples of letters that they write.

Extend Learning

- Repeat the lesson with groups of letters (two or three at a time) until children can form letters efficiently and correctly.

- Repeat the lesson if children are not getting and putting away handwriting books properly. It is very important for this routine to become automatic.

▶ Connect with Home

Tell caregivers about the handwriting books and explain that children will be bringing them home when they are filled up. Give family members a copy of the Letter Formation Charts so that they can use them at home. Encourage caregivers to have their children form letters using finger paint, watercolors and a brush, a brush in water on the sidewalk, or their finger or a stick in a sandbox.

Form Letters with Writing Tools

Plan

▶ Consider Your Children

This lesson is best introduced after children have worked with the class name chart and have sorted letters. Each child should be able to write his or her name accurately. Select a consistent way to show children the movements for writing the selected letter. [See the Verbal Path for the Formation of Letters for simple language to describe letter formation.] Children will have begun to learn how to use the handwriting books. At first, have them all write at the same time. After the routine has been established, they can practice in the book independently. In this lesson, you show children how to evaluate their own handwriting. The Letters Made in Similar Ways chart depicts an order for teaching letter formations that begin the same way. You can teach two or three letters at a time. See the Letter Formation Charts for specific directions for forming uppercase and lowercase letters.

▶ Working with English Language Learners

If children have not learned the handwriting-book routines well enough to follow them automatically, provide more demonstrations. The Verbal Path for the Formation of Letters will be helpful to English language learners, but they need to understand what the descriptive words mean and how to use them. Have them say these words in unison as they make letters. You may want to use unlined newsprint at first so they can concentrate on movement. Show them what "best" means in terms of self-evaluating their handwriting.

UNDERSTAND THE PRINCIPLE

Young children need to learn to form letters with efficient and consistent motions. Using consistent motions while saying aloud the steps to make individual letters improves children's memory of letters and words and develops children's writing fluency. An additional benefit is the growing legibility of their handwriting. Handwriting lessons take only a few minutes a day, are easy to manage, and are a way to help children practice regularly. Frequent practice will help children become more efficient and fluent at handwriting.

YOU WILL NEED

PWS **Ready Resources**
- ▶ Letter Formation Charts
- ▶ Verbal Path for the Formation of Letters

Online Resources
- ▶ LK 19 Action Tags

Other Materials
- ▶ magnetic drawing board, dry-erase marker and whiteboard, or chart paper on easel
- ▶ individual handwriting books
- ▶ large version of a handwriting book

✔ Generative Lesson

A generative lesson has a simple structure that you can use to present similar content or concepts. You can use this lesson structure to teach children how to form a variety of letters.

EXPLAIN THE PRINCIPLE

Make the shape of a letter.

Say the steps you use to make a letter.

Check to see if a letter looks right.

Comprehensive Phonics, Spelling, and Word Study Guide

Refer to:
page **23**, row **14**

ACTIVITY:
HANDWRITING BOOKS

INSTRUCTIONAL
PROCEDURE

SAY AND WRITE

See page 36 for detailed
descriptions of Instructional
Procedures.

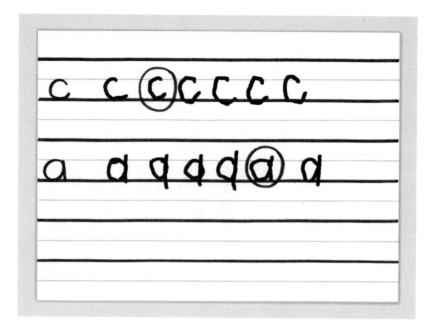

EXPLAIN THE PRINCIPLE

Make the shape of a letter.

Say the steps you use to make a
letter.

Check to see if a letter looks
right.

Comprehensive
Phonics, Spelling,
and Word Study
Guide

Refer to:
page **23**, row **14**

Teach

1. Explain to the children that they are going to learn more about how to make letters and how to check the letters in their writing.

2. Select an easy letter that most children know and can make. *I'm going to make c. To make a lowercase c, pull back and around.* Make the letter slowly as you describe the movement. At first, make a large letter so children see the large motor movements. Use a whiteboard, chart paper, or a magnetic drawing board (a thick writing instrument is most effective).

3. Make the letter again and invite the children to say the verbal path aloud with you as you write.

4. Have children make the letter in the air and on the floor as they softly repeat the verbal path.

5. Show the children your large handwriting book. Open it and demonstrate writing the letter *c* several times next to the model while you say the motions. Point out that the letter is formed within a set of lines. Show the children your line of *c*'s. *Now I'm going to choose the best c that I have made. I'm going to circle it with a colored marker.* Then close the book.

6. *Now you will work on a page in your own handwriting books. On the left, at the beginning of each line, you will see the letter I want you to practice today. Trace over it and say the name of the letter as you write it. ● Then write it several more times until you fill the line. Be sure to leave spaces between the letters you practice. When you bring your handwriting book to me, I'll help you choose your best letter.*

7. Help the children choose their best letter and tell them why the letter is "best." Choosing a best letter will gradually become routine for children as they learn to evaluate their handwriting.

8. Children who finish first can look at books (or do some other activity) while you work with the children who need more time.

Fountas & Pinnell Phonics, Spelling, and Word Study Lessons, Kindergarten

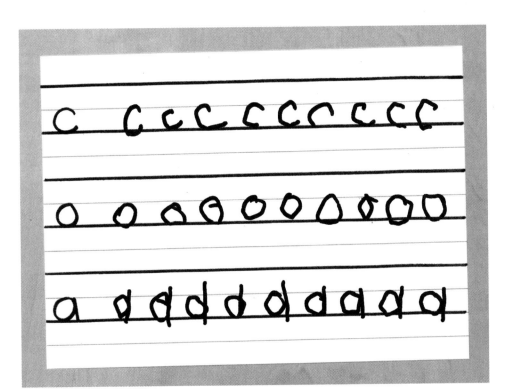

ACTIVITY:
HANDWRITING BOOKS

INSTRUCTIONAL
PROCEDURE

SAY AND WRITE

See page 36 for detailed
descriptions of Instructional
Procedures.

ACTION TAGS

say
write
circle

Apply

Have the children use their handwriting books to practice writing the letter on each line. Help them circle their best letter with a colored marker before they return their handwriting books to the colored boxes.

Share

Ask several children to share their handwriting. Have them put a finger under the best letter.

Bring the children together in a circle again and invite one or two children to the board to make a "beautiful *c*."

Assess

- Observe the children as they write to determine their ability to use efficient directional movements.
- Dictate letters to children and then look at their work. Check off the letters they are representing well. Eventually you will want to evaluate their formation of all letters.
- You may wish to use Letter Knowledge Assessment B or E.

Connect Learning Across Contexts

Interactive Read-Aloud Read aloud alphabet books that draw attention to the shapes of letters.

> IRA *A, My Name Is Alice* by Jane Bayer

> IRA *Alphabet Under Construction* by Denise Fleming

Shared Reading See "I Clap My Hands" in *Words That Sing* (2019). If you don't have these poetry charts, enlarge the print of this poem or other poems such as "My Little Sister" or "See-saw, Margery Daw" in *Sing a Song of Poetry,* and have children use highlighter tape to find a letter you make on the whiteboard. You may also wish to use the following Shared Reading title from *Fountas & Pinnell Classroom*™ to look at more letters.

> SR *City ABCs* by Finnoula Louise

Interactive Writing After a piece of writing is finished, ask children to locate a "really good *c*" or other letter.

Independent Writing Encourage children to check their writing and point out letters that they have made well. If children are having difficulty with letter formation, support them with language from the Verbal Path for the Formation of Letters.

Extend Learning

- Individualize the handwriting books by giving children different letters to practice.
- Design lessons focusing on particular letters that children need to practice.
- After children are able to make letters easily, have them write high-frequency words or simple sentences in the books.

▶ Connect with Home

Let children take home pieces of lined paper for writing practice. Also send home handwriting books that children have filled. Explain to caregivers that the circled letters are the child's best efforts. The development of fine-motor coordination contributes to a child's ability to use small hand movements to form letters. Describe activities that can be done at home that help children develop fine motor skills: for example, working with clay or pipe cleaners; finger painting; tracing (dot to dot); building with small blocks; stringing macaroni, beads, popcorn, or cranberries.

Recognize Uppercase Letters and Lowercase Letters

Plan

▶ Consider Your Children

This lesson is best used after you have worked with children on handwriting. Children should have some experience noticing letter features and thinking about the directional movements for forming letters. You want them to be able to recognize letters fluently and automatically. Generally lowercase letters are more difficult to learn. Connecting the uppercase form and the lowercase form of each letter will help children begin to recognize and name each lowercase letter more easily. (In some schools the terms are *capital* and *small*).

▶ Working with English Language Learners

In this lesson, English language learners will be using the terms *uppercase* and *lowercase* to describe letters. It will take many experiences working with letters to help children distinguish uppercase from lowercase letters and match uppercase and lowercase letter pairs. Provide as many demonstrations as necessary to help them notice the differences and similarities between uppercase and lowercase letters. Work with children in a small group to make sure that they understand the sorting process.

UNDERSTAND THE PRINCIPLE

Becoming familiar with the alphabet is an important step for emergent readers. Children need to be familiar with the idea that each letter has an uppercase form and a lowercase form. Moreover, the name of the letter stays the same regardless of uppercase or lowercase form.

YOU WILL NEED

PWS Ready Resources
- ▶ Alphabet Linking Chart
- ▶ Uppercase and Lowercase Letter Cards
- ▶ Letter Formation Charts

Online Resources
- ▶ LK 20 Action Tags
- ▶ LK 20 Two-Way Sorts

Other Materials
- ▶ *Chicka Chicka Boom Boom* by Bill Martin Jr. and John Archambault (or another large-print alphabet book that shows both uppercase and lowercase forms of letters)
- ▶ whiteboard or magnetic drawing board

Generative Lesson ✓

A generative lesson has a simple structure that you can use to present similar content or concepts. You can use this lesson structure to teach children the differences between uppercase and lowercase forms with a variety of letters.

EXPLAIN THE PRINCIPLE

There are two kinds of letters. One is uppercase (or capital), and the other is lowercase (or small).

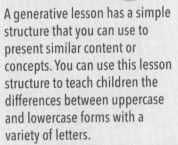 Comprehensive Phonics, Spelling, and Word Study Guide

Refer to: page **22**, row **3**

ACTIVITY: UPPERCASE AND LOWERCASE LETTERS

INSTRUCTIONAL PROCEDURE

NOTICE PARTS

See page 36 for detailed descriptions of Instructional Procedures.

EXPLAIN THE PRINCIPLE

There are two kinds of letters. One is uppercase (or capital), and the other is lowercase (or small).

Comprehensive Phonics, Spelling, and Word Study Guide

Refer to: page **22**, row **3**

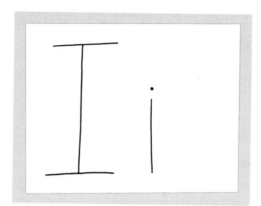

Teach

1. Tell children that they are going to learn more about letters.

2. Select an alphabet book that children are familiar with. Books like *Chicka Chicka Boom Boom* are very appealing because they incorporate rhyme and rhythm.

3. *Today we'll read one of our favorite alphabet books.* Discuss the uppercase and lowercase letters. If you are using *Chicka Chicka Boom Boom*, you can talk about how the mamas, papas, uncles, and aunts are represented by uppercase letters, whereas children are represented by lowercase letters. Have some fun with the page where the uppercase letters are hugging the lowercase letters. Read the book with the children joining in.

4. After the first reading, ask one child to point to a lowercase letter on a page of the book, and ask another child to find the same lowercase letter on the Alphabet Linking Chart. *In this book we see some uppercase letters. Sometimes these are called "capital letters."* Show an example of an uppercase letter. *And we also see lowercase letters. Sometimes these are called "small letters."* Show an example of a lowercase letter.

5. Choose a letter and write the uppercase and lowercase forms on a whiteboard or magnetic drawing board so the children can see them clearly.

6. *This is uppercase I, and this is lowercase i. They have the same name. They're both called I, but one is uppercase and one is lowercase. What do you notice about the uppercase I and the lowercase i?* Children may offer answers like "One is taller" or "One has a dot." Ask them to be specific and to name them as uppercase (or capital) *I* and lowercase (or small) *i*.

7. Repeat this action with several more letters.

8. Finally, have the children read the lowercase letters on the Alphabet Linking Chart in various ways: (1) read every other line; (2) read every other letter; (3) read down the columns; (4) read the letters with circles; (5) read the letters with long sticks; (6) read the letters with no curves; (7) read the letters with tails; (8) read the letters with tunnels.

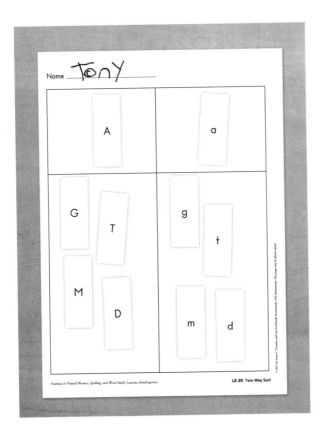

INSTRUCTIONAL PROCEDURE

FIND AND MATCH

See page 36 for detailed descriptions of Instructional Procedures.

ACTION TAGS

take
put
match
write

Apply

- Give each child a bag or small container of selected pairs of uppercase letter cards and lowercase letter cards. On a two-way sort, have children put an uppercase letter on the left and the matching lowercase letter on the right. They continue until they have matched all of the letters in their bag. Then they can use an additional two-way sort to write the two forms of each letter.

- Have children swap containers of letters and repeat.

Share

Have an Alphabet Linking Chart available. Ask children what they noticed about how uppercase letters and lowercase letters are alike or different. Have them point to and talk about specific examples.

Assess

- Notice the children's ability to recognize high-frequency words and whether they start with an uppercase letter or a lowercase letter.

- Observe the children's use of uppercase letters and lowercase letters in their writing.

- Use uppercase letter cards and lowercase letter cards to check knowledge of individual letters.

- You may wish to use Letter Knowledge Assessment C or F.

Connect Learning Across Contexts

Interactive Read-Aloud Read aloud alphabet books. Point out uppercase letters and lowercase letters.

> IRA *B Is for Bulldozer* by June Sobel

> IRA *ABC I Like Me* by Nancy Carlson

Shared Reading See "How Many Days?" in *Words That Sing* (2019). If you don't have these poetry charts, enlarge the print of this poem or other poems such as "The Whole Duty of Children" in *Sing a Song of Poetry,* and have children use highlighter tape to identify uppercase letters and lowercase letters. You may also wish to use the following Shared Reading title from *Fountas & Pinnell Classroom*™ to point out more uppercase and lowercase letters.

> SR *Spin, Spin, Spin* by Alina Kirk

Interactive Writing When you are writing a word, ask children whether you should use an uppercase letter or a lowercase letter.

Independent Writing Compliment children when they use lowercase letters in their writing. Encourage them to use an uppercase letter at the beginning of a name and to use lowercase letters for the rest of the name.

Extend Learning

- Go back to *Chicka Chicka Boom Boom.* Read the book again and look at the endpapers, which show both letter forms. Using the whiteboard or chart paper, write a lowercase letter and ask a volunteer to come up and write the corresponding uppercase letter (or vice versa). Check it with the book.

- Make a voice recording of an alphabet book. Have children listen to the recording while following along in the book. Then give each child a personal copy of letter formation charts for uppercase and lowercase letters. Have children listen to the tape again, this time pointing to the letters on one or both of their charts as the letters are mentioned.

▶ **Connect with Home**

Children can take home a copy of the Alphabet Linking Chart to read to their families. They might also take home their personal letter formation charts to share with family members.

Plan

▶ Consider Your Children

Use this lesson after children have had some experience matching pictures with beginning sounds. They will be using the same procedure to match uppercase and lowercase letter forms. Children who already have rapid automatic recognition of all forms of letters and recognize similarities and differences between uppercase and lowercase forms will not need this lesson.

▶ Working with English Language Learners

By the time you use this lesson, English language learners should be familiar with the Alphabet Linking Chart, the concept of letters, and the names of many of the letters that make up the alphabet. They should have noticed that there are two forms for each letter, but recognition of each form may not be automatic. Provide clear demonstrations of how to compare and match the two forms of each letter, making sure to use the terms *uppercase* and *lowercase*, or *big* and *little*. Continue to reinforce that some uppercase and lowercase forms look the same, whereas some uppercase and lowercase forms look different.

YOU WILL NEED

PWS Ready Resources
- ▶ Blank Pocket-Chart Cards
- ▶ Alphabet Linking Chart
- ▶ Lowercase Letter Cards
- ▶ Uppercase Letter Cards

Online Resources
- ▶ **LK 21** Action Tags
- ▶ **LK 21** Lotto and Bingo Game Boards
- ▶ **LK 21** Directions for Lotto and Bingo

Other Materials
- ▶ pocket chart

Generative Lesson

A generative lesson has a simple structure that you can use to present similar content or concepts. You can use this lesson structure to teach children the differences between the uppercase and lowercase forms of a variety of letters.

UNDERSTAND THE PRINCIPLE

Children need to be able to discern the distinctive features that make one letter different from every other letter. Some uppercase and lowercase letters look the same. However, other pairs of uppercase and lowercase letters look quite different. Connecting uppercase and lowercase letter forms will help children recognize and name the lowercase letters more easily.

EXPLAIN THE PRINCIPLE

Some uppercase letters and lowercase letters look the same [e.g., W, w].

Some uppercase letters and lowercase letters look different [e.g., R, r].

Comprehensive Phonics, Spelling, and Word Study Guide

Refer to: page **22**, row **4**

ACTIVITY: UPPERCASE AND LOWERCASE LETTER FORMS

INSTRUCTIONAL PROCEDURE

FIND AND MATCH

See page 36 for detailed descriptions of Instructional Procedures.

EXPLAIN THE PRINCIPLE

Some uppercase letters and lowercase letters look the same [e.g., W, w].

Some uppercase letters and lowercase letters look different [e.g., R, r].

Comprehensive Phonics, Spelling, and Word Study Guide

Refer to: page **22**, row **4**

Teach

1. In preparation for the lesson, prepare pocket-chart cards with uppercase and lowercase forms of letters in your handwriting.

2. Explain to the children that they are going to learn more about uppercase and lowercase letters.

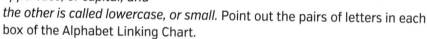
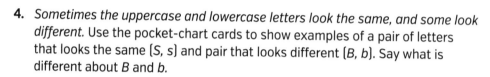

3. *Remind children that each letter of the alphabet has two kinds. One is called uppercase, or capital, and the other is called lowercase, or small.* Point out the pairs of letters in each box of the Alphabet Linking Chart.

4. *Sometimes the uppercase and lowercase letters look the same, and some look different.* Use the pocket-chart cards to show examples of a pair of letters that looks the same [S, s] and pair that looks different [B, b]. Say what is different about *B* and *b*.

5. On the pocket chart, place twelve uppercase letter cards, three in each row. *Today we are going to play a game called Lotto. In this game you will match uppercase and lowercase letters then tell whether they look the same or different. Let's start with the letters I put in the pocket chart. These are uppercase letters, aren't they? Let's read them.* Read through the letters on the pocket chart.

6. *Now, on these cards, I have written some lowercase letters. I'll mix them all up and then pick one.* Hold up a card. *I'm going to see if it goes with one of the uppercase letters on the chart. Does it?*

7. Model checking the lowercase letter with the uppercase letter on the chart, using the Alphabet Linking Chart as needed: A–a. *We have a match!* Then say whether the two forms of the letter look the same or whether the two forms of the letter look different from each other. *Uppercase* A *and lowercase* a *look different. Uppercase* A *has only straight lines; lowercase* a *has a straight line and a curvy line.*

8. Continue to draw cards one at a time, modeling how to check each lowercase letter against the uppercase letters and describe any differences in form. Place matching cards on top of corresponding letters. Place cards that don't match letters on the chart to the side, facedown.

9. Continue until all spaces are covered. *I've covered all the spaces. That's what you do to win Lotto. As you check your matches, remember to say the name of the uppercase and lowercase letters and say whether they look the same or different.*

10. Demonstrate the game with three children in a circle on the floor. Show them how to take turns drawing cards and matching them to the letters on their cards. The first child to fill the Lotto game board wins.

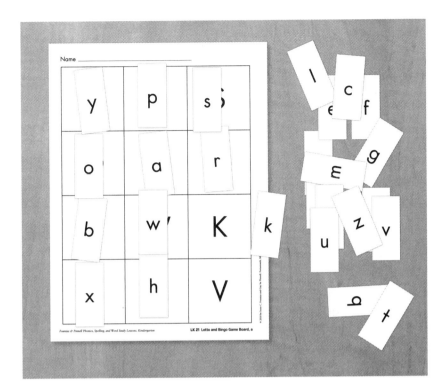

ACTIVITY: LOTTO

INSTRUCTIONAL PROCEDURE

FIND AND MATCH

See page 36 for detailed descriptions of Instructional Procedures.

ACTION TAGS

take

match

cover

check

Apply

Have children play Lotto using the Lotto game boards and lowercase letter cards. If you have enough letter cards and game boards, several games can be played at once. When children are done, have them discuss which letter pairs look the same and which letter pairs look different.

Share

Give each child a letter. Have each child, in turn, say the letter name and tell whether it is the lowercase form or the uppercase form.

Assess

■ Notice whether children are able to identify letters by name.

■ Point to a capital letter and ask the child to find the corresponding lowercase letter, or vice versa. Select letters that you think are more difficult rather than using the entire alphabet.

■ Show a selection of uppercase letter cards and ask the child to say whether the lowercase letter form looks the same or different.

■ You may wish to use Letter Knowledge Assessment C or F.

Letter Knowledge: Distinguish the Differences Between Uppercase and Lowercase Forms of a Letter

Connect Learning Across Contexts

Interactive Read-Aloud Read aloud alphabet books.

IRA *On Market Street* by Arthur Lobel and Anita Lobel

IRA *B Is for Bulldozer* by June Sobel

Shared Reading Read the Alphabet Linking Chart. Have children give a thumbs up if the uppercase and lowercase forms of a letter look the same and a thumbs down if the two forms of a letter look different. You may also wish to use the following Shared Reading title from *Fountas & Pinnell Classroom*™.

SR *City ABCs* by Finnoula Louise

Interactive Writing When the class is thinking about how to write a word, have children say the word slowly and connect it to a name or another word that starts with the same letter.

Independent Writing Encourage children to say words slowly when they are writing and to connect those words to names or other words that start with the same letter. If children are trying to think of the correct lowercase letter form, ask them to think about whether it looks the same or different as the letter's uppercase form.

Extend Learning

- Repeat the lesson. Have the children use uppercase letter cards and match them to lowercase letters on the Lotto game board. You also may wish to customize gameboards using Gamemaker in Online Resources.

- Play Concentration, having children match pairs of one uppercase letter card with one lowercase letter card. When they are done, have them work together to sort letter pairs into two groups: uppercase and lowercase letter forms that look the same, and uppercase and lowercase letter forms that look different. Have children describe any differences between two forms.

▶ Connect with Home

Have children take home uppercase and lowercase letter cards reproduced on heavy paper so they can cut them apart and match them. Then they can describe to a family whether the letter pairs look the same or different. You may also want to give them copies of the Lotto game boards so they can play the game with family members.

Recognize That Letters Can Be Consonants or Vowels

Plan

▶ Consider Your Children

This lesson is best used after children know most of the letters and can recognize and name them quickly in words. They should also know the terms *first, middle*, and *last* as applied to letters in words and know simple high-frequency words as well as some words that have regular spellings. As children notice consonants and vowels in words, they may have questions about the words *my* and *why*. Simply explain that in some words, *y* is a vowel.

▶ Working with English Language Learners

You may need many demonstrations and repetitions to help English language learners learn the labels *consonants* and *vowels*. Once children learn these terms, they can use them often to talk about letters and words. Have children work not only with magnetic letters but with letter cards, letter tiles, and other manipulatives. Practice having children say and locate the vowels *a, e, i, o*, and *u*. Once they can find these letters quickly and identify them as vowels, they can notice that the rest of the letters are consonants. Be sure to demonstrate the sorting task.

YOU WILL NEED

PWS Ready Resources
▶ Lowercase Letter Cards

Online Resources
▶ **LK 22** Action Tags
▶ **LK 22** Vowel Strips
▶ **LK 22** Two-Way Sorts
▶ **LK 22** Blank Word Cards

Other Materials
▶ magnetic letters
▶ magnetic surface

UNDERSTAND THE PRINCIPLE

The words *consonants* and *vowels* are useful labels that will allow children to talk about letters and how how letters make up words. Learning these two terms–and the broad categories they represent–early will help children explore more complex principles later, such as ones involving the relationships between sounds and letters.

EXPLAIN THE PRINCIPLE

Some letters are consonants: b, c, d, f, g, h, j, k, l, m, n, p, q, r, s, t, v, w, x, y, z.

Some letters are vowels: a, e, i, o, u, *and sometimes* y.

Every word has at least one vowel.

Comprehensive Phonics, Spelling, and Word Study Guide

Refer to: page **23**, row **7**

ACTIVITY: MAGNETIC LETTERS

INSTRUCTIONAL PROCEDURE

SAY AND SORT

See page 36 for detailed descriptions of Instructional Procedures.

EXPLAIN THE PRINCIPLE

Some letters are consonants: b, c, d, f, g, h, j, k, l, m, n, p, q, r, s, t, v, w, x, y, z.

Some letters are vowels: a, e, i, o, u, *and sometimes* y.

Every word has at least one vowel.

Comprehensive Phonics, Spelling, and Word Study Guide

Refer to: page **23**, row **7**

Teach

1. Using magnetic letters, display the alphabet on the left side of a magnetic surface. Tell the children that they are going to learn something new about letters.

2. *Today we are going to learn which letters are consonants and which letters are vowels. Say the words* consonant *and* vowel. • *Knowing which letters are consonants and which letters are vowels will help you spell words better.*

3. Make the word *cat* with additional magnetic letters. *Here is a word that you know. What is this word?* • *In this word the first letter,* c, *is a consonant. The middle letter,* a, *is a vowel, and the last letter,* t, *is another consonant.*

4. *Now I am going to show the letters that are vowels.* Place additional magnetic letters of the vowels on the blank half of the surface. *The vowels are* a, e, i, o, *and* u. *We're going to hunt for the vowels as we say the alphabet. The first one we'll look for is* a. *Who can find it?* Have a child find the *a* on the left side and place it on the blank side.

5. Repeat for each additional vowel, each time telling children what to look for and asking them to clap when you come to it. Then have them say the vowels as a group: *a, e, i, o, u.*

6. Place the vowels back in the alphabet, but display one set of vowels on the right as a model. Go through the process again more quickly, this time without telling the children what vowel to look for.

7. Use the magnetic letters to make several simple words consisting of a consonant-vowel-consonant pattern (e.g., *dog, cat*) and a vowel-consonant combination (e.g., *at, in*). In each instance, have children find the vowel and ask them what they notice about the word.

8. Children may say vowels are "in the middle." *A vowel is often in the middle of a word. In some words, a vowel is at the beginning. Sometimes a vowel is even at the end of the word. Now, do you know what you can find in every word?* • *That's right, every word has at least one vowel in it. Many words have more than one vowel.*

9. Turn to the class name chart and have children determine which names begin with a consonant and which names begin with a vowel.

10. Tell children that they are going to sort letters into consonants and vowels, and quickly show them how to do this. Then, explain how children can check each letter in the vowel column by trying to find it on the list of vowels on the letter strip.

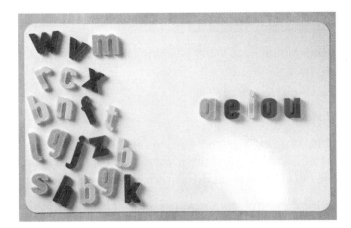

ACTIVITY: TWO-WAY LETTER SORT

INSTRUCTIONAL PROCEDURE

SAY AND SORT

See page 36 for detailed descriptions of Instructional Procedures.

ACTION TAGS

say

sort

check

Apply

Have children place a collection of magnetic letters on a flat or vertical surface (or lowercase letter cards beside a two-way sort). Have children place all of the consonants on the left and all of the vowels on the right, saying the name of each letter as they sort it. Have vowel strips handy so children can check their work. Provide more than one of each letter to make the task more complex.

Share

Have children look at a set of name cards (prepared from blank word cards) and count the number of vowels in each name. Then have each child say the name of each vowel.

Assess

■ Notice whether the children are able to identify vowels quickly.

■ Observe whether the children are able to locate the vowels in words.

Connect Learning Across Contexts

Interactive Read-Aloud Read aloud an alphabet book. Have children clap when you come to a vowel.

    IRA *ABC I Like Me* by Nancy Carlson

    IRA B *Is for Bulldozer* by June Sobel

Shared Reading Read the Alphabet Linking Chart twice, first reading just the consonants and then reading just the vowels. Ask children to point out the vowels and/or consonants in a word that they locate in a familiar text.

Interactive Writing When a word is written, have children check to see whether it has a vowel and name it. Invite children to say the vowel's position—first, middle, or last—in the word.

Independent Writing Encourage children to check words they have written to be sure that each has at least one vowel.

Extend Learning

Play Follow the Path with a game board containing a consonant or a vowel in each space. Have children throw the die, land on a letter, say the name of the letter, and tell whether it is a consonant or a vowel. See the directions for Follow the Path in Online Resources. You may also wish to customize gameboards using Gamemaker in Online Resources.

▶ Connect with Home

Have children take home uppercase and lowercase letter cards to sort into consonants and vowels. Have caregivers help children find uppercase and lowercase letters in their home and environment: for example, on signs, on magazine or newspaper pages, on food labels. Also suggest that caregivers ask children to sort consonants and vowels using magnetic letters or letter cards. You may wish to provide them with a copy of 25 Ways to Use Magnetic Letters at Home (see Online Resources).

Recognize the Order of the Alphabet

Plan

▶ Consider Your Children

Once children have learned letter names and can locate them easily, it is useful for them to understand the alphabet as a tool. They may be able to say or sing the alphabet, but that does not necessarily mean they understand alphabetical order. This lesson will help children use the order of the alphabet to help them find information they need.

▶ Working with English Language Learners

This lesson will give English language learners more experience in connecting letter shapes and letter names. Learning alphabetical order will give them an additional tool for understanding the way written language is organized. Provide as many repetitions as necessary to help children understand the order of the letters in the alphabet. Work with a small group to help them use the Alphabet Linking Chart to put their magnetic letters in order. Then show them how to check the order by saying the alphabet or checking letter by letter with the chart.

YOU WILL NEED

PWS Ready Resources
- ▶ Alphabet Strips
- ▶ Lowercase Letter Cards

Online Resources
- ▶ LK 23 Action Tags

Other Materials
- ▶ magnetic letters
- ▶ magnetic board or other magnetic surface

Generative Lesson ✓

A generative lesson has a simple structure that you can use to present similar content or concepts. You can use this lesson structure to teach children to recognize and sort the order of the alphabet in a variety of ways.

UNDERSTAND THE PRINCIPLE

Children need to develop a working knowledge of the twenty-six letter names and their order so they will be able to talk about letters. Knowing letter order also gives them a tool for referring to the word wall.

EXPLAIN THE PRINCIPLE

The alphabet has twenty-six letters.

The letters are in a special order.

Comprehensive Phonics, Spelling, and Word Study Guide

Refer to: page **22**, row **6**

ACTIVITY: MAGNETIC LETTERS

INSTRUCTIONAL PROCEDURE

SAY AND SORT

See page 36 for detailed descriptions of Instructional Procedures.

EXPLAIN THE PRINCIPLE

The alphabet has twenty-six letters.

The letters are in a special order.

Comprehensive Phonics, Spelling, and Word Study Guide

Refer to: page **22**, row **6**

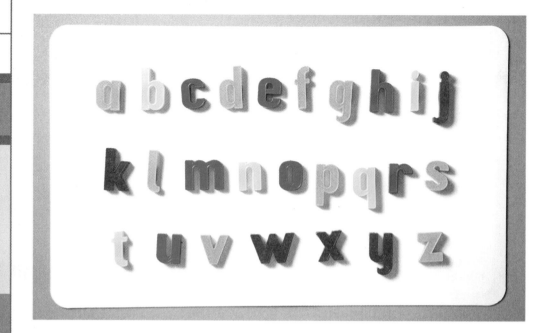

Teach

1. Tell children that there are twenty-six letters in the alphabet and that these letters go in a special order. Then explain to the children that they are going to learn how to put the letters of the alphabet in order.

2. Show the series of lowercase magnetic letters arranged in alphabetical order on a magnetic board or other magnetic surface. Count the letters with the children to reinforce that there are twenty-six letters in the alphabet.

3. Mix up the letters.

4. Explain to the group that they are going to put the letters of the alphabet in order. Invite individual children to place two or three letters at a time in alphabetical order and say the names of the letters.

5. After two or three children take their turns, have a child come up to point to each letter while the other children read the sequence of letters.

6. Continue until the whole alphabet is in the correct order.

7. Show the children the alphabet strips and explain how to complete the alphabetical order activity. You may wish to cut horizontally across the alphabet strips to make separate the printed letters and the lines for children to write letters.

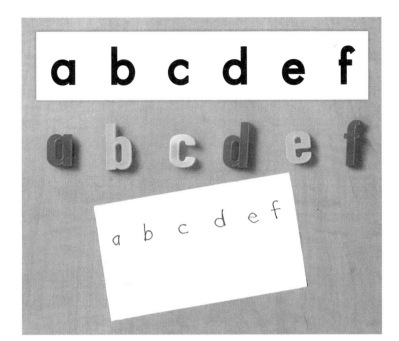

ACTIVITY: ALPHABET STRIPS

INSTRUCTIONAL PROCEDURE

SAY AND WRITE

See page 36 for detailed descriptions of Instructional Procedures.

ACTION TAGS

match

say

write

Apply

- Have children put the magnetic letter *a* under the matching *a* on the alphabet strip, and say the name of the letter. They should continue in this way through the alphabet in order.
- Then have children write the letters of the alphabet in order on the blank write-on line.

Share

Give each child a letter as she comes to the group meeting. Play a quick alphabet game. One child says the letter she is holding and the next child tells the letter that comes after it. That child then names the letter she is holding, and the process is repeated.

Assess

- Notice the children's ability to navigate the word wall using alphabetical order.
- Ask the children to tell you how many letters are in the alphabet.
- Observe the children as they put lowercase letter cards in alphabetical order on a long paper strip.

Letter Knowledge: Recognize the Order of the Alphabet

Connect Learning Across Contexts

Interactive Read-Aloud Read aloud alphabet books. Have the children predict each upcoming letter.

> IRA *On Market Street* by Arnold Lobel and Anita Lobel

> IRA *Miss Bindergarten Gets Ready for Kindergarten* by Joseph Slate

Shared Reading See "There Was an Old Woman Who Lived in a Shoe" in *Words That Sing* (2019). If you don't have these poetry charts, enlarge the print of a song or poem such as "Teeter-totter" or Christina Rossetti's "Mix a Pancake" in *Sing a Song of Poetry*. Have children use highlighter tape to find letters during a game of "I'm thinking of . . . for example, *I'm thinking of a word that starts with the letter that comes after* b. You may also wish to use the following Shared Reading title from *Fountas & Pinnell Classroom*™.

> SR *Country ABCs* by Finnoula Louise

Interactive Writing After a text has been written, have children find particular letters.

Independent Writing Invite children to refer to the word wall (which is displayed in alphabetical order) to find a word they want to write.

Extend Learning

- Repeat the lesson with uppercase letters.
- Have children place the lowercase letters on the alphabet strips and match the corresponding uppercase letters below them.
- Using the alphabet strips, block out some of the letters with white paper and tape. Invite children to place all the magnetic letters in order, including those that go on top of the visible letters and those that belong in spaces where the letters aren't visible.

▶ Connect with Home

Have caregivers ask their children to mix up magnetic letters or copies of the lowercase letter cards and put them in alphabetical order.

Recognize the Order of the Alphabet

Plan

▶ Consider Your Children

This lesson is best used after children can recognize and name most of the letters of the alphabet and can read and write their names. This lesson helps consolidate their knowledge and helps them understand alphabetical order. Once children learn how to play this game, you can vary the task.

▶ Working with English Language Learners

This lesson will help English language learners understand how to use the alphabet as a tool and also give them experience with the entire set of twenty-six letters. Be sure that English language learners have plenty of opportunities to say the alphabet while pointing to each letter in turn. Also be sure that children know how to play Follow the Path; introduce the game in a small group, if needed.

UNDERSTAND THE PRINCIPLE

Children need to develop a working knowledge of the twenty-six letter names and their order so they will be able to talk about letters. Knowing letter order also gives them a tool for referring to the word wall. The alphabet is a very important tool for emergent and early readers, and knowledge of alphabetical order is a helpful organizational tool.

YOU WILL NEED

PWS Ready Resources
- ▶ Alphabet Linking Chart
- ▶ Lowercase Letter Cards

Online Resources
- ▶ LK 24 Action Tags
- ▶ LK 24 Follow the Path Game Boards
- ▶ LK 24 Directions for Follow the Path

Other Materials
- ▶ dice
- ▶ game markers

Generative Lesson

A generative lesson has a simple structure that you can use to present similar content or concepts. You can use this lesson structure to teach children to recognize and sort the order of the alphabet in a variety of ways.

EXPLAIN THE PRINCIPLE

The alphabet has twenty-six letters.

The letters are in a special order.

Comprehensive Phonics, Spelling, and Word Study Guide

Refer to: page **22**, row **6**

**ACTIVITY: ALPHABET
LINKING CHART**

**INSTRUCTIONAL
PROCEDURE**

SEE AND SAY

*See page 36 for detailed
descriptions of Instructional
Procedures.*

EXPLAIN THE PRINCIPLE

*The alphabet has twenty-six
letters.*

The letters are in a special order.

Comprehensive
Phonics, Spelling,
and Word Study
Guide

Refer to:
page **22**, row **6**

Teach

1. Explain to the children that
they are going to learn more
about the alphabet.

2. Using the Alphabet Linking
Chart as a reference, invite
children to sing "The Alphabet
Song":

    A – B – C – D – E – F – G,

    H – I – J – K ,

    L – M – N – O – P,

    Q – R – S,

    T – U – V,

    W – X,

    Y and Z.

    Now I've said my ABCs.

    *Tell me what you think of
    me.*

3. *You know many of the letters
on our chart. Let's name some
of the letters on the Alphabet Linking Chart.* Point quickly to different letters
and have children name them. Then have them tell you how many letters are
in the alphabet. *Today we're going to learn how to play a game about the
special order of the letters in the alphabet. The special order of the letters is
called alphabetical order. Can you say* alphabetical order? • *The Alphabet
Linking Chart shows the special order of the twenty-six letters in the alphabet.
When you say the alphabet, you always say it in the same special order.*

4. Show children the Follow the Path game board. Have them read letters on the
game board as you point to each one. *Look at the letters on this game board.
Are these letters in alphabetical order?* • *The letters are* not *in alphabetical
order. We're going to play Follow the Path to help us remember the special
order of the letters in the alphabet.*

5. Ask a volunteer to come up and play the game with you as your partner.
Demonstrate how to throw the die and advance the marker the appropriate
number of spaces. Demonstrate saying the letter you land on. *When you land
on a letter, say the name of the letter and tell the next two letters in the
alphabet. Where could you look if you can't remember them?* • *Your partner
will have a small copy of the Alphabet Linking Chart. Your partner's job is to
check to see whether you said the right letters.*

6. Take a few turns until the children understand how to play. Explain that the
person who reaches the end first is the winner of the game.

Fountas & Pinnell Phonics, Spelling, and Word Study Lessons, Kindergarten

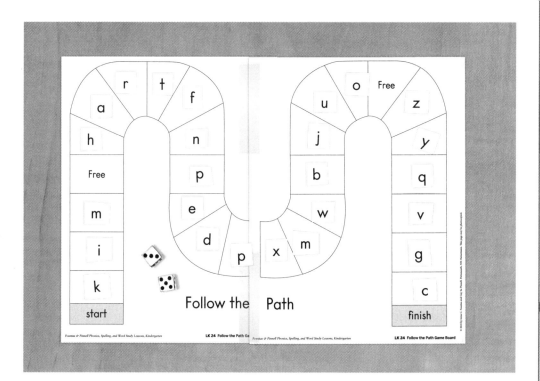

INSTRUCTIONAL PROCEDURE

SEE AND SAY

See page 36 for detailed descriptions of Instructional Procedures.

ACTION TAGS

toss
move
say

Apply

Working with a partner, children play Follow the Path two times. You also may wish to customize gameboards using Gamemaker in Online Resources.

Share

Suggest letters to children and have them say the next two letters without looking at the chart.

Assess

Check children's knowledge by giving them a set of lowercase letter cards and asking them to put the letters in alphabetical order.

Connect Learning Across Contexts

Interactive Read-Aloud Read aloud alphabet books. Pause and ask children to predict the next letter.

🔲 *ABC I Llike Me* by Nancy Carlson

🔲 *On Market Street* by Arthur and Anita Lobel

Shared Reading Have children read the Alphabet Linking Chart in different ways: for example, read consonants, read vowels, read pictures, read words in every other box, sing it, read the first box and clap or snap the next box, read it in reverse order (starting at the end), and read letters with circles. You may also wish to use the following Shared Reading title from *Fountas & Pinnell Classroom*™.

🔲 *City ABCs* by Finnoula Louise

Interactive Writing Use the Alphabet Linking Chart to locate and connect letters in the words children are writing.

Independent Writing Encourage children to check the letters they write against the Alphabet Linking Chart.

Extend Learning

- Have children name the two letters that come *before* the one they land on.
- Have children name the letter that comes *before* the one they land on, as well as the letter that comes *after* the one they land on.
- Make new game boards with different letter arrangements.
- Make new game boards with uppercase and lowercase letters.

▶ Connect with Home

Send a copy of the Follow the Path game board home with each child. Give each child a small, numbered die or one made from simple pieces of paper with the numbers 1, 2, 3, or directions ("Extra Turn," "Miss a Turn") written on them. Be sure children know how to play the game, but also provide simple directions for family members.

Letter-Sound Relationships

The sounds of oral language are related in both simple and complex ways to the twenty-six letters of the alphabet. Learning the connections between sounds and letters is basic to understanding written language. Children first learn simple relationships that are regular in that one phoneme is connected to one grapheme, or letter. But sounds can also be consonant digraphs (e.g., *ch, ph, sh, th, wh*), which stand for a sound that is different from either of the individual consonant sounds. Long vowel sounds can be represented by letter combinations (e.g., *ai, ea, igh, oa, ue*) that stand for the sound of the name of the first vowel. (Some exceptions exist, usually in words adopted from other languages.) Children learn to look for and recognize these letter combinations as units, which makes their word solving more efficient. It is important to remember that children will be able to hear and connect the easy-to-identify consonants and vowels early and progress to the harder-to-hear and more difficult letter-sound relationships. You will want to connect initial letter sounds to the Alphabet Linking Chart (see *Ready Resources*). It is not necessary to teach every letter as a separate lesson. When using the children's names to teach about words, substitute *name* for *word* when explaining the principle.

Connect to Assessment

See related (optional) LSR Assessment tasks in Online Resources.

- Assessment A: Matching Consonant Letters and Sounds at the Beginning of Words
- Assessment B: Matching Consonant Letters and Sounds at the End of Words
- Assessment C: Class Record

Develop Your Professional Understanding

See *The Fountas & Pinnell Comprehensive Phonics, Spelling, and Word Study Guide*. Related pages: 2–12, 26–31.

See *The Fountas & Pinnell Literacy Continuum: A Tool for Assessment, Planning, and Teaching*. 2017. Portsmouth, New Hampshire: Heinemann. Related pages: 357–397.

See *Word Matters: Teaching Phonics and Spelling in the Reading/Writing Classroom* by G. S. Pinnell and I. C. Fountas. 1998. Portsmouth, New Hampshire: Heinemann. Related pages: 46–48, 71–72, 72–73, 90–93, 123, 141.

Jenny

book

ball

bird.

Flower

Frog

Recognize Beginning Consonant Sounds and the Letters That Represent Them

Plan

▶ Consider Your Children

This lesson is best used after children have demonstrated that they can hear and isolate sounds in words, understand the concept of matching sounds and letters, and can name most letters of the alphabet. You can use any of the picture cards for beginning consonant sounds. Select first consonants that you think most children know or "nearly know."

▶ Working with English Language Learners

Be sure that children say and understand the name for each picture. Have them say the words rather than just listening to your pronunciation. Demonstrate saying the names of the letters and matching letters with the sounds in words represented in the picture cards. Begin with a small set of letters that are easy to hear. Then repeat the lesson, gradually increasing the number of sounds and letters children will match. Demonstrate the application task using the two-way sort; you may want to work with a small group to be sure they understand the task.

YOU WILL NEED

PWS **Ready Resources**
▶ LSR 1 Pocket-Chart Picture Cards
▶ LSR 1 Pocket-Chart Letter Cards
▶ Lowercase Letter Cards

Online Resources
▶ LSR 1 Action Tags
▶ LSR 1 Two-Way Sorts
▶ LSR 1 Two-Column Sorts
▶ LSR 1 Picture Cards

Other Materials
▶ pocket chart

Generative Lesson
A generative lesson has a simple structure that you can use to present similar content or concepts. You can use this lesson structure to teach children beginning consonant sounds with a variety of letters.

UNDERSTAND THE PRINCIPLE

Connecting the initial sound of a word with a letter helps children begin to use the alphabet to solve words while reading. Once children can identify initial sounds and connect letters to them, they can use this information to monitor their reading and distinguish between words. Children can check letter-sound information with their sense of meaning and language structure as they read.

EXPLAIN THE PRINCIPLE

Say a word slowly and listen for the first sound.

Match sounds and letters at the beginning of a word.

Comprehensive Phonics, Spelling, and Word Study Guide

Refer to: page **26**, row **2**

ACTIVITY: PICTURE AND LETTER MATCH

INSTRUCTIONAL PROCEDURE

FIND AND MATCH

See page 36 for detailed descriptions of Instructional Procedures.

EXPLAIN THE PRINCIPLE

Say a word slowly and listen for the first sound.

Match sounds and letters at the beginning of a word.

Comprehensive Phonics, Spelling, and Word Study Guide

Refer to: page **26**, row **2**

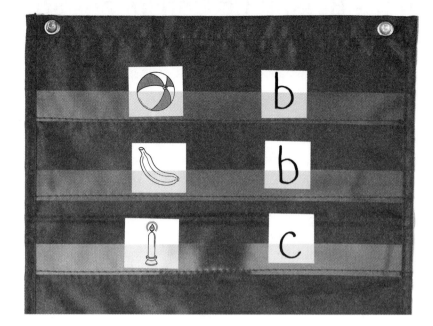

Teach

1. Explain to the children that they are going to learn more about sounds and letters.

2. *Today you are going to match sounds and letters at the beginning of words. First, let's say the names of each picture in the pocket chart. And let's listen for the sound at the beginning of each word.* Invite children to say the name of each picture.

3. *I'm going to take a letter card from this stack. I'm going to see if I can match a letter to a beginning sound in a word shown in one of the pictures.*

4. Hold up the first letter card. *What is this letter? ● This is* b. *Now I'm going to see if there is a picture of a word that has the sound of* b *at the beginning. Can anyone see a picture of a word that starts with a* b *sound? ●* Provide an example of a *b* word if necessary.

5. Match *b* with *ball* and place the letter card of *b* next to the picture of the ball.

6. Draw letter cards one at a time, asking children to say the letter and matching it with a word shown in a picture each time. (If a letter doesn't match any word pictured on the chart, return that letter card to the bottom of the pile.) Continue until all pictured words have a matching letter.

7. Show the children a two-way sort with a key picture on the left (e.g., a snake) and a letter card that matches the initial sound of the picture's name on the right (e.g., the letter s).

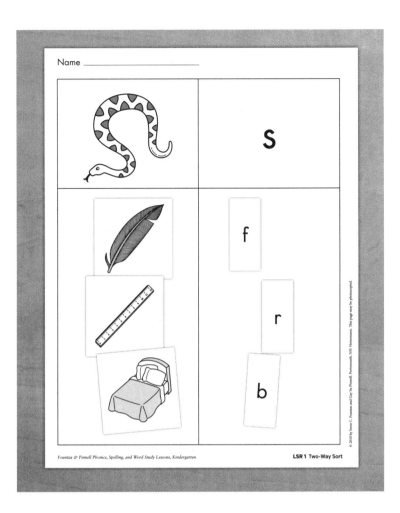

Name _____

S

f

r

b

Fountas & Pinnell Phonics, Spelling, and Word Study Lessons, Kindergarten   **LSR 1** Two-Way Sort

© 2018 by Irene C. Fountas and Gay Su Pinnell. Portsmouth, NH: Heinemann. This page may be photocopied.

ACTIVITY: TWO-WAY PICTURE AND LETTER MATCH

INSTRUCTIONAL PROCEDURE

FIND AND MATCH

See page 36 for detailed descriptions of Instructional Procedures.

ACTION TAGS

choose
say
find
match

Apply

Give children a number of picture cards, a number of corresponding letter cards, a two-way sort with a key picture and a letter as an example at the top, and a two-column sort. Invite children to choose a picture card, say the word, find the consonant letter that represents the sound at the beginning of that word, and place or glue the matching picture card and letter card on the sort.

Share

Ask the children to tell about some of the beginning sounds and consonant letters they matched in words.

Assess

■ Place picture cards in the pocket chart and ask individual children to match beginning sounds and letters.

■ Notice whether the children can isolate and say the first sound of a word while reading.

■ Check whether the children can use the first sound and/or first letter of a word to monitor and check their reading.

■ Observe whether the children are able to generate the first letters of words during writing.

■ You may wish to use Letter-Sound Relationships Assessment A or C.

Letter-Sound Relationships: Recognize Beginning Consonant Sounds and the Letters That Represent Them

Connect Learning Across Contexts

Interactive Read-Aloud Read aloud stories that emphasize words that begin with the same sound.

> IRA *Cat's Colors* by Jane Cabrera

> IRA *Over on the Farm* by Marianne Berkes

Shared Reading See "Three Blind Mice" in *Words That Sing* (2019). If you don't have these poetry charts, enlarge the print of this poem or other poems such as "Snail, Snail" in *Sing a Song of Poetry*, and cover the first letter of a word with a stick-on note. Ask children to read up to the word and to predict the first letter by thinking about the sound. You may also wish to use the following Shared Reading title from *Fountas & Pinnell Classroom*™ to find further examples of beginning consonant sounds.

> SR *Pitter Patter* by Miriam David

Interactive Writing Before writing a word, have children say it slowly and think about what the first letter is likely to be.

Independent Writing When they are writing, encourage children to say words slowly and to write the first letter. Accept approximations that represent good sound analysis (for example, *cit* for *kite*).

Extend Learning

- Repeat the lesson with other pictures and letters.
- Repeat the lesson with more difficult consonant sounds (for example, *w* or *y*).

▶ Connect with Home

- Make reproducible pictures and letters that children can take home, cut apart, and match.
- Have family members play "I Say, You Say." The caregiver says a word that begins with a certain letter (for example, "I say *dish*") and then the child says one that begins with the same letter ("I say *dog*"). They do this with several letters.

Recognize Beginning Consonant Sounds and the Letters That Represent Them

Plan

▶ Consider Your Children

This lesson is best used after children have demonstrated that they can hear and isolate sounds in words, understand the concept of matching sounds and letters, and can name most letters of the alphabet. You will want to use this lesson with just two or three consonants at first: *s, m, t,* and *b* are among the easiest to distinguish. Then continue with three or four other consonants at a time (*f, r, n, p, d, h, c, g, j, l, k, v, w, z, qu, y*).

▶ Working with English Language Learners

By the time you use this lesson with English language learners, they should be familiar with the words shown on a large number of picture cards. Avoid any words that involve concepts that are likely to be outside their experiences. Children should be able to say the words, identify the initial sound, and recognize the corresponding letter. Work with a small group as needed to be sure that they understand the task and are checking their work by saying the words.

YOU WILL NEED

PWS Ready Resources
- ▶ **LSR 2** Pocket-Chart Alphabet Cards
- ▶ **LSR 2** Pocket-Chart Picture Cards
- ▶ **LSR 2** Pocket-Chart Word Cards

Online Resources
- ▶ **LSR 2** Action Tags
- ▶ **LSR 2** Three-Way Sorts
- ▶ **LSR 2** Picture Cards
- ▶ **LSR 2** Word Cards

Other Materials
- ▶ pocket chart, easel, or whiteboard

Generative Lesson ✓

A generative lesson has a simple structure that you can use to present similar content or concepts. You can use this lesson structure to teach children beginning consonant sounds with a variety of letters.

UNDERSTAND THE PRINCIPLE

Connecting the initial sound of a word with a letter helps children begin to use the alphabet to solve words while reading. Once children can identify initial sounds and connect letters to them, they can use this information to monitor their reading and distinguish between words. Children can check letter-sound information with their sense of meaning and language structure as they read.

EXPLAIN THE PRINCIPLE

Match sounds and letters at the beginning of a word.

When you know the sound, you can find the letter.

Find a word by saying it and thinking about the first sound.

Comprehensive Phonics, Spelling, and Word Study Guide

Refer to: page **26**, row **2**

ACTIVITY: LETTER AND PICTURE MATCH

INSTRUCTIONAL PROCEDURE

SAY AND SORT

See page 36 for detailed descriptions of Instructional Procedures.

EXPLAIN THE PRINCIPLE

Match sounds and letters at the beginning of a word.

When you know the sound, you can find the letter.

Find a word by saying it and thinking about the first sound.

Comprehensive Phonics, Spelling, and Word Study Guide

Refer to: page **26**, row **2**

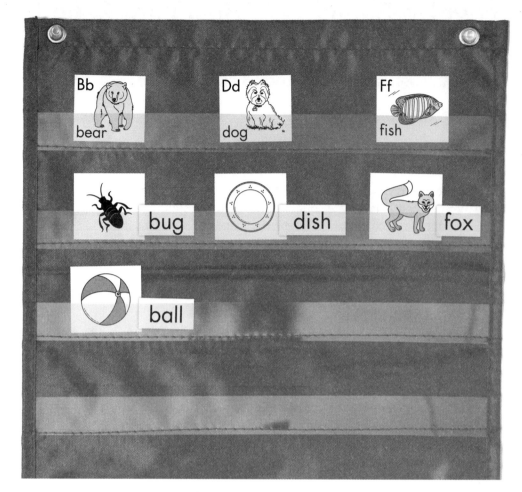

Teach

1. Explain to children that they are going to learn more about sounds and letters at the beginning of words.

2. Place key Pocket-Chart Alphabet Cards at the top of three columns in a pocket chart or on an easel or whiteboard.

3. *Look at the first picture. What word is this?* • *Yes, it's* bear. *What sound do you hear first in the word* bear? As you say *bear* make sure to enunciate each phoneme clearly. • *What letter would you expect to see first in* bear? •

4. *Now, can you think of another word that begins with the letter* b? • *Yes, the word* bug *begins with the letter* b. Invite a child to place the picture of *bug* underneath the picture of *bear*.

5. Repeat with other words beginning with consonants that correspond to the words shown on the key picture cards.

6. *You have looked at many words today and matched the sound and the letter at the beginning of each word. When you know the sound, you can find the letter.*

Name Chantall

Bb bear	Mm moon	Ss sun
bug	mitten	snake
ball	mouse	

Fountas & Pinnell Phonics, Spelling, and Word Study Lessons, Kindergarten

LSR 2 Three-Way Sort

© 2017 by Irene C. Fountas and Gay Su Pinnell. Portsmouth, NH: Heinemann. This page may be photocopied.

INSTRUCTIONAL PROCEDURE

SAY AND SORT

See page 36 for detailed descriptions of Instructional Procedures.

ACTION TAGS

say

sort

read

underline

Apply

Have children sort pictures and words using a three-way sort, saying each word and placing each picture and word under the appropriate key picture. Then have them read each column with a partner. Finally, have them underline the first letter in each word.

Share

Have children read their three-column sorts to a new partner. Have two or three children share with the group what they have noticed about matching sounds and letters.

Assess

- Give the children a sheet with pictures and letters and have them draw lines to match them.
- Observe the children to determine how well they are matching sounds and letters at the beginnings of words. Have any child who seems confused match the picture cards and letter cards individually as you observe which ones cause her confusion.
- You may wish to use Letter-Sound Relationships Assessment A or C.

Letter-Sound Relationships: Recognize Beginning Consonant Sounds and the Letters That Represent Them

Connect Learning Across Contexts

Interactive Read-Aloud Read aloud books that emphasize the beginning sounds in words.

> IRA *A, My Name is Alice* by Jane Bayer
>
> IRA *One Duck Stuck* by Phyllis Root

Shared Reading See "Willaby, Wallaby, Woo" in *Words That Sing* (2019). If you don't have these poetry charts, enlarge the print of this poem or other poems such as "Chickery, Chickery, Cranny, Crow" in *Sing a Song of Poetry*, and cover the last part of a word with a stick-on note. Ask children to read up to the word and to predict the word by thinking about the first letter. You may also wish to use the following Shared Reading title from *Fountas & Pinnell Classroom*™ to engage children in the same process of using the first letter to predict the word using the text meaning.

> SR *In the Arctic* by Tess Fletcher

Interactive Writing When children want to write the next word in a sentence, ask them to say the word and think about the first sound and *identify* the first letter.

Independent Writing Remind children to say a word and write the letter *that stands for* the first sound.

Extend Learning

Repeat the lesson with a focus on various consonants and other words, using other picture cards and word cards from Online Resources.

▶ Connect with Home

Send home sheets of pictures and words for children to cut out and match.

Recognize Beginning Consonant Sounds and the Letters That Represent Them

Plan

▶ Consider Your Children

This lesson is best used after children have demonstrated that they can hear and isolate sounds in words, understand the concept of matching sounds and letters, and can name most letters of the alphabet. Learning letters and sounds together will accelerate learning letter-sound relationships and allow children to apply that knowledge to solving words. Children who are very proficient at identifying first letters and sounds will not need this lesson.

▶ Working with English Language Learners

For this lesson, children need to associate the name of each picture with a letter representing the first sound in the word. It will help your English language learners if you select pictures with which they are familiar. Be sure that children understand how to do a three-way sort. You may need to do an extra demonstration for a small group to be sure that they can perform the application task independently. Recognize and accept answers that show they are using names in their own language and categorizing them, for example, *luna* (moon) under *l*.

YOU WILL NEED

PWS Ready Resources
- ▶ Blank Pocket-Chart Cards
- ▶ LSR 3 Pocket-Chart Picture Cards
- ▶ LSR 3 Pocket-Chart Letter Cards

Online Resources
- ▶ LSR 3 Action Tags
- ▶ LSR 3 Three-Way Sorts
- ▶ LSR 3 Three-Column Sorts
- ▶ LSR 3 Picture Cards

Other Materials
- ▶ pocket chart

Generative Lesson
A generative lesson has a simple structure that you can use to present similar content or concepts. You can use this lesson structure to teach children beginning consonant sounds with a variety of letters.

UNDERSTAND THE PRINCIPLE

Connecting the initial sound of a word with a letter helps children begin to use the alphabet to solve words while reading. Once children can identify initial sounds and connect letters to them, they can use this information to monitor their reading and distinguish between words. Children can check letter-sound information with their sense of meaning and language structure as they read.

EXPLAIN THE PRINCIPLE

Match sounds and letters at the beginning of a word.

When you know the sound, you can find the letter.

Find a word by saying it and thinking about the first sound.

Comprehensive Phonics, Spelling, and Word Study Guide

Refer to: page **26**, row **2**

EARLY **MIDDLE** LATE

INSTRUCTIONAL PROCEDURE

SAY AND SORT

See page 36 for detailed descriptions of Instructional Procedures.

EXPLAIN THE PRINCIPLE

Match sounds and letters at the beginning of a word.

When you know the sound, you can find the letter.

Find a word by saying it and thinking about the first sound.

Comprehensive Phonics, Spelling, and Word Study Guide

Refer to: page **26**, row **2**

Teach

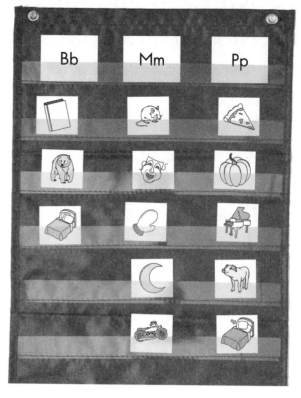

1. Explain to children that they are going to learn more about sounds and letters at the beginning of words.

2. In the first column of a pocket chart, show the picture card for *book*, leaving one space at the top of the column. *Look at this picture. What is this?* ● *The word is* book. Place the picture card for *bear* underneath the book. *Now look at this picture. What is this?* ● *It is a* bear. *Where should I put it?* Repeat for bed. *What do you notice about these words?* ● *Each of these words starts with the letter* b. Place the *Bb* pocket-chart card at the top of the column. *I'm going to put the letter* Bb *at the top because all of these words begin with the letter* b.

3. Moving to the next column, repeat the process with a few picture cards for words beginning with *m*. Moving to the next column, repeat the process with a few picture cards for words beginning with *p*.

4. *Now, I'm going to take a picture card from this stack. I want you to think about the sound at the beginning of the word and see if we can match the word with any of the letters in the pocket chart.*

5. Hold up the first picture card. *This is a pizza. Say* pizza. ● *What sound do you hear first in* pizza? ● *Where should I put it? I'll place the* pizza *with the other words that begin with the letter* p. Model checking /p/, *pizza, p.*

6. Continue holding up picture cards that represent words beginning with the letters *b, m,* and *p*. Have the children say each word and the letter that represents the first sound of the word. Then place the picture card in the corresponding column. If a word does not begin with any of the three letters, put the card aside. Continue to do so until all of the picture cards have been placed into the pocket chart or put aside.

7. *Today you learned that you can match sounds and letters at the beginning of a word. When you know the sound in a word, you can say and find the letter.*

ACTIVITY:
THREE-WAY SORT

INSTRUCTIONAL
PROCEDURE

SAY AND SORT

See page 36 for detailed descriptions of Instructional Procedures.

ACTION TAGS

take

say

sort

check

Apply

Give the children a three-way sort with the key letters at the top of the columns, as well as a three-column sort and picture cards, some with names that match the key letters and some that don't. One child takes each card, says the word, and sorts it according to the first sound of the word and the letter that stands for that sound. The child's partner listens, watches, and checks the completed sort. Then they mix the cards up and switch roles.

Share

Ask children which pictures they have matched with which letters. Invite them to give one more word for each letter in the chart.

Assess

- Place letter cards in the pocket chart and ask individual children to match a limited set of pictures quickly.
- Observe whether the children say the first sound of a word while reading.
- Notice whether the children use the first letter-sound of a word to monitor and check on their reading.
- Notice whether the children are able to write the first letters of words.
- You may wish to use Letter-Sound Relationships Assessment A or C.

Letter-Sound Relationships: Recognize Beginning Consonant Sounds and the Letters That Represent Them

Connect Learning Across Contexts

Interactive Read-Aloud Read aloud stories that emphasize beginning sounds.

IRA *A House Is a House for Me* by Mary Ann Hoberman

IRA *Fireman Small* by Wong Herbert Yee

Shared Reading See "Hickory, Dickory, Dare!" in *Words That Sing* (2019). If you don't have these poetry charts, enlarge the print of this poem or other poems such as "This is the Way We Wash Our Face" in *Sing a Song of Poetry*, and cover the first letter of a word with a stick-on note. Ask children to read up to the word and to predict the first letter by thinking about the sound. You may also wish to use the following Shared Reading title from *Fountas & Pinnell Classroom*™ to engage children in the same process of using the first letter to predict the word using the meaning of the text.

SR *Crunch: A Story for Two Voices* by David Edwin

Interactive Writing When they are thinking how to write a word, have children say the word slowly and decide what the first letter is likely to be.

Independent Writing Encourage children to say words slowly when they are writing and to write the first letter.

Extend Learning

- Extend the activity by increasing the number and variety of letters.
- Mix children's names and high-frequency word cards (see Online Resources) into the picture card set so that they are matching both pictures and words with the letters.

▶ Connect with Home

- Reproduce picture cards and letters (see Online Resources) that children can take home, cut apart, and match.
- Have family members make letter posters with the children. They write a letter at the top of a sheet and draw (or cut out from a magazine) pictures of objects whose names start with that letter. Have them check the beginning sound of the name with the first letter.

Recognize Beginning Consonant Sounds and the Letters That Represent Them

Plan

▶ Consider Your Children

This lesson is best used after children have demonstrated that they can hear and isolate sounds in words, understand the concept of matching sounds and letters, and can name most letters of the alphabet. Learning letters and sounds together will accelerate learning letter-sound relationships and allow children to apply that knowledge to solving words. Children who are very proficient at identifying first letters and sounds will not need this lesson. The directions below assume that children already know how to play Lotto (see the directions in Online Resources). To play, you need to place one card in each square until all the squares are filled.

▶ Working with English Language Learners

Some children may be only beginning to notice letters and sounds, and they may be doing so in both their own languages and English. If you can, provide an example of a word in their own language that has the same beginning sound and letter. Repeat the English words many times, using pictures and explanations, so that the words become meaningful to them. Eliminate any words that are meaningless to them. Even though children will be matching sounds, their learning will be limited if they are not working with words they understand. Do a quick check to be sure that children know all the names for the pictures in the Lotto game.

UNDERSTAND THE PRINCIPLE

Connecting the initial sound of a word with a letter helps children begin to use the alphabet to solve words while reading. Once children can identify initial sounds and connect letters to them, they can use this information to monitor their reading and distinguish between words. Children can check letter-sound information with their sense of meaning and language structure as they read. Children do not need to know all letters of the alphabet before reading stories, but knowing letters and their relationship to sounds in words is valuable information as they read their first storybooks.

YOU WILL NEED

PWS **Ready Resources**
- ▶ LSR 4 Pocket-Chart Picture Cards
- ▶ LSR 4 Pocket-Chart Letter Cards
- ▶ Alphabet Linking Chart
- ▶ Lowercase Letter Cards

Online Resources
- ▶ LSR 4 Action Tags
- ▶ LSR 4 Lotto and Bingo Game Boards
- ▶ LSR 4 Letter Cards
- ▶ LSR 4 Directions for Lotto and Bingo

Other Materials
- ▶ pocket chart

Generative Lesson

A generative lesson has a simple structure that you can use to present similar content or concepts. You can use this lesson structure to teach children beginning consonant sounds with a variety of letters.

EXPLAIN THE PRINCIPLE

Match sounds and letters at the beginning of a word.

When you know the sound, you can find the letter.

Find a word by saying it and thinking about the first sound.

Comprehensive Phonics, Spelling, and Word Study Guide

Refer to: page **26**, row **2**

ACTIVITY: LETTER AND PICTURE MATCH

INSTRUCTIONAL PROCEDURE

FIND AND MATCH

See page 36 for detailed descriptions of Instructional Procedures.

EXPLAIN THE PRINCIPLE

Match sounds and letters at the beginning of a word.

When you know the sound, you can find the letter.

Find a word by saying it and thinking about the first sound.

Comprehensive Phonics, Spelling, and Word Study Guide

Refer to: page **26**, row **2**

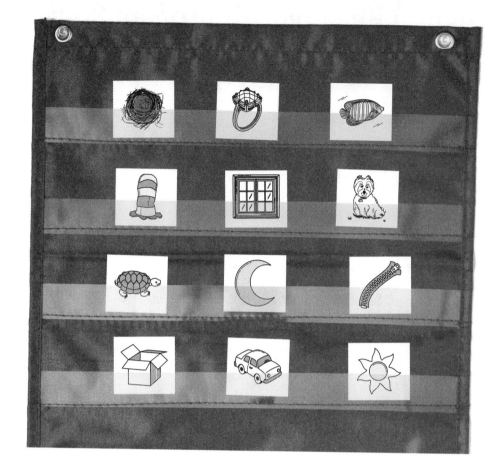

Teach

1. Tell the children they are going to learn more about letters and sounds.

2. Using the pocket chart, place picture cards in a rectangular pattern.

3. *Today we are going to play Lotto. Remember that you take turns taking a card and matching it to the pictures on your game card. This time we are going to use cards that have letters on them. Say the names of each of the pictures and listen for the first sound of the word.* Have children say the names of each picture.

4. *I'm going to take a letter card from this stack and see if I can match it to one of the pictures on my game card.*

5. Hold up the first letter card. *This is t. Now I'm going to see if there is a picture on my game card that has the sound of* t *at the beginning. Can anyone see the picture of a word that starts with a t sound?* Provide an example of a *t* word if necessary.

6. Model checking *t, turtle* and place the *t* card on the picture of the turtle.

7. Take cards one at a time, demonstrating how to say the letter and the name of the picture. Some letters will not match any word pictured on the pocket chart and will be placed facedown again.

8. *I've covered all the spaces on the pocket chart. That's what you do to win the Lotto game. Remember to say the letter and the name of the picture to check your matches. If you are not sure, you can look at the Alphabet Linking Chart.*

ACTIVITY: LOTTO (SMALL GROUPS)

INSTRUCTIONAL PROCEDURE

FIND AND MATCH

See page 36 for detailed descriptions of Instructional Procedures.

ACTION TAGS

take

say

match

Apply

Have children play Lotto in groups of three or four, each with a different game board. They take turns taking a letter card and saying the name of the picture that matches it. If there is a match, they place the letter card on the picture on the game board. If there is no match, the card is returned to the bottom of the card pile. The game continues until one child fills her card.

Share

Ask children to share some of the letters and pictured words they matched while playing Lotto.

Assess

- Place picture cards in the pocket chart and ask children to match sounds with letters.
- Notice whether the children can say the first sound of a word while reading.
- Notice whether the children can use the first letter-sound of a word to monitor and check their reading.
- Observe whether the children are able to generate beginning letters of words when they are writing.
- You may wish to use Letter-Sound Relationships Assessment A or C.

Letter-Sound Relationships: Recognize Beginning Consonant Sounds and the Letters That Represent Them

Connect Learning Across Contexts

Interactive Read-Aloud Read aloud stories that draw attention to beginning letters and sounds.

> IRA *Charlie Parker Played Be Bop* by Chris Raschka
>
> IRA *Fish Eyes* by Lois Ehlert

Shared Reading See "Diddlety, Diddlety, Dumpty!" in *Words That Sing* (2019). If you don't have these poetry charts, enlarge the print of this poem or other poems such as "Two Little Black Birds" in *Sing a Song of Poetry*, and cover the first letter of a word with a stick-on note. Ask children to read up to the word and to predict the first letter by thinking about the sound. You may also wish to use the following Shared Reading title from *Fountas & Pinnell Classroom*™ to engage children in the same process of using the first letter to predict the word using the meaning of the text.

> SR *Animal Masks* by Jennifer Blizin Gillis

Interactive Writing When thinking how to write a word, have children say it slowly and think about what the first letter will to be.

Independent Writing Encourage children to say words slowly when they are writing and to write the first letter.

Extend Learning

Extend the Lotto game by varying the pictures. You may customize gameboards using Gamemaker in Online Resources. Start with pictures that represent simple initial sounds, such as those suggested in this lesson, but gradually increase the complexity of the game and/or eliminate the easy-to-match sounds.

▶ Connect with Home

Have family members make an alphabet book of objects from their home. Send home twenty-six plain pieces of paper stapled together. Caregivers write one uppercase and the matching lowercase letter at the bottom of each page–e.g., *Aa*, *Bb*. (You can also duplicate letters and assemble these books yourself.) With the child, caregivers identify an object in the home that has a name that starts with each letter. The child draws the object on the appropriate page and the family member writes the word (for example, *table* for *t*, *lamp* for *l*, *pillow* for *p*, and *refrigerator* for *r*).

Recognize Beginning Consonant Sounds and the Letters That Represent Them

Plan

▶ Consider Your Children

Use this lesson after children can recognize some beginning sounds in words and connect them to letters of the alphabet. They should have had some experience writing words in interactive writing and should also understand the concept of first as it applies to words. The overall expectation is that children will be able to notice and locate words and first letters that are embedded in text.

▶ Working with English Language Learners

Go over the poem in an enjoyable way many times until English language learners know it and can say it with little support. Point to the words as you have them read the text; if they know the poem well, you may want to have individual children point to the words with some support. Talk about the meaning of the words in the poem—for example, *jelly* and *plate*—so that you are sure children know the individual words and what they mean. Invite them to share their own experiences and make connections to the poem. Once the poem is well known, the words will be more available to children and you can have them locate words, match letters, and so on.

YOU WILL NEED

Online Resources
- ▶ LSR 5 Poem: Jelly on the Plate
- ▶ LSR 5 Action Tags
- ▶ LSR 5 Poem, verses a, b, c

Other Materials
- ▶ chart paper and/or whiteboard
- ▶ masking card or highlighter tape

Generative Lesson ✓

A generative lesson has a simple structure that you can use to present similar content or concepts. You can use this lesson structure to teach children beginning consonant sounds with a variety of letters.

UNDERSTAND THE PRINCIPLE

Connecting the initial sound of a word with a letter helps children begin to use the alphabet to solve words while reading. Once children can identify initial sounds and connect letters to them, they can use this information to monitor their reading and distinguish between words. Children can check letter-sound information with their sense of meaning and language structure as they read. Children do not need to know all letters of the alphabet before reading stories, but knowing letters and their relationship to sounds in words is valuable information as they read their first storybooks.

EXPLAIN THE PRINCIPLE

Match sounds and letters at the beginning of a word.

When you know the sound, you can find the letter.

Find a word by saying it and thinking about the first sound.

Comprehensive Phonics, Spelling, and Word Study Guide

Refer to:
page **26**, row **2**

ACTIVITY: JELLY ON THE PLATE

INSTRUCTIONAL PROCEDURE

FIND AND MATCH

See page 36 for detailed descriptions of Instructional Procedures.

EXPLAIN THE PRINCIPLE

Match sounds and letters at the beginning of a word.

When you know the sound, you can find the letter.

Find a word by saying it and thinking about the first sound.

Comprehensive Phonics, Spelling, and Word Study Guide

Refer to: page **26**, row **2**

Jelly on the Plate

Jelly on the plate.
Jelly on the plate.
Wibble, wobble,
Wibble, wobble,
Jelly on the plate.

Pudding in the pan.
Pudding in the pan.
Ooey, gooey,
Ooey, gooey,
Pudding in the pan.

Soup in the pot.
Soup in the pot.
Bubble, bubble,
Bubble, bubble,
Soup in the pot.

Teach

1. Explain to the children that they are going to learn more about letters and sounds.

2. Invite the children to read and enjoy the poem several times.

3. *I see a word in this poem that starts with the letter* p. *Can you find it?* • Children may come up with *plate, pudding, pan,* and *pot.*

4. Say the *p* words and write them on another piece of chart paper or a whiteboard. *Let's read the words* plate, pudding, pan, pot. *Each of these words starts with the letter* p.

5. Have several children, using a masking card or highlighter tape, locate the words in the text that start with *p.* Read the text again to discover how these words fit into the whole text. At this point, children probably will not know how to discriminate between *pan* and *pot,* and that is not important now. They will be able to read the words because they're learning them in the poem.

6. *Can you think of any other words that start with the letter* p? • Children can get ideas for words from their own experience, from the class name chart, or from the word wall. Add any *p* words they suggest to the list. Display the list beside the poem.

7. Help children notice the *p* at the beginning of each word.

Pudding in the pan.
Pudding in the pan.
Ooey, gooey,
Ooey, gooey,
Pudding in the pan.

Soup in the po
Soup in the po
Bubble, bubble,
Bubble, bubble,
Soup in the po

Jelly on the plate.
Jelly on the plate.
Wibble, wobble,
Wibble, wobble,
Jelly on the plate.

ACTIVITY: VERSES FROM A POEM

INSTRUCTIONAL PROCEDURE

NOTICE PARTS

See page 36 for detailed descriptions of Instructional Procedures.

ACTION TAGS

say
draw
circle

Apply

Give the children printed pages with verses from the poem. The children can point and say the text to a partner, illustrate it, and circle the *p*'s at the beginning of words.

Share

Have the children say the poem together again as a group, and ask individuals to point to words that start with *p*.

Assess

- Notice whether the children are able to categorize words by beginning sound and letter.
- Observe whether the children can locate words in the text by saying the word and predicting the first letter.
- Notice whether the children are representing first letters in words they try to write in stories.
- You may wish to use Letter-Sound Relationships Assessment A or C.

Letter-Sound Relationships: Recognize Beginning Consonant Sounds and the Letters That Represent Them

Connect Learning Across Contexts

Interactive Read-Aloud Read aloud stories that feature words that have the same first letters and sounds. Point out that *k* and *c* often have the same sound, as in *kangaroo* and *cricket*.

IRA *Mouse Was Mad* by Linda Urban

IRA *Little Red Hen* by Paul Galdone

Shared Reading See "I Clap My Hands" in *Words That Sing* (2019). If you don't have these poetry charts, enlarge the print of this poem or poems such as "Teddy Bear, Teddy Bear" in *Sing a Song of Poetry*, and cover the first letter of a word with a stick-on note. Ask children to read up to the word and to predict the first letter by thinking about the sound. You may also wish to use the following Shared Reading title from *Fountas & Pinnell Classroom*™ to engage children in the same process of using the first letter to predict the word using the meaning of the text.

SR *Stars* by Catherine Friend

Interactive Writing When they are thinking how to write a word, have the children say it slowly and think about what the first sound is and what the first letter is likely to be. Connect the word with other words that start the same and locate those words on the word wall.

Independent Writing When children want to write a word, encourage them to say it slowly, isolate the first sound, and write the first letter. Make connections to other words they know that start the same.

Extend Learning

- Repeat the activity with other poems. *Sing a Song of Poetry* contains many other appropriate poems, such as "Pease Porridge Hot" and "Peter, Peter, Pumpkin-eater."

- Have children take a clipboard, go around the room looking for words (or objects with names) that start with a particular letter, and copy those words on a piece of paper.

▶ Connect with Home

Send home copies of simple poems or songs from *Sing a Song of Poetry*. Explain to family members how to point under each word with a pencil or chopstick as they read the text so children will be looking in the right place. Then caregivers can have children point under words that begin with a particular letter.

Recognize Beginning Consonant Sounds and the Letters That Represent Them

Plan

▶ Consider Your Children

Before you select this lesson, be sure children know what letters are, understand the concept of *consonants,* know the names of some letters and some associated sounds, and have worked with letters in simple ways. This lesson will be effective in helping children bring together their growing knowledge of letters and sounds, with a focus on the consonants that are very often found at the beginning of words.

▶ Working with English Language Learners

This lesson will help children systematize their knowledge of consonants (with associated key words) and the sounds they represent. It is especially important for English language learners to acquire these key words so that they can utilize them as resources when they are working with new words. Be sure that children understand the names of the pictures in the class consonants book. Have them talk about and use the names of the familiar objects that will be represented on the pages. Reread the book several times so that they can say the names of the objects on each page, noticing the first sounds and saying the name of each consonant.

YOU WILL NEED

PWS **Ready Resources**
- ▶ Alphabet Linking Chart
- ▶ LSR 6 Pocket-Chart Alphabet Cards

Online Resources
- ▶ LSR 6 Action Tags
- ▶ LSR 6 Book Pages

Other Materials
- ▶ class book, assembled from large pieces of card stock or folded craft paper that are stapled or held together by rings, with a letter card of a consonant in upper-right corner of each page
- ▶ camera

Generative Lesson ✓

A generative lesson has a simple structure that you can use to present similar content or concepts. You can use this lesson structure to teach children beginning consonant sounds with a variety of letters.

UNDERSTAND THE PRINCIPLE

Beginning readers need to recognize that the first letter of a word is on the left and is connected to a sound that they can say. Once this concept is established, children notice the first letter and learn to say the sound associated with it, which is the beginning of learning to decode and blend the sounds of complete words.

EXPLAIN THE PRINCIPLE

Match sounds and letters at the beginning of a word.

When you know the sound, you can find the letter.

Find a word by saying it and thinking about the first sound.

Comprehensive Phonics, Spelling, and Word Study Guide

Refer to: page **26**, row **2**

ACTIVITY: CLASS CONSONANTS BOOK

INSTRUCTIONAL PROCEDURE

SEE AND SAY

See page 36 for detailed descriptions of Instructional Procedures.

EXPLAIN THE PRINCIPLE

Match sounds and letters at the beginning of a word.

When you know the sound, you can find the letter.

Find a word by saying it and thinking about the first sound.

Comprehensive Phonics, Spelling, and Word Study Guide

Refer to: page **26**, row **2**

Teach

1. Tell the children that they are going to use what they know about beginning letters and sounds to make a class book about consonants.

2. You may want to use the Alphabet Linking Chart to quickly review the letter-sound relationships of the consonants. Point to the letter *Bb. What sound does the letter* b *stand for?* • *Yes, /b/, bear.* Continue with the remaining consonants.

3. Explain that children will spend a few days making a consonants book to show the consonants and their sounds. Flip through the class book you have prepared, pointing out the consonant in the upper-right corner of each page. *On each page, we're going to add photos or drawings of objects or people whose names begin with the consonant. What are some things we could add to the letter* Bb *page?* • Children might suggest adding a picture of a bird, a picture of a ball, or a drawing of a book.

4. Over a period of several days, guide children to brainstorm objects or people whose names begin with each consonant. Then work with children to take photos around the classroom or school, draw pictures, or cut out images to glue on the appropriate page. You may wish to assign individual pages to partners or small groups to create and assemble. Include the letter *x*, explaining to children that the letter appears at the beginning of very few words and that when it does, it says its name.

5. Each day, read together the pages completed so far to review words with the same beginning sound.

6. Read through the completed class consonants book during shared reading and refer to it during other phonics and word study lessons. You may wish to insert additional pages for vowels once you have introduced those letter-sound relationships.

INSTRUCTIONAL PROCEDURE

SEE AND SAY

See page 36 for detailed descriptions of Instructional Procedures.

ACTION TAGS

| draw |
| cut |
| glue |
| write |
| read |

Apply

Have children make their own books, creating one page for each consonant. Children may choose to draw pictures or cut out and glue picture cards or magazine images. Guide them to write labels for each picture. Encourage them to say the word slowly and think of the letters that stand for them. Encourage them to use lowercase letters. Encourage children to include at least three images and labels for each consonant. (If children get stuck on the letter *x*, explain that the letter *x* appears at the beginning of very few words and that when it does, it says its name.) This project will take several days.

Share

■ Read the class book together.

■ Have children read their completed books to a partner.

Assess

■ Observe children's ability to write the first letter of words in independent writing.

■ Ask individual children to say a word that starts with each consonant.

■ You may wish to use Letter-Sound Relationships Assessment A or C.

Letter-Sound Relationships: Recognize Beginning Consonant Sounds and the Letters That Represent Them

Connect Learning Across Contexts

Interactive Read-Aloud Read aloud a variety of alphabet books, drawing children's attention to the letter-sounds of various beginning consonants.

> [IRA] *A, My Name Is Alice* by Jane Bayer

> [IRA] *B Is for Bulldozer* by June Sobel

Shared Reading See "Five Fingers on Each Hand" in *Words That Sing* (2019). If you don't have these poetry charts, enlarge the print of this poem or other poems such as "Five Little Froggies" in *Sing a Song of Poetry*, and cover the first letter of a word with a stick-on note. Ask children to read up to the word and to predict the first letter by thinking about the sound. You may also wish to use the following Shared Reading title from *Fountas & Pinnell Classroom*™ to engage children in an alphabet book reading while examining the beginning letter sounds of various consonants.

> [SR] *City ABCs* by Finnoula Louise

Interactive Writing When you write labels for the pictures in the class consonants book, encourage children to write the first letter of words and any other letters they know.

Independent Writing Model how to say a word slowly and write the first letter. Encourage children to do this for themselves as they write words.

Extend Learning

Create other class consonant books based on a theme, such as foods, animals, or clothing.

▶ Connect with Home

Send home copies of the Alphabet Linking Chart. Have family members take turns saying the sound a letter stands for and having the next player name the letter. For example, "I'm thinking of a food that stands for the sound of the letter *d*."

Recognize Beginning Consonant Sounds and the Letters That Represent Them

Plan

▶ Consider Your Children

Use this lesson after children have learned to distinguish letters by their features, can recognize and name most letters, and can match words by beginning sound. This lesson will help them systematize and summarize their knowledge because it includes all twenty-six letters. Some teachers like to use a theme for the pictures related to the letters of the alphabet. One possibility is the concept of food: for example, *animal cracker, bean, carrot.* Ahead of time, prepare grab bags containing small objects–or pictures of small objects–with names that begin with each sound/letter. Facsimiles (or picture cards) may be used for many items–cutouts of jelly beans, ice cream cones, and so forth. For some groups of children, you may want to show all of the objects and pictures and review their names to build vocabulary prior to the lesson.

▶ Working with English Language Learners

This lesson gives children experience relating sounds and letters. Moreover, it can help children widen their English vocabularies by learning words that are related to one another by meaning. You may wish to discuss with children the concept of inventions and to remind them that the words in this lesson are connected by this concept. Be sure that you introduce the objects in the bags to children and have them say the name. It's important for them to know the English labels for objects before they begin the activity. Alternatively, work with a small group so that when children encounter an object, you can give them the label and have them repeat it.

UNDERSTAND THE PRINCIPLE

Connecting the initial sound of a word with a letter helps children begin to use the alphabet to solve words while reading. Once children can identify initial sounds and connect letters to them, they can use this information to monitor their reading and distinguish between words.

YOU WILL NEED

Online Resources
  ▶ **LSR 7** Action Tags
  ▶ **LSR 7** Picture Cards

Other Materials
  ▶ bulletin board with area for each letter of the alphabet
  ▶ heavy paper
  ▶ twenty-six bags for each letter of the alphabet
  ▶ objects–or photographs, facsimiles, and/or letter cards showing objects–for all letters

Generative Lesson
A generative lesson has a simple structure that you can use to present similar content or concepts. You can use this lesson structure to teach children beginning consonant sounds with a variety of letters.

EXPLAIN THE PRINCIPLE

Match sounds and letters at the beginning of a word.

Comprehensive Phonics, Spelling, and Word Study Guide

Refer to: page **26**, row **2**

ACTIVITY: GRAB BAGS

INSTRUCTIONAL PROCEDURE

SAY AND WRITE

See page 36 for detailed descriptions of Instructional Procedures.

EXPLAIN THE PRINCIPLE

Match sounds and letters at the beginning of a word.

Comprehensive Phonics, Spelling, and Word Study Guide

Refer to: page **26**, row **2**

Teach

1. Explain to the children that they are going to learn more about sounds and letters at the beginning of words.

2. Show children the bulletin board with the twenty-six letters displayed in uppercase and lowercase forms. *You've been learning about letters and their sounds. Today you are going to decorate the letters of the alphabet while you learn more.*

3. Hand each child a sheet of heavy paper with a letter lightly drawn on it as a guide.

4. *I have a grab bag for every letter of the alphabet. How many bags do I have?* • *I'm going to take one of these grab bags and open it. Watch what I do so that you will know what to do with your grab bag.*

5. Demonstrate opening the bag and looking at the contents. In each bag are items that begin with the letter. For example, in the *b* bag there could be objects or pictures of objects such as a ball, a baby, and a bag.

6. Take each object or picture out of the bag and say the word associated with it. Have the children repeat the name.

7. Help the children think about the sound they hear at the beginning of each word and name the letter that represents the sound.

8. Show the children how to form a large letter. They can use the letter you've already drawn lightly as a guide. Then show them how to trace the letter with glue and then how to stick on the objects or pictures in the shape of the letter.

9. When the project is dry, have each child hang his letter on the bulletin board in the area for the particular letter.

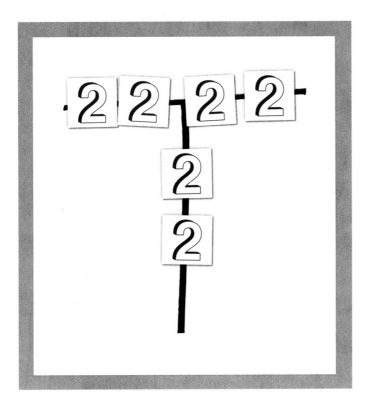

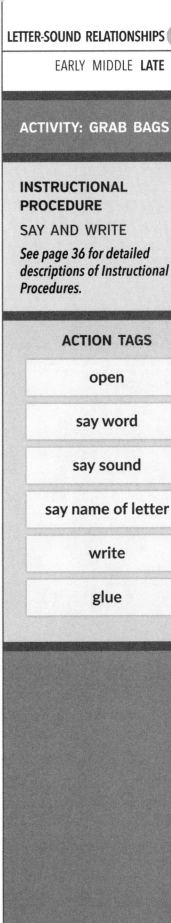

ACTIVITY: GRAB BAGS

INSTRUCTIONAL PROCEDURE

SAY AND WRITE

See page 36 for detailed descriptions of Instructional Procedures.

ACTION TAGS

open

say word

say sound

say name of letter

write

glue

Apply

Review the steps before sending each child off with one bag:

Open the bag.

For each object or picture inside the bag, say the word, say the sound, and say the name of the first letter.

Write the capital letter on your paper. (Fill the paper to make a big letter.)

Glue your objects on the line to make the shape of the letter.

Alternatively, provide large letters on sheets of paper. The children can then trace the letter before making their letter.

Share

Have each child share his letter, name the objects glued to it, and put the letter on the wall.

Assess

- Notice whether the children are linking the first sounds of words to their names and other words.

- Show the children three to five pictures and have them tell the letter for the first sound.

- You may also wish to use Letter-Sound Relationships Assessment A or C.

Letter-Sound Relationships: Recognize Beginning Consonant Sounds and the Letters That Represent Them

Connect Learning Across Contexts

Interactive Read-Aloud Read aloud alphabet books to reinforce learning of beginning consonant sounds.

> IRA *Alphabet Under Construction* by Denise Fleming
>
> IRA *I Love Our Earth* by Bill Martin, Jr.

Shared Reading See "Here Is a House" in *Words That Sing* (2019). If you don't have these poetry charts, enlarge the print of this poem or other poems such as "Diddlety, Diddlety, Dumpty!" or "Chickery, Chickery, Cranny, Crow" in *Sing a Song of Poetry*, and cover the first letter of a word with a stick-on note. Ask children to read up to the word and to predict the first letter by thinking about the sound. You may also wish to use the following Shared Reading title from *Fountas & Pinnell Classroom*™ to reinforce learning of beginning consonant sounds.

> SR *Pitter Patter* by Miriam David

Interactive Writing Create labels for objects in the classroom, emphasizing saying the word and listening for the first sound.

Independent Writing Encourage children to record at least the first letter of every word they want to write. If appropriate, invite the children to write the first letter of the name of each object in their pictures.

Extend Learning

Repeat the lesson with each child getting another grab bag so they work with different letters over time. Increase the number of pictures/objects in the bags by asking children to bring in objects and pictures from home.

▶ Connect with Home

- Send the children home with a paper bag that has a consonant letter written on it, and have them work with family members to put in objects or pictures of objects with names that begin with the letter. Have them bring the bag back to school.

- Have the children find an object or a picture of an object at home for each letter of the alphabet.

- Have the children find several objects or pictures of objects whose names start like their names.

Recognize Ending Consonant Sounds and the Letters That Represent Them

Plan

▶ Consider Your Children

Use this lesson after children are able to identify and connect words by beginning sounds and letters. To make children more flexible in using their knowledge, focus on hearing dominant consonant sounds at the end of words and connecting them with letters. Children may also begin to notice vowels in words. Select picture cards that represent easy three-letter words with easy-to-hear consonants.

▶ Working with English Language Learners

This lesson will help English language learners become more flexible as they think about the sounds in words and as they look at words. Be sure that the pictures and words you use in this lesson are those that children have seen before and/or know. Work with a small group if necessary to be sure that they understand the task of taking picture cards, saying the word matching the word and picture, and writing the word.

UNDERSTAND THE PRINCIPLE

Recognizing and knowing the letter-sound relationships for ending consonants gives children strong visual information with which to check the accuracy of their reading as well as solve new words. Becoming familiar with words that have regular letter-sound correspondence will help children learn this word-solving process.

YOU WILL NEED

 Ready Resources
- ▶ LSR 8 Pocket-Chart Picture Cards
- ▶ LSR 8 Pocket-Chart Letter Cards
- ▶ Lowercase Letter Cards

Online Resources
- ▶ LSR 8 Action Tags
- ▶ LSR 8 Two-Way Sorts
- ▶ LSR 8 Two-Column Sorts
- ▶ LSR 8 Picture Cards
- ▶ LSR 8 Letter Cards

Other Materials
- ▶ pocket chart

Generative Lesson

A generative lesson has a simple structure that you can use to present similar content or concepts. You can use this lesson structure to teach children ending consonant sounds with a variety of letters.

EXPLAIN THE PRINCIPLE

Listen for the sound at the end of a word.

Match sounds and letters at the end of a word.

When you know the sound, you can find the letter or letters.

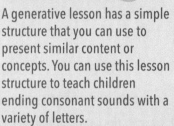

Comprehensive Phonics, Spelling, and Word Study Guide

Refer to: page **27**, row **4**

ACTIVITY: PICTURE AND LETTER MATCH

INSTRUCTIONAL PROCEDURE

FIND AND MATCH

See page 36 for detailed descriptions of Instructional Procedures.

EXPLAIN THE PRINCIPLE

Listen for the sound at the end of a word.

Match sounds and letters at the end of a word.

When you know the sound, you can find the letter or letters.

Comprehensive Phonics, Spelling, and Word Study Guide

Refer to: page **27**, row **4**

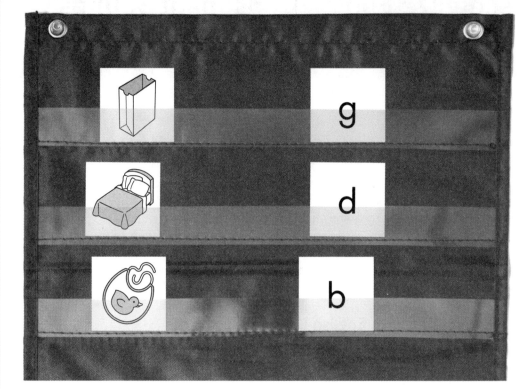

Teach

1. Explain to the children that they are going to learn more about sounds and letters. Put picture cards for *bag, log,* and *pig* in the pocket chart and have children say all three words. *What do you notice about these three words?* • *They have the same sound at the end.*

2. *Today we are going to match sounds and letters at the end of words. Let's say the names of each picture in the pocket chart. And let's listen for the sound at the end of each word.* Invite children to say the name of each picture.

3. *I'm going to take a letter card from this stack. I'm going to see if I can match a letter to an ending sound in a word shown in one of the pictures.*

4. Hold up the first letter card. *What is the letter?* • *Now I'm going to see if there is a picture of a word that has the sound of* b *at the end. Can anyone see a picture of a word that ends with a* b *sound?* • Provide an example of a word ending in *b* if necessary.

5. Match *b* with *bib* and place the letter card of *b* next to the picture of the *bib.*

6. Draw letter cards one at a time, saying the letter and matching it with a word shown in a picture each time. (If a letter doesn't match any word pictured on the chart, return that letter card to the bottom of the pile.) Continue until all pictured words have a matching letter.

7. Show the children a two-way sort with a key picture on the left (e.g., a snake) and a letter card that matches the ending sound of the picture's name on the right (e.g., the letter *k*).

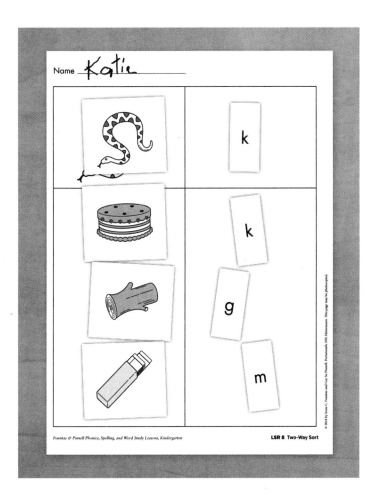

ACTIVITY: TWO-WAY PICTURE AND LETTER MATCH

INSTRUCTIONAL PROCEDURE

FIND AND MATCH

See page 36 for detailed descriptions of Instructional Procedures.

ACTION TAGS

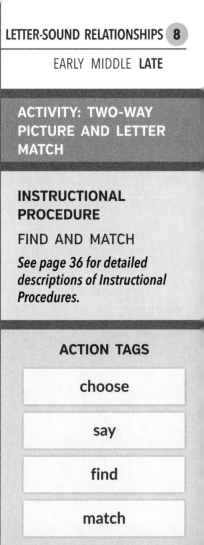

choose

say

find

match

Apply

Give children a number of picture cards, a number of corresponding letter cards, a two-way sort with a key picture and a letter as an example at the top, and a two-column sort. Invite children to choose a picture card, say the word, find the consonant letter that represents the sound at the end of that word, and place the matching picture card and letter card on the sort.

Share

Ask the children to tell some of the ending sounds and consonant letters they matched in words.

Assess

- Place picture cards in the pocket chart and ask individual children to match ending sounds and letters.
- Notice whether the children can isolate and say the last sound of a word while reading.
- Check whether the children can use the ending sound and/or ending letter of a word to monitor and check their reading.
- Observe whether the children are able to generate the last letters of words during writing.
- You may wish to use Letter-Sound Relationships Assessment B or C.

Letter-Sound Relationships: Recognize Ending Consonant Sounds and the Letters That Represent Them

Connect Learning Across Contexts

Interactive Read-Aloud Read aloud books that emphasize consonant sounds in words.

    IRA *ABC I Like Me* by Nancy Carlson

    IRA *On Market Street* by Arthur and Anita Lobel

Shared Reading See "Five Fat Pumpkins" in *Words That Sing* (2019). If you don't have these poetry charts, enlarge the print of this poem or other poems such as "Pease Porridge Hot" or "Little White Rabbit" in *Sing a Song of Poetry*, and ask the children to say a word, tell the last letter, and highlight the word in the poem after reading. You may also wish to use the following Shared Reading title from *Fountas & Pinnell Classroom*™ to reinforce learning of ending consonant sounds.

    SR *Miss Mary Mack* retold by Susannah Franco

Interactive Writing Invite the children to say words slowly and contribute last sounds in words you write together.

Independent Writing Model saying words slowly and listening for the ending sounds. Encourage the children to write ending sounds in words they are trying to write.

Extend Learning

- Repeat the lesson with other pictures and letters.
- Repeat the lesson with other consonant sounds (for example, *f, l,* or *w*).

▶ Connect with Home

Send home sheets of picture cards and letter cards. Have the children build each picture name using the letter cards or magnetic letters.

Spelling Patterns

Phonograms are spelling patterns that represent the sounds of rimes. In a one-syllable word, the *rime* is the ending part containing the letters that represent the vowel sound and the letters that follow. The part before the vowel is called the *onset.* Phonograms are sometimes called *word families*. You will not need to teach children the technical word *phonogram*, although you may want to use *pattern* or *word part*. We have included a large list of common phonograms in *Ready Resources* that will be useful to primary-age children in reading or writing, but you will not need to teach every phonogram separately. Once children understand that there are patterns and learn how to look for patterns, they will quickly discover more for themselves.

Another way to look at phonograms is to examine the way simple words and syllables are put together. Here we include the consonant-vowel-consonant (CVC) pattern in which the vowel often has a short, or terse, sound; and the consonant-vowel-consonant-silent *e* (CVC*e*) pattern in which the vowel usually has a long, or lax, sound. Knowing spelling patterns helps children notice and use larger parts of words, thus making word solving faster and more efficient. Patterns are also helpful to children in writing words because children will quickly write down the patterns rather than laboriously work with individual sounds and letters. The fourteen most common phonograms are marked with an asterisk in rows 8 and 9 of the Spelling Patterns section of *The Fountas & Pinnell Comprehensive Phonics, Spelling, and Word Study Guide* (page 35).

Connect to Assessment

See related (optional) SP Assessment tasks in Online Resources.

- Assessment A: Matching Pictures of Words That Contain the Same Phonogram Pattern

- Assessment B: Matching Words That Contain the Same Phonogram Pattern

- Assessment C: Matching Pictures with Words That Contain the Phonogram Pattern

- Assessment D: Reading Words with the CVC Pattern in Unfamiliar Text

- Assessment E: Reading Words with Phonogram Patterns

- Assessment F: Writing Words with Phonogram Patterns

- Assessment G: Class Record (Reading Phonogram Patterns)

- Assessment H: Class Record (Writing Phonogram Patterns)

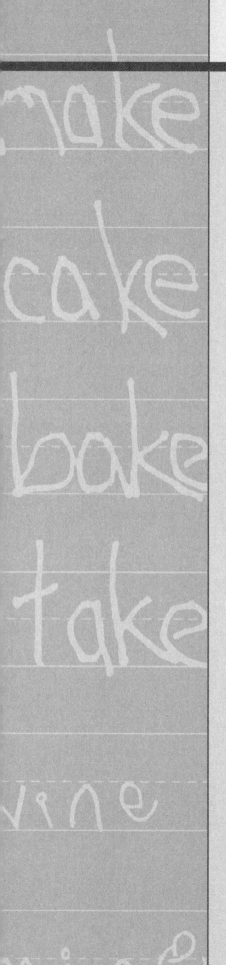

Develop Your Professional Understanding

See *The Fountas & Pinnell Comprehensive Phonics, Spelling, and Word Study Guide.* 2017. Portsmouth, New Hampshire: Heinemann. Related pages: 1–12, 34–38.

See *The Fountas & Pinnell Literacy Continuum: A Tool for Assessment, Planning, and Teaching.* 2017. Portsmouth, New Hampshire: Heinemann. Related pages: 357–397.

See *Word Matters: Teaching Phonics and Spelling in the Reading/Writing Classroom* by G. S. Pinnell and I. C. Fountas. 1998. Portsmouth, New Hampshire: Heinemann. Related pages: 65, 82, 95, 236.

Recognize and Use the CVC Pattern

Plan

▶ Consider Your Children

This lesson lays the foundation for the next two phonogram lessons. Children should understand what words are, have grasped the idea of *first, middle*, and *last* as it applies to the component parts of words, know the concepts of vowels and consonants, and have learned the short sound for each vowel. This lesson is best used with the shared reading of texts that prominently feature CVC words. The goal of this lesson is to draw children's attention to a spelling pattern or part that they can begin to look for and recognize in texts. While children don't need to learn the abbreviation *CVC*, they do need to use the labels *vowel* and *consonant* readily in talking about this pattern.

▶ Working with English Language Learners

It may be helpful to review the five vowels and each consonant with English language learners before the lesson. Articulate the words clearly for children, and make sure they can pronounce them clearly, although there may be some approximation. You may need to use the words in sentences or with accompanying pictures and concrete objects to make sure that children understand the meanings of the words. Work with a small group and help them practice making words.

YOU WILL NEED

 Ready Resources
- Lowercase Letter Cards

Online Resources
- SP 1 Action Tags
- SP 1 List Sheets

Other Materials
- magnetic letters
- magnetic surface

Generative Lesson

A generative lesson has a simple structure that you can use to present similar content or concepts. You can use this lesson structure to teach children a variety of CVC spelling patterns with a variety of words.

UNDERSTAND THE PRINCIPLE

Words that contain the consonant-vowel-consonant pattern are very common, appearing frequently in early texts. Because the pattern is also very stable, with the vowel nearly always standing for its short sound when it appears between two consonants, it is particularly useful for children to learn and easy for them to apply. The CVC pattern is the foundation for many common phonograms, or word families, each with many exemplar words. Learning the CVC pattern encourages children to notice patterns as part of their word-solving actions and helps them recognize and build words quickly.

EXPLAIN THE PRINCIPLE

Some words have a consonant, a vowel, and then another consonant. The vowel sounds like the a *in* apple, *the* e *in* egg, *the* i *in* in, *the* o *in* octopus, *or the* u *in* umbrella.

Comprehensive Phonics, Spelling, and Word Study Guide

Refer to: page **34**, row **2**

INSTRUCTIONAL PROCEDURE

MAKE WORDS

See page 36 for detailed descriptions of Instructional Procedures.

EXPLAIN THE PRINCIPLE

Some words have a consonant, a vowel, and then another consonant. The vowel sounds like the a in apple, the e in egg, the i in in, the o in octopus, or the u in umbrella.

Comprehensive Phonics, Spelling, and Word Study Guide

Refer to:
page **34**, row **2**

Teach

1. Tell the children that they are going to learn to look for and use a spelling pattern that is found in many words.

2. Using magnetic letters, display the vowels *a, e, i, o,* and *u* in a column on a magnetic surface. *Who can tell the name for this group of letters?* • *The letters* a, e, i, o, *and* u *are vowels.* Have children say the letters with you as you point to each one. *All of the other letters in the alphabet are consonants.*

3. Build the word *pat*, borrowing the *a* from the group of vowels. Have children read the word with you. *How many letters are in the word* pat? • *What are the three letters?* • *Where is the vowel in this word?* • *Where are the consonants in this word?* • If needed, help children notice that the consonant *p* is at the beginning, the vowel *a* is in the middle, and the consonant *t* is at the end. *Many words have this spelling pattern–a consonant, then a vowel, and then another consonant. When you see this pattern in a word, the vowel* a *stands for its short sound, /ă/, like the* a *in apple.*

4. Replace the letter *a* with the letter *o*, and have children read the word *pot* with you. Talk about the spelling pattern of the word. *The pattern is the same: a consonant, then a vowel, and then another consonant. So the vowel* o *stands for its short sound, /ŏ/, like the* o *in octopus.*

5. Continue replacing the vowel to build the word *pet*. Point out that the vowel *e* stands for the sound /ĕ/ like the *e* in *egg.*

6. Build more CVC words, replacing a consonant or vowel one at a time. As you build new words, describe the changes you are making. *I'm going to change the first consonant in* put *to a* b. *What is the new word?* • *I'm going to change the vowel in* but *to an* a. *What is the new word?*

7. Once children have successfully read new CVC words with all five vowels, reinforce the principle. *You have read a lot of words this morning with the same spelling pattern: a consonant at the beginning, a vowel in the middle, and a consonant at the end. When you see this pattern, you know that the vowel stands for its short sound.*

ACTIVITY: CVC WORDS

INSTRUCTIONAL PROCEDURE

MAKE WORDS

See page 36 for detailed descriptions of Instructional Procedures.

ACTION TAGS

make
write
read

Apply

- Have children use magnetic letters, letter tiles, or lowercase letter cards to make words with a variety of CVC spelling patterns. Children may make words that the class built together during the lesson, but encourage them to discover a few new words that fit the pattern.

- Have children write each word they build on a list sheet. They can read the list to a partner and bring it to sharing time.

Share

Ask each child to share one word. You may wish to build any new words using magnetic letters and have the class read them together.

Assess

- Ask individual children to make and read a CVC word with magnetic letters.

- Observe children as they read to determine whether they are noticing and using the CVC pattern to solve new words.

- You may wish to use Spelling Patterns Assessment A, B, C, D, or G.

Spelling Patterns: Recognize and Use the CVC Pattern

Connect Learning Across Contexts

Interactive Read-Aloud Read aloud books that prominently include words with the CVC spelling pattern.

> IRA *Have You Seen My Cat?* by Eric Carle

> IRA *The Little Red Hen* by Paul Galdone

Shared Reading See "A Frog Sat on a Log" in *Words That Sing* (2019). If you don't have these poetry charts, enlarge the print of this poem or other poems such as "I Can Do It Myself" and "Five Fat Pumpkins" in *Sing a Song of Poetry*, and have children use highlighter tape to match words that contain the spelling pattern. You may also wish to use the following Shared Reading title from *Fountas & Pinnell Classroom*™ to call attention to words with the CVC spelling pattern.

> SR *Ten in the Bed* illustrated by Inna Chernyak

Interactive Writing Invite children to help you write words with the CVC pattern, or have them use a known word that contains the pattern to write a new word.

Independent Writing Encourage children to use their knowledge of parts or spelling patterns as a resource to write words.

Extend Learning

Ask children to look for CVC words in texts that the class has read during Interactive Read-Aloud and Shared Reading. Have them write each word they find on a blank word card. As a whole class, have children share the words they found and then sort the words by different criteria, for example, by vowel or by words that rhyme.

▶ Connect with Home

Encourage family members to go on a word hunt around their home, searching for at least one CVC word for each vowel. Children can write each word that is found, and family members can then read the list of words together.

Recognize and Use Phonograms: *-an*

Plan

▶ Consider Your Children

This lesson builds on the previous phonogram lesson and is best used after children have had extensive experience hearing and recognizing rhymes, can distinguish most letters, and know many consonant sounds. They should also understand the concept of a word and have grasped the ideas of *first* and *last* as they apply to the component parts of words. Knowing some high-frequency words or simple words from the word wall also helps. The goal of this lesson is to draw children's attention to a spelling pattern that they can begin to look for and recognize in texts. In this lesson, children learn a vowel and consonant (VC) pattern, *-an*. Children don't need to learn the label *phonogram;* the term *spelling pattern* or *word part* will be more useful and meaningful.

▶ Working with English Language Learners

Be sure that you begin with some *-an* words that English language learners already know and can read and write. Use them in sentences and invite children to repeat your sentences or make sentences of their own. Be sure to articulate words slowly and carefully and have children repeat the words themselves.

YOU WILL NEED

PWS Ready Resources
- ▶ Lowercase Letter Cards

Online Resources
- ▶ SP 2 Action Tags
- ▶ SP 2 List Sheets

Other Materials
- ▶ blank chart paper
- ▶ magnetic letters

UNDERSTAND THE PRINCIPLE

A phonogram, also referred to as a spelling pattern or word family, is a group of letters that forms a common word ending. It is the equivalent of the rime, the part of a word or syllable that comprises a vowel sound and the consonant sounds that follow. Children easily hear the break between the first part of a word and the rime, for example, *f-an, p-an*. Learning common phonograms provides useful information about written language and helps children recognize and build words quickly.

EXPLAIN THE PRINCIPLE

Look at the spelling pattern to read a word.

Use the spelling pattern to write a word.

Comprehensive Phonics, Spelling, and Word Study Guide

Refer to:
page **34**, row **3**

ACTIVITY: PHONOGRAM AND WORD CHART

INSTRUCTIONAL PROCEDURE

NOTICE PARTS

See page 36 for detailed descriptions of Instructional Procedures.

EXPLAIN THE PRINCIPLE

Look at the spelling pattern to read a word.

Use the spelling pattern to write a word.

Comprehensive Phonics, Spelling, and Word Study Guide

Refer to: page **34**, row **3**

-an

man
an
can

van
fan
ran
Anne
Andrea
Andrew
Anessa
Dan

Teach

1. Show a few words ending in -*an* that children know, such as *man, an,* and *can*. Write the words on chart paper, and have children read them aloud. *What do you notice about these words?* • *Each of these words has the letters -an in it. The word* an *is a word by itself, but you also see these letters at the end of other words.*

2. Cover the first letter of each word as you point out the ending pattern. Then write the spelling pattern -*an* above the column of words. *You can look at this spelling pattern to read each word. What else do you notice about these words?* • *The words* man, an, *and* can *all rhyme.*

3. *Today you are going to make more words that end with -an.* Invite the children to say two or three more words that end with the spelling pattern -*an*. Guide children to make sure the words they suggest are real words by thinking about how to use them in a sentence.

4. If any children's names include the spelling pattern -*an*, draw attention to those names and include them on the chart.

5. Ask children to reread the list of words, and then reinforce the principle. *You can look for and use spelling patterns, such as -an, to help you read and write words.* Display the chart on the wall as a reference for children to use when building words. Continue to add to the chart as children encounter new -*an* words.

ACTIVITY: PHONOGRAM AND WORD CHART

INSTRUCTIONAL PROCEDURE

NOTICE PARTS

See page 36 for detailed descriptions of Instructional Procedures.

ACTION TAGS

make

write

read

Apply

- Have children use magnetic letters, letter tiles, or lowercase letter cards to make words with the spelling pattern -*an*. For this phonogram, include *a, c, f, h, m, n, p, r, t,* and *v*. Children may build words that are on the chart, but encourage them to think of at least one or two additional words with the -*an* pattern.

- Then have children write the words they made on a list sheet. They can read the list to a partner and bring it to sharing time.

Share

Ask each child to share one -*an* word that he wrote. Add to the chart any new -*an* words that children have discovered.

Assess

- Ask individual children to read the -*an* phonogram chart or make a word containing the -*an* phonogram with magnetic letters.

- Observe children as they read to determine whether they are noticing and using the -*an* pattern to solve new words.

- You may wish to use Spelling Patterns Assessment A, B, C, E, F, G, or H.

Connect Learning Across Contexts

Interactive Read-Aloud Read aloud rhyming books, drawing children's attention to spelling patterns that they have learned.

IRA *Red Is a Dragon* by Grace Lin

IRA *From Head to Toe* by Eric Carle

Shared Reading See "There Once Was an Old Woman" in *Words That Sing* (2019). If you don't have these poetry charts, enlarge the print of this poem or other poems such as "This Old Man," "We Can," and "The Muffin Man" in *Sing a Song of Poetry*, and have children use highlighter tape to point out words that contain the spelling pattern, *-an*. You may also wish to use the following Shared Reading title from *Fountas & Pinnell Classroom*™ to call attention to words with the spelling pattern *-an*.

SR *Alligator Hide-and-Seek* by Reese Brooks

Interactive Writing Invite children to help you write words with the *-an* pattern, or have them use a known word that contains *-an* to write a new word. When writing is finished, revisit it to highlight any *-an* words that are in it.

Independent Writing Encourage children to use their knowledge of spelling patterns as a resource to write words. When children are writing rhyming texts, remind them to make use of the spelling pattern charts.

Extend Learning

Use other rhyme books to help children hear and notice other spelling patterns. If a text includes *-an* words, draw children's attention to them and build a few of the words after reading.

▶ Connect with Home

- Reproduce letter cards and the pattern chart for *-an* for children to take home, cut apart, and use to build and read words.

- Send home copies of nursery rhymes containing *-an* words, such as "This Old Man" from *Sing a Song of Poetry,* after children have read them in shared reading. Encourage family members to read them together and find all the words ending in *-an*.

Recognize and Use Phonograms: -at

Plan

▶ Consider Your Children

This lesson and the next four introduce simple phonograms, or common spelling patterns. These lessons are best used after children have had extensive experience hearing and recognizing rhymes, can distinguish most letters, and know many consonant sounds. They should also understand what words are and have grasped the ideas of *first* and *last* as they apply to the component parts of words. Knowing some high-frequency words or simple words from the word wall also helps. The goal of this lesson is to draw children's attention to a spelling pattern that they can begin to look for and recognize in texts. They will be working with one syllable words but will eventually use these patterns to take apart multisyllable words. In this lesson, children learn a vowel and consonant (VC) pattern, *-at*. Children don't need to learn the label *phonogram*; the term *spelling pattern* or *word part* will be more useful and meaningful.

▶ Working with English Language Learners

English language learners' previous work with rhymes will form a foundation for learning about spelling patterns. Articulate the words clearly for children, and also make sure that they understand the words and can pronounce them clearly, although there may be some approximation. You may need to use the words in sentences or use pictures and concrete objects where appropriate. Work with a small group and help them practice making words. Observe them writing words with *-at*.

UNDERSTAND THE PRINCIPLE

A phonogram, also referred to as a spelling pattern or word family, is a group of letters that forms a common word ending. It is the equivalent of the rime, the part of a word or syllable that comprises a vowel sound and the consonant sounds that follow. Children easily hear the break between the first part of a word and the rime, for example, *b–at, s–at*. Learning common phonograms provides useful information about written language and helps children recognize and build words quickly.

YOU WILL NEED

PWS Ready Resources
▶ Lowercase Letter Cards

Online Resources
▶ SP 3 Action Tags
▶ SP 3 List Sheets

Other Materials
▶ blank chart paper
▶ magnetic letters

EXPLAIN THE PRINCIPLE

Look at a part or pattern to read a word.

Use the part or pattern to write a word.

Comprehensive Phonics, Spelling, and Word Study Guide

Refer to: page **34**, row **3**

ACTIVITY: PHONOGRAM AND WORD CHART

INSTRUCTIONAL PROCEDURE

NOTICE PARTS

See page 36 for detailed descriptions of Instructional Procedures.

EXPLAIN THE PRINCIPLE

Look at a part or pattern to read a word.

Use the part or pattern to write a word.

Comprehensive Phonics, Spelling, and Word Study Guide

Refer to: page **34**, row **3**

-at

cat
at
hat

bat
sat
Pat
Matt

Teach

1. Show a few words ending in -*at* that children know, such as *cat, at,* and *hat.* Write the words on chart paper, and have children read them aloud. *What do you notice about these words?* • *Each of these words has the letters* -at *in it. The word* at *is a word by itself, but you also see these letters at the end of other words.*

2. Cover the first letter of each word as you point out the ending pattern. Then write the spelling pattern -*at* above the column of words. *You can look at this spelling pattern to read each word. What else do you notice about these words?* • *Yes, the words* cat, at, *and* hat *all rhyme.*

3. *Today you're going to make more words that end with* -at. Invite the children to say two or three more words that end with the spelling pattern -*at.* Guide children to make sure the words they suggest are real words by thinking about how to use them in a sentence.

4. If any children's names include the spelling pattern -*at,* draw attention to those names and include them on the chart.

5. Ask children to reread the list of words, and then reinforce the principle. *You can look for and use spelling patterns, such as* -at, *to help you read and write words.* Display the chart on the wall as a reference for children to use when building words. Continue to add to the chart as children encounter new -*at* words.

INSTRUCTIONAL PROCEDURE

NOTICE PARTS

See page 36 for detailed descriptions of Instructional Procedures.

ACTION TAGS

make

write

read

Apply

- Have children use magnetic letters, letter tiles, or lowercase letter cards to make words with the spelling pattern -*at.* For this phonogram, provide the letters *a, b, c, f, h, m, p, r, s,* and *t.* Children may build words that are on the chart, but encourage them to think of at least one or two additional words with the -*at* pattern.

- Then have children write the words they made on a list sheet. They can read the list to a partner and bring it to sharing time.

Share

Ask each child to share one -*at* word. Add to the chart any new -*at* words that children have discovered.

Assess

- Ask individual children to read the -*at* phonogram chart or make a word containing the -*at* phonogram with magnetic letters.

- Observe children as they read to determine whether they are noticing and using the -*at* pattern to solve new words.

- You may wish to use Spelling Patterns Assessment A, B, C, E, F, G, or H.

Connect Learning Across Contexts

Interactive Read-Aloud Read aloud rhyming books, drawing children's attention to spelling patterns that they have learned.

> IRA *Have You Seen My Cat?* by Eric Carle

> IRA *Top Cat* by Lois Ehlert

Shared Reading See "My Head" in *Words That Sing* (2019). If you don't have these poetry charts, enlarge the print of this poem or other poems such as "Make a Pancake" or "The Cat" in *Sing a Song of Poetry*, and have children use highlighter tape to mark words that contain the spelling pattern, *-at*. You may also wish to use the following Shared Reading title from *Fountas & Pinnell Classroom*™ to call attention to words with that end in *-at*.

> SR *The House That Jack Built* adapted by David Edwin

Interactive Writing Invite children to help you write words with the *-at* pattern, or have them use a known word that contains *-at* to write a new word. Use highlighter tape to identify words with the *-at* pattern.

Independent Writing Encourage children to use their knowledge of spelling patterns as a resource to write words. When children are writing rhyming texts, remind them to make use of the spelling pattern charts.

Extend Learning

Use other rhyme books to help children hear and notice other spelling patterns. If a text includes *-at* words, draw children's attention to them and build a few of the words after reading.

▶ Connect with Home

- Reproduce letter cards and the pattern chart for *-at* for children to take home, cut apart, and use to build and read words.

- Send home copies of nursery rhymes containing *-at* words, such as "Jack Sprat" or "Pat-a-cake" from *Sing a Song of Poetry*, after children have read them in shared reading. Encourage family members to read them together and find all the words ending in *-at*.

Recognize and Use
Phonograms: -ay

Plan

▶ Consider Your Children

This lesson builds on the previous phonogram lesson and is best used after children have had extensive experience hearing and recognizing rhymes, can distinguish most letters, and know many consonant sounds. They should also understand what words are and have grasped the ideas of *first* and *last* as they apply to the component parts of words. Knowing some high-frequency words or simple words from the word wall also helps. The goal of this lesson is to draw children's attention to a spelling pattern that they can begin to look for and recognize in texts. In this lesson, children learn a vowel and consonant (VC) pattern, *-ay*. Children don't need to learn the label *phonogram;* the term *part, pattern, spelling pattern* or *word part* will be more useful and meaningful.

▶ Working with English Language Learners

Begin with words that English language learners have in their speaking vocabularies and also have encountered as high-frequency words or in shared reading. You may want to refer to the word wall or to the calendar. Be sure they know the meaning of the words that you create. Remember that English language learners will not necessarily know that substitutions they suggest do not create real words (for example, *tay*). Recognize their efforts and give them feedback as to which words are real by using them in a sentence.

YOU WILL NEED

 Ready Resources
- ▶ Lowercase Letter Cards

Online Resources
- ▶ SP 4 Action Tags
- ▶ SP 4 List Sheets

Other Materials
- ▶ blank chart paper
- ▶ magnetic letters

UNDERSTAND THE PRINCIPLE

A phonogram, also referred to as a spelling pattern or word family, is a group of letters that forms a common word ending. It is the equivalent of the rime, the part of a word or syllable that comprises a vowel sound and the consonant sounds that follow. Children easily hear the break between the first part of a word and the rime, for example, *h-ay, s-ay.* Learning common phonograms provides useful information about written language and helps children recognize and build words quickly.

EXPLAIN THE PRINCIPLE

Look at a part or pattern to read a word.

Use the part or pattern to write a word.

 Comprehensive Phonics, Spelling, and Word Study Guide

Refer to: page **34**, row **3**

ACTIVITY: PHONOGRAM AND WORD CHART

INSTRUCTIONAL PROCEDURE

NOTICE PARTS

See page 36 for detailed descriptions of Instructional Procedures.

EXPLAIN THE PRINCIPLE

Look at a part or pattern to read a word.

Use the part or pattern to write a word.

Comprehensive Phonics, Spelling, and Word Study Guide

Refer to: page **34**, row **3**

−ay

day
may
play

say
stay
way
Kayla

Teach

1. Show a few words ending in *-ay* that children know, such as *day, may,* and *play*. Write the words on chart paper, and have children read them aloud. *What do you notice about these words?* • *Each of these words has the letters* -ay *in it. The letters* a *and* y *together stand for /ā/.*

2. Cover the first letter of each word as you point out the ending pattern. Then write the spelling pattern *-ay* above the column of words. *You can look at this spelling pattern to read each word. What else do you notice about these words?* • *Yes, the words* day, may, *and* play *all rhyme.*

3. *Today you're going to make more words that end with* -ay. Invite the children to say two or three more words that end with the spelling pattern *-ay*. Guide children to make sure the words they suggest are real words by thinking about how to use them in a sentence.

4. If any children's names include the spelling pattern *-ay*, draw attention to those names and include them on the chart.

5. Ask children to reread the list of words, and then reinforce the principle. *You can look for and use spelling patterns, such as* -ay, *to help you read and write words.* Display the chart on the wall as a reference for children to use when building words. Continue to add to the chart as children encounter new *-ay* words.

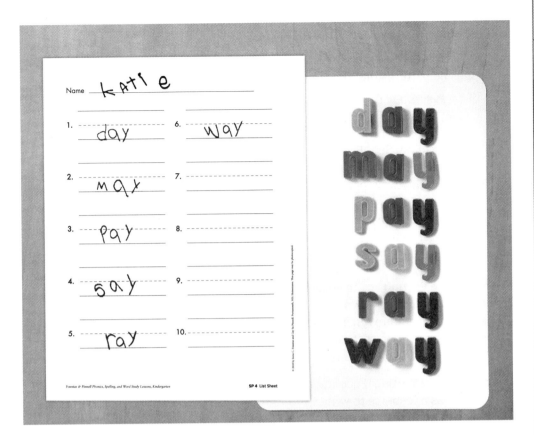

**INSTRUCTIONAL
PROCEDURE**

NOTICE PARTS

*See page 36 for detailed
descriptions of Instructional
Procedures.*

ACTION TAGS

make

write

read

Apply

- Have children use magnetic letters, letter tiles, or lowercase letter cards to make words with the spelling pattern -*ay*. For this phonogram, include *a, b, d, h, j, l, m, p, r, s, w,* and *y.* Children may build words that are on the chart, but encourage them to think of at least one or two additional words with the -*ay* pattern.
- Then have children write the words they made on a list sheet. They can read the list to a partner and bring it to sharing time.

Share

Ask each child to share one -*ay* word that he wrote. Add to the chart any new -*ay* words that children have discovered. If children have encountered the word *today,* you may want to bring it to their attention and add it to the chart.

Assess

- Ask individual children to read the -*ay* phonogram chart or make a word containing the -*ay* phonogram with magnetic letters.
- Observe children as they read to determine whether they are noticing and using the -*ay* pattern to solve new words.
- You may wish to use Spelling Patterns Assessment A, B, C, E, F, G, or H.

Connect Learning Across Contexts

Interactive Read-Aloud Read aloud rhyming books, drawing children's attention to spelling patterns that they have learned.

> [IRA] *Alicia's Happy Day* by Meg Starr

> [IRA] *The Gingerbread Boy* by Paul Galdone

Shared Reading See "Five Little Snowmen" in *Words That Sing* (2019). If you don't have these poetry charts, enlarge the print of this poem or other poems such as "Rain, Rain, Go Away" and "How Many Days?" in *Sing a Song of Poetry*, and have children use highlighter tape to point out words that contain the spelling pattern, -*ay*. You may also wish to use the following Shared Reading title from *Fountas & Pinnell Classroom*™ to call attention to words with the spelling pattern -*ay*.

> [SR] *Hand in Hand: Poems About Friends*

Interactive Writing Invite children to help you write words with the -*ay* pattern, or have them use a known word that contains -*ay* to write a new word. Revisit pieces produced through interactive writing to look for spelling patterns that have been taught in phonics lessons. Use highlighter tape and have the child read the word and identify the pattern.

Independent Writing Encourage children to use their knowledge of spelling patterns as a resource to write words. When children are writing rhyming texts, remind them to make use of the spelling pattern charts.

Extend Learning

Use other rhyme books to help children hear and notice other spelling patterns. If a text includes -*ay* words, draw children's attention to them and build a few of the words after reading.

▶ Connect with Home

- Reproduce letter cards and the pattern chart for -*ay* for children to take home, cut apart, and use to build and read words.

- Send home copies of nursery rhymes containing -*ay* words, such as "Rain, Rain, Go Away" or "London Bridge" (second and third verses) from *Sing a Song of Poetry*, after children have read them in shared reading. Encourage family members to read them together and find all the words ending in -*ay*.

Recognize and Use Phonograms with a VCe Pattern: *-ake*

Plan

▶ Consider Your Children

Building on previous phonogram lessons, this lesson is part of a sequence of lessons that help children develop systems for noticing and learning word patterns. By the time you use this lesson, children will be aware of the concept that many words have patterns that they can look for and recognize in texts. In this lesson, children learn the vowel-consonant-silent *e* (VCe) pattern.

▶ Working with English Language Learners

If some of your English language learners are having difficulty using spelling patterns, work with them in a small group and focus on easier phonograms. Be sure they understand and can pronounce the words. Use the words in context, and use pictures and real objects when possible. Appreciate their efforts to use patterns even when their constructions are invented rather than actual English words.

YOU WILL NEED

 Ready Resources
- ▶ Lowercase Letter Cards

Online Resources
- ▶ SP 5 Action Tags
- ▶ SP 5 List Sheets

Other Materials
- ▶ blank chart paper
- ▶ magnetic letters

UNDERSTAND THE PRINCIPLE

A phonogram, also referred to as a spelling pattern or word family, is a group of letters that forms a common word ending. It is the equivalent of the rime, the part of a word or syllable that comprises a vowel sound and the consonant sounds that follow. Children easily hear the break between the first part of a word and the rime, for example, *b-ake, t-ake*. Learning common phonograms provides useful information about written language and helps children recognize and build words quickly.

EXPLAIN THE PRINCIPLE

Some words have a vowel, a consonant, and silent e. The vowel sound is usually the name of the first vowel.

 Comprehensive Phonics, Spelling, and Word Study Guide

Refer to:
page **35**, row **5**

INSTRUCTIONAL PROCEDURE

NOTICE PARTS

See page 36 for detailed descriptions of Instructional Procedures.

EXPLAIN THE PRINCIPLE

Some words have a vowel, a consonant, and silent e. The vowel sound is usually the name of the first vowel.

Comprehensive Phonics, Spelling, and Word Study Guide

Refer to: page **35**, row **5**

-ake

make
cake
bake

rake
take
Jake

Teach

1. Show a few words ending in -*ake* that children know, such as *make, cake,* and *bake.* Write the words on chart paper, and have children read them aloud. *What do you notice about all of these words?* • *Each of these words has the letters -ake in it. What kind of letter is the letter* a? • *The letter* a *is a vowel. What kind of letter is the letter* k? • *The letter* k *is a consonant. When you see a vowel and a consonant followed by the letter* e *at the end of a word, the vowel sound is usually its name and the* e *is silent–/āk/,* make.

2. Cover the first letter of each word as you point out the ending pattern. Then write the spelling pattern -*ake* above the column of words. *You can look at this spelling pattern to read each word. What else do you notice about these words?* • *The words* make, cake, *and* bake *all rhyme. They have* -ake *and the* e *is silent.*

3. *Today you're going to make more words that end with* -ake. Invite the children to say two or three more words that end with the spelling pattern -*ake*. Guide children to make sure the words they suggest are real words by thinking about how to use them in a sentence.

4. If any children's names include the spelling pattern -*ake*, draw attention to those names and include them on the chart.

5. Ask children to reread the list of words, and then reinforce the principle. *You can look for and use spelling patterns, such as* -ake, *to help you read and write words.* Display the chart on the wall as a reference for children to use when building words. Continue to add to the chart as children encounter new -*ake* words.

ACTIVITY: PHONOGRAM AND WORD CHART

INSTRUCTIONAL PROCEDURE

NOTICE PARTS

See page 36 for detailed descriptions of Instructional Procedures.

ACTION TAGS

make

write

read

Apply

■ Have children use ┌─ ┐ netic letters, letter tiles, or lowercase letter cards to make words └ ┘ elling pattern *-ake.* For this phonogram, include *a, b, c, e, f, h, k* ┌ ┐ nd *w.* Children may build words that are on the chart, bเ └ ┘ think of at least one or two additional words with the

┌ ┐ children write the words they made on a list sheet. They can read the └ ┘ a partner and bring it to sharing time.

Share

Ask each child to share one *-ake* word that he wrote. Add to the chart any new *-ake* words that children have discovered.

Assess

■ Ask individual children to read the *-ake* phonogram chart or make a word containing the *-ake* phonogram with magnetic letters.

■ Observe children as they read to determine whether they are noticing and using the *-ake* pattern to solve new words.

■ You may wish to use Spelling Patterns Assessment E.

Spelling Patterns: Recognize and Use Phonograms with a VCe Pattern: -ake

Connect Learning Across Contexts

Interactive Read-Aloud Read aloud rhyming books, drawing children's attention to spelling patterns that they have learned.

> IRA *Sleepy Bears* by Mem Fox

> IRA *Over on the Farm* by Marianne Berkes

Shared Reading See "Hiccup, Hiccup" in *Words That Sing* (2019). If you don't have these poetry charts, enlarge the print of this poem or other poems such as "Pat-a-cake" and "As I Was Walking" in *Sing a Song of Poetry*, and have children use highlighter tape to point out words that contain the spelling pattern, *-ake*. You may also wish to use the following Shared Reading title from *Fountas & Pinnell Classroom*™ to call attention to words with spelling patterns.

> SR *Smash! Crash!* by Catherine Friend

Interactive Writing Invite children to help you write words with the *-ake* pattern, or have them use a known word that contains *-ake* to write a new word. Revisit pieces of interactive writing to hunt for, identify, and highlight known patterns.

Independent Writing Encourage children to use their knowledge of spelling patterns as a resource to write words. When children are writing rhyming texts, remind them to make use of the spelling pattern charts.

Extend Learning

Use other rhyme books to help children hear and notice other spelling patterns. If a text includes *-ake* words, draw children's attention to them and build a few of the words after reading.

▶ Connect with Home

■ Reproduce letter cards and the pattern chart for *-ake* for children to take home, cut apart, and use to build and read words.

■ Send home copies of nursery rhymes containing *-ake* words, such as "Pat-a-cake" and "Blow, Wind, Blow" from *Sing a Song of Poetry,* after children have read them in shared reading. Encourage family members to read them together and find all the words ending in *-ake.*

Recognize and Use Phonograms with a VCe Pattern: *-ine*

Plan

▶ Consider Your Children

Building on previous phonogram lessons, this lesson is part of a sequence of lessons that help children develop systems for noticing and learning word patterns. By the time you use this lesson, children will be aware of the concept that many words have patterns that they can look for and recognize in texts. In this lesson, children learn the vowel-consonant-silent *e* (VCe) pattern.

▶ Working with English Language Learners

If some of your English language learners are having difficulty using spelling patterns, work with them in a small group and focus on easier phonograms. Be sure they understand and can pronounce the words. Use the words in context, and use pictures and real objects when possible. Appreciate their efforts to use patterns even when their constructions are invented rather than actual English words. As English language learners take on new phonograms, you may want to have them go back and review others in random order so that they grasp the larger principle of words that are the same at the end. This process will give them generative power over words. Understanding these word patterns will greatly expand their ability to spell. Help children pronounce the words with the long *i* sound.

YOU WILL NEED

 Ready Resources
- ▶ Lowercase Letter Cards

Online Resources
- ▶ SP 6 Action Tags
- ▶ SP 6 List Sheets

Other Materials
- ▶ blank chart paper
- ▶ magnetic letters

UNDERSTAND THE PRINCIPLE

A phonogram, also referred to as a spelling pattern or word family, is a group of letters that forms a common word ending. It is the equivalent of the rime, the part of a word or syllable that comprises a vowel sound and the consonant sounds that follow. Children easily hear the break between the first part of a word and the rime, for example, *l-ine, f-ine*. Learning common phonograms provides useful information about written language and helps children recognize and build words quickly.

EXPLAIN THE PRINCIPLE

Some words have a vowel, a consonant, and silent e. The vowel sound is usually the name of the first vowel.

 Comprehensive Phonics, Spelling, and Word Study Guide

Refer to: page **35**, row **5**

ACTIVITY: PHONOGRAM AND WORD CHART

INSTRUCTIONAL PROCEDURE

NOTICE PARTS

See page 36 for detailed descriptions of Instructional Procedures.

EXPLAIN THE PRINCIPLE

Some words have a vowel, a consonant, and silent e. The vowel sound is usually the name of the first vowel.

Comprehensive Phonics, Spelling, and Word Study Guide

Refer to: page **35**, row **5**

-ine

line
nine

mine
fine
Adeline

Teach

1. Show a few words ending in *-ine* that children know, such as *line* and *nine*. Write the words on chart paper, and have children read them aloud. *What do you notice about all of these words? • Each of these words has the letters -ine in it. What kind of letter is the letter* i? *• The letter* a *is a vowel. What kind of letter is the letter* n? *• The letter* n *is a consonant. When you see a vowel and a consonant followed by the letter* e *at the end of a word, the vowel sound is usually its name and the* e *is silent–/īn/,* line.

2. Cover the first letter of each word as you point out the ending pattern. Then write the spelling pattern *-ine* above the column of words. *You can look at this spelling pattern to read each word. What else do you notice about these words? • The words* line *and* nine *rhyme and they have a vowel, a consonant, and a silent* e.

3. *Today you're going to make more words that end with* -ine. Invite the children to say two or three more words that end with the spelling pattern *-ine*. Guide children to make sure the words they suggest are real words by thinking about how to use them in a sentence.

4. If any children's names include the spelling pattern *-ine*, draw attention to those names and include them on the chart.

5. Ask children to reread the list of words, and then reinforce the principle. *You can look for and use spelling patterns, such as* -ine, *to help you read and write words.* Display the chart on the wall as a reference for children to use when building words. Continue to add to the chart as children encounter new *-ine* words.

ACTIVITY: PHONOGRAM AND WORD CHART

INSTRUCTIONAL PROCEDURE

NOTICE PARTS

See page 36 for detailed descriptions of Instructional Procedures.

ACTION TAGS

make

write

read

Name KAtie

1. LiNE   6.
2. Nine   7.
3. mine   8.
4.   9.
5.   10.

Fountas & Pinnell Phonics, Spelling, and Word Study Lessons, Kindergarten   **SP 6 List Sheet**

Apply

- Have children use magnetic letters, letter tiles, or lowercase letter cards to make words with the spelling pattern *-ine.* For this phonogram, include *d, e, f, i, l, m, n, p, v,* and *w.* Children may build words that are on the chart, but encourage them to think of at least one or two additional words with the *-ine* pattern.
- Then have children write the words they made on a list sheet. They can read the list to a partner and bring it to sharing time.

Share

Ask each child to share one *-ine* word that he wrote. Add to the chart any new *-ine* words that children have discovered.

Assess

- Ask individual children to read the *-ine* phonogram chart or make an *-ine* word with magnetic letters.
- Observe children as they read to determine whether they are noticing and using the *-ine* pattern to solve words.
- You may wish to use Spelling Patterns Assessment E.

Spelling Patterns: Recognize and Use Phonograms with a VCe Pattern: -ine

Connect Learning Across Contexts

Interactive Read-Aloud Read aloud rhyming stories that emphasize words whose ending parts sound alike.

> IRA *When it Starts to Snow* by Phillis Gershator

> IRA *Feathers for Lunch* by Lois Ehlert

Shared Reading See "Go to Bed Early" in *Words That Sing* (2019). If you don't have these poetry charts, enlarge the print of this poem or other poems such as "The Elephant Goes Like This" or "Pease Porridge Hot" in *Sing a Song of Poetry*, and have children use highlighter tape to point out words that contain familiar spelling patterns. You may also wish to use the following Shared Reading title from *Fountas & Pinnell Classroom*™ to call attention to words with the spelling pattern -*ine* and other spelling patterns.

> SR *Giggles: Poems to Make You Laugh*

Interactive Writing Draw the children's attention to phonograms they have learned, or have them use a known word that contains the phonogram to write a new word. Following the writing, have children use highlighter tape to mark words with the phonogram patterns they have learned.

Independent Writing Encourage the children to use their knowledge of phonograms as a resource to write words.

Extend Learning

Use other rhyme books to help children hear and notice other spelling patterns. If a text includes -*ine* words, draw children's attention to them and build a few of the words after reading.

▶ Connect with Home

- Reproduce letter cards and the pattern chart for -*ine* for children to take home, cut apart, and use to build and read words.

- Send home copies of nursery rhymes containing -*ine* words, such as "Elsie Marley," "Billy, Billy," "Cuckoo, Cuckoo," "Dormy, Dormy, Dormouse," or "Pease Porridge Hot" (see *Sing a Song of Poetry*) after children have read them in shared reading. Encourage family members to read them together and find all the words ending in -*ine*.

Recognize Letter Patterns

Plan

▶ Consider Your Children

Knowing common patterns will make reading and writing more efficient. Use words from the word wall that have easy spelling patterns, such as *it, not, got, but,* or *is* (which are arranged alphabetically by beginning letter), so that children will have already encountered them in interactive writing, shared reading, or a word study lesson. There should be about thirty words on the word wall before you teach this lesson.

▶ Working with English Language Learners

Looking at visual features of words will help children connect words and build the networks of word knowledge that will accelerate learning. Be sure that all of the words you use for this lesson are within children's oral vocabularies and that most are easily recognizable words.

UNDERSTAND THE PRINCIPLE

As children become familiar with letters and words, they begin to notice visual patterns, which is an important step in understanding how words work. Children are able to use the patterns they know to figure out new words.

YOU WILL NEED

PWS Ready Resources
- ▶ SP 7 Pocket-Chart Cards
- ▶ Blank Pocket-Chart Cards
- ▶ High-Frequency Word Cards

Online Resources
- ▶ SP 7 Action Tags
- ▶ SP 7 Word Cards
- ▶ SP 7 Blank Word Cards

Other Materials
- ▶ pocket chart

✓ Generative Lesson

A generative lesson has a simple structure that you can use to present similar content or concepts. You can use this lesson structure to teach children to recognize letter patterns in a variety of words.

EXPLAIN THE PRINCIPLE

Some words have parts or patterns that are the same.

Notice parts or patterns that are the same in many words.

Comprehensive Phonics, Spelling, and Word Study Guide

Refer to: page **34**, row **1**

ACTIVITY: WORD SORT

INSTRUCTIONAL PROCEDURE

NOTICE PARTS

See page 36 for detailed descriptions of Instructional Procedures.

EXPLAIN THE PRINCIPLE

Some words have parts or patterns that are the same.

Notice parts or patterns that are the same in many words.

Comprehensive Phonics, Spelling, and Word Study Guide

Refer to: page **34**, row **1**

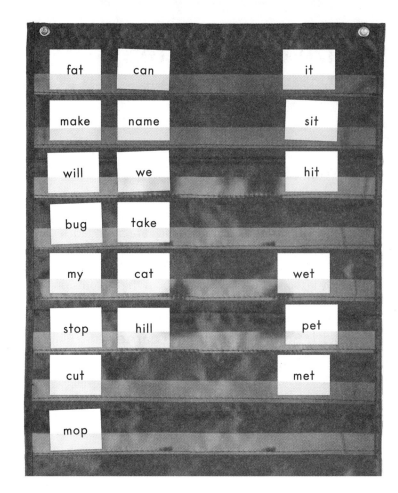

Teach

1. Explain to children that they are going to notice different ways in which words are the same.

2. Give each child a card with a word from your word wall as a "ticket" to the group meeting. Select the words from those provided to reflect your children's knowledge. Ask children to read aloud the word and then place it on the left side of the pocket chart.

3. Select a few words with a common pattern or part, such as words containing the part *-ot,* and hold up one card after another, asking the group to read each word. Take the word cards for *hot, got,* and *not* out of the group of words and place them together on the right side of the pocket chart. *What do you notice about these words?* Guide children to discover what the words have in common.

4. Continue until children are able to identify several different patterns successfully. At this point, any patterns they notice are helpful. Reinforce the principle as you review the lesson. *You can find patterns that are the same in some words. Some patterns appear in many words.*

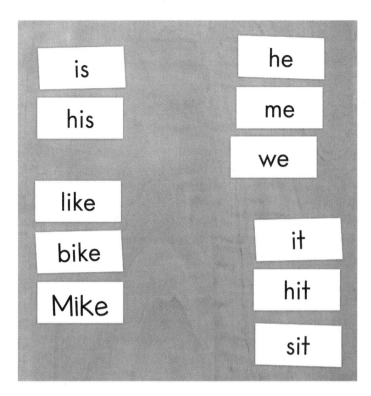

INSTRUCTIONAL PROCEDURE

NOTICE PARTS

See page 36 for detailed descriptions of Instructional Procedures.

ACTION TAGS

read

sort

tell

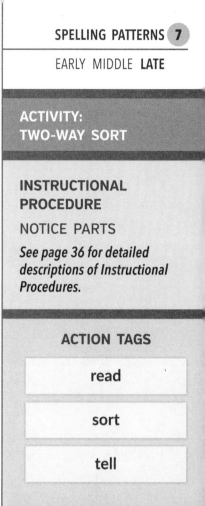

Apply

- Give partners a set of word cards that contain words children have learned (the words can be the same ones you used in the lesson). Have partners read all of the words.

- Have children take turns choosing a part or pattern that some of the words have in common, such as words beginning with *i*, and placing the word cards in a column. After the words are sorted, the partner reads the list and tells how the words are alike (categorized).

Share

Ask partners to talk about how they sorted words during the activity. Then invite one or two children to do a "mystery sort" for the whole group and have children guess how the words are alike.

Assess

- Notice whether children are representing word patterns in their writing.

- Observe whether children are noticing words with similar patterns in shared or guided reading.

- You may wish to use Spelling Patterns Assessment A, B, C, or G.

Spelling Patterns: Recognize Letter Patterns

Connect Learning Across Contexts

Interactive Read-Aloud Read aloud books that emphasize connections and similarities among words.

> IRA *Creak! Said the Bed* by Phyllis Root
>
> IRA *Rattletrap Car* by Phyllis Root

Shared Reading See "Go to Bed Early" in *Words That Sing* (2019). If you don't have these poetry charts, enlarge the print of this poem or other poems such as "Teeter-totter" in *Sing a Song of Poetry*, and have children use highlighter tape to call attention to words that have similar letter patterns. You may also wish to use the following Shared Reading title from *Fountas & Pinnell Classroom™* to call attention to words that end with the letter pattern *-ed*.

> SR *Splish Splash!* by Susan F. Rank

Interactive Writing Make explicit connections between words on the word wall and words children are writing. After writing, point out common patterns among the words in the text. Sometimes you can ask children to use yellow highlighter tape to make patterns stand out. An interactive writing piece is very meaningful to children because they have participated actively in constructing it.

Independent Writing Encourage children to use the word wall as a resource for spelling words accurately in their writing. When they know a word with an ending pattern it will help them with another word, for example, *is, his; and, hand, band*.

Extend Learning

Introduce the idea that a word may fit into more than one group or have more than one pattern or feature–for example, words that have two letters *and* end in *e*, such as *he, me,* and *we*.

▶ Connect with Home

Send home cards with words from the word wall for children to read to their families and caregivers. Encourage children to share different ways to sort the words with their family members.

High-Frequency Words

A core of known high-frequency words is a valuable resource as children build their reading and writing processes. Young children notice words that appear frequently in the simple texts they read; eventually, their recognition of these words becomes automatic. In this way, their reading becomes more efficient, enabling them to decode new words using phonics as well as to attend to comprehension.

Readers are more able to engage in problem-solving when they do it against a backdrop of accurate reading. They have more information available to them (i.e., language structure, meaning). Also, they can use connections between words in problem solving. Known high-frequency words are powerful examples that help them grasp that a word is always written the same way. They can use known high-frequency words to check on the accuracy of their reading and as resources for solving other words (for example, *this* starts like *the*). In general, children learn the simpler words earlier and in the process develop efficient systems for learning words. They continuously add to the core of high-frequency words they know. Lessons on high-frequency words help them look more carefully at words and develop more efficient systems for word recognition.

Connect to Assessment

See related (optional) HFW Assessment tasks in Online Resources.

- Assessment A: Reading Words
- Assessment B: Writing Words
- Assessment C: Individual Record
- Assessment D: Class Record (Reading 25 High-Frequency Words)
- Assessment E: Class Record (Writing 25 High-Frequency Words)

Develop Your Professional Understanding

See *The Fountas & Pinnell Comprehensive Phonics, Spelling, and Word Study Guide*. Related pages: 2–12, 40–41.

See *The Fountas & Pinnell Literacy Continuum: A Tool for Assessment, Planning, and Teaching*. 2017. Portsmouth, New Hampshire: Heinemann. Related pages: 357–397.

See *Word Matters: Teaching Phonics and Spelling in the Reading/Writing Classroom* by G. S. Pinnell and I. C. Fountas. 1998. Portsmouth, New Hampshire: Heinemann. Related pages: 35–41, 44–46, 71–72, 88–90, 237–238.

the
and
is
can
enjoy
look

Recognize and Use High-Frequency Words with One, Two, or Three Letters

Plan

▶ Consider Your Children

Use this lesson after children know the concept of "word" and are familiar with a few high-frequency words. Children will already have encountered some high-frequency words many times in shared reading, interactive writing, and guided reading. You will have placed at least some of them on the word wall. In this lesson and the next three, you will make sure that children know as many as twenty-five high-frequency words in detail and teach them a procedure for learning and remembering words by sight.

▶ Working with English Language Learners

Building and writing high-frequency words will help English language learners attend to the details that they will need to remember when reading or writing the words. Knowing some common English words in detail will help them make connections between their own pronunciation and how the letters and letter combinations that they see relate to the English sound system. Be sure that children can say (in approximated form) the words they are building and writing.

UNDERSTAND THE PRINCIPLE

Children use a core of known high-frequency words as anchors to monitor and check their reading. These known words help them read simple texts with greater fluency and engage in the behaviors of reading, such as moving from left to right across the page and matching word by word. Known words are powerful exemplars because children connect new words to these familiar words by beginning letters or sounds.

YOU WILL NEED

PWS Ready Resources
- ▶ HFW 1 Pocket-Chart Cards

Online Resources
- ▶ HFW 1 Action Tags
- ▶ HFW 1 Read-Make-Write Sheets
- ▶ HFW 1 Word Cards
- ▶ HFW 1 Letter Cards

Other Materials
- ▶ whiteboard
- ▶ magnetic letters
- ▶ wipe-off markers

Generative Lesson
A generative lesson has a simple structure that you can use to present similar content or concepts. You can use this lesson structure to teach children to recognize and use a variety of high-frequency words.

EXPLAIN THE PRINCIPLE

Some words have one letter.

Some words have two letters.

Some words have three letters.

You see some words many times when you read.

You need to learn words that you see many times because they help you read and write.

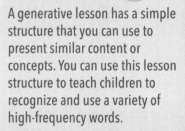

Comprehensive Phonics, Spelling, and Word Study Guide

Refer to:
page **40**, row **1**

EARLY MIDDLE LATE

ACTIVITY: READ-MAKE-WRITE SHEET

INSTRUCTIONAL PROCEDURE

WORDS TO KNOW

See page 36 for detailed descriptions of Instructional Procedures.

EXPLAIN THE PRINCIPLE

Some words have one letter.

Some words have two letters.

Some words have three letters.

You see some words many times when you read.

You need to learn words that you see many times because they help you read and write.

Comprehensive Phonics, Spelling, and Word Study Guide

Refer to: page **40**, row **1**

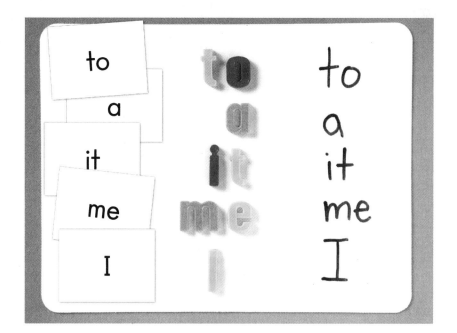

Teach

1. Explain to your children that there are some words they will read and write many times. *Today you will look carefully at some words so that you will know them every time you see them.*

2. Place the word cards *to, a, it, me,* and *I* one at a time in a left column on the magnetic whiteboard. (If children already know these words well, choose other one-, two-, and three-letter high-frequency words to practice and reinforce. If children have little experience building words, use fewer words so that it is easier for them to focus on each one.)

3. *You're going to read, make, and write some words today.*

4. Hold up the word *to. What is this word? You read it. ● What are the two letters in this word? Let's spell it from left to right.*

5. *Now I'll make the word* to *with magnetic letters. I'm looking for a* t. *Place the* t *on the board, and then demonstrate looking for and placing the* o. *I want to be sure that every letter is in the right order.* Demonstrate how to check by pointing to each letter in both words, in order: *t–t, o–o, to.*

6. *Now I'll write the word: t, o. I'll check it letter by letter. ● Now let's read all three examples of the word: to, to, to.*

7. Continue reading, building, checking, writing, and rereading each of the remaining words.

8. Place the words on the word wall for reference, if they aren't already there.

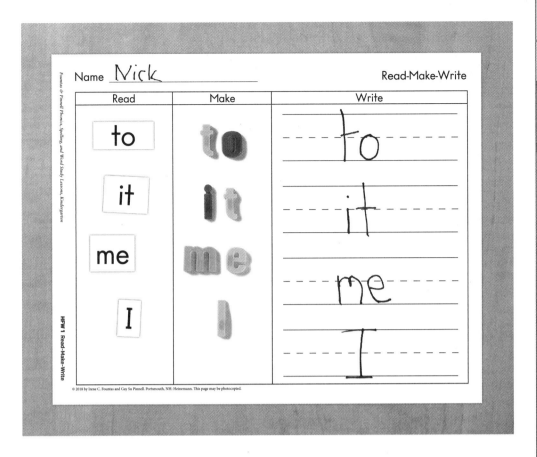

ACTIVITY: READ-MAKE-WRITE SHEET

INSTRUCTIONAL PROCEDURE

WORDS TO KNOW

See page 36 for detailed descriptions of Instructional Procedures.

ACTION TAGS

read

make

write

Apply

- Explain to children that they will now practice reading, making, and writing the words for themselves.
- Give each child two read-make-write sheets, a set of the lesson's small word cards, and a set of either magnetic letters or the lesson's letter cards.
- Have children place each word card in the first column of the sheet and read it, make the word in the middle column, and write the word in the last column.
- Partners can check each other's completed list.

Share

- Have children read their list of words to a different partner.
- Ask children to point to and read words on the word wall that they have learned to make and write.
- Show the word cards one at a time. Ask children to read each word quickly.

Assess

- Notice whether children are able to recognize high-frequency words quickly when reading.
- Notice whether children can write high-frequency words accurately.
- You may wish to use High-Frequency Words Assessment A, B, C, D, or E.

High-Frequency Words: Recognize and Use High-Frequency Words with One, Two, or Three Letters

Connect Learning Across Contexts

Interactive Read-Aloud Read aloud books such as the examples below. Reread a few sentences and have children listen for any easy high-frequency words.

> IRA *Fish Eyes* by Lois Ehlert

> IRA *The Bus for Us* by Suzanne Bloom

Shared Reading See "My Head" in *Words That Sing* (2019). If you don't have these poetry charts, enlarge the print of this poem or other poems such as "As I Was Going Along" or "To Market, to Market" in *Sing a Song of Poetry*, and have children use highlighter tape to locate one-, two-, and three-letter high-frequency words after reading. You may also wish to use the following Shared Reading title from *Fountas & Pinnell Classroom*™ to have children highlight easy high-frequency words after reading.

> SR *The Dog Park* by Jackson Pace

Interactive Writing Have a child write a high-frequency word quickly while others locate it on the word wall. If all children can write the word, write it yourself to save time, but have children check it letter by letter for accuracy.

Independent Writing As children begin to write, have them recall words they know by sight. Encourage them to write those words quickly and then to check for accuracy by comparing to the word wall. In conferences, point out words that children write quickly because they know them.

Extend Learning

Each time children learn a new high-frequency word, give them a card to add to their collection of words in a bag or on rings. Have them practice reading all the words in the bag or on the ring.

▶ Connect with Home

Send home two sets of high-frequency word cards and encourage children to play Concentration with family members. Be sure to include a set of directions (see Online Resources), even though children will have learned to play at school. Send home copies of rhymes and songs from *Sing a Song of Poetry* that contain high-frequency words that children are learning at school.

Recognize and Use High-Frequency Words with One, Two, or Three Letters

Plan

▶ Consider Your Children

Use this lesson after children know the conecpt of words and are familiar with a few high-frequency words. This is the second lesson in becoming familiar with up to twenty-five short high-frequency words. Children will already have encountered these words many times in shared reading, interactive writing, and guided reading. In this lesson, you continue to reinforce a procedure for learning and remembering words by sight.

▶ Working with English Language Learners

Be sure to use high-frequency words that children can understand and repeat. Help them articulate the words and locate them in print in different types of text (books, poems, charts). Work with them in a small group to be sure that they are building words left to right. Have them read each form of the words–word card, word built in magnetic letters, word written by the child–several times to emphasize that a word in any form is made up of the same letters.

UNDERSTAND THE PRINCIPLE

Children use a core of known high-frequency words as anchors to monitor and check their reading. These known words help them read simple texts with greater fluency and engage in the behaviors of reading, such as moving from left to right across the page and matching word by word. Known words are powerful exemplars because children connect new words to these familiar words by beginning letters or sounds.

YOU WILL NEED

PWS Ready Resources
- ▶ HFW 2 Pocket-Chart Cards

Online Resources
- ▶ HFW 2 Action Tags
- ▶ HFW 2 Read-Make-Write Sheets
- ▶ HFW 2 Word Cards
- ▶ HFW 2 Letter Cards

Other Materials
- ▶ whiteboard
- ▶ magnetic letters
- ▶ wipe-off markers

Generative Lesson ✓
A generative lesson has a simple structure that you can use to present similar content or concepts. You can use this lesson structure to teach children to recognize and use a variety of high-frequency words.

EXPLAIN THE PRINCIPLE

Some words have one letter.

Some words have two letters.

Some words have three letters.

You see some words many times when you read.

You need to learn words that you see many times because they help you read and write.

Comprehensive Phonics, Spelling, and Word Study Guide

Refer to: page **40**, row **1**

EARLY **MIDDLE** LATE

ACTIVITY: READ-MAKE-WRITE SHEET

INSTRUCTIONAL PROCEDURE

WORDS TO KNOW

See page 36 for detailed descriptions of Instructional Procedures.

EXPLAIN THE PRINCIPLE

Some words have one letter.

Some words have two letters.

Some words have three letters.

You see some words many times when you read.

You need to learn words that you see many times because they help you read and write.

Comprehensive Phonics, Spelling, and Word Study Guide

Refer to: page **40**, row **1**

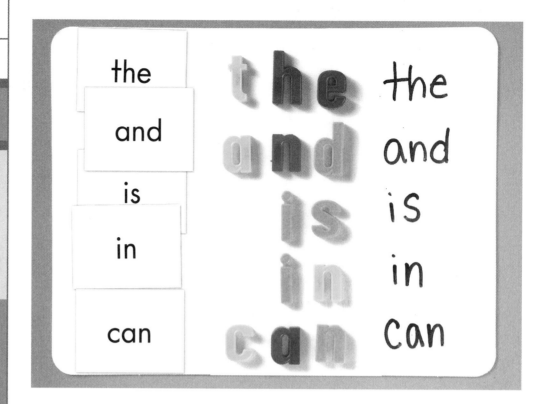

Teach

1. Remind children that there are certain words they will read and write many times. *Today we will look carefully at some of these words so that you can read them every time you see them.*

2. Place the pocket-chart cards *the, and, is, in,* and *can* one at a time in a left column on the magnetic whiteboard. (If children already know these words well, choose other one-, two-, and three-letter high-frequency words to practice and reinforce. If children have little experience building words, use fewer words so that it is easier for them to focus on each one.)

3. *You're going to read, make, and write some words today.*

4. Hold up the word *the. What is this word? You read it.* • *What are the three letters in this word? Let's spell it from left to right.*

5. *Now I'll make the word* the *with magnetic letters. I'm looking for a* t*. Place the* t *on the board, and then demonstrate looking for and placing the* h *and* e*. I want to be sure that every letter is in the right order.* Demonstrate how to check by pointing to each letter in both words, in order: *t–t, h–h, e–e, the.*

6. *Now I'll write the word:* t, h, e*. I'll check it letter by letter.* • *Now let's read all three examples of the word:* the, the, the.

7. Continue reading, building, checking, writing, and rereading each of the remaining words.

8. Place the words on the word wall for reference, if they aren't already there.

Name Taneisha   Read-Make-Write

Read	Make	Write
the	the	the
and	and	and
is	is	is
can	can	can

Fountas & Pinnell Phonics, Spelling, and Word Study Lessons, Kindergarten

HFW 2 Read-Make-Write

© 2018 by Irene C. Fountas and Gay Su Pinnell. Portsmouth, NH: Heinemann. This page may be photocopied.

ACTIVITY: READ-MAKE-WRITE SHEET

INSTRUCTIONAL PROCEDURE
WORDS TO KNOW

See page 36 for detailed descriptions of Instructional Procedures.

ACTION TAGS

read
make
write

Apply

- Explain to children that they will now practice reading, making, and writing the words for themselves.
- Give each child two read-make-write sheets, a set of the lesson's small word cards, and a set of either magnetic letters or the lesson's letter cards.
- Have children place each word card in the first column of the sheet and read it, make the word in the middle column, and write the word in the last column.
- Partners can check each other's completed lists.

Share

- Have children read their list of words to a different partner.
- Ask children to point to and read words on the word wall that they have learned to make and write.
- Show the word cards one at a time. Ask children to read each word quickly.

Assess

- Notice whether children are able to recognize high-frequency words quickly when reading.
- Notice whether children can write high-frequency words accurately.
- You may wish to use High-Frequency Words Assessment A, B, C, D, or E.

Connect Learning Across Contexts

Interactive Read-Aloud Read aloud books such as the examples below. Reread a few sentences and have children listen for any easy high-frequency words.

IRA *Does a Kangaroo Have a Mother, Too?* by Eric Carle

IRA *Lola at the Library* by Anna McQuinn

Shared Reading See "Puppies and Kittens" in *Words That Sing* (2019). If you don't have these poetry charts, enlarge the print of this poem or other poems such as "Fiddle-de-dee," "Did You Ever See a Lassie?" or "Jack-in-the-box" in *Sing a Song of Poetry,* and have children use highlighter tape to locate one-, two-, and three-letter high-frequency words. You may also wish to use to the following Shared Reading title from *Fountas & Pinnell Classroom*™ to have children highlight easy high-frequency words after reading.

SR *Spots* by Judy Kentor Schmauss

Interactive Writing Have a child write a high-frequency word quickly while others locate it on the word wall. If all children can write the word, write it yourself to save time, but have children check it letter by letter for accuracy.

Independent Writing As children begin to write, have them recall words they know by sight. Encourage them to write those words quickly and then to check for accuracy by comparing to the word wall. In conferences, point out words that children write quickly because they know them.

Extend Learning

Reinforce the principle that some words have one, two, or three letters. Ask children to read from the word wall all the one-letter words. Repeat for two- and three-letter words.

▶ Connect with Home

Send home a set of high-frequency word cards and encourage children to play a word guessing game with family members. The family member begins by giving a clue, such as "I'm thinking of a word that begins with the letter *a* and has three letters." When the child correctly guesses the word, players switch roles. Be sure to include a set of directions (see Online Resources), even though children will have learned to play the game at school.

Plan

▶ Consider Your Children

Use this lesson after children understand that knowing common words by sight will help them read and write more quickly. Lotto is similar to Bingo except that players cover every space, providing additional practice in recognizing words. In this game, children will be matching words by reading them aloud and looking carefully at their visual features. They can help one another in this activity, so every player does not have to know every word in isolation to play the game.

▶ Working with English Language Learners

Working with high-frequency words will help English language learners monitor their own reading of beginning texts. It will also make words more available to them phonologically. Provide many repetitions, and be sure that children know how to use each high-frequency word in comprehensible sentences. Create some simple sentences that children can repeat. For example, "It is time to play" and "I can jump."

UNDERSTAND THE PRINCIPLE

Children use a core of known high-frequency words as anchors to monitor and check their reading. These known words help them read simple texts with greater fluency and engage in the behaviors of reading, such as moving from left to right across the page and matching word by word. Known words are powerful exemplars because children connect new words to these familiar words by beginning letters or sounds.

YOU WILL NEED

PWS Ready Resources
- ▶ HFW 3 Pocket-Chart Cards

Online Resources
- ▶ HFW 3 Action Tags
- ▶ HFW 3 Lotto and Bingo Game Boards
- ▶ HFW 3 Word Cards
- ▶ HFW 3 Directions for Lotto and Bingo

Other Materials
- ▶ pocket chart

Generative Lesson

A generative lesson has a simple structure that you can use to present similar content or concepts. You can use this lesson structure to teach children to recognize and use a variety of high-frequency words.

EXPLAIN THE PRINCIPLE

Some words have one letter.

Some words have two letters.

Some words have three letters.

You see some words many times when you read.

You need to learn words that you see many times because they help you read and write.

Comprehensive Phonics, Spelling, and Word Study Guide

Refer to: page **40**, row **1**

ACTIVITY: LOTTO

INSTRUCTIONAL PROCEDURE

WORDS TO KNOW

See page 36 for detailed descriptions of Instructional Procedures.

EXPLAIN THE PRINCIPLE

Some words have one letter.

Some words have two letters.

Some words have three letters.

You see some words many times when you read.

You need to learn words that you see many times because they help you read and write.

Comprehensive Phonics, Spelling, and Word Study Guide

Refer to: page **40**, row **1**

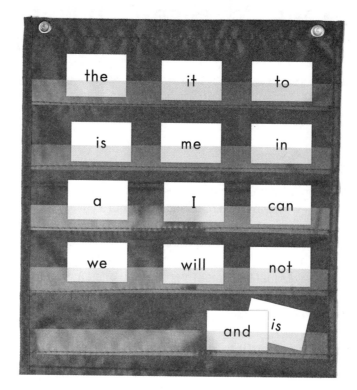

Teach

1. Tell children they are going to play a word-matching game.

2. Arrange the pocket-chart cards in rows in the pocket chart.

3. *Today you are going to play a game called Lotto. In this game you will match words. Let's try it with the words I have in the pocket chart. I'm going to take a word card from the stack and see if I can match it to a word on my chart.*

4. Hold up the first card, for example, *is. What is this word?* • *Now I'm going to look for the word* is *on my chart. Can anyone find* is *on my chart?*

5. Model checking the word *is* on the card with the word *is* on the chart by pointing to each letter in both words, in order: *i–i, s–s, is.* Then place the card you drew over the word on the chart.

6. Continue to draw one card at a time, modeling how to read, find, and check each word until all words on the chart are covered. (Words that don't match any on the chart are put at the bottom of the stack.)

7. *I've covered all the spaces on my chart. That's how you win the Lotto game.*

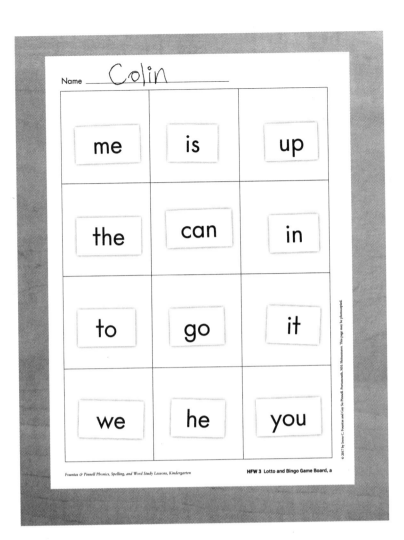

Name Colin

me	is	up
the	can	in
to	go	it
we	he	you

Fountas & Pinnell Phonics, Spelling, and Word Study Lessons, Kindergarten   **HFW 3** Lotto and Bingo Game Board, a

© 2017 by Irene C. Fountas and Gay Su Pinnell. Portsmouth, NH: Heinemann. This page may be photocopied.

ACTIVITY: LOTTO

INSTRUCTIONAL PROCEDURE

WORDS TO KNOW

See page 36 for detailed descriptions of Instructional Procedures.

ACTION TAGS

take

read

match

Apply

- Have children play Lotto in groups of three or four. Distribute game boards so that each child in a group receives a different board. Place a set of word cards in the center of each group. Each set should have multiple cards for each word.

- Explain how to play the game. *Take turns taking a card and reading the word. If you have a matching word on your game board, place the card on the matching word. If you don't have a match, return the card to the bottom of the stack. Keep taking turns until someone in your group has covered all the words with matching word cards.*

Share

Ask volunteers to read the words on their game boards. Ask children to talk about how they "know" (recognize) a word. This elicitation will give you information about their thinking processes.

Assess

- Notice whether children are able to recognize high-frequency words quickly when reading.

- Notice whether children can write high-frequency words accurately.

- You may wish to use High-Frequency Words Assessment A, B, C, D, or E.

High-Frequency Words: Recognize and Use High-Frequency Words with One, Two, or Three Letters

Connect Learning Across Contexts

Interactive Read-Aloud Read aloud books such as the examples below. Reread a few sentences and have children listen for any easy high-frequency words.

IRA *Head to Toe* by Eric Carle

IRA *Piggies* by Audrey Wood

Shared Reading See "Why Rabbits Jump" in *Words That Sing* (2019). If you don't have these poetry charts, enlarge the print of this poem or other poems such as "The Elephant Goes Like This" or "Puppies and Kittens" in *Sing a Song of Poetry*, and have children use highlighter tape to locate one-, two-, and three-letter high-frequency words. You may also wish to use the following Shared Reading title from *Fountas & Pinnell Classroom*™ to have children highlight easy high-frequency words after reading.

SR *Stripes* by Catherine Friend

Interactive Writing Have a child write a high-frequency word quickly while others locate it on the word wall. If all children can write the word, write it yourself to save time, but have children check it letter by letter for accuracy. Revisit finished pieces of interactive writing to practice quickly locating high-frequency words.

Independent Writing As children begin to write, have them recall words they know by sight. Encourage them to write those words quickly and then to check for accuracy by comparing to the word wall. In conferences, point out words that children write quickly because they know them.

Extend Learning

Have children create their own set of high-frequency word cards and then swap with a partner to read aloud quickly. You may also wish to customize word cards using Gamemaker in Online Resources.

▶ Connect with Home

Give each child a set of high-frequency word cards to practice reading at home. Explain to family members that these are words that appear often in books, so children need to learn to read them quickly. (For example, you may wish to point out that *I, the,* and *and* make up ten percent of all printed text.) Explain that children's ability to recognize these words automatically will help them read more smoothly and use parts of these words to figure out other words.

Recognize and Use High-Frequency Words with Three or More Letters

Plan

▶ Consider Your Children

Use this lesson to continue expanding children's knowledge of high-frequency words. Children will already have encountered these words many times in shared reading, interactive writing, and guided reading. As you continue to reinforce a procedure for learning and remembering words by sight, children will also be learning how to check the spelling of the words they write. If your assessment indicates that children already know these words, select others and/or move on to the next lesson.

▶ Working with English Language Learners

As English language learners say, build, and write high-frequency words, they will also be acquiring a system for learning new words and noticing how letters work together to make words. Be sure that children say the words while building them and read each form of a word—the word on a word card, the word built with magnetic letters, the word as written by the child—after completing the activity to emphasize that a word in any form is made up of the same letters.

UNDERSTAND THE PRINCIPLE

Children use a core of known high-frequency words as anchors to monitor and check their reading. These known words help them read simple texts with greater fluency and engage in the behaviors of reading, such as moving from left to right across the page and matching word by word. Known words are powerful exemplars because children can connect new words to these familiar words by beginning letters or sounds.

YOU WILL NEED

 **Ready Resources**
- ▶ HFW 4 Pocket-Chart Cards

Online Resources
- ▶ HFW 4 Action Tags
- ▶ HFW 4 Read-Make-Write Sheets
- ▶ HFW 4 Word Cards
- ▶ HFW 4 Letter Cards

Other Materials
- ▶ whiteboard
- ▶ magnetic letters
- ▶ wipe-off markers

Generative Lesson
A generative lesson has a simple structure that you can use to present similar content or concepts. You can use this lesson structure to teach children to recognize and use a variety of high-frequency words.

EXPLAIN THE PRINCIPLE

Some words have three or more letters.

You see some words many times when you read.

You need to learn words that you see many times because they help you read and write.

 Comprehensive Phonics, Spelling, and Word Study Guide

Refer to: page **40**, row **4**

ACTIVITY: READ-MAKE-WRITE SHEET

INSTRUCTIONAL PROCEDURE

WORDS TO KNOW

See page 36 for detailed descriptions of Instructional Procedures.

EXPLAIN THE PRINCIPLE

Some words have three or more letters.

You see some words many times when you read.

You need to learn words that you see many times because they help you read and write.

Comprehensive Phonics, Spelling, and Word Study Guide

Refer to: page **40**, row **4**

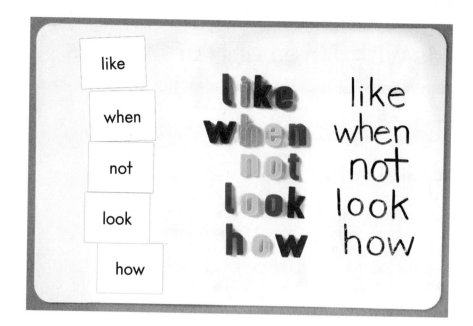

Teach

1. Remind children that there are certain words they will read and write many times. *Today you will look carefully at more words you use many times so that you get to know them by how they look.*

2. One at a time, place the pocket-chart cards *like, when, not, look,* and *how* in a left column on the magnetic whiteboard. (If children already know these words well, choose other high-frequency words with three or more letters to practice and reinforce. If children have little experience building words, use fewer words so that it is easier for them to focus on each one.)

3. *You're going to read, make, and write some words today. Let's read the first word on the board.*

4. *The first word is* like. *You read it.* • *What are the four letters in this word?*

5. *Now I'll make the word* like *with magnetic letters. I'm looking for an* l. *Place the* l *on the board, and then demonstrate looking for and placing the* i, k, *and* e. *I want to be sure that every letter is in the right order.* Demonstrate how to check by pointing to each letter in both words, in order: *l–l, i–i, k–k, e–e,* like.

6. *Now I'll write the word:* l, i, k, e. *I'll check it letter by letter.* • *Now let's read all three examples of the word:* like, like, like.

7. Continue reading, building, checking, writing, and rereading each of the remaining words.

8. Place the words on the word wall for reference, if they aren't already there.

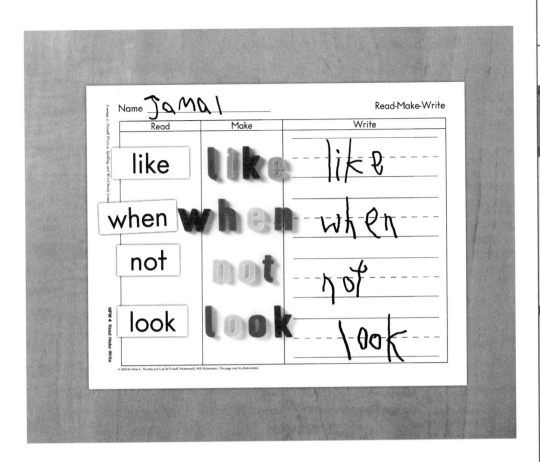

INSTRUCTIONAL PROCEDURE

WORDS TO KNOW

See page 36 for detailed descriptions of Instructional Procedures.

ACTION TAGS

put

read

make

write

check

Apply

- Explain to children that they will now practice reading, making, and writing the words for themselves.
- Give each child two read-make-write sheets, a set of the lesson's word cards, and a set of either magnetic letters or the lesson's letter cards.
- Have children place each word card in the first column of the sheet and read it, make the word in the middle column, and write the word in the last column.
- Partners can check each other's completed list.

Share

- Have children read their list of words to a different partner.
- Ask children to point to and read words on the word wall that they have learned to make and write.
- Show the word cards one at a time. Ask the children to read each word quickly.

Assess

- Notice whether children are able to recognize high-frequency words with three or more letters quickly when reading.
- Notice whether children can write high-frequency words with three or more letters accurately.
- You may wish to use High-Frequency Words Assessment A, B, C, D, or E.

High-Frequency Words: Recognize and Use High-Frequency Words with Three or More Letters

Connect Learning Across Contexts

Interactive Read-Aloud Read aloud books such as the examples below. Reread a few sentences and have children listen for any easy high-frequency words.

> IRA *ABC I Like Me* by Nancy Carlson

> IRA *Alicia's Happy Day* by Meg Starr

Shared Reading See "When Ducks Get Up in the Morning" in *Words That Sing* [2019]. If you don't have these poetry charts, enlarge the print of this poem or other poems such as "Pease Porridge Hot" or "Little Jack Sprat" in *Sing a Song of Poetry,* and have children use highlighter tape to locate and identify one or two high-frequency words. You may also wish to use the following Shared Reading title from *Fountas & Pinnell Classroom*™ and have children place highlighter tape on easy high-frequency words after reading.

> SR *Up in the Cloud Forest* by Tess Fletcher

Interactive Writing Have a child write a high-frequency word quickly while others locate it on the word wall. If all children can write the word, write it yourself to save time, but have children check it letter by letter for accuracy. Revisit completed pieces to practice locating known high-frequency words quickly.

Independent Writing As children begin to write, have them recall words they know by sight. Encourage them to write those words quickly and then to check for accuracy by comparing to the word wall. In conferences, point out words that children have written quickly because they know them.

Extend Learning

Reinforce the principle that some words have three letters and some have more than three. Ask children to read from the word wall all the three-letter words. Repeat for words with four letters. You may also wish to customize word cards using Gamemaker in Online Resources.

▶ Connect with Home

Send home two sets of high-frequency word cards with each child and encourage children to play Concentration with family members. Be sure to include a set of directions, even though children will have learned to play at school.

Recognize and Use High-Frequency Words with Three or More Letters

Plan

▶ Consider Your Children

This lesson is part of a series of lessons designed to expand children's knowledge of high-frequency words by helping them establish flexible familiarity with twenty-five short high-frequency words. Children will already have encountered these words many times in shared reading, interactive writing, and guided reading. In this lesson, you continue to reinforce a procedure for learning and remembering words by sight. You may want to assess children's knowledge to determine whether more lessons on high-frequency words will be needed.

▶ Working with English Language Learners

By the time you use this lesson, English language learners will know a small core of high-frequency words that they can say, build, and write. Encourage them to look carefully at words in order to learn more words. Use the words in very simple but meaningful sentences to help children understand them. Be sure to check their ability to recognize and say the words before they take home word cards. If there are no English speakers in the home, show children how to use the cards to practice independently.

UNDERSTAND THE PRINCIPLE

Children use a core of known high-frequency words as anchors to monitor and check their reading. These known words help them read simple texts with greater fluency and engage in the behaviors of reading, such as moving from left to right across the page and matching word by word. Known words are powerful exemplars because children can connect new words to these familiar words by beginning letters or sounds.

YOU WILL NEED

 **Ready Resources**
- ▶ HFW 5 Pocket-Chart Cards

Online Resources
- ▶ HFW 5 Action Tags
- ▶ HFW 5 Read-Make-Write Sheets
- ▶ HFW 5 Word Cards
- ▶ HFW 5 Letter Cards

Other Materials
- ▶ whiteboard
- ▶ magnetic letters
- ▶ wipe-off markers

✓ Generative Lesson

A generative lesson has a simple structure that you can use to present similar content or concepts. You can use this lesson structure to teach children to recognize and use a variety of high-frequency words.

EXPLAIN THE PRINCIPLE

Some words have three or more letters.

You see some words many times when you read.

You need to learn words that you see many times because they help you read and write.

Comprehensive Phonics, Spelling, and Word Study Guide

Refer to:
page **40**, row **4**

ACTIVITY: READ-MAKE-WRITE SHEET

INSTRUCTIONAL PROCEDURE

WORDS TO KNOW

See page 36 for detailed descriptions of Instructional Procedures.

EXPLAIN THE PRINCIPLE

Some words have three or more letters.

You see some words many times when you read.

You need to learn words that you see many times because they help you read and write.

Comprehensive Phonics, Spelling, and Word Study Guide

Refer to: page **40**, row **4**

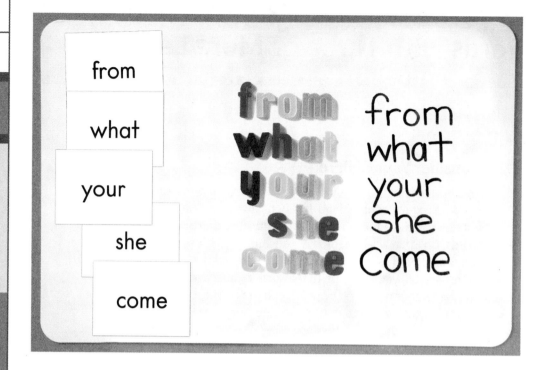

Teach

1. Remind children that there are certain words they will read and write *many times. Today you will look carefully at more words so that you get to know them by how they look and you can read them quickly.*

2. One at a time, place the pocket-chart cards *from, what, your, she,* and *come* in a left column on the magnetic whiteboard. (If children already know these words well, choose other high-frequency words with three or more letters to practice and reinforce. If children have little experience building words, use fewer words so that it is easier for them to focus on each one.)

3. *You're going to read, make, and write these words today. Let's read each word on the board.*

4. *The first word is* from. *You read it.* • *What are the four letters in this word?*

5. *Now I'll make the word* from *with magnetic letters. I'm looking for an* f. Place the *f* on the board, and then demonstrate looking for and placing the *r, o,* and *m. I want to be sure that every letter is in the right order.* Demonstrate how to check by pointing to each letter in both words, in order: *f–f, r–r, o–o, m–m, from.*

6. *Now I'll write the word: f, r, o, m. I'll check it letter by letter.* • *Now let's read all three examples of the word: from, from, from.*

7. Continue reading, building, checking, writing, and rereading each of the remaining words.

8. Place the words on the word wall for reference, if they aren't already there.

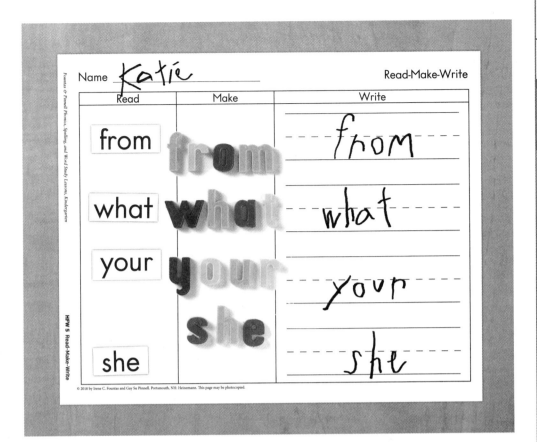

INSTRUCTIONAL PROCEDURE

WORDS TO KNOW

See page 36 for detailed descriptions of Instructional Procedures.

ACTION TAGS

put
read
make
write
check

Apply

- Explain to children that they will now practice reading, making, and writing the words for themselves.
- Give each child two read-make-write sheets, a set of the lesson's word cards, and a set of either magnetic letters or the lesson's letter cards.
- Have children put each word card in the first column of the sheet and read it, make the word in the middle column, and write the word in the last column.
- Partners can check each other's completed list.

Share

- Have children read their list of words to a different partner.
- Ask children to point to and read words on the word wall that they have learned to make and write.
- Show the word cards one at a time. Ask children to read each word quickly.

Assess

- Notice whether children are able to recognize high-frequency words with three or more letters quickly when reading.
- Notice whether children can write high-frequency words with three or more letters accurately. You may wish to dictate words from previous high-frequency word lessons that you have taught, ask children to write them, and then focus another lesson on words that most of your children do not yet know.
- You may wish to use High-Frequency Words Assessment A, B, C, D, or E.

High-Frequency Words: Recognize and Use High-Frequency Words with Three or More Letters

Connect Learning Across Contexts

Interactive Read-Aloud Read aloud books such as the examples below. Reread a few sentences and have children listen for any easy high-frequency words.

[IRA] *Market Day* by Lois Ehlert

[IRA] *Snowballs* by Lois Ehlert

Shared Reading See "There Once Was a Queen" in *Words That Sing* (2019). If you don't have these poetry charts, enlarge the print of this poem or other poems such as "Who Stole the Cookies?" "Twinkle, Twinkle, Little Star," or "Clap Your Hands" in *Sing a Song of Poetry,* and have children use highlighter tape to locate and identify one or two high-frequency words. You may also wish to use the following Shared Reading title from *Fountas & Pinnell Classroom*™ to have children highlight easy high-frequency words after reading.

[SR] *A Bear and His Honey* by Fannie Morris

Interactive Writing Have a child write a high-frequency word quickly while others locate it on the word wall. If all children can write the word, write it yourself to save time, but have children check it letter by letter for accuracy. Remember that when a child knows a word very well and can write it quickly and automatically, you will want to write the word yourself to move the lesson along. Focus attention on words an individual nearly knows.

Independent Writing As children begin to write, have them recall words they know by sight. Encourage them to write those words quickly and then to check for accuracy by comparing to the word wall. In conferences, point out words that children have written quickly because they know them.

Extend Learning

Each time children learn a new high-frequency word, give them a card to add to their collection of words in a bag or on rings. Have them practice reading all the words in the bag or on the ring.

▶ Connect with Home

Send home a set of word cards and encourage children to play a word guessing game with family members. The family member begins by giving a clue, such as "I'm thinking of a word that rhymes with the word *free* and has three letters." When the child correctly guesses the word, players switch roles. Be sure to include a set of directions, even though children will have learned to play the game at school.

Recognize and Use High-Frequency Words with Three or More Letters

Plan

▶ Consider Your Children

This lesson is part of a series of lessons designed to expand children's knowledge of high-frequency words by helping them establish flexible familiarity with twenty-five short high-frequency words. Children will already have encountered these words many times in shared reading, interactive writing, and guided reading. In this lesson, you continue to reinforce a procedure for learning and remembering words by sight. Emphasize working quickly and checking spelling.

▶ Working with English Language Learners

Acquiring a core of high-frequency words that they know in every detail and can automatically recognize and read will be very helpful to English language learners. Most high-frequency words are abstract in that they function in sentences but are not concrete nouns. For English language learners, it will be especially important to use these words in the context of sentences so that they become familiar with hearing them and see how they are used in sentences. Construct sentences for each word that will be meaningful to children and that they can repeat–for example: "I see John." (John says, "I see Mike." Children repeat the phrase as a way of calling on others in the group.) Sentences will become more complex–for example: "Johnny can ride his bike up the mountain. So can I." Be sure the high-frequency words you use are available to English language learners with your support.

UNDERSTAND THE PRINCIPLE

Children use a core of known high-frequency words as anchors to monitor and check their reading. These known words help them read simple texts and engage in the behaviors of reading, like moving from left to right across the page and matching word by word. Known words are powerful exemplars because children connect new words to these familiar words by beginning letters or sounds.

YOU WILL NEED

PWS Ready Resources
- ▶ HFW 6 Pocket-Chart Cards

Online Resources
- ▶ HFW 6 Action Tags
- ▶ HFW 6 Read-Make-Write Sheets
- ▶ HFW 6 Word Cards
- ▶ HFW 6 Letter Cards

Other Materials
- ▶ magnetic whiteboard
- ▶ magnetic letters
- ▶ wipe-off markers

Generative Lesson

A generative lesson has a simple structure that you can use to present similar content or concepts. You can use this lesson structure to teach children to recognize and use a variety of high-frequency words.

EXPLAIN THE PRINCIPLE

Some words have three or more letters.

You see some words many times when you read.

You need to learn words that you see many times because they help you read and write.

Comprehensive Phonics, Spelling, and Word Study Guide

Refer to: page **40**, row **4**

EARLY   MIDDLE   **LATE**

ACTIVITY: READ-MAKE-WRITE SHEET

INSTRUCTIONAL PROCEDURE

WORDS TO KNOW

See page 36 for detailed descriptions of Instructional Procedures.

EXPLAIN THE PRINCIPLE

Some words have three or more letters.

You see some words many times when you read.

You need to learn words that you see many times because they help you read and write.

Comprehensive Phonics, Spelling, and Word Study Guide

Refer to: page **40**, row **4**

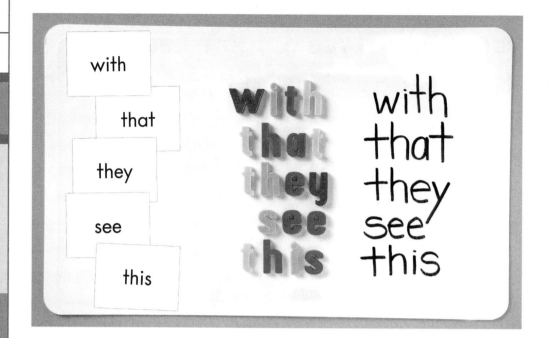

Teach

1. Remind children that there are certain words they will read and write many times. *Today we will look carefully at more words so that you get to know them by how they look.*

2. One at a time, place the pocket-chart cards *with, that, they, see,* and *this* in a left column on the magnetic whiteboard. [If children already know these words well, choose other high-frequency words with three or more letters to practice and reinforce. If children have little experience building words, use fewer words so that it is easier for them to focus on each one.]

3. *You're going to read, make, and write more words today. Let's read each word on the board.*

4. *The first word is* with. *You read it.* • *What are the four letters in this word?*

5. *Now I'll make the word* from *with magnetic letters. I'm looking for a* w. Place the *w* on the board, and then demonstrate looking for and placing the *i, t,* and *h. I want to be sure that every letter is in the right order.* Demonstrate how to check by pointing to each letter in both words, in order: *w–w, i–i, t–t, h–h, with.*

6. *Now I'll write the word: w, i, t, h. I'll check it letter by letter.* • *Now let's read all three examples of the word: with, with, with.*

7. Continue reading, building, checking, writing, and rereading each of the remaining words.

8. Place the words on the word wall for reference, if they aren't already there.

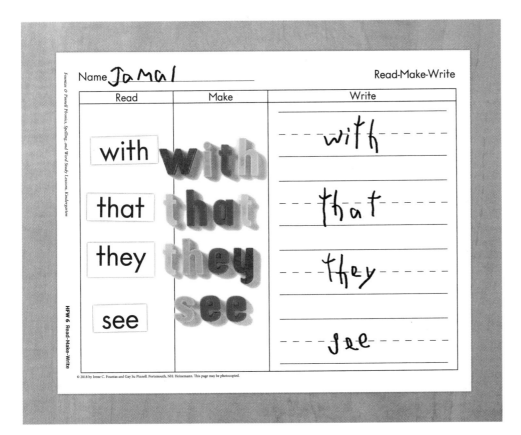

ACTIVITY: READ-MAKE-WRITE SHEET (PAIRS)

INSTRUCTIONAL PROCEDURE

WORDS TO KNOW

See page 36 for detailed descriptions of Instructional Procedures.

ACTION TAGS

put

read

make

write

check

Apply

- Explain to children that they will now practice reading, making, and writing the words for themselves.
- Give each child two read-make-write sheets, a set of the lesson's word cards, and a set of either magnetic letters or the lesson's letter cards.
- Have children place each word card in the first column of the sheet and read it, make the word in the middle column, and write the word in the last column.
- Partners can check each other's completed list.

Share

- Ask the children to show on the word wall some of the words they have learned to make and write.
- Show high-frequency word cards one at a time for a quick review.
- Have the children read their list of words to a different partner.

Assess

- Notice whether the children are able to recognize high-frequency words when reading.
- Notice whether the children can write high-frequency words with three or more letters quickly and accurately.
- Take a quick inventory by dictating a list of words for children to write. Have them practice words they do not yet know.
- You may wish to use High-Frequency Words Assessment A, B, C, D, or E.

High-Frequency Words: Recognize and Use High-Frequency Words with Three or More Letters

Connect Learning Across Contexts

Interactive Read-Aloud Read aloud books that have large print. Reread a few sentences and have children listen for any easy high-frequency words.

IRA *Rain* by Manya Stojic

IRA *The Feelings Book* by Todd Parr

Shared Reading See "Here We Go" in *Words That Sing* (2019). If you don't have these poetry charts, enlarge the print of this poem or other poems such as "Hey Diddle Diddle," "Baby Mice," or "Blow, Wind, Blow" in *Sing a Song of Poetry,* and have children use highlighter tape to locate and identify one or two high-frequency words. You may also wish to use the following Shared Reading title from *Fountas & Pinnell Classroom*™ to have children highlight easy high-frequency words after reading.

SR *Playing Basketball* by Louis Petrone

Interactive Writing Have a child write a high-frequency word quickly while others locate it on the word wall. If all children can write the word, write it yourself to save time, but have children check it with their eyes.

Independent Writing Encourage the children to recognize that they know some words really well. They can write them quickly as they write stories. Have them check their spelling.

Extend Learning

- Have children match pairs of word cards with high-frequency words.
- Each time children learn a new high-frequency word, give them a card to add to their collection of words in a bag or on rings. Have them practice reading all the words in the bag or on the ring.

▶ Connect with Home

Send home two sets of high-frequency words on cards and encourage children to play Concentration. Be sure to include a set of directions, even though the children will have learned to play at school. You may also wish to customize word cards using Gamemaker in Online Resources.

Locate and Read High-Frequency Words in Continuous Text

Plan

▶ Consider Your Children

Use this lesson after you have read a favorite poem, rhyme, song, or chant several times to your children and several more times from an enlarged text during shared reading. Any favorite text containing known high-frequency words is suitable. Lessons such as this one help children realize how they can use their knowledge of known words to check the accuracy of their reading and to read quickly.

▶ Working with English Language Learners

While this lesson uses "Pat-a-cake" as a model for finding high-frequency words in text, you may select any shared reading text that has meaning for the English language learners in your class. After selecting the text, act it out with children and repeat it enough times for them to be comfortable reading it and matching word by word.

YOU WILL NEED

PWS Ready Resources
- ▶ HFW 7 Pocket-Chart Cards

Online Resources
- ▶ HFW 7 Action Tags
- ▶ HFW 7 Rhyme

Other Materials
- ▶ chart paper
- ▶ highlighter tape
- ▶ *Words That Sing* or *Sing a Song of Poetry*

Generative Lesson ✓

A generative lesson has a simple structure that you can use to present similar content or concepts. You can use this lesson structure to teach children to recognize and use a variety of high-frequency words.

UNDERSTAND THE PRINCIPLE

Learning to discriminate and identify words that occur frequently in text helps children build a core of known words that makes reading longer passages less intimidating and is useful for monitoring reading. This ability also reinforces the concept of "word," as defined in print, which is important basic knowledge as children begin to read.

EXPLAIN THE PRINCIPLE

Find a word when you know how it looks.

When you know a word, you can read it every time you see it.

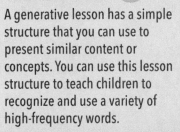

Comprehensive Phonics, Spelling, and Word Study Guide

Refer to: page **40**, row **3**

ACTIVITY: RHYME

INSTRUCTIONAL PROCEDURE

WORDS TO KNOW

See page 36 for detailed descriptions of Instructional Procedures.

EXPLAIN THE PRINCIPLE

Find a word when you know how it looks.

When you know a word, you can read it every time you see it.

Comprehensive Phonics, Spelling, and Word Study Guide

Refer to: page **40**, row **3**

Pat-a-cake
Pat-a-cake, pat-a-cake.
Baker's man!
Bake me a cake
As fast as you can.
Pat it, and prick it,
And mark it with a T,
Put it in the oven
For Tommy and me.

Teach

1. Display a shared reading poem from *Words That Sing* (2019) that contains one or more high-frequency words that your children are learning: for example, the rhyme "This Is the Way We Go to School" containing the word *to*. If you don't have these poetry charts, enlarge "Pat-a-cake" from *Sing a Song of Poetry*, which contains the word *it*.

2. Tell children that today they are going to practice finding words they know in this poem.

3. Read the text with children, pointing to the words. Read and enjoy the text several times.

4. Have children locate a known high-frequency word. *You can find a word you know. What are the two letters in the word* it? • *This time when we read, stop when you come to the word* it. Read the rhyme with children, stopping at the first instance of the word *it*.

5. Invite a child to place highlighter tape over the word on the chart.

6. *Now use your eyes to find* it *again.* Invite children to take turns underlining, circling, or placing highlighter strips over each instance of the word.

7. Repeat the process with other high-frequency words that children have learned. If you're using highlighter tape, remove the strips from the previous word each time so that children can focus on finding the new word.

8. Reinforce the principle as you review the words that children have found. *You were able to find these words because you knew how they looked. When you know a word, you can read it every time you see it.*

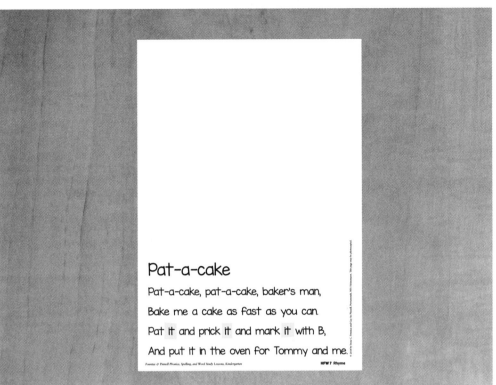

Pat-a-cake

Pat-a-cake, pat-a-cake, baker's man,

Bake me a cake as fast as you can.

Pat it and prick it and mark it with B,

And put it in the oven for Tommy and me.

Fountas & Pinnell Phonics, Spelling, and Word Study Lessons, Kindergarten

HFW 7 Rhyme

ACTIVITY: RHYME

INSTRUCTIONAL PROCEDURE

WORDS TO KNOW

See page 36 for detailed descriptions of Instructional Procedures.

ACTION TAGS

| read |
| find |
| circle |
| draw |

Apply

Give children a copy of the rhyme "Pat-a-cake." Display a word card. Have children read the rhyme and find and use highlighter tape to mark the word each time it appears. Repeat with the remaining high-frequency words. Then have them illustrate the poem.

Share

Have partners take turns reading aloud the rhyme to each other. Then have partners share how many instances of each high-frequency word they found, for example, four instances of the word *it,* two instances of the word *me,* and so on.

Assess

- Notice whether children are able to locate high-frequency words in their shared reading texts.
- Observe whether children can read high-frequency words automatically.

Interactive Read-Aloud Read aloud books that include familiar rhymes and songs. Reread a few sentences and have children listen for any easy high-frequency words.

> **IRA** *I'm a Little Teapot* by Iza Trapani

> **IRA** *It's Raining, It's Pouring* by Kin Eagle

Shared Reading See "Five Fingers on Each Hand" in *Words That Sing* (2019). If you don't have these poetry charts, enlarge the print of this poem or other poems such as "Little Red Apple" or "I Clap My Hands" in *Sing a Song of Poetry,* and have children use highlighter tape to locate and identify one or two high-frequency words. You may also wish to use the following Shared Reading title from *Fountas & Pinnell Classroom*™ to have children highlight easy high-frequency words after reading.

> **SR** *Coco Steps Out* by Lionel Page

Interactive Writing Draw attention to words that children can write quickly because they have seen them before. Remind children of these words on the word wall and in the poems, rhymes, songs, and chants that they have encountered in shared reading.

Independent Writing Encourage children to use the texts they know from shared reading as resources for their writing.

Extend Learning

Repeat the lesson using other shared reading texts and different high-frequency words. Vary the Apply activity by giving clues about the high-frequency word children must find. *I see a word that begins with the letter* a *and has three letters. You know this word. What word is it?* • *How many times do you see the word* and *in this poem?*

▶ Connect with Home

Give each child a copy of the rhyme "Pat-a-cake" to take home and enjoy. You may also wish to send home a set of word cards. Children can work with family members to find each word in text around their home.

Word Meaning/Vocabulary

Children need to know the meaning of the words they are learning to read and write. It is important for them to expand their speaking, reading, writing, and vocabulary constantly as well as to develop a more complex understanding of words they already know. The category of Word Meaning/Vocabulary includes concept words such as numbers and days of the week that are often used in the texts that children read, and they will want to use these words in their own writing. When children learn concept words (color words are another example), they can learn how to form categories that help in retrieving these words when needed. In our complex language, meaning and spelling are intricately connected. Often you must know the meaning of the word you want to spell or read before you can spell it accurately, and vocabulary is certainly a very important element of reading comprehension.

Connect to Assessment

See related (optional) WMV Assessment tasks in Online Resources.

- Assessment A: Understanding Color Words
- Assessment B: Understanding Number Words
- Assessment C: Class Record (Concept Words)

Develop Your Professional Understanding

See *The Fountas & Pinnell Comprehensive Phonics, Spelling, and Word Study Guide.* 2017. Related pages: 2–12, 44–49.

See *The Fountas & Pinnell Literacy Continuum: A Tool for Assessment, Planning, and Teaching.* 2017. Portsmouth, New Hampshire: Heinemann. Related pages: 357–397.

See *Word Matters: Teaching Phonics and Spelling in the Reading/Writing Classroom* by G. S. Pinnell and I. C. Fountas. 1998. Portsmouth, New Hampshire: Heinemann. Related pages: 78–81, 88–89, 199–205.

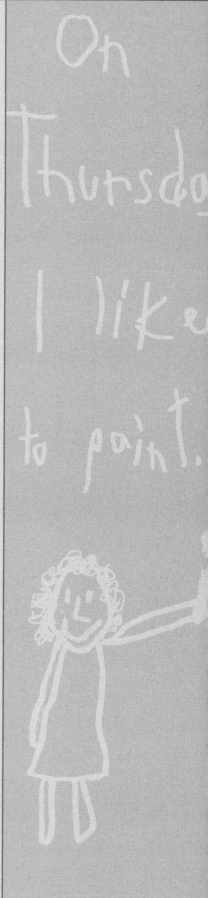

On Thursday I like to paint.

Recognize and Use Concept Words: Color Names

Plan

▶ Consider Your Children

Decide how many words to include in the first lesson. Children should understand what a word is and should have worked with their names. They should have had some experience reading color names in shared reading and interactive writing. They do not have to know all of the letters and sounds to do this activity successfully. If they are inexperienced, start with just three or four color names. It is a good idea to conduct an informal assessment to determine which color words children already know. Begin the lesson with a word that most of the children know. Color names should be written in black (not in the color) because children need to learn to attend to the features of the letters to distinguish the words.

▶ Working with English Language Learners

Color names are helpful for English language learners to know. You'll need to consider whether they know the concept and word in their own language or whether they have not yet connected the concept/color with the label in any language. In either case, present many different examples so that you are sure children are attending to the characteristic–color–and know that the label applies to all objects that have that characteristic. Once children understand the concept, they will rapidly acquire the labels.

YOU WILL NEED

PWS Ready Resources
- ▶ WMV 1 Pocket-Chart Cards
- ▶ Color Word Cards

Online Resources
- ▶ WMV 1 Action Tags
- ▶ WMV 1 Two-Column Sorts
- ▶ WMV 1 Word Cards

Other Materials
- ▶ chart paper
- ▶ colored markers
- ▶ glue sticks
- ▶ crayons

Generative Lesson ✓

A generative lesson has a simple structure that you can use to present similar content or concepts. You can use this lesson structure to teach children a variety of concept words.

UNDERSTAND THE PRINCIPLE

Good word solvers are able to connect words by their meanings. Using meaning to group words into categories creates a useful mental map for early readers and writers. Children can then use these words in writing and recognize them quickly in reading, making connections between these words and others that they want to read or write. Color names are especially helpful in interactive writing, where many early stories feature colors.

EXPLAIN THE PRINCIPLE

A color has a name.

Read and write the names of colors.

Comprehensive Phonics, Spelling, and Word Study Guide

Refer to: page **44**, row **1**

**ACTIVITY:
READ-WRITE CHART**

**INSTRUCTIONAL
PROCEDURE**

MAP WORDS

*See page 36 for detailed
descriptions of Instructional
Procedures.*

EXPLAIN THE PRINCIPLE

A color has a name.

*Read and write the names of
colors.*

Comprehensive
Phonics, Spelling,
and Word Study
Guide

Refer to:
page **44**, row **1**

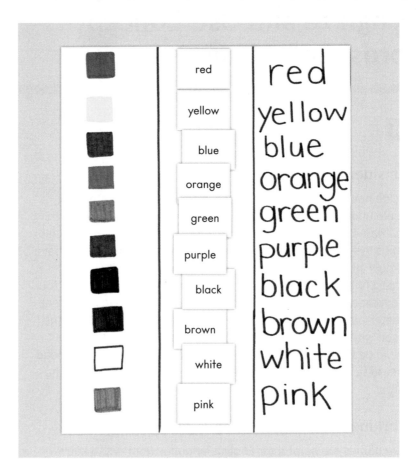

Teach

1. Tell children that they're going to learn to read and write the names of colors.

2. Display chart paper with squares of the following colors along the left side: red, yellow, blue, orange, green, purple, black, brown, white, and pink. Point to each square and ask children to say the name of the color.

3. Hold up the pocket-chart card for *red* as you guide children to read the word. *This is the word* red. *Read it with me.* • *What letters make the word* red? • Place the pocket-chart card beside the red square.

4. *Now I'll write the word: r, e, d. Did I write it correctly?* • *Let's check it letter by letter.* Demonstrate how to check by pointing to each letter in both words, in order: *r–r, e–e, d–d, red.*

5. Continue reading, writing, and checking each of the remaining words.

6. Reinforce the principle as you guide children to reread the list of words. *You can read and write the names of all of these colors.*

ACTIVITY:
READ-WRITE CHART

INSTRUCTIONAL PROCEDURE

MAP WORDS

See page 36 for detailed descriptions of Instructional Procedures.

ACTION TAGS

read

glue

color

write

Apply

- Distribute two-column sorts and a set of word cards to each child. *You will now practice reading and writing the names of colors.*

- Have children read the word cards, glue them in a list in the left column, and then color each word card with its corresponding color. Encourage children to refer to the chart paper as needed.

- Then have children write the name of each color in the right column. After they have completed their lists, remind children to check their written words letter by letter.

Share

Have partners exchange papers and read each other's list. Guide children to tell what they noticed about color names. They may observe and compare characteristics such as:

"*Purple* has more letters than *red*."

"*Black* and *blue* both have *b* and *l* at the beginning."

"*Purple* has the same number of letters as *orange*."

"*Red* is the shortest."

Assess

- Have individual children read a set of word cards.

- Have children match color names written on two sets of cards.

- You may wish to use Word Meaning/Vocabulary Assessment A or C.

Word Meaning/Vocabulary: Recognize and Use Concept Words: Color Names

Connect Learning Across Contexts

Interactive Read-Aloud Read aloud books that focus children's attention on colors and color names.

> IRA *What Color Is Nature?* by Stephen R. Swinburne

> IRA *Cat's Colorful Day* by Emma Dodd

Shared Reading See "Red, White, and Blue" in *Words That Sing* (2019). If you don't have these poetry charts, enlarge the print of this poem or other poems such as "Color Song" from *Sing a Song of Poetry*, and have children use highlighter tape to highlight color names. You may also wish to use the following Shared Reading title from *Fountas & Pinnell Classroom*™ to examine more color words.

> SR *A Rainbow of Fruit* by Brooke Matthews

Interactive Writing Innovate using mentor texts such as *Brown Bear, Brown Bear, What Do You See?* by Bill Martin Jr. and Eric Carle. Create a new text–such as "Green Frog, Green Frog, What Do You See?"–that allows children to explore the use of color names in their writing.

Independent Writing When appropriate, encourage children to include color names in their writing. For example, if a child is writing a story about her house, ask what color it is.

Extend Learning

- Have partners sort the word cards into various categories, such as words that begin with the letter *b,* words with four letters, words with five letters, and words with a double letter in the middle. After each sort, have children read the words in the category.

- You may also wish to have children make a stapled word book that features a color name and a corresponding picture on each page. Children may choose to draw pictures, print images that they find online, or cut out photos and illustrations from magazines.

▶ Connect with Home

Give each child a set of word cards to practice reading at home. Invite family members to go on a color hunt around their home, attaching a word card to an object that represents the color.

Recognize and Use Concept Words: Color Names

Plan

▶ Consider Your Children

Decide how many color names and sentences you will use in the lesson. Children should have worked with their own names and other words and also have had some experience reading color names in shared reading and interactive writing. They do not have to know all the letters and sounds to locate color names successfully. If children are inexperienced, create a verse with just one or two sentences and use only two or three colors.

▶ Working with English Language Learners

Be sure that English language learners have had opportunities to explore color concepts in various ways and to use color names in oral language as well as see the words in print. The repetitive sentences in this lesson will help them gain familiarity with English syntax. Provide many opportunities for repetition, substituting different colors.

YOU WILL NEED

PWS Ready Resources
- ▶ WMV 2 Pocket-Chart Cards
- ▶ Blank Sentence Strips
- ▶ Color Word Cards

Online Resources
- ▶ WMV 2 Action Tags

Other Materials
- ▶ pocket chart
- ▶ colored markers or crayons

Generative Lesson ✓

A generative lesson has a simple structure that you can use to present similar content or concepts. You can use this lesson structure to teach children a variety of color words.

UNDERSTAND THE PRINCIPLE

Good word solvers are able to connect words by their meanings. Using meaning to group words into categories creates a useful mental map for early readers and writers. Children can then use these words in writing and recognize them quickly in reading, making connections between these words and others that they want to read or write. Color names are especially helpful in interactive writing, where many early stories feature colors.

EXPLAIN THE PRINCIPLE

A color has a name.

Read and write the names of colors.

Find the names of colors.

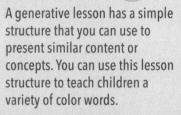

Comprehensive Phonics, Spelling, and Word Study Guide

Refer to: page **44**, row **1**

ACTIVITY:
COLOR-NAME VERSE

INSTRUCTIONAL PROCEDURE

MAP WORDS

See page 36 for detailed descriptions of Instructional Procedures.

EXPLAIN THE PRINCIPLE

A color has a name.

Read and write the names of colors.

Find the names of colors.

Comprehensive Phonics, Spelling, and Word Study Guide

Refer to:
page **44**, row **1**

Teach

1. Tell children that they are going to read and find color names.

2. In the pocket chart, create a verse template using color names. You may want children to choose the object to complete the third line. You may also want to add a small picture or a dot of color at the beginning or end of the verse to support emergent readers.

3. Read the verse with children several times, pointing under each word as you read.

4. Ask a child to come up and point to the word *green*. Guide children to notice characteristics of the word. *What letter does the word* green *begin with?* • *The letter* g *can be uppercase or lowercase. How many letters does the word* green *have?* • *How many times does the word* green *appear in this verse?*

5. *Now let's make a new verse with a new color.* Replace the five pocket-chart cards with others showing the word *red*. Invite children to suggest a red object to complete the third line (for example, strawberries). Write the word on a blank card and insert it into the verse. You may want to quickly draw a corresponding picture next to the word as a clue to support children's understanding.

6. Reread the verse with children several times and then guide them to notice characteristics of the word *red.*

7. Repeat the process, possibly over several days, with the other color names: *yellow, white, orange, blue, purple, brown, black, pink.*

I LIKe purPLe.

ACTIVITY:
COLOR-NAME VERSE

INSTRUCTIONAL PROCEDURE

MAP WORDS

See page 36 for detailed descriptions of Instructional Procedures.

ACTION TAGS

write

draw

read

Apply

Invite children to write their own verse using color names. Children may use the verse in the pocket chart as a model, or they may choose to make up their own verse. As they write, encourage them to recall words that they know by sight, such as *I* and *like,* and to refer to the word wall and pocket chart as needed. Have them draw two or three objects that correspond to the color(s) in their verse.

Share

Have children read their verse to a partner. Guide children to tell what they noticed about color names. They may observe and compare characteristics such as:

Color names can start with uppercase or lowercase letters.

Orange is the same name for the color and the fruit.

White and *blue* have an *e* at the end.

Orange and *green* both have a *g*, but it sounds different.

Assess

■ See how many color names individual children can recognize without clues.

■ You may wish to use Word Meaning/Vocabulary Assessment A or C.

Connect Learning Across Contexts

Interactive Read-Aloud Read aloud books that focus children's attention on colors and color words, such as:

IRA *Red Is a Dragon* by Roseanne Thong

IRA *Dog's Colorful Day* by Emma Dodd

Shared Reading See "Gray Squirrel" in *Words That Sing* (2019). If you don't have these poetry charts, enlarge the print of this poem or other poems such as "Roses Are Red" or "Who Is Wearing Red?" from *Sing a Song of Poetry*, and have children use highlighter tape to highlight color names. You may also wish to use the following Shared Reading title from *Fountas & Pinnell Classroom*™ to read about more color words.

SR *A Rainbow of Fruit* by Brooke Matthews

Shared or Interactive Writing Help children conduct a survey of class members' favorite colors and graph the results. Use interactive writing to write a sentence or two about their conclusions.

Independent Writing Encourage children to use a color name chart or colors on the word wall as a resource in writing.

Extend Learning

Have partners work together to build color names with magnetic letters.

▶ Connect with Home

Encourage family members to have children draw a rainbow with crayons or watercolors and then label each color of the rainbow.

Recognize and Use Concept Words: Number Names

Plan

▶ Consider Your Children

This lesson is best used after children have read poems with number words, such as "One, Two, Buckle My Shoe" in *Sing a Song of Poetry*, and after they are able to count objects. Children should understand what a word is and should have worked with their own names. They should have encountered numerals and the names of numbers in shared reading and interactive writing. If children are inexperienced, start with just three number words. It is a good idea to conduct an informal assessment before this lesson to determine which numerals and number words children already know. Begin the lesson with a number word that most of the children know. This lesson will help children learn that words can be sorted into categories.

▶ Working with English Language Learners

English language learners need to understand the concept of numbers as well as the fact that numbers have names in English. Children may know number concepts and labels in their own languages, or they may still be developing number concepts and just beginning to learn labels in any language. Number concepts take some time to acquire; for example, children must be able to match one by one (count) and must understand the number word as the label for the accumulation of objects. Then the child must be able to match the number concepts and spoken words with written symbols—both the numeral and the word. Explicit, clear explanations and many opportunities to count (matching one by one) and say number labels will help children establish the concept and learn to use the labels with automaticity.

YOU WILL NEED

PWS **Ready Resources**
- ▶ WMV 3 Pocket-Chart Cards
- ▶ Blank Pocket-Chart Cards
- ▶ Blank Sentence Strips

Online Resources
- ▶ WMV 3 Action Tags
- ▶ WMV 3 Four-Box Sheets
- ▶ WMV 3 Word Cards

Other Materials
- ▶ chart paper
- ▶ glue sticks
- ▶ crayons
- ▶ pocket chart

UNDERSTAND THE PRINCIPLE

Good word solvers are able to connect words by their meanings. Using meaning to group words into categories, such as the names of numbers, creates a useful mental map for early readers and writers. Children can then use these words in writing and recognize them quickly in reading. They can make connections between these words and others that they want to read or write.

EXPLAIN THE PRINCIPLE

A number has a name.

Read and write the names of numbers.

Comprehensive Phonics, Spelling, and Word Study Guide

Refer to: page **44**, row **1**

ACTIVITY: NUMBER-WORDS CHART

INSTRUCTIONAL PROCEDURE

MAP WORDS

See page 36 for detailed descriptions of Instructional Procedures.

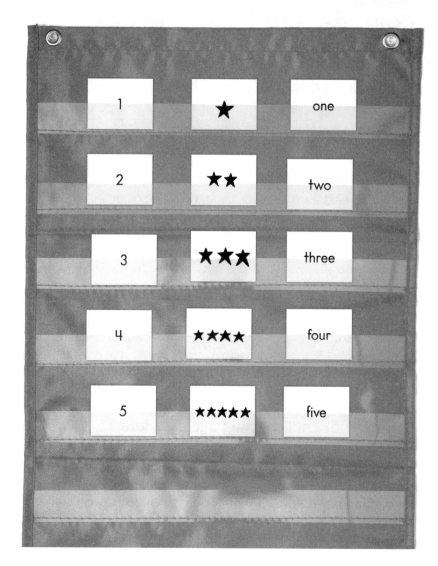

EXPLAIN THE PRINCIPLE

A number has a name.

Read and write the names of numbers.

Comprehensive Phonics, Spelling, and Word Study Guide

Refer to: page **44**, row **1**

Teach

1. Tell children that they're going to learn to read and write the names of numbers.

2. Display pocket-chart cards 1–5 down the left side. You may wish to draw dots or stars on blank sentence strips to emphasize the quantity that each numeral represents. Point to each numeral and ask children to say the name of the number.

3. Hold up the pocket-chart card for *one* as you guide children to read the word. *This is the word* one. *Read it with me.* ● *What letters make the word* one? ● Place the card beside the numeral *1*.

4. *Now I'll write the word: o, n, e. Did I write it correctly? Let's check it letter by letter.* Demonstrate how to check by pointing to each letter in both forms of the word, in order: *o–o, n–n, e–e, one.*

5. Continue reading, writing, and checking each of the remaining number words.

6. Reinforce the principle as you guide children to reread the list of words. *You can read and write the names of the numbers 1–5.*

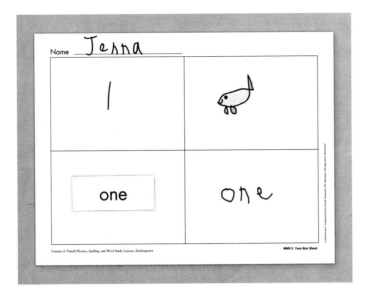

INSTRUCTIONAL PROCEDURE

MAP WORDS

See page 36 for detailed descriptions of Instructional Procedures.

ACTION TAGS

draw

glue

read

write

check

Apply

- Distribute five four-box sheets and a set of word cards to each child. *Today you are going to make your own number words book.* (If making entire books takes too much time, complete the activity over two days. You may want to staple the books in advance.)

- Point to a completed page as you explain how to create the book. *Turn your paper so that the long side is toward you. In the upper-left box, you'll write a number. In the upper-right box, you'll draw a picture that shows how many the number stands for. In the lower-left box, you'll glue the word card that matches the number. In the lower-right box, you'll write the name for the number. You'll make a page for each number, 1–5.* Display the completed page so that children can refer to it as they work.

- As children work, guide them to read each word card and check their written words letter by letter.

- Assist children in stapling their sheets together to assemble a book. You may wish to have them create a cover page.

Share

Invite children to share their number-word books with classmates by reading the words and describing their pictures on each page. As they share, guide children to tell what they noticed about number words. They may observe and compare characteristics such as:

Two and *three* start with the same letter–*t*.

Three has the most letters.

Four and *five* both start with an *f*.

One and *two* each have three letters.

Assess

- Have individual children read a set of the lesson's word cards.

- Have children match number words written on two sets of cards.

- You may wish to use Word Meaning/Vocabulary Assessment B or C.

Connect Learning Across Contexts

Interactive Read-Aloud Read aloud books that contain number words.

IRA *One Moose, Twenty Mice* by Clare Beaton

IRA *1, 2, 3 to the Zoo* by Eric Carle

Shared Reading See "One, Two, Three, Four" or "One Potato, Two Potato" in *Words That Sing* (2019). If you don't have these poetry charts, enlarge the print of one of these poems from *Sing a Song of Poetry*, and have children use highlighter tape to highlight number words. You may also wish to use the following Shared Reading title from *Fountas & Pinnell Classroom*™ to read more about number words.

SR *Counting on the Farm* by Tess Fletcher

Interactive Writing Construct texts similar to "One, Two, Buckle My Shoe" to help children explore number words in their writing. For example, "One, two, look at you; three, four, tap on the floor...."

Independent Writing Encourage children to use the number-words chart as a resource as they write. Guide them to write number words instead of numerals in their stories.

Extend Learning

Repeat the lesson for the numbers 6–10 and have children add to their number-words book.

▶ Connect with Home

Give each child a set of the lesson's word cards to practice reading at home. Suggest that family members go on a number hunt around their home to find a numeral (e.g., on a calendar or as part of a house number) that corresponds to each word card.

Recognize and Use Concept Words: Number Names

Plan

▶ Consider Your Children

Decide how many lines of the verse and how many numbers to include in the lesson. You may choose to use only the first two lines (with the numbers 1 through 5) or all four lines (with the numbers 1 through 10). If you use all four lines, children should have completed the Extend Learning activity in the previous lesson. Children should also understand what words are and should have worked with their own names. They should have encountered number words in shared reading and interactive writing. They do not have to know all of the letters and sounds to locate number words successfully. Prepare for the lesson by reading the verse several days in shared reading. This lesson will help children learn that words can be sorted into categories.

▶ Working with English Language Learners

Reinforce the concept of the numbers 1 through 5 by counting with children on fingers or counting objects. Children may understand the concept but not the English word. Once they understand the concept, show them the numeral and then the word. Spend some time counting and matching. All children may need help understanding that a *hare* is really a rabbit. If this is a difficult concept, substitute other words such as *bird*, *bug*, or *bee*. Act out the poem to support understanding, and provide many repetitions.

YOU WILL NEED

PWS Ready Resources
- ▶ WMV 4 Pocket-Chart Cards (long)
- ▶ Blank Pocket-Chart Cards

Online Resources
- ▶ WMV 4 Action Tags

Other Materials
- ▶ pocket chart
- ▶ pencils
- ▶ colored markers or crayons

UNDERSTAND THE PRINCIPLE

Good word solvers are able to connect words by their meanings. Using meaning to group words into categories, such as the names of numbers, creates a useful mental map for early readers and writers. Children can then use these words in writing and recognize them quickly in reading. They can make connections between these words and others that they want to read or write. Number words are especially helpful in interactive writing and early reading because many texts include number concepts and words.

EXPLAIN THE PRINCIPLE

A number has a name.

Read and write the names of numbers.

Find the names of numbers.

Comprehensive Phonics, Spelling, and Word Study Guide

Refer to: page **44**, row **1**

ACTIVITY:
NUMBER-WORDS VERSE

INSTRUCTIONAL
PROCEDURE

MAP WORDS

See page 36 for detailed
descriptions of Instructional
Procedures.

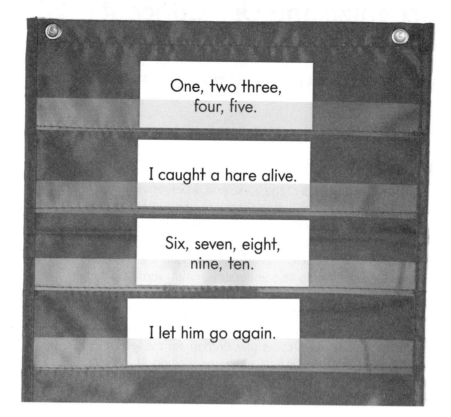

One, two three,
four, five.

I caught a hare alive.

Six, seven, eight,
nine, ten.

I let him go again.

EXPLAIN THE PRINCIPLE

A number has a name.

Read and write the names of
numbers.

Find the names of numbers.

Comprehensive
Phonics, Spelling,
and Word Study
Guide

Refer to:
page **44**, row **1**

Teach

1. Tell children that they are going to read and find number words.

2. In the pocket chart, create a verse template using number words. Read the verse with children several times, pointing under each word as you read. *What do you notice about the last words in the first line and the second line?* • *What about the last words in the third line and the fourth line?* • As needed, point out that each pair of words rhymes.

3. Ask a child to come up and point to the word *one*. Guide children to notice characteristics of the word. *What letter does the word* one *begin with?* • *The letter* o *can be uppercase or lowercase. How many letters does the word* one *have?* • Repeat the process with two or three additional number words.

4. *Now let's make a new verse with these number words.* Have children work together to replace lines 2 and 4 with new lines that end with words that rhyme with *five* and *ten,* for example "Bees are buzzing in the hive" and "Who's that clucking? It's the hen." To help children generate new lines, have them brainstorm words that rhyme with *five,* such as *hive, drive, dive,* and *arrive,* and words that rhyme with *ten,* such as *hen, men, den, when,* and *pen.* Write the new lines on blank pocket-chart cards and insert them into the pocket chart.

5. Read the new verse with children several times and then guide them to notice characteristics of several additional number words.

6. Repeat the process, possibly over several days, until children have discussed all of the number words. As you celebrate children's creative work, reinforce the principle. *You created some amusing verses, and you can read and find the names of the numbers 1–10.*

I have a fish.
One, two, three.
I like her.
She likes me.

**ACTIVITY:
NUMBER-WORDS VERSE**

**INSTRUCTIONAL
PROCEDURE**

MAP WORDS

*See page 36 for detailed
descriptions of Instructional
Procedures.*

ACTION TAGS

write

draw

read

Apply

Invite children to write their own verse using number words. Children may use the verse in the pocket chart as a model, or they may choose to make up their own verse. As they write, encourage them to recall words that they know by sight, referring to the word wall and pocket chart as needed. Encourage them to add drawings to their verse.

Share

Have children read their verse to a partner. Guide children to tell what they noticed about number words. They may observe and compare characteristics such as:

Two, *three*, and *ten* start with *t*.

One, *two*, *six*, and *ten* each have three letters.

Six and *seven* start with the same letter.

Assess

- Notice how many number words individual children can recognize without clues.
- You may wish to use Word Meaning/Vocabulary Assessment B or C.

Connect Learning Across Contexts

Interactive Read-Aloud Read aloud books that focus children's attention on numerals and number words.

IRA *Fish Eyes* by Lois Ehlert

IRA *One Duck Stuck* by Phyllis Root

Shared Reading See "Five Fat Pumpkins" or "Jumping Beans" in *Words That Sing* (2019). If you don't have these poetry charts, enlarge the print of one of these poems from *Sing a Song of Poetry*, and have children use highlighter tape to highlight number words. You may also wish to use the following Shared Reading title from *Fountas & Pinnell Classroom™* to read more about number words.

SR *Ten Big Elephants* by Susan F. Rank

Shared or Interactive Writing Have children conduct surveys that involve numbers (for example, "How many letters are in your name?"). Graph the class results and write about them. The sentences you write with the children will contain many number words.

Independent Writing Encourage children to use the number-words chart as a resource in writing. Remind them to write number words instead of numerals in their stories.

Extend Learning

Have partners work together to build number words with magnetic letters.

▶ Connect with Home

Reproduce the poem "One, Two, Three, Four" from *Sing a Song of Poetry* (or another number poem you have taught the children) and send it home with children. Suggest that family members have their children read the poem and highlight the number words with a colored highlighter.

Recognize and Use Concept Words: Days of the Week

Plan

▶ Consider Your Children

Use this lesson after children have heard you read aloud stories that present the days of the week in context, such as *Cookie's Week* by Cindy Ward or *The Very Hungry Caterpillar* by Eric Carle. Refer to the calendar often during your morning meeting, so that children hear and see the days of the week regularly and notice that they have a consistent, recurring order. If children fully understand these words and concepts, you will not need to spend much time on this lesson.

▶ Working with English Language Learners

Most kindergarten children, whatever their language background, will just be beginning to understand time as measured by the calendar. Using the calendar as a visual aid, help children understand time as it passes by marking the days and helping them pronounce the names of the days of the week. After children have had some experience with the calendar, you can begin to make this knowledge systematic by helping them focus on the seven days of the week.

YOU WILL NEED

 Ready Resources
- ▶ **WMV 5** Pocket-Chart Cards
- ▶ Blank Pocket-Chart Cards

Online Resources
- ▶ **WMV 5** Action Tags
- ▶ **WMV 5** Two-Column Sorts
- ▶ **WMV 5** Word Cards

Other Materials
- ▶ calendar
- ▶ glue sticks

UNDERSTAND THE PRINCIPLE

Good word solvers are able to connect words by their meanings. Using meaning to group words into categories, such as the names of days of the week, creates a useful mental map for early readers and writers. Children can then use these words in writing and recognize them quickly in reading. They can make connections between these words and others that they want to read or write. Texts are sometimes organized around categories of words, such as the days of the week.

EXPLAIN THE PRINCIPLE

A day has a name.

Every week the days happen in the same order.

Read and write the names of days.

 Comprehensive Phonics, Spelling, and Word Study Guide

Refer to:
page **44**, row **1**

ACTIVITY:
READ-WRITE CHART

INSTRUCTIONAL
PROCEDURE

MAP WORDS

See page 36 for detailed
descriptions of Instructional
Procedures.

EXPLAIN THE PRINCIPLE

A day has a name.

Every week the days happen in
the same order.

Read and write the names of
days.

Comprehensive
Phonics, Spelling,
and Word Study
Guide

Refer to:
page **44**, row **1**

Teach

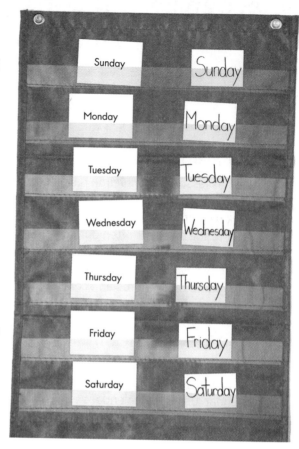

1. Tell children that they're going to learn to read and write the names of days.

2. Point to or hold up a calendar. *A calendar lists the days of the week across the top.* Read the names of the days in order, Sunday through Saturday. *Now let's read them together.* Point to each word as children read it with you.

3. *Days happen in the same order each week. What is the first day of the week?* • *That's right. What day comes after Sunday?* • *Monday always follows Sunday. What day comes after Monday?* • *Tuesday always follows Monday. Then Wednesday, then Thursday, then Friday, and finally Saturday—always in the same order each week.*

4. In a pocket chart, display the days of the week on word cards in random order. *These days of the week are all mixed up. Can you help me put the days in the right order? Which word should come first?* • Have children help you place the word cards in the correct order.

5. Point to the word card for *Sunday. What letters make the word* Sunday? • *I'm going to write the word* Sunday. Write the word on a blank word card, saying each letter as you write. Place your written word next to the word card for *Sunday* in the pocket chart. *Did I write it correctly? Let's check it letter by letter.* Demonstrate how to check by pointing to each letter in both words, in order: *s–s, u–u, n–n, d–d, a–a, y–y,* Sunday.

6. Continue reading, writing, and checking each of the remaining days.

7. Reinforce the principles as you guide children to reread the names of the days. *Days happen in the same order each week. You can name the days in order, and you can read and write the name of each day.*

Apply

- Distribute to each child a two-column sort and a set of word cards for the days of the week in a random order. *You will now practice reading and writing the names of days.*

- Have children read the word cards, put the days of the week in the correct order, and then glue them in a list in the left column. Encourage children to refer to the pocket chart or calendar as needed.

- Then have children write the name of each day in the right column. After they have completed their lists, remind children to check their written words letter by letter.

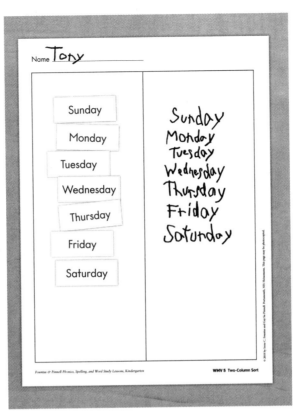

Name Tony

Sunday
Monday
Tuesday
Wednesday
Thursday
Friday
Saturday

Sunday
Monday
Tuesday
Wednesday
Thursday
Friday
Saturday

Fountas & Pinnell Phonics, Spelling, and Word Study Lessons, Kindergarten   **WMV 5 Two-Column Sort**

**ACTIVITY:
READ-WRITE CHART**

INSTRUCTIONAL PROCEDURE

MAP WORDS

See page 36 for detailed descriptions of Instructional Procedures.

ACTION TAGS

read
put
glue
write

Share

Have children tell what they noticed about the names of the days of the week. If they do not spontaneously offer observations, model the process by saying what you are noticing. They may notice features and similarities such as:

Tuesday and *Thursday* both start with *T*.

All the days start with a capital (or uppercase) letter.

They all have *day* at the end.

Saturday and *Sunday* start the same.

Assess

- Have individual children put in order a set of word cards for the days of the week.

- Have individual children read the names of days on a calendar.

Connect Learning Across Contexts

Interactive Read-Aloud Read aloud books that are structured around the days of the week.

IRA *Cookie's Week* by Cindy Ward

IRA *Dear Daisy, Get Well Soon* by Maggie Smith

Shared Reading See "How Many Days?" in *Words That Sing* (2019). If you don't have these poetry charts, enlarge the print of this poem or other poems such as "Tommy Snooks" from *Sing a Song of Poetry*, and have children use highlighter tape to highlight days-of-the-week words.

Interactive Writing Write texts structured around the days of the week. For example, "On Monday, we go to the library." These texts can later be used for shared reading.

Independent Writing When appropriate, encourage children to use the days of the week in their writing. For example, if a child is writing about an event, ask what day of the week the event occurred. Remind children to refer to the calendar as a resource.

Extend Learning

Cut up the word cards into syllables (*Sun-day, Mon-day, Tues-day,* and so on) and have children build and read the words with a partner.

▶ Connect with Home

Encourage family members to use a calendar with their children at home. They can point out and read together the names of the days of the week.

Recognize and Use Concept Words: Days of the Week

Plan

▶ Consider Your Children

Decide how many days and what kinds of sentences to include in the lesson. Children should have worked with the names of the days of the week as well as be familiar with a calendar. Also, children should be familiar with high-frequency words such as *we, like, on,* and *to*. The example in this lesson shows what the chart will look like after you have worked with it for several days. On the first day, write only two or three sentences.

▶ Working with English Language Learners

This lesson requires children to use their knowledge of the words representing days of the week as they read a series of sentences. For English language learners, you may want to use the sentences as a shared reading task and be sure that they understand the key activities (for example, "read books"). Act out any verbs that English language learners may not fully understand and have them repeat the language structure. Have children locate the names of the days of the week around the room and connect them to the calendar.

YOU WILL NEED

 Ready Resources
▶ Blank Pocket-Chart Cards (long)

Online Resources
▶ WMV 6 Action Tags

Other Materials
▶ blank chart paper
▶ markers
▶ pencils
▶ colored markers or crayons

UNDERSTAND THE PRINCIPLE

Proficient word solvers are able to connect words by their meanings. Using meaning to group words into categories, such as the names of days of the week, creates a useful mental map for early readers and writers. Children can then use these words in writing and recognize them quickly in reading. They can make connections between these words and others that they want to read or write. Texts are sometimes organized around categories of words, such as the days of the week. The days of the week are helpful in interactive writing and early reading because many texts include these concepts and words.

EXPLAIN THE PRINCIPLE

A day has a name.

Every week the days happen in the same order.

Read and write the names of days.

Find the names of days.

 Comprehensive Phonics, Spelling, and Word Study Guide

Refer to: page **44**, row **1**

ACTIVITY: SHARED WRITING

INSTRUCTIONAL PROCEDURE

MAP WORDS

See page 36 for detailed descriptions of Instructional Procedures.

EXPLAIN THE PRINCIPLE

A day has a name.

Every week the days happen in the same order.

Read and write the names of days.

Find the names of days.

Comprehensive Phonics, Spelling, and Word Study Guide

Refer to: page **44**, row **1**

Teach

1. Tell children that together you are going to write sentences using the names of the days of the week and that they will then find and read those words.

2. *Let's write about things we like to do each day at school. We'll post this list in our classroom so that visitors can learn what we like to do as a class.* Have children brainstorm favorite activities that they do throughout the week. Then, through shared writing, guide children to compose sentences as you write. For example, "We like to read books on Monday. On Tuesday, we like to write stories." You may wish to point out that you can vary the sentence structure to make your writing more interesting. *I put the name of the day near the beginning of this sentence. Beginning sentences in different ways makes our writing more interesting to read.*

3. Reread the sentences with children.

4. Guide children to find and read each day of the week. *What is the first day of our school week?* • Ask a child to come up and point to the word *Monday*. Guide children to notice characteristics of the word. *What letter does the word* Monday *begin with?* • *How many letters does the word* Monday *have?* • *When I cover the first part of the word, what smaller word is left?* • Repeat the process with the additional days of the school week.

5. Post the list in your classroom as you reinforce the principle. *You can find and read the names of the days of the week.*

On Thursday,
I like to paint.

ACTIVITY: DAYS-OF-THE-WEEK SENTENCES

INSTRUCTIONAL PROCEDURE

MAP WORDS

See page 36 for detailed descriptions of Instructional Procedures.

ACTION TAGS

| write |
| draw |
| read |

Apply

Invite children to write their own sentences about what they like to do each day at school. Children may use the list that the class created as a model. As they write, encourage them to recall words that they know by sight, referring to the word wall, calendar, and the list of sentences as needed. Encourage them to add drawings to illustrate their sentences.

Share

Have children read their sentence(s) to a partner.

Assess

Use word cards to check how many days of the week each child can recognize.

Word Meaning/Vocabulary: Recognize and Use Concept Words: Days of the Week

Connect Learning Across Contexts

Interactive Read-Aloud Read aloud books that are structured around the days of the week.

 *One Monday Morning* by Uri Shulevitz

 *Today Is Monday* by Eric Carle

Shared Reading See "How Many Days?" in *Words That Sing* (2019). If you don't have these poetry charts, enlarge the print of this poem or other poems such as "Today" from *Sing a Song of Poetry*, and have children use highlighter tape to highlight days-of-the-week words.

Interactive Writing Have children choose a favorite day and graph the class results. Then construct some simple sentences about the results, such as "Many children like Friday because our class goes to art."

Independent Writing: Encourage children to use the calendar or the list of sentences that the class created as a resource when writing days of the week.

Extend Learning

Have partners work together to build the names of days with magnetic letters.

▶ Connect with Home

Reproduce the poem "How Many Days?" from *Sing a Song of Poetry* and send it home with children. Suggest that family members have their children read the poem and highlight the days of the week with a colored highlighter.

Recognize Related Words

Plan

▶ **Consider Your Children**

This lesson is intended to help children focus directly on related words and should be used after reading aloud stories that include examples from the category, so that the children can experience the words in multiple contexts. As you use this lesson and repeat it, continue to read stories with related words. The lesson deals with very simple relationships, but you can expand it to increase children's knowledge of word meanings. You can use this lesson early in kindergarten and repeat it with different sets of words as often as necessary throughout the year.

▶ **Working with English Language Learners**

Knowing the meaning of words in English is an important factor in English language learners' literacy. Unless they have an understanding of the words they encounter in reading, decoding will be meaningless. Repeating this lesson with various categories will help English language learners become aware of related words, building mental maps that make learning vocabulary more effective and efficient. You will want to have pictures representing the words you are using and also to be sure that children say the words themselves. Having children use the same language structures repeatedly will help them develop word meaning and natural usage. For example, "Marisa has one sister. Raquel has one brother and two sisters." Encourage English language learners to share different names they may have for family members, adding interest to the lesson for all children.

UNDERSTAND THE PRINCIPLE

Words that are in children's spoken vocabulary are easier for them to decode. Knowing the meanings of words in oral language helps children comprehend the texts that they read. The texts children read should consist mostly of words that they already know, which is why it is important that children continuously expand their speaking vocabularies.

Children benefit from knowing not only individual word meanings but also the important relationships among words. When children form categories that connect words, they are able to increase their speaking and listening vocabulary more readily and are more aware of subtle shades of meaning that are often necessary for deep comprehension.

YOU WILL NEED

 Ready Resources
  ▶ **WMV 7** Pocket-Chart Picture Cards
  ▶ **WMV 7** Pocket-Chart Word Cards

Online Resources
  ▶ **WMV 7** Action Tags

Other Materials
  ▶ pocket chart
  ▶ pencils
  ▶ colored markers or crayons

Generative Lesson

A generative lesson has a simple structure that you can use to present similar content or concepts. You can use this lesson structure to teach children to connect a variety of words by meaning.

EXPLAIN THE PRINCIPLE

Some words go together because they are the same in some way.

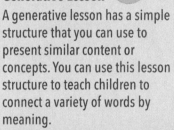 Comprehensive Phonics, Spelling, and Word Study Guide

Refer to: page **45**, row **3**

ACTIVITY: FAMILY WORDS

INSTRUCTIONAL PROCEDURE

MAP WORDS

See page 36 for detailed descriptions of Instructional Procedures.

EXPLAIN THE PRINCIPLE

Some words go together because they are the same in some way.

Comprehensive Phonics, Spelling, and Word Study Guide

Refer to: page **45**, row **3**

Teach

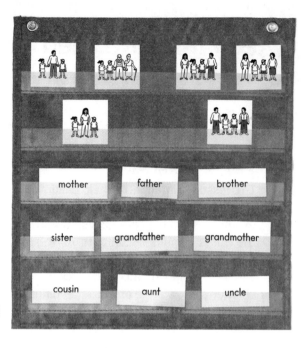

1. Explain to the children that today they will be learning about words that go together because they are alike in some way.

2. Place pictures of families in the pocket chart. Be sure to show diversity among families—for example, a grandmother and children; a father, mother, and several children; a mother, grandmother, and child; a father and child; or several generations of a family. You may wish to include a picture of your own family.

3. *What do you notice about these pictures?* • *They are families. What do you notice about the words?* • *We have special names for people in our families. What do you call the people in your families?* Allow children time to talk generally about the people in their families. Point out that families are different because people are different, but there are certain words that we can all use to tell about specific people in our families.

4. *One important family word is* mother. Add the word card for *mother* to the pocket chart. *Who can point to someone in a picture who looks like the* mother? • *Do you know some other words for* mother? • Encourage children to talk about what they call their mothers, such as *mommy, mama, mom,* or words in a language other than English.

5. *A word that often goes with* mother *is the word* father. Add the word card for *father* to the pocket chart and repeat the process.

6. Continue the process for *sister/brother* and *grandmother/grandfather.* Children may also offer other family words, such as *cousins* or *aunt/uncle.*

7. Encourage children to talk about family members who are not actually related to them but are considered family or function as caregivers and have special names. Explain that special people can be part of a family even if they are not related to you.

8. Read the family words in the pocket chart with children as you reinforce the principle. *These words go together because they are alike in some way. Each of these words refers to a member of a family. We can also think of other words that go together because of what they mean.*

ACTIVITY: FAMILY PICTURES

INSTRUCTIONAL PROCEDURE

MAP WORDS

See page 36 for detailed descriptions of Instructional Procedures.

ACTION TAGS

draw

write

Apply

Have children draw a picture of their families, or a selected member of their family, and label the picture with words. Expect approximated spelling.

Share

Have children share their family pictures and locate family words on the chart.

Assess

- Observe children's use of family words in their oral language.
- Perform a quick oral assessment by asking children to generate additional connected words when you say a few family words, such as *mother, sister, grandmother,* and so on.
- Notice whether children can accurately identify categories of words while reading simple texts.

Connect Learning Across Contexts

Interactive Read-Aloud Read aloud books such as the following that feature family themes. As you read, point out words such as *parents* that can be added to the "family" category.

> IRA *Do Like Kyla* by Angela Johnson

> IRA *Jonathan and His Mommy* by Irene Smalls

Shared Reading See "Five Little Ducks Went in for a Swim" in *Words That Sing* (2019). If you don't have these poetry charts, enlarge the print of this poem or other poems such as "Five Little Monkeys on the Bed" or "My Little Sister" from *Sing a Song of Poetry*, and have children use highlighter tape to highlight family words. You may also wish to use the following Shared Reading title from *Fountas & Pinnell Classroom*™ to read more about family words.

> SR *Coco Steps Out* by Lionel Page

Interactive Writing Have children write sentences about their families—for example, "Javon has two brothers." You may wish to draw children's attention to singular and plural forms of words.

Independent Writing Have children make a family book, which can also include pictures and labels of friends and caregivers.

Extend Learning

Repeat the lesson with other categories of words.

> clothing: *hat, shirt, skirt, shoes, socks, T-shirt, jacket, coat, gloves, mittens, belt, dress, sweatshirt*

> weather: *hot, warm, cold, windy, sunny, rainy, snowy; snow, rain, sleet, drizzle, wind*

> animals: *cow, horse, cat, dog, sheep, elephant, gerbil, turtle, monkey.* You may wish to form subcategories for pets, farm animals, and animals at the zoo.

> food: *breakfast, lunch, supper or dinner; juice, cereal, apples, oranges, peanut butter, chicken, steak, hamburger.* You may wish to form subcategories for breakfast foods, lunch foods, and dinner foods. Emphasize that people often have different preferences. For example, some people might eat fish and rice for breakfast, whereas others eat pancakes or cereal.

Place charts of related words together in one part of the room so that children can use the categories and groups of words for reference during interactive and independent writing. Add to the charts as children encounter new words related to the categories.

▶ Connect with Home

Have children share their pictures with family members. Encourage families to take the opportunity to talk about extended family members with whom children may be unacquainted, as well as special names that older family members used for grandparents and other relatives.

Word Structure

Looking at the structure of words will help children learn how words are related to each other and how words can be changed by adding letters. Being able to recognize syllables, for example, helps children break down words into smaller units that are easier to analyze. Kindergarten children can be expected to recognize syllables by clapping them, and that is a prelude to breaking down words later.

Endings that are added to words signal meaning. Principles related to word structure include understanding the meaning and structure of contractions and plurals as well as knowing how to make and use them accurately. In shared and interactive writing, children will begin to recognize the *-ing* and *-s* endings and to understand to take notice of word endings.

Connect to Assessment

See related (optional) WS Assessment tasks in Online Resources.

- Assessment A: Repeating Sentences with Singular and Plural Nouns

- Assessment B: Selecting Sentences with Plural Nouns

- Assessment C: Individual Record (Sentence Repetition A)

- Assessment D: Class Record (Sentence Repetition A)

- Assessment E: Individual Record (Sentence Repetition B)

- Assessment F: Class Record (Sentence Repetition B)

Develop Your Professional Understanding

See *The Fountas & Pinnell Comprehensive Phonics, Spelling, and Word Study Guide*. 2017. Related pages: 2–12, 51–73.

See *The Fountas & Pinnell Literacy Continuum: A Tool for Assessment, Planning, and Teaching*. 2017. Portsmouth, New Hampshire: Heinemann. Related pages: 357–397.

See *Word Matters: Teaching Phonics and Spelling in the Reading/Writing Classroom* by G. S. Pinnell and I. C. Fountas. 1998. Portsmouth, New Hampshire: Heinemann. Related pages: 97–98.

with
that
they
see

EMILY

Hear, Say, and Identify Syllables

Plan

▶ Consider Your Children

This lesson will be effective for children who have had experience saying words slowly to identify word parts and are familiar with clapping syllables.

▶ Working with English Language Learners

It will be very important to use words that English language learners can pronounce and to say each syllable so that they can hear and clap it. Begin with simple words they know and remind them of how to listen for and clap the parts. You may need to perform this task individually a few times with children who have difficulty coordinating the action with words that they are just beginning to learn in English. Work with a small group to help them understand the sorting task and be sure to include only pictures that they can say and understand.

YOU WILL NEED

PWS Ready Resources
- ▶ WS 1 Pocket-Chart Cards

Online Resources
- ▶ WS 1 Action Tags
- ▶ WS 1 Two-Way Sorts
- ▶ WS 1 Two-Column Sorts
- ▶ WS 1 Picture Cards

Other Materials
- ▶ magnetic letters
- ▶ pocket chart
- ▶ glue sticks

Generative Lesson
A generative lesson has a simple structure that you can use to present similar content or concepts. You can use this lesson structure to teach children to hear, say, and notice the number of syllables in a variety of words.

UNDERSTAND THE PRINCIPLE

Recognizing how many syllables a word has is an effective way for readers and writers to break down words into smaller units that are easier to analyze.

EXPLAIN THE PRINCIPLE

Listen for the syllables in words.

Some words have one syllable.

Some words have more than one syllable.

Look at the syllables in a word to read it. Say and clap the syllables to notice them in a word.

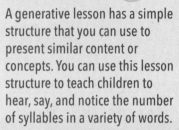 Comprehensive Phonics, Spelling, and Word Study Guide

 Refer to: page **52**, row **2**

ACTIVITY: TWO-WAY SYLLABLE SORT

INSTRUCTIONAL PROCEDURE

SAY AND SORT

See page 36 for detailed descriptions of Instructional Procedures.

EXPLAIN THE PRINCIPLE

Listen for the syllables in words.

Some words have one syllable.

Some words have more than one syllable.

Look at the syllables in a word to read it. Say and clap the syllables to notice them in a word.

Comprehensive Phonics, Spelling, and Word Study Guide

Refer to: page **52**, row **2**

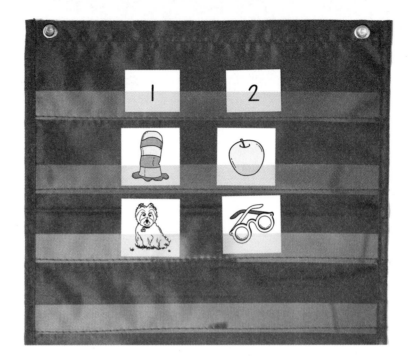

Teach

1. Using magnetic letters, make and display three or four one-syllable words, one word at a time. (e.g., *hat*).

2. Point to the first word you've made on the board. *What word is this?* • *The word is* cat. *How many parts do you hear in* cat? • *There's one part in* cat. *Now, say the word again and clap the part you hear.* • *Let's look at another word.* Have the children clap the part in a few other one-syllable words.

3. Make the word *airplane* on the board. *What word is this?* • *The word is* airplane. *How many parts do you hear in* airplane? • *There are two parts in* airplane. *Now, say the word again and clap the parts you hear.* • *Let's look at another word.* Have the children clap the parts in a few other two-syllable words.

4. *You can hear the parts in words.* Point to each column of words as you ask children the question. *What do you notice about the words in this column, and what do you notice about the words in this column?* • *Some words have one part. Some words have more than one part.* Explain that these parts in a word are called *syllables*.

5. Place the cards with the numerals *1* and *2* at the top of a pocket chart. *We are going to look at some more words.* Show a picture of a hat. *What word is this?* • *How many parts do you hear in* hat? • *There is one part in* hat. *Now, say the word again and clap the part you hear.* • Invite one of the children to place the *hat* under the numeral *1* in the pocket chart.

6. *Let's look at another word.* Continue holding up picture cards, each time asking the children how many parts are in the word. The children should place each picture under 1 or 2, according to the number of syllables they hear in the word.

7. Explain to the children that they will see a 1 and a 2 at the top of the columns of a two-way sort. Then they will take a picture, say the word it represents, and clap the part or parts of the word. Then they will glue the picture in the column under the appropriate number.

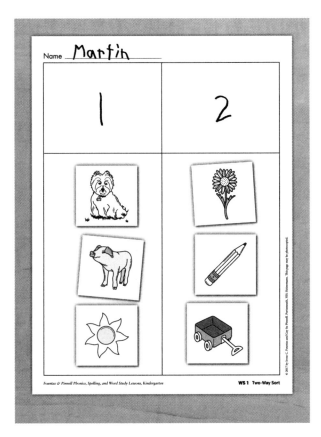

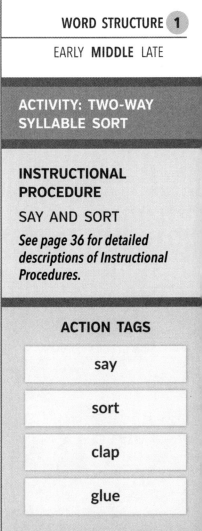

**INSTRUCTIONAL
PROCEDURE**

SAY AND SORT

*See page 36 for detailed
descriptions of Instructional
Procedures.*

ACTION TAGS

say
sort
clap
glue

Apply

Have the children complete the two-way sort, using an additional two-column
sort as needed.

Share

Have each child choose one word and clap the syllable or syllables.

Assess

- Look at children's sort sheets to determine the extent to which children
  understood the task and were able to place pictures in the appropriate
  categories.

- Have a small group of children take turns clapping syllables of new words.
  Observe and note their behavior.

Word Structure: Hear, Say, and Identify Syllables

Interactive Read-Aloud Enjoy various books, stopping to clap a few of the one- and two-syllable words.

IRA *Wemberly Worried* by Kevin Henkes

IRA *Stone Soup* by Marcia Brown

Shared Reading See "What's the Weather?" or "Charlie over the Ocean" in *Words That Sing* (2019). If you don't have these poetry charts, enlarge the print of these poems from *Sing a Song of Poetry*, and have children find and clap three or four words with one-syllable or two-syllables. You may also wish to use the following Shared Reading title from *Fountas & Pinnell Classroom*™ to clap syllables.

SR *Up in the Cloud Forest* by Tess Fletcher

Interactive Writing Before writing a two-syllable word, have children clap the parts so that they can hear them more clearly.

Independent Writing Encourage children to listen for syllables in words as they try to write them.

Extend Learning

Repeat the lesson with additional pictures of one- and two-syllable words. You may also wish to customize picture cards using Gamemaker in Online Resources.

▶ **Connect with Home**

Suggest to family members that they play the clapping syllables game in the market or on a walk. The child picks out words and the family member says and claps the syllables. Then they reverse roles.

Understand the Concept of a Contraction

Plan

▶ Consider Your Children

Use this lesson after children have encountered contractions in reading and interactive writing. Children may already know how to read the words *isn't, can't,* and *don't,* but in this lesson you will be using them to explain the concept. If your children are familiar with the idea of contractions in general, you may want to include several more in this lesson.

▶ Working with English Language Learners

For some English language learners, contractions may be a new word structure. If you know parallels in their first language, use them in your explanation. If not, use plenty of simple sentences to help them understand the way in which contractions work. For example, *he is not sad; he isn't sad.*

UNDERSTAND THE PRINCIPLE

Children use contractions in their oral language and often attempt to use them in their writing. They also encounter common contractions in many early texts. Understanding the concept of contractions and how they are formed will help children understand their meanings and promote correct and conventional use in writing.

YOU WILL NEED

 Ready Resources
  - ▶ Lowercase Letter Cards

Online Resources
  - ▶ WS 2 Action Tags

Other Materials
  - ▶ magnetic letters
  - ▶ magnetic surface

Generative Lesson
A generative lesson has a simple structure that you can use to present similar content or concepts. You can use this lesson structure to help children understand contractions.

EXPLAIN THE PRINCIPLE

A contraction is one or more words put together. A letter or letters are left out, and an apostrophe takes the place of the missing letter or letters.

 Comprehensive Phonics, Spelling, and Word Study Guide

Refer to: page **54**, row **19**

ACTIVITY: MAGNETIC LETTERS

INSTRUCTIONAL PROCEDURE

MAKE WORDS

See page 36 for detailed descriptions of Instructional Procedures.

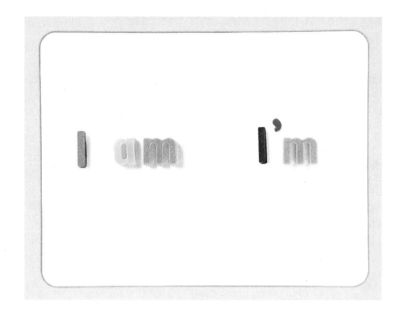

EXPLAIN THE PRINCIPLE

A contraction is a one or more words put together. A letter or letters are left out, and an apostrophe takes the place of the missing letter or letters.

Comprehensive Phonics, Spelling, and Word Study Guide

Refer to: page **54**, row **19**

Teach

1. Using magnetic letters, build the words *is* and *not* on a magnetic surface. *What are these words?* • *The words are* is *and* not. *In talking and writing, the words* is *and* not *are sometimes put together to make one word,* isn't.

2. With the magnetic letters, create the contraction *isn't. What do you notice about this new word?* • *The word* isn't *is made up of the two words* is *and* not. *Do you notice anything else?* • *The word is missing the letter* o. *There is an apostrophe to take the place of the missing letter* o. *Read the new word with me.* • *When you put words together this way using an apostrophe for missing letters, the word you make is called a* contraction. *Say* contraction.

3. Demonstrate taking apart the contraction and forming the words *is* and *not,* and make the contraction again. *Does the meaning change when we use the word* isn't *instead of* is not? • *How do you know that?* • *The meaning of the two words stays the same when you make a contraction, whether you are talking or writing. For example, I can say "she is not home," or I can say "she isn't home." The meaning is the same.*

4. Repeat the procedure to build the contraction *can't* and ask the children what they notice about the new word. Once children understand the contraction *can't,* repeat the same steps with the word *don't.*

5. *A contraction is one or more words put together. When a letter is taken out, an apostrophe takes the place of the missing letter or letters.* Add the words *isn't, can't,* and *don't* to the word wall, if they aren't already there, and read them again with children.

INSTRUCTIONAL PROCEDURE

MAKE WORDS

See page 36 for detailed descriptions of Instructional Procedures.

ACTION TAGS

make
read

Apply

Distribute lowercase letter cards to partners. Have children take turns making and reading the words *is not*, *cannot*, and *do not* and then forming contractions for each.

Share

Have partners share how they built a contraction by talking through each step.

Assess

- Select one or two contractions and have children write them.
- Notice whether children can locate a contraction in a text and state the two words that form the contraction.

Connect Learning Across Contexts

Interactive Read-Aloud Briefly draw children's attention to contractions when you encounter them in books.

IRA *It's Raining, It's Pouring* by Kin Eagle

IRA *Don't You Feel Well, Sam?* by Amy Hest

Shared Reading See "I'm a Little Acorn Brown" or "There Was an Old Woman Who Lived in a Shoe" in *Words That Sing* (2019). If you don't have these poetry charts, enlarge the print of these poems or others such as "Color Song" or "Fuzzy Wuzzy" from *Sing a Song of Poetry*, and have children use highlighter tape to point out contractions. You may also wish to use the following Shared Reading title from *Fountas & Pinnell Classroom*™ to give children the opportunity to notice and read contractions.

SR *Coming Around the Mountain* by Norma Morris

Interactive Writing When composing a text together, ask children to decide which sounds better–a contraction or the full words–in a sentence or story. (For example, a contraction might sound good in dialogue.) Guide children to form a contraction with an apostrophe, when appropriate.

Independent Writing As you begin to introduce new contractions to children, encourage them to use the contractions in their writing, where appropriate. Point out when a sentence sounds more natural because a child has chosen to use a contraction.

Extend Learning

Once children understand the concept of contractions, begin to point out new contractions during shared reading.

▶ Connect with Home

Send home copies of rhymes that contain contractions for children to read with family members. Encourage families to look for contractions in print around their home.

Understand the Concept of Plural

Plan

▶ Consider Your Children

This lesson is best used after children can count and group objects. You will be introducing or reinforcing the concept of more than one, specifically noting and finding words that represent the concept. This lesson lays the foundation for future lessons that describe how the structures of words are changed to indicate a plural form. Most speakers of English will have an internalized sense of how to form and use plurals in oral language. Build on children's sense of what "sounds right" as you draw their attention to plurals in print.

▶ Working with English Language Learners

English language learners may have difficulty understanding the word structures for plurals and will need many experiences talking about concrete objects—for example: "I see one pencil. I see two pencils." Provide many opportunities for them to use singular and plural forms to talk about pictures and to talk about the stories that you read aloud to them.

YOU WILL NEED

PWS Ready Resources
▸ WS 3 Pocket-Chart Word Cards
▸ WS 3 Pocket-Chart Picture Cards

Online Resources
▸ WS 3 Action Tags
▸ WS 3 Poem: Here Are My Ears

Other Materials
▸ chart paper
▸ highlighter pens

UNDERSTAND THE PRINCIPLE

By giving attention to plurals, children become aware that word structures change to represent more than one. While the concept of more than one will be completely familiar to children, the understanding that words are altered in oral language and in writing to represent this concept is likely to be new.

EXPLAIN THE PRINCIPLE

Plural means "more than one."

Comprehensive Phonics, Spelling, and Word Study Guide

Refer to:
page **56**, row **27**

ACTIVITY: "HERE ARE MY EARS"

INSTRUCTIONAL PROCEDURE

SAY AND SORT

See page 36 for detailed descriptions of Instructional Procedures.

EXPLAIN THE PRINCIPLE

Plural means "more than one."

Comprehensive Phonics, Spelling, and Word Study Guide

Refer to: page **56**, row **27**

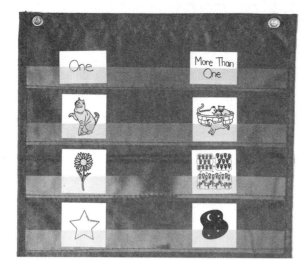

Here Are My Ears

Here are my ears.
Here is my nose.
Here are my fingers.
Here are my toes.

Here are my eyes
Both open wide.
Here is my mouth
With white teeth inside.

Here is my tongue
That helps me speak.
Here is my chin
And here are my cheeks.

Here are my hands
That help me play.
Here are my feet
For walking today.

Teach

1. Place the word cards *One* and *More Than One* into the top of the pocket chart.

2. Hold up the picture card for *cat. What do you notice about this picture? • Is there one or more than one? • There's one.* Place the picture card into the first column underneath *One.* Hold up the picture card for *cats. Is there one or more than one? • How many cats are in this picture? • Three cats.* Place the picture card into the second column, underneath *More Than One.*

3. Continue to ask the children if there is *one* or *more than one* with *flower/flowers* and *star/stars.*

4. Point to the first column. *What do you notice about the pictures in the first column? • There's just one of each thing. Now, what do you notice about the pictures in the second column? • There's more than one of each thing.*

5. *When a word stands for more than one, it is plural. The words* cats, flowers, *and* stars *are plural because they stand for more than one cat, more than one flower, and more than one star. What do you notice about how these words end? • You hear the /s/ sound.*

6. Display the poem "Here Are My Ears" and read the title. If you don't have these charts, enlarge the poem from *Sing a Song of Poetry. This poem tells about parts of our body, such as our ears. Do you have one ear, or more than one ear? • How many ears do we have? •* Enjoy reading the poem along with children.

7. *Let's read the poem again, and this time notice which parts of our body are just one and which parts of our body are more than one.* After reading, guide children in a discussion of how many of each body part we have, for example, two ears, one nose, etc. Ask what they notice as they look at *ears, fingers, toes,* and *eyes. They are plural, so they have an* s. Point out the plurals in the poem to reinforce the principle. *The words* ears, fingers, toes, eyes, teeth, cheeks, hands, *and* feet *are plural because they tell about more than one.*

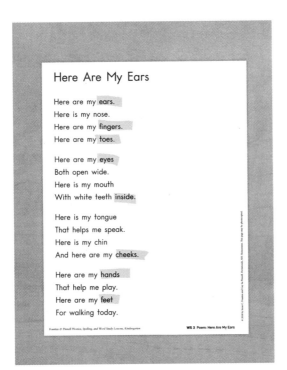

Here Are My Ears

Here are my ears.
Here is my nose.
Here are my fingers.
Here are my toes.

Here are my eyes
Both open wide.
Here is my mouth
With white teeth inside.

Here is my tongue
That helps me speak.
Here is my chin
And here are my cheeks.

Here are my hands
That help me play.
Here are my feet
For walking today.

Fountas & Pinnell Phonics, Spelling, and Word Study Lessons, Kindergarten

WS 3 Poem: Here Are My Ears

**ACTIVITY: "HERE
ARE MY EARS"**

**INSTRUCTIONAL
PROCEDURE**

SAY AND SORT

*See page 36 for detailed
descriptions of Instructional
Procedures.*

ACTION TAGS

read
find
mark

Apply

Distribute copies of the poem "Here Are My Ears" and highlighter pens to partners.
Ask children to reread the poem together, find the words that tell about more than
one, and mark them with their highlighter pens.

Share

Ask children to read the plurals that they highlighted. Children may observe that
most of the plurals have the letter -s at the end. Affirm their observation and
explain that they will soon learn more about how words change to stand for more
than one of something.

Assess

- Notice whether children use plurals accurately in their oral language.
- Notice whether children find all of the plurals in the poem and any observations
  they make about the structure of the words.
- You may wish to use Word Structure Assessment A, B, C, D, E, or F.

Word Structure: Understand the Concept of Plural

Connect Learning Across Contexts

Interactive Read-Aloud While reading aloud, briefly draw children's attention to plurals. The concept of more than one is central to the plot of the following stories.

> IRA *The Three Bears* by Paul Galdone

> IRA *Three Hens and a Peacock* by Lester Laminack

Shared Reading See "Five Fingers on Each Hand" or "Puppies and Kittens" in *Words That Sing* (2019). If you don't have these poetry charts, enlarge the print of these poems or others from *Sing a Song of Poetry*, and have children use highlighter tape to point out plural words. You may also wish to use the following Shared Reading title from *Fountas & Pinnell Classroom*™ to read and locate plurals.

> SR *The Log* by Joseph Petronaci

Interactive Writing As you construct a text together, draw children's attention to words that are plural. Have children say the word to hear the last sound.

Independent Writing While conferring with children, point out plurals that they have included in their writing.

Extend Learning

Distribute copies of additional texts that you have read together in shared reading, and have children find and name the plurals.

▶ **Connect with Home**

Encourage family members to use objects around their home to discuss the concept of plurals, for example, one banana, five bananas.

Recognize and Use Plurals That Add -s

Plan

▶ Consider Your Children

This lesson is best used after children can count and group objects and know the concept of plural. They should also be able to identify sounds at the end of words. Use nouns that children know.

▶ Working with English Language Learners

English language learners may have difficulty understanding English word structure for plurals and will need many experiences talking about concrete objects: for example, *I see one pencil. I see two pencils.* In many languages and dialects, plurality is not signaled by change in the word, so this idea may be new. They can also use singular forms and plural forms to talk about pictures and to talk about the stories that you read aloud to them. Be sure to articulate clearly, slightly emphasizing the final sound on plural nouns. Drawing attention to the s at the end of the plural will help children realize that the sound is added.

YOU WILL NEED

Online Resources
- ▶ WS 4 Action Tags
- ▶ WS 4 Game Cards
- ▶ WS 4 Directions for Concentration

Other Materials
- ▶ chart paper or magnetic letters

UNDERSTAND THE PRINCIPLE

Children need to attend to word endings that indicate more than one of something, or a plural. The /s/ or /z/ sound at the end of a word often indicates that someone is talking about more than one.

EXPLAIN THE PRINCIPLE

Add -s to some words to make them plural.

You can hear the s at the end of the word.

Comprehensive Phonics, Spelling, and Word Study Guide

Refer to: page **56**, row **28**

INSTRUCTIONAL PROCEDURE

NOTICE PARTS

See page 36 for detailed descriptions of Instructional Procedures.

EXPLAIN THE PRINCIPLE

Add -s to some words to make them plural.

You can hear the s at the end of the word.

Comprehensive Phonics, Spelling, and Word Study Guide

Refer to: page **56**, row **28**

Add -s to some
words to make them plural.

dog	dogs
ca	cats
boy	boys
girl	girls
ball	balls
tree	trees
mom	moms
dad	dads
sister	sisters
brother	brothers

Teach

1. Tell the children you are going to show them something new about words.

2. Begin by having children generate plural forms of simple nouns orally. *I'll say the word for one thing, and you say the word for more than one.* Demonstrate by saying *one cat* and then *two cats*. Ask children what sound they can hear at the end of *cats*. Follow with words such as *tree, can, boy,* and *girl*.

3. After the children generate plurals by adding -s, write some simple words on the left side of a chart, or make them with magnetic letters. Invite children to write each word and to add an s on the right side of the word. If you are using magnetic letters, you can have a child add -s and read the new plural form.

4. Ask the children what they have noticed about the words. Be sure to help them understand that you add -s when there are two or more things. You may demonstrate. Comments like these indicate that children are analyzing words and thinking about the principle:

   "You add -s."

   "Some sound like *z* and some sound like *s* at the end."

   "*Boy* is one boy and *boys* is two boys."

5. With the children, formulate the principle "Add -s to some words to make them plural. The s at the end of the word can be heard." Reinforce that the s at the end of the word will make a /s/ or a /z/ sound, depending on which word it is added to.

6. With two children, demonstrate how to play the card game Concentration. The goal is to match a singular noun with its plural form. The player who makes the most pairs wins the game.

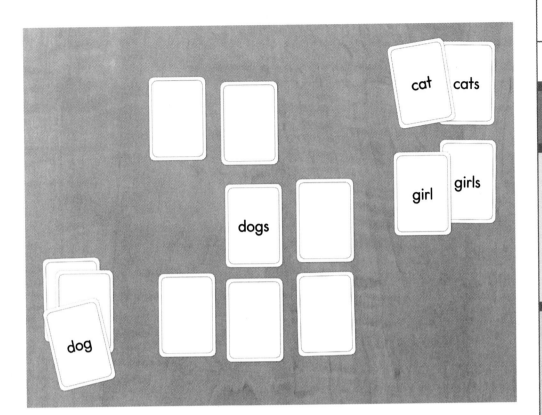

**INSTRUCTIONAL
PROCEDURE**

FIND AND MATCH

*See page 36 for detailed
descriptions of Instructional
Procedures.*

ACTION TAGS

turn

read

match

Apply

Have children play Concentration with the words from the lesson. You may also
wish to customize game cards using Gamemaker in Online Resources.

Share

Ask the children to show one plural word. Place one or two examples on the word
wall.

Assess

■ Notice whether the children are using conventional spelling for simple plurals in
their writing.

■ You may wish to use Word Structure Assessment A, B, C, D, E, or F.

Connect Learning Across Contexts

Interactive Read-Aloud While reading a story, point out an interesting new plural word for children that illustrates the principle of this lesson.

IRA *Flower Garden* by Eve Bunting

IRA *A Fruit Is a Suitcase for Seeds* by Jean Richards

Shared Reading See "All by Myself" in *Words That Sing* (2019). If you don't have these poetry charts, enlarge the print of this poem or others such as "Hot Cross Buns" or "Here Are My Ears" from *Sing a Song of Poetry*, and have children use highlighter tape to find plural nouns that are made by adding -s. You may also wish to use the following Shared Reading title from *Fountas & Pinnell Classroom*™ to read and locate words in the plural form.

SR *The Log* by Joseph Petronaci

Interactive Writing Call attention to the principle. Invite the children who are having difficulty to come up to the easel and write the plural ending for a simple noun.

Independent Writing Draw attention to the principle while conferring with children.

Extend Learning

When children are familiar with all the simple plurals you have used, remove the singular forms from the matching. Then have them sort the plurals by the ending sound (/s/or /z/). This extension will help children understand that the *s* at the end can have either sound.

▶ Connect with Home

Send home copies of word cards with the singular form and the plural form of simple nouns so that children can cut them apart and match them.

Word-Solving Actions

Word-solving actions are the strategic moves readers and writers make when they use their knowledge of the language system to solve words. These strategies are "in-the-head" actions that are invisible, although we can infer them from some overt or observable behavior. The principles listed in this area represent children's ability to use the principles in all previous areas of *The Fountas & Pinnell Comprehensive Phonics, Spelling, and Word Study Guide*.

Classroom lessons developed around these principles should provide opportunities for children to apply concepts in active ways—for example, through sorting, building, locating, reading, or writing. Lessons related to word-solving actions demonstrate to children how they can problem-solve by working on words in isolation or while reading or writing continuous text. The more children can integrate these strategies into their reading and writing systems, the more flexible they will become in solving words.

Connect to Assessment

See related (optional) WSA Assessment tasks in Online Resources.

- Assessment A: Sorting Names
- Assessment B: Using Letter-Sound Relationships to Solve New Words
- Assessment C: Recognizing and Reading Known Words Quickly
- Assessment D: Using Onsets and Rimes in Known Words to Solve New Words
- Assessment E: Using Onsets and Rimes in Known Words to Solve New Words
- Assessment F: Individual Record (Using Parts of Known Words to Solve New Words, 1 and 2)
- Assessment G: Individual Record (Name Chart)
- Assessment H: Class Record
- Assessment I: Class Record (Name Chart)

Develop Your Professional Understanding

See *The Fountas & Pinnell Comprehensive Phonics, Spelling, and Word Study Guide*. 2017. Related pages: 2–12, 76–83.

See *The Fountas & Pinnell Literacy Continuum: A Tool for Assessment, Planning, and Teaching*. 2017. Portsmouth, New Hampshire: Heinemann. Related pages: 357–397.

See *Word Matters: Teaching Phonics and Spelling in the Reading/ Writing Classroom* by G. S. Pinnell and I. C. Fountas. 1998. Portsmouth, New Hampshire: Heinemann. Related pages: 46–47, 63–64, 90–93, 95, 222–228, 237–244.

katie

ray

ma,

ay

pay

way

Recognize and Find Names

Plan

▶ Consider Your Children

This lesson is best used after you have made a class name chart with the children (see Early Literacy Concepts 1) and after they have done a great deal of interactive writing in which you have made connections between their names and the words they want to write. Your goal is to teach children that words they know are a good resource for learning to read and write new words.

▶ Working with English Language Learners

This lesson will help children use their names as resources for learning more about English words. It also sets up the expectation that they can actively search for connections rather than waiting to be taught new words. Be sure that English language learners can pronounce (with some understandable variation) the words they are using to make connections with their names. Limit the set at first so that children can find examples easily. Encourage them to use words from the word wall.

UNDERSTAND THE PRINCIPLE

Making connections between how words look is a powerful word-solving strategy that helps children develop categories of words and derive principles for how words work. Comparing a specific aspect of a familiar word (such as a name) with that aspect of other names and other words helps children understand that they can use their knowledge to expand their vocabularies and to organize how they think about the parts of words.

YOU WILL NEED

Online Resources
- ▶ WSA 1 Action Tags
- ▶ WSA 1 Lotto and Bingo Game Boards
- ▶ WSA 1 Blank Word Cards
- ▶ WSA 1 Lotto and Bingo Game Boards

Other Materials
- ▶ class name chart
- ▶ game pieces/markers

✓ Generative Lesson

A generative lesson has a simple structure that you can use to present similar content or concepts. You can use this lesson structure to teach children to use known words as a resource in reading and writing.

EXPLAIN THE PRINCIPLE

Connect a name with other words.

The first letter in a name is the same as the first letter in some other names.

The first letter in a name is the same as the first letter in some other words.

You can find the first letter in a name in some other words.

Comprehensive Phonics, Spelling, and Word Study Guide

Refer to: page **76**, row **2**

ACTIVITY: CLASS NAME CHART

INSTRUCTIONAL PROCEDURE

SEE AND SAY

See page 36 for detailed descriptions of Instructional Procedures.

EXPLAIN THE PRINCIPLE

Connect a name with other words.

The first letter in a name is the same as the first letter in some other names.

The first letter in a name is the same as the first letter in some other words.

You can find the first letter in a name in some other words.

Comprehensive Phonics, Spelling, and Word Study Guide

Refer to: page **76**, row **2**

Teach

1. Explain to the children that they are going to use their names to learn about other words.

2. *You have been using the class name chart to help you write words. Now we are going to talk about one way the class name chart helps you. We are going to make connections between your name and other words.*

3. Read the class name chart aloud with the children.

4. *You can use what you know about the letters in your name to help you read and write other words. Let's look at an example. What is the first letter in the name Marcus? ● Right, it's an m. What do you notice about the first letter in the name Michael? ● That's right, this name starts with the same letter, an m. These two words are the same at the beginning–both words start with the letter m.* Write the words *Marcus* and *Michael* on the whiteboard. *Can you think of another word–not a name–that starts with the letter m? ● Yes, the word mop starts with m, doesn't it? All three of these words are the same at the beginning.*

5. The primary focus here is the letter match; however, confirming it with the matching /m/ sound is a way to help children begin making connections with how words sound as well.

6. Make additional connections between children's names and other words:

   "*Annesa* and *away* start the same."

   "*Sara* and *Suzanne* start the same."

   "*Suzanne* and *sun* start the same."

   "*Billy* and *box* start the same."

   "*Peter* and *play* start the same."

7. Tell children that they are now going to play Lotto with partners in pairs or small groups.

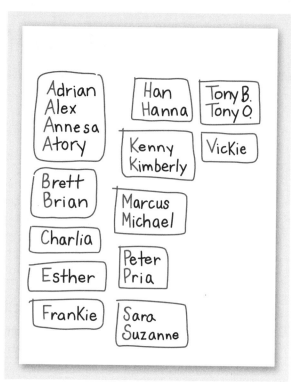

ACTIVITY: LOTTO (PAIRS)

INSTRUCTIONAL PROCEDURE

SEE AND SAY

See page 36 for detailed descriptions of Instructional Procedures.

ACTION TAGS

take

say the name

say another word

cover

Apply

- Prepare three or four 3 x 4 Lotto game boards that are different from each other. (You may wish to photocopy each of these boards for use by additional children.) Write names from the class name chart in the individual spaces on a game board. Then prepare word cards containing names from the class name chart. Children can play with partners.

- To play, a child takes a word card, says the name on the card, and says a word that has the same beginning letter as that name. Then, if the name card matches a name on her game board, the child covers the space with a marker (button, penny, or paper square). The first child to cover the names on her board wins the game.

Share

Go around the group quickly and ask each child to say his or her name and a word that starts the same.

Assess

- Notice whether the children can connect names with other words when reading and writing.

- You may wish to use Word-Solving Actions Assessment A, B, G, or I.

Connect Learning Across Contexts

Interactive Read-Aloud Read aloud books that focus on how children's names connect to other words.

> IRA *Miss Bindergarten Gets Ready for Kindergarten* by Joseph Slate

> IRA *Lola at the Library* by Anna McQuinn

Shared Reading See "Grandpa Grig" in *Words That Sing* (2019). If you don't have these poetry charts, enlarge the print of this poem or other poems such as "Little Jack Horner" or "Little Miss Muffet" from *Sing a Song of Poetry*, and have children point out the words that connect to the names in the poems. You may also wish to use the following Shared Reading title from *Fountas & Pinnell Classroom™* to make more connections to other words by using names.

> SR *Dancing in the Mud* by Nancy K. Wallace

Interactive Writing Post the class name chart next to the easel where you write. Help children make connections with names to spell unknown words. *What is the beginning sound of this name? • Do you know a word that starts with the same beginning sound?*

Independent Writing Remind the children to use the class name chart as a resource in spelling words they want to write.

Extend Learning

When children have good control of initial sounds, you may also connect names to other words using ending sounds or using consonant digraphs (*Shaun* or *Shayla* with *short*).

▶ Connect with Home

Write the child's first name on a piece of paper and have him look for a small object or picture of something that begins like his name. Have him bring the picture or object to school to glue on a special version of the class name chart.

Recognize and Read Known Words Quickly

Plan

▶ Consider Your Children

This lesson is best used after children know and have worked with some high-frequency words. The purpose is to give children opportunities to notice how they can read many words quickly and easily because they know them. This lesson can be repeated with many other simple texts that are only a few lines long.

▶ Working with English Language Learners

When you prepare a simple text for English language learners to read on their own, be sure that the topic is familiar, that the words are known and understood in oral language, and that children have had exposure to the language structure through hearing it read aloud and in shared reading. If necessary, work with a small group of children who need more repetition. Observing children perform this task will tell you about their ability to use knowledge of letters, sounds, and words while reading text. Repeat this lesson with easy sentences over several days.

YOU WILL NEED

PWS Ready Resources
▶ **WSA 2** Sentence Strips

Online Resources
▶ **WSA 2** Action Tags

Other Materials
▶ chart paper displaying a new, unfamiliar text
▶ pointer
▶ scissors
▶ blank paper
▶ glue sticks

Generative Lesson
A generative lesson has a simple structure that you can use to present similar content or concepts. Use this lesson structure to help children recognize and read a large number of high-frequency words.

UNDERSTAND THE PRINCIPLE

Children use a core of known high-frequency words as anchors to monitor their reading. They can use known words to check on the accuracy of their reading. Also, knowing a core of rapidly recognized words promotes fluency.

EXPLAIN THE PRINCIPLE

When you know a word, you can read the word quickly.

 Comprehensive Phonics, Spelling, and Word Study Guide

Refer to: page **77**, row **8**

ACTIVITY: LETTER TO CLASS

INSTRUCTIONAL PROCEDURE

WORDS TO KNOW

See page 36 for detailed descriptions of Instructional Procedures.

EXPLAIN THE PRINCIPLE

When you know a word, you can read the word quickly.

Comprehensive Phonics, Spelling, and Word Study Guide

Refer to:
page **77**, row **8**

Teach

1. In preparation for the lesson, write on chart paper the beginning of a letter addressed to the children in your classroom. After a salutation, you may wish to write a simple text (one sentence per line) such as "I am proud of you."

2. Tell the children they are going to learn more about reading words.

3. *Today you are going to read something together. Do you know why I'm not going to read this letter to you?* • *Because you already know so much about reading. I'll tell you some of the words, but there are lots of words you already know.*

4. *This is a letter to the kids in this classroom. What's the first word?* • *You know the word* to. *Let's read the beginning together.* Read the salutation with the children.

5. Go on to the first line. *Now you can read the first line.* Children will read *I* and *am,* and they may pause on the word *proud.* Join in to read *proud of* with them, but drop out again on *you. You read the whole first sentence. Were you right?* • *You know some of the words, don't you?* • *Checking on words you know helps you know that you are right.*

6. Have a child come up and read the first line as he points underneath each word. Assist on *proud of* if necessary. Ask other children to check whether the child read accurately. Have children locate known high-frequency words or put highlighter tape over the known words in the first line.

7. Have children read the second line, helping if needed. Point out that they will usually see some words they know in the stories they are reading. Knowing these words helps them read faster and also helps them check their reading.

8. Go back and read the salutation and first two lines together again quickly, using the pointer.

9. *You did such a great job that I am going to add two more lines to my letter. Watch me write two more lines. You can think about what I'm writing, but don't say it out loud.*

10. Write two more lines that are easy and that have some high-frequency words in them. For example: "I like the way you read books" and "We can read books together." Read these additional lines with the children and have them locate known words.

Dear Room 5 kids,

You read lots of books.

We can read lots of books together.

You work very hard.

I am proud of you.

Love,

Mrs. Hawkins

Dear Room 5 kids,

You read lots of books.

We can read lots of books together.

You work very hard.

I am proud of you.

Love,
Mrs. Hawkins

ACTION TAGS

cut

mix

find

glue

read

Apply

Give each child a copy of your class letter, including the lines you added. Have them cut the letter into sentence strips. Then they should mix up the strips. Using the original chart paper as a reference if needed, have children re-create the note by gluing the strips on a blank sheet of paper. Have them point under each word as they read it to a partner.

Share

Invite one or two children to read the letter to the class while another child points under each word.

Assess

- Notice whether the children are able to recognize high-frequency words when they read.
- You may wish to use Word-Solving Actions Assessment C.

Connect Learning Across Contexts

Interactive Read-Aloud Read aloud standard-size books that have large bold print that the class can easily see. As you read aloud, invite children to read some of the words with you, particularly on second and third readings.

> IRA *Two Homes* by Claire Masurel

> IRA *Lost* by David McPhail

Shared Reading See "Five Fingers on Each Hand" in *Words That Sing* (2019). If you don't have these poetry charts, enlarge the print of this poem or other poems such as "Bouncing Ball" from *Sing a Song of Poetry*, and have children predict a word or two and check whether they were right. You may also wish to use the following Shared Reading title from *Fountas & Pinnell Classroom*™ to recognize known words.

> SR *A Bear and His Honey* by Fannie Morris

Guided Reading After reading a text, have children locate two or three high-frequency words.

Shared or Interactive Writing Remind the children of words they know how to read and write. Write them quickly yourself to demonstrate how to write them from beginning to end without stopping.

Independent Writing Encourage the children to use conventional spelling for the words they know in detail and to reread their writing and notice these words.

Extend Learning

- Repeat this lesson with other simple texts that you write yourself. Include as many high-frequency words as you can. (Start each sentence on a new line.)

- Bring together a group of children who are waiting for help and not actively solving words. Read new texts with them and demonstrate strategies explicitly. Stick with easy texts with only one or two words to solve.

▶ Connect with Home

Have the children take home copies of the letter to read to family members.

Change the Beginning Sound or Sounds to Make and Solve a New Word

Plan

▶ Consider Your Children

The oral activities in this lesson provide a foundation for a strategic approach to reading and writing of new words. Children should have some familiarity with (though not a thorough knowledge of) consonant sounds.

▶ Working with English Language Learners

Be sure that English language learners have worked with and can isolate sounds in simple words. If they have difficulty with the task, make connections with known words. Children should understand *first* and *last* and have experience in working with beginning sounds.

YOU WILL NEED

PWS Ready Resources
- ▸ WSA 3 Pocket-Chart Cards

Online Resources
- ▸ WSA 3 Action Tags
- ▸ WSA 3 Picture Cards
- ▸ WSA 3 Two-Column Sorts

Other Materials
- ▸ pocket chart

Generative Lesson

A generative lesson has a simple structure that you can use to present similar content or concepts. You can use this lesson structure to teach children to make and solve a variety of new words.

UNDERSTAND THE PRINCIPLE

Competent word solvers recognize the connections between words and can flexibly manipulate the sounds in words to make and solve new words.

EXPLAIN THE PRINCIPLE

Change the first sound or sounds in a word to make another word.

Comprehensive Phonics, Spelling, and Word Study Guide

Refer to: page **78**, row **20**

ACTIVITY: PICTURE CARDS

**INSTRUCTIONAL
PROCEDURE**

HEAR AND SAY

*See page 36 for detailed
descriptions of Instructional
Procedures.*

EXPLAIN THE PRINCIPLE

*Change the first sound or
sounds in a word to make
another word.*

Comprehensive
Phonics, Spelling,
and Word Study
Guide

Refer to:
page **78**, row **20**

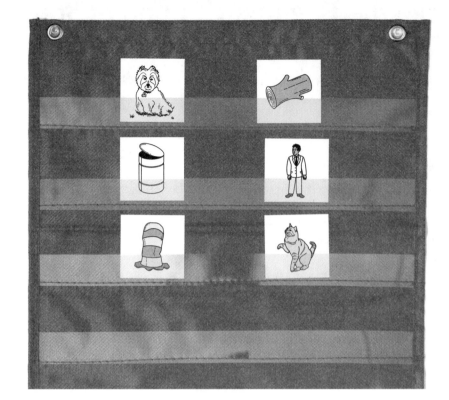

Teach

1. Tell the children they are going to learn something new about words.

2. Place the picture of the *dog* and the *log* in the pocket chart. Point to the dog and say *dog* aloud. Now point to the log and say *log* aloud. *What do you notice about these two words?* • *Both* dog *and* log *end with the same sound, -og. What sound do you hear first in* dog? • *What about* log? • *Both words sound different in the beginning of the word, but they sound the same at the end of the word. Let's look at more words.*

3. Children may make comments such as these:

   "They rhyme."

   "They sound the same at the end."

   "*Dog* has *a* /d/ sound and *log* has an /l/ sound."

4. *What word does this picture show?* • *That's right, it is a can.* • *What is the first sound in* can? • *Right, the first sound in* can *is* /k/. *Let's change the first sound to* /m/. *What word did we make?* Invite children to solve the word by saying *can* and the new word, *man*.

5. Follow the same procedure with *hat, cat*.

6. Then point to the pictures on the pocket chart as you say the word pairs. Tell children that each pair of words (*dog* and *log, can* and *man,* and *hat* and *cat*) has different first sounds but the rest of the word sounds the same. You can change the first sound in a word to make another word.

7. Explain to the children that they will be working with a partner to change the beginning sound of a word to make a new word.

ACTIVITY:
TWO-WAY SORT

INSTRUCTIONAL PROCEDURE

SAY AND SORT

See page 36 for detailed descriptions of Instructional Procedures.

ACTION TAGS

say
match
put
say
change
check

Apply

■ Give pairs of children a number of picture cards and a two-column sort. Have partners work together to say the name of each picture. Then have them match each picture with another picture of a word that rhymes with the word shown in the first picture but that has a different beginning sound: for example, *dog, log; hat, bat; pan, van; fish, dish.* Children should put one picture in the left-hand column and one in the right-hand column.

■ Ask them to take turns explaining to their partner how they can change the first sound of the word on the left to make the word on the right. Ask them to explain using this format: "The first sound in *dog* is /d/. When I change the first sound to /l/, I make the word *log.*" Once they are done, have them say the pairs of words to check.

Share

Invite children to describe how they changed the first sound in a word to make a new word.

Assess

■ Notice whether the children can use known words to figure out new words.

■ Say three words and ask a child to change the first sound of each to make a new word.

Word-Solving Actions: Change the Beginning Sound or Sounds to Make and Solve a New Word

Connect Learning Across Contexts

Interactive Read-Aloud Read aloud books that help children attend to words that are alike in some of their sounds.

IRA *Charlie Parker Played Be Bop* by Chris Raschka

IRA *Creak! Said the Bed* by Phyllis Root

Shared Reading See "Hiccup, Hiccup" in *Words That Sing* (2019). If you don't have these poetry charts, enlarge the print of this poem or other poems such as "Elsie Marley" from *Sing a Song of Poetry*, and play a game; *I'm thinking of a word from the poem that sounds like* say (or another word). *Do you know what it is?* Reinforce the principle that you can change the first sound of a word to make a new word. You may also wish to use the following Shared Reading title from *Fountas & Pinnell Classroom*™ to find more words that sound alike.

SR *Wiggles: Poems to Make You Wiggle Your Fingers and Toes*

Interactive Writing Help children make new words by making connections to words they know. Encourage them to think of a word that is like the word they are trying to write: *Do you know another word that sounds the same at the end?* Use the whiteboard to demonstrate making new words by changing the beginning sound. In this case, children will be changing the beginning sound and seeing the letter change at the same time.

Independent Writing Encourage children to use words they know to help them write new words. Demonstrate by saying a word they know or writing it on a small piece of paper or stick-on note. Show how to change one sound or letter to make the word they want to write (*hot, not*).

Extend Learning

■ As you work with children to make new words by changing first sounds, include examples of words that have initial blends or digraphs: for example, *sled, bed; bee, tree; clock, sock; more, shore*.

■ Alternate changing first sounds and last sounds to make new words. This will help children become more flexible in word solving.

▶ Connect with Home

Send home a copy of selected picture cards. Have children match cards that sound the same at the end and say the names of the picture pairs to family members. Then have them explain how they can change the first sound of one word to create a new word.

Change the Beginning Sound or Sounds to Make and Solve a New Word

Plan

▶ Consider Your Children

The oral activities in this lesson provide a foundation for a strategic approach to reading and writing of new words. Children should have some familiarity with (though not a thorough knowledge of) consonant sounds. This lesson is best used after children understand the concept of words and the concept of *first* relative to the sequence of sounds in a word.

▶ Working with English Language Learners

Be sure that English language learners have worked with and can isolate sounds in simple words. If they have difficulty with the task, make connections with known words. Children should understand *first* and *last* and have experience in working with beginning sounds. You may need to start by saying some words that sound the same at the end but have different first sounds. Let them notice and talk about the connections. Then explicitly demonstrate how you can take one word and change the first sound to make the other word. Provide many opportunities for practice.

YOU WILL NEED

 Ready Resources
- ▶ WSA 4 Pocket-Chart Cards

Online Resources
- ▶ WSA 4 Action Tags
- ▶ WSA 4 Picture Cards

Other Materials
- ▶ pocket chart

Generative Lesson ✓

A generative lesson has a simple structure that you can use to present similar content or concepts. You can use this lesson structure to teach children to make and solve a variety of new words.

UNDERSTAND THE PRINCIPLE

Competent word solvers recognize the connections between words and can flexibly manipulate the sounds in words to make and solve new words. As children become more aware of the sounds within words, they learn that words are made up of individual sounds. These sounds can be changed to make new words. Taking away the first sound of a word and substituting another helps children understand a basic principle of how words work. This understanding helps them recognize connections between words and use their knowledge to solve words during reading or writing.

EXPLAIN THE PRINCIPLE

Change the first sound or sounds in a word to make another word.

 Comprehensive Phonics, Spelling, and Word Study Guide

Refer to: page **78**, row **20**

ACTIVITY: ANIMAL NAMES

INSTRUCTIONAL PROCEDURE

HEAR AND SAY

See page 36 for detailed descriptions of Instructional Procedures.

EXPLAIN THE PRINCIPLE

Change the first sound or sounds in a word to make another word.

Comprehensive Phonics, Spelling, and Word Study Guide

Refer to: page **79**, row **20**

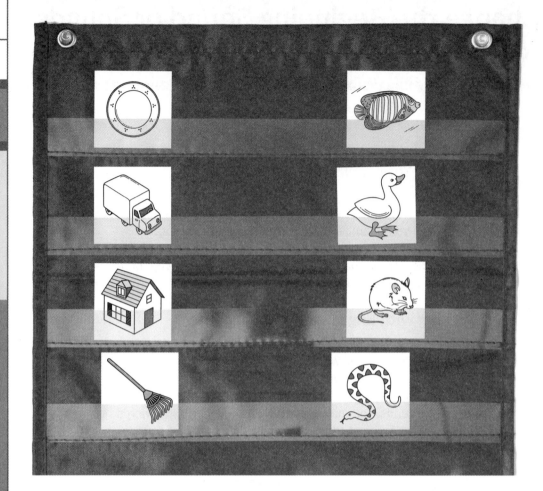

Teach

1. Explain to children that they are going to play a fun word game. They will change words into names of animals.

2. Display the picture of the dish on the pocket chart. *What word does this picture show?* • *It's a dish. Say* dish. • Now place the picture of *fish* on the chart. *What word does this picture show?* • *It's a fish. Talk about the words* dish *and* fish. • *If I change the first sound of* dish *to /f/, the word is* fish.

3. *Let's try another one.* Display the picture of the truck. *What word does this picture show?* • *Listen carefully as I say the word:* truck. *What is the first sound in* truck? • *It's /t/. What is the second sound in* truck? *Say the word again, slightly emphasizing the* r *sound. It is /r/. The /t/ and the /r/ sounds go together at the beginning of this word. Now let's change the /t/ /r/ to another sound–/d/. What word do we have now?* • *The new word is* duck. Truck, duck. *We changed the /t//r/ to /d/.*

4. Provide one or two more examples if needed (*house, mouse; rake, snake*). Have children explain how they change the beginning sound or sounds to make a new word.

5. *Today you are going to make words by changing only the first sound or sounds.*

ACTIVITY: THREE NEW WORDS

INSTRUCTIONAL PROCEDURE

HEAR AND SAY

See page 36 for detailed descriptions of Instructional Procedures.

ACTION TAGS

say
change
say
tell

Apply

Give pairs of children a picture of a hat and then have them say *hat.* Explain to the children that they will be working with a partner to change the first sound in *hat* to make several new words. Have partners take turns changing only the first sound to make a new word and telling what they changed: "*Hat, rat.* I changed the /h/ to /r/." "*Rat, flat.* I changed the /r/ to /f/ /l/." Have them come up with at least three new words. If they need help, suggest that they think about other animal names that end like *hat* (*cat, bat*)*.* They may also come up with *mat, pat,* and *sat.*

Share

Have children demonstrate how they made a new word by changing only the first sound.

Assess

■ Observe the children's ability to use what they know to figure out new words.

■ Say three words and ask each child to change the first sound of each word to make a new word.

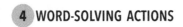

Connect Learning Across Contexts

Interactive Read-Aloud Read aloud books with simple rhymes.

IRA *When It Starts to Snow* by Phillis Gershator

IRA *The Doorbell Rang* by Pat Hutchins

Shared Reading See "Hiccup, Hiccup" in *Words That Sing* (2019). If you don't have these poetry charts, enlarge the print of this poem or other poems such as "Elsie Marley" from *Sing a Song of Poetry*, and play a game. *I'm thinking of a word from the poem that sounds like* say (or another word). *Do you know what it is?* Reinforce the principle that you can change the first sound of a word to make a new word. You may also wish to use the following Shared Reading title from *Fountas & Pinnell Classroom*™ to find more words that sound alike.

SR *Wiggles: Poems to Make You Wiggle Your Fingers and Toes*

Interactive Writing Within the texts children compose, look for opportunities to connect words by changing the first sound or sounds (and letter or letters). Use the whiteboard to demonstrate. For example, if they want to write *be* and they know *me*, show them on the whiteboard how to go from *me* to *be*. Children will be changing the first sound and seeing the letter change at the same time.

Independent Writing Encourage the children to make connections to known words when writing new words. Demonstrate by saying a word they know or writing it on a small piece of paper or stick-on note. Show how to change one letter to make the word they want to write (*like, bike*).

Extend Learning

Repeat the lesson without picture support, starting with words with common endings -*an*, -*ad*, -*in*, -*ot*, or -*it.* Starting with–or asking children to think of–words that have two sounds in the onset (such as *plan, glad, spin,* and *spot*) can make the task more challenging.

▶ Connect with Home

Send home a selection of pictures. Have children say the names of the pictures and show how they can change the first sound or sounds to make other words that sound the same at the end.

Hear Sounds in Sequence

Plan

▶ Consider Your Children

This lesson focuses on saying words slowly and then writing them. It is best used when children have done a great deal of interactive writing and can hear initial and final consonants in words. Interactive writing is a powerful context for teaching children to say words slowly and record the individual sounds and is especially effective because the writing is for authentic purposes. You'll want to show explicitly how children can use this technique in their own writing.

▶ Working with English Language Learners

Saying words slowly to hear individual sounds is a technique that will help English language learners make connections between the letters and the sounds in words. At first, encourage them to write words that they can pronounce easily, avoiding those that require sounds that are hard for them to say. (For some words, they will have to remember how they *look*.) Saying words slowly will help English language learners understand English pronunciations.

YOU WILL NEED

PWS Ready Resources
- ▶ WSA 5 Pocket-Chart Cards

Online Resources
- ▶ WSA 5 Action Tags
- ▶ WSA 5 Picture Cards
- ▶ WSA 5 Two-Way Sorts
- ▶ WSA 5 Two-Column Sorts

Other Materials
- ▶ pocket chart
- ▶ chart paper or whiteboard
- ▶ writing materials
- ▶ glue sticks

Generative Lesson

A generative lesson has a simple structure that you can use to present similar content or concepts. You can use this lesson structure to teach children to hear sounds in a variety of words.

UNDERSTAND THE PRINCIPLE

Saying a word slowly helps beginning readers attend to and hear the individual sounds in the word. Children begin to develop the concept that words are made up of sequences of sounds. This concept is basic to connecting sounds to letters, letter clusters, and letter patterns.

EXPLAIN THE PRINCIPLE

Saying a word slowly makes it easier to hear each sound in order from first to last.

Comprehensive Phonics, Spelling, and Word Study Guide

Refer to: page **78**, row **17**

INSTRUCTIONAL PROCEDURE

HEAR AND SAY

See page 36 for detailed descriptions of Instructional Procedures.

EXPLAIN THE PRINCIPLE

Saying a word slowly makes it easier to hear each sound in order from first to last.

Comprehensive Phonics, Spelling, and Word Study Guide

Refer to:
page **78**, row **17**

Teach

1. Explain to the children that they are going to learn how to say words slowly and listen for sounds so they can write words.

2. Show the children one of the pocket-chart picture cards. Have them look at your mouth while you say the name of the picture slowly (*cat*, for example).

3. Have the children say the word slowly with you.

4. *What sound do you hear first in* cat*? • The first sound is /k/. What is a letter that stands for the sound /k/? • The letter c stands for /k/. What sound do you hear last in the word* cat*? • What letter stands for /t/? • The letter* t. Place the pocket-chart word card next to the picture card. Point out the first letter, *c*, and the last letter, *t*.

5. Repeat this procedure with many easy words. For beginners, focus only on words with two or three sounds. Include easy-to-hear middle vowel sounds if the children are well in control of beginning and ending consonant sounds. Possible pictures include *bat, bus, cake, can, cat*.

Name _Lisa_

cak

ball

car

Fountas & Pinnell Phonics, Spelling, and Word Study Lessons, Kindergarten

© 2018 by Irene C. Fountas and Gay Su Pinnell. Portsmouth, NH: Heinemann. This page may be photocopied.

WSA 5 Two-Way Sort

**ACTIVITY:
TWO-WAY SORT**

**INSTRUCTIONAL
PROCEDURE**

HEAR AND SAY

SAY AND WRITE

*See page 36 for detailed
descriptions of Instructional
Procedures.*

ACTION TAGS

glue

say

hear

write

read

Apply

- Give the children a two-way sort and a few picture cards. Demonstrate how to say the word *cake* aloud sound by sound and to write the letter for each sound in sequence.

- Invite children to glue each picture card on the left, say each word slowly, write the first sound, and attempt to write the middle and last sounds as well, depending on what they can control. (As long as all three sounds in a word are represented, the word does not have to be spelled conventionally.) Finally, have them read their lists to a partner while they point at each word.

- Some children will be able to represent only one or two sounds in the words, so you should expect differences. For extra space, children can use the back of the paper or an additional two-column sort.

Share

Invite individual children to the chalkboard or easel to say one of their words slowly and write the sounds.

Assess

- Notice whether the children are representing more sounds in the new words they attempt to spell.

- Notice whether the children are using letter-sound relationships to solve words.

Word-Solving Actions: Hear Sounds in Sequence

Connect Learning Across Contexts

Interactive Read-Aloud Read aloud books that help the children attend to the sounds in words.

> 📖 *It's Raining, It's Pouring* by Kin Eagle

> 📖 *Elephants Swim* by Linda Capus Riley

Shared Reading See "The Mockingbird" in *Words That Sing* (2019). If you don't have these poetry charts, enlarge the print of this poem or other poems such as "Who Stole the Cookies?" or "Little Red Apple" from *Sing a Song of Poetry*, and have children say the words slowly to think about what they hear and what letters they might see. Then have them check the letters to see if they are right. You may also wish to use the following Shared Reading title from *Fountas & Pinnell Classroom*™ to look at more word sounds.

> 📖 *Fuzzy and Buzzy* by Aaron Mack

Interactive Writing Select words that will expand children's ability to hear sounds. Have children say them slowly and think what letters would be at the beginning, middle, and end of the word. Have one child write the word or parts of the word.

Independent Writing Remind children to say words slowly and think about what letters to write at the beginning, middle, and end of words.

Extend Learning

- Repeat the lesson with other pictures or objects.
- Move from words with three sounds to some words with four sounds.

▶ Connect with Home

Suggest to family members that they play "Listen for the Sounds" with their children. They give the child a clue about a word ("I'm thinking of a fruit that is yellow," "I'm thinking of a fruit that is huge," "I'm thinking of a vegetable that is green"), and she guesses the word (*banana, watermelon, spinach*) and tells the letter it starts with (*b, w, s*).

Use Onsets and Rimes in Known Words to Read and Write Other Words with the Same Parts

Plan

▶ Consider Your Children

Use this lesson after children can recognize between ten and twenty high-frequency words. They should also have some experience changing the beginning sound in a word to make a new word. Don't work on all the words in the rhyme in any one lesson because that can decrease children's enjoyment and sense of purpose. Extend learning by making additional connections in successive readings.

▶ Working with English Language Learners

In this lesson, children are using their knowledge of known words and their awareness of parts of words to figure out the words in a poem for themselves. You may want to provide extra support to English language learners in a small group at first, but this is also a time to observe their problem solving. If they have difficulty with the four lines, try some very simple sentences that use words they know and one new word that they know enough to figure out. Doing this will set up the expectation that they need to search for what they know to solve words in reading.

YOU WILL NEED

Online Resources
- ▶ WSA 6 Action Tags
- ▶ WSA 6 Poem: After a Bath

Other Materials
- ▶ chart with new unfamiliar rhyme for shared reading
- ▶ pointer
- ▶ whiteboard
- ▶ scissors
- ▶ glue
- ▶ sheets of paper
- ▶ magnetic letters

Generative Lesson ✓

A generative lesson has a simple structure that you can use to present similar content or concepts. You can use this lesson structure to teach children to use known words and parts of known words to solve a variety of other words.

UNDERSTAND THE PRINCIPLE

Children use a core of known high-frequency words as anchors to monitor their reading. Children use known words and parts of known words to solve other words they are trying to read or write.

EXPLAIN THE PRINCIPLE

Sometimes a part of a word you know can be found in another word.

Use parts of words you know to read or write another word with the same parts.

Comprehensive Phonics, Spelling, and Word Study Guide

Refer to:
page **77**, row **11**

EARLY MIDDLE **LATE**

ACTIVITY: AFTER A BATH

INSTRUCTIONAL PROCEDURE

NOTICE PARTS

See page 36 for detailed descriptions of Instructional Procedures.

EXPLAIN THE PRINCIPLE

Sometimes a part of a word you know can be found in another word.

Use parts of words you know to read or write another word with the same parts.

Comprehensive Phonics, Spelling, and Word Study Guide

Refer to: page **77**, row **11**

Teach

1. Tell the children they are going to read a new poem.

2. *Today we are going to read something together. I'll tell you some of the words, but there are lots of words you already know. This is a new rhyme that you haven't heard before. It's a little bit funny. It's about what you do after a bath. You take a towel and you wipe yourself dry, don't you?*

3. *What is the first word?* • *You know the word* after. *Let's read the first line about what happens after a bath.*

> After a Bath
>
> After my bath
>
> I try, try, try
>
> To wipe myself until
>
> I'm dry, dry, dry.

4. Point and read *After* with the children, but drop out for the rest of the line. Children should be able to read *my* and *bath*, drawing from both the meaning and their knowledge of the words and word parts.

5. Go on to the next line. Children may be able to read *try*, but if not, ask them what they notice about it. Then say, *I'm going to show you a way to figure out the word* try. *Do you know another word that sounds like this at the end? Say* try.

6. Write *my* on the whiteboard. *What is this word?* • Draw a vertical line between the onset (*m*) and the rime (*y*). *I'm going to take away the* m *and put* t *and* r *at the beginning of the word. The word is* t r . . . • *That's right, the word is* try. *Let's see if it makes sense in our rhyme.* Point and read from the beginning through line 2.

7. Go on to the next line, helping children with "wipe myself until."

8. Quickly use the whiteboard to help children see *my* in *myself*. (Remember, don't encourage them to look for the "little word inside the big word," which is not an effective strategy.) *Myself has two parts. Can you clap it?* • *I'll write the first part,* my. • *You know the word* my. *There it is, right in the first line of this poem.* Write the rest of the word *myself*, and have children read it.

9. Read the last line of the rhyme with the children. Repeat the procedure in step 6 to separate the onset (*dr*) and the rime (*y*). *Do you remember the ending part of the word* try? *That same part is in this word. Do you see it?* • *This word is* dry. *You can use parts of words you know to read or write another word with the same parts.*

10. Read the poem together again quickly, using the pointer.

After a Bath

After
I
bath, until try,
dry, dry. try
a I'm To wipe
myself try,
dry,

ACTIVITY: CUT-UP POEM

INSTRUCTIONAL PROCEDURE

NOTICE PARTS

See page 36 for detailed descriptions of Instructional Procedures.

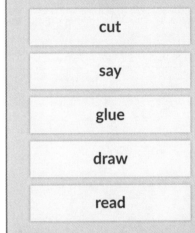

ACTION TAGS

cut

say

glue

draw

read

Apply

Give children a photocopy of a rhyme such as "After a Bath." Have them cut apart the words. Then they can say and glue each word onto another sheet of paper in the appropriate order. Help them with the order of the punctuated words as needed. Then have them illustrate the poem and read it to a partner.

Share

Read the rhyme together again. Have some children make words from the poem on the easel with magnetic letters, and have a child demonstrate going from a known word to a new word.

Assess

- Observe whether the children are able to recognize words that contain the same parts as other words when they read.
- Notice whether the children can write high-frequency words quickly.
- You may wish to use Word-Solving Actions Assessment D, E, F, H.

Connect Learning Across Contexts

Interactive Read-Aloud Read aloud books that encourage the manipulation of sounds.

> IRA *Charlie Parker Played Be Bop* by Chris Raschka
>
> IRA *Rattletrap Car* by Phyllis Root

Shared Reading See "Rig-a-jig-jig" in *Words That Sing* (2019). If you don't have these poetry charts, enlarge the print of this poem or other poems such as "Chickery, Chickery, Cranny, Crow" from *Sing a Song of Poetry*, and point out words that have the same onset or rime. You may also wish to use the following Shared Reading title from *Fountas & Pinnell Classroom*™ to find more words that sound alike.

> SR *Giggles: Poems to Make You Laugh*

Interactive Writing When solving new words, use as resources words from the word wall that have the same onset or the same rime.

Independent Writing Encourage the children to write words they know rather than consult the word wall.

Extend Learning

Repeat the lesson with other unfamiliar rhymes or songs.

▶ Connect with Home

Send home a copy of the rhyme for children to read with family members.

Use Onsets and Rimes in Known Words to Read and Write Other Words with the Same Parts

Plan

▶ Consider Your Children

This lesson is best used after children are aware of the connections between sounds and letters in words and have learned some letter-sound relationships and between ten and twenty-five high-frequency words. Although they need not be familiar with the terms *onset* and *rime*, they should know that when you say "parts of a word" you are referring to the first part of a word (the letter or letters before the vowel) and to the last part of a word (the vowel and the letters that come after). The understanding established in this lesson will be reinforced every time children engage in shared and guided reading.

▶ Working with English Language Learners

In this lesson, children use their knowledge of known words–and their awareness of parts of words–to solve the words in the poem for themselves. You will want English language learners to be generally familiar with the text (although they should not have it memorized). You may want to work with children in a small group and remind them of words they know that can be connected to the new words they are trying to solve. Be sure that the text they are reading is comprehensible and that it does not have too many words that are hard for them to understand.

YOU WILL NEED

Online Resources
- ▶ WSA 7 Action Tags
- ▶ WSA 7 Poem: Here Is a House

Other Materials
- ▶ chart with text of poem "Here Is a House"
- ▶ pointer
- ▶ whiteboard
- ▶ scissors
- ▶ glue
- ▶ sheets of paper
- ▶ magnetic letters

Generative Lesson
A generative lesson has a simple structure that you can use to present similar content or concepts. You can use this lesson structure to teach children to use known words and parts of known words to solve a variety of new words.

UNDERSTAND THE PRINCIPLE

Children use a core of known high-frequency words as anchors to monitor their reading. Children use known words and parts of known words to solve other words they are trying to read or write. Knowing about onsets and rimes can help children read and write other words that have the same parts.

EXPLAIN THE PRINCIPLE

Sometimes a part of a word you know can be found in another word.

Use parts of words you know to read or write another word with the same parts.

Comprehensive Phonics, Spelling, and Word Study Guide

Refer to: page **77**, row **11**

**INSTRUCTIONAL
PROCEDURE**

NOTICE PARTS

*See page 36 for detailed
descriptions of Instructional
Procedures.*

EXPLAIN THE PRINCIPLE

*Sometimes a part of a word you
know can be found in another
word.*

*Use parts of words you know to
read or write another word with
the same parts.*

Comprehensive
Phonics, Spelling,
and Word Study
Guide

Refer to:
page **77**, row **11**

Teach

1. Tell the children they are
going to learn more about
solving new words as they
read a poem.

2. *Today we are going to
read a poem together. I'll
tell you some of the
words, but this poem has
lots of words you already
know. This poem is about
a very big house. The title
of this poem is "Here Is a
House."*

3. *Let's look at the first line
of the poem. The first
words in this line are the
same words as the title.
Let's read the first line
together.* Point and read
the first line. Children should be able to read the words *here, is, a, house,* and
up, drawing from both the meaning and their knowledge of the words and
word parts.

4. *Now let's look at the second line. What is this word?* • *You know the word* with.
Go on to the next words. Children may be able to read *tall,* but if not, ask what
they notice about the word. *Do you know a word that ends like that?* • *I'm
going to show you a way to figure out the word* tall.

5. Write *ball* on the whiteboard. *What is this word?* • Draw a vertical line between
the onset [b] and the rime [all]. *I'm going to take away the* b *and put* t *at the
beginning of the word. The word is* t . . . • *The word is* tall. *Let's see if it makes
sense in the poem.* Point and read from the beginning through the end of line
2, helping children with "chimneys."

6. Repeat the procedure in step 5, writing the word *by* on the whiteboard and
separating the onset [sk] and the rime [y]. *I can take away the* b *and put* sk *at
the beginning of the word. The word is* s-k . . . • *The word is* sky.

7. Go on to the next lines, helping children with "windows," "peep," "inside," and
"We'll." Repeat the procedure in step 5, writing the word *house* on the
whiteboard and separating the onset [h] and the rime [ouse]; the same
procedure can be used for *door* and *floor.*

8. Read the poem together again quickly, using the pointer.

Here Is a House

Here is a house built up high,

With two tall chimneys reaching the sky.

Here are the windows.

Here is the door.

If we peep inside

We'll see a mouse on the floor.

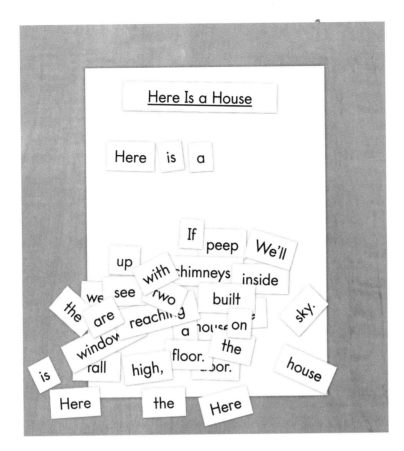

ACTIVITY: CUT-UP POEM

INSTRUCTIONAL PROCEDURE

NOTICE PARTS

See page 36 for detailed descriptions of Instructional Procedures.

ACTION TAGS

cut
say
glue
draw
read

Apply

Give children a photocopy of a poem such as "Here Is a House." Have them cut apart the words. Then they can say and glue each word onto another sheet of paper in the appropriate order. Help them with the order of the punctuated words as needed. Then have them illustrate the poem and read it to a partner.

Share

Read the poem again with the group. Have some children make words from the poem on the easel with magnetic letters, and have a child demonstrate going from a known word to a new word.

Assess

- Observe whether the children are able to recognize words that contain the same parts as other words when they read.
- Note whether children can write the high-frequency words quickly.
- You may wish to use Word-Solving Actions Assessment D, E, F, H.

Word-Solving Actions: Use Onsets and Rimes in Known Words to Read and Write Other Words with the Same Parts

Connect Learning Across Contexts

Interactive Read-Aloud Read aloud books that draw attention to words that have the same word parts.

> IRA *The Bus for Us* by Suzanne Bloom

> IRA *Where Are You Going, Little Mouse?* by Robert Kraus

Shared Reading See "Five Little Snowmen" or "Go to Bed Early" in *Words That Sing* (2019). If you don't have these poetry charts, enlarge the print of one of these poems from *Sing a Song of Poetry*, and show children how to figure out words they do not know and to check their reading by noticing word parts. You may also wish to use the following Shared Reading title from *Fountas & Pinnell Classroom*™ to find more words that sound alike.

> SR *Jump and Hop: Poems to Make You Move*

Interactive Writing Prompt children to think about word parts in the words they are writing. Ask, "Do you see a part you know?"

Independent Writing Prompt children to use their knowledge of word parts to spell words.

Extend Learning

- Repeat the lesson using other texts children have read during shared reading. Take words out of the text and write them on a whiteboard, showing onsets and rimes, so the children will notice them. Then read the text to be sure the words they solve make sense and sound right.

- You may want to repeat the lesson with other onsets and rimes you have taught.

▶ Connect with Home

When you are sure that the children can read the texts you have used in the lesson, send home copies for children to read with caregivers.

Change the Ending Sound or Sounds to Make and Solve a New Word

Plan

▶ Consider Your Children

Use this lesson after children can recognize some simple high-frequency words, are able to relate most letters to the sounds they represent, and have had some experience constructing words in interactive writing and on their own. They should also have had experience changing the first sound of a word to make new words. This lesson helps children understand that they can make new words by changing parts of words they know. It lays the foundation for a flexible range of connections that will help them solve words.

▶ Working with English Language Learners

This lesson will help children realize that they can use what they know to figure out what they do not know. Be sure to begin with words that English language learners know well in oral language. Say the names of the pictures with them and help them articulate individual sounds, especially the last sound, which they will be changing.

YOU WILL NEED

Online Resources
- ▶ **WSA 8** Action Tags
- ▶ **WSA 8** Two-Column Sorts
- ▶ **WSA 8** Picture Cards

Other Materials
- ▶ magnetic whiteboard
- ▶ magnetic letters

Generative Lesson ✓

A generative lesson has a simple structure that you can use to present similar content or concepts. You can use this lesson structure to teach children to make connections to sounds in a variety of words.

UNDERSTAND THE PRINCIPLE

Good readers and writers solve words by drawing on what they already know. They make connections to sounds in words. Connections to known words help children form powerful strategies that will make them rapid, flexible word solvers.

EXPLAIN THE PRINCIPLE

Change the last sound or sounds in a word to make another word.

Comprehensive Phonics, Spelling, and Word Study Guide

Refer to: page **78**, row **21**

INSTRUCTIONAL PROCEDURE

MAKE WORDS

See page 36 for detailed descriptions of Instructional Procedures.

EXPLAIN THE PRINCIPLE

Change the last sound or sounds in a word to make another word.

Comprehensive Phonics, Spelling, and Word Study Guide

Refer to: page **78**, row **21**

Teach

1. Tell children that they are going to learn more about changing sounds in words to make new words.

2. *You have been learning how to tell which sounds are the same in words. And you have been making new words by changing beginning sounds in words. Today you are going to make new words by changing the ending sounds.* You may wish to show the word *is* in magnetic letters and to have the magnetic letters *t, n,* and *f* off to the side.

3. *Say is. What is the first sound?* • /i/. *What is the last sound in is?* • /z/. *Now say is again, but change the /z/ to /t/. What word did I make?* • *I made the word it. Now say it, then change the /t/ to /n/. What word did you make?* • *You made the word in. Now, what if you change the last sound to /f/? What word would you make?*

4. Repeat using *as, at, am; cat, can, cap;* and *an, at.* Sometimes it is helpful to change back to the original word before making the new word. The more explicit this teaching is, the more effective it will be.

5. *When you are thinking about how to write a word or read a word, it can help you to think about the sounds of the words you already know.*

6. Explain to children that they will be working with pairs of words that sound the same at the beginning but have different last sounds.

Name _____

Fountas & Pinnell Phonics, Spelling, and Word Study Lessons, Kindergarten

WSA 8 Two-Column Sort

© 2018 by Irene C. Fountas and Gay Su Pinnell. Portsmouth, NH: Heinemann. This page may be photocopied.

ACTIVITY: TWO-WAY SORT (PAIRS)

INSTRUCTIONAL PROCEDURE

FIND AND MATCH

See page 36 for detailed descriptions of Instructional Procedures.

ACTION TAGS

say
match
put
say

Apply

Give pairs of children the picture cards and a two-column sort. Partners work together to name each picture, slowly pronouncing the individual sounds. Then have them find and match pairs of pictures representing words that sound the same except for the last sound. Children can place one picture in the left-hand column and one in the right-hand column (*bug, bus; pin, pig; bag, bat; mat, map; bell, bed*). Ask them to take turns telling their partner what the last sound is in each of the two words. Have them say the pairs of words to check.

Share

Have children explain how they can change the last sound of a particular word to make a new word.

Assess

- Observe how the children use words they know to make new words.
- Listen as individual children explain how to change the last sound in three words to make three new words.

Word-Solving Actions: Change the Ending Sound or Sounds to Make and Solve a New Word

Connect Learning Across Contexts

Interactive Read-Aloud Read aloud books that help children make connections among words according to the sounds in words.

> IRA *A, My Name Is Alice* by Jane Bayer

> IRA *"Slowly, Slowly, Slowly," Said the Sloth* by Eric Carle

Shared Reading See "Three Men In a Tub" in *Words That Sing* (2019). If you don't have these poetry charts, enlarge the print of this poem or other poems such as "Blackberries" in *Sing a Song of Poetry*. After reading and enjoying a text, play a word game: *I am thinking of a word that I can make if I change the last sound of the word* bag. (If children are very proficient, they can give the clues for the game.) Reinforce the principle that you can change the last sound or sounds of a word to make a new word. Help children locate the words in the text. You may also wish to use the following Shared Reading title to change more ending sounds to create new words.

> SR *Splish Splash!* by Susan F. Rank

Interactive Writing When the children are writing a new word, help them connect it to a word they already know.

Independent Writing Encourage the children to use words they know to help them spell new words.

Extend Learning

Play an oral game in which children create strings of words by changing the last sounds: *pig/pit/pin; hug/hum/hut; pet/pen/pep/pest.* Include one or two examples of words that have two last sounds (final consonant blends) to make the task more challenging.

▶ Connect with Home

Send home picture cards that children can use to change last sounds to make new words. Ask them to explain to a family member how they can change the last sound in the pictured word to make another word.

Change the Ending Sound or Sounds to Make and Solve a New Word

Plan

▶ Consider Your Children

Use this lesson after children have made words by substituting beginning sounds. This lesson helps children realize that they can make words by changing ending sounds of words they know. Knowing that they can change first *and* last sounds of words lays the foundation for a flexible range of connections that will help them take words apart as they decode and spell.

▶ Working with English Language Learners

When English language learners know some basic information about sounds in words, they can approach words more flexibly. In this lesson they connect words by last sounds. They need to know that learning about words is not just a matter of memorizing them but of recognizing, changing, and putting together sounds— and the letters associated with those sounds. Have them work with words and pictures they know, or explain any words or pictures ahead of time as needed.

YOU WILL NEED

PWS Ready Resources
▶ WSA 9 Pocket-Chart Cards

Online Resources
▶ WSA 9 Action Tags
▶ WSA 9 Picture Cards

Other Materials
▶ pocket chart
▶ chart paper

Generative Lesson
A generative lesson has a simple structure that you can use to present similar content or concepts. You can use this lesson structure to teach children to make connections between words to solve them.

UNDERSTAND THE PRINCIPLE

Proficient readers and writers solve words by drawing on what they already know. They make connections to sounds in words. Connections to known words help children form powerful strategies that will make them rapid, flexible word solvers.

EXPLAIN THE PRINCIPLE

Change the last sound or sounds in a word to make another word.

Comprehensive Phonics, Spelling, and Word Study Guide

Refer to:
page **78**, row **21**

ACTIVITY: WORD LINKS

INSTRUCTIONAL PROCEDURE

HEAR AND SAY

See page 36 for detailed descriptions of Instructional Procedures.

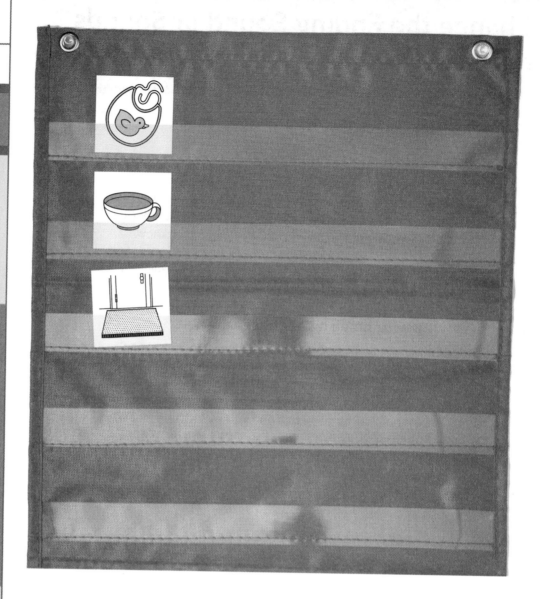

EXPLAIN THE PRINCIPLE

Change the last sound or sounds in a word to make another word.

Comprehensive Phonics, Spelling, and Word Study Guide

Refer to: page **78**, row **21**

Teach

1. Tell the children that today they are going to learn more about making a new word by changing the last sound of a word.

2. Display the pocket-chart card for the word *bib*. Say the word *bib* slowly, accentuating each the three sounds. *What is the last sound you hear?* • /b/. *Now I'm going to change the last sound to /t/. Now I have...* • *Now I have the word* bit. *You can change the last sound in a different way. Let's change the last sound from /b/ to /g/. What word do you have now?* • *You made the word* big.

3. Repeat with these different strings of words: *cup, cut, cub; mat, mad, man, map, mask.* Sometimes it is helpful to say the original word before making the new word. The more explicit this teaching is, the more effective it will be.

4. *Just think about how many words you can make by changing ending sounds. When you are thinking about how to write a word or read a word, think about how the words you know can help you.*

ACTIVITY: WORD LINKS (PAIRS)

INSTRUCTIONAL PROCEDURE

HEAR AND SAY

See page 36 for detailed descriptions of Instructional Procedures.

ACTION TAGS

| glue |
| say |
| change |
| say |
| draw |

Apply

Give pairs of children the picture cards for *man* and *bug* and have them glue the pictures on a piece of chart paper. Have children work together to make and say aloud one or two new words by changing the last sound of each pictured word (e.g., *mat, map, mad; bus, bun, but, bud, buzz*). Then have each child in the pair choose one new word to illustrate in some way. They can position their illustrations next to the picture of the word that is almost like the new word they made.

Share

Invite children to say a word and suggest a different ending sound that would make a new word. Then have the class say the new word together.

Assess

Ask a child to change the last part of a word. Look for flexibility and independence.

Word-Solving Actions: Change the Ending Sound or Sounds to Make and Solve a New Word

Connect Learning Across Contexts

Interactive Read-Aloud Read aloud books that help children make connections among the sounds in words.

> IRA *Alicia's Happy Day* by Meg Starr

> IRA *Flower Garden* by Eve Bunting

Shared Reading See "Five Fat Pumpkins" in *Words That Sing* (2019). If you don't have these poetry charts, enlarge the print of this poem or other poems such as "Dance a Merry Jig" in *Sing a Song of Poetry*. After reading and enjoying a text, play a word game: *I'm thinking of a word that I can make by changing the last sound of the word* it. You may also wish to use the following Shared Reading title to change more ending sounds to create new words.

> SR *Fly Away* by Alina Kirk

Interactive Writing As children try to write new words, prompt them to think of a similar word: *Do you know another word that starts like that?* Encourage children to try to write the first few letters and then help them identify the last sound.

Independent Writing Encourage the children to use words they know to help them spell words that sound the same. The word wall can be a useful reference.

Extend Learning

- Say a selection of words that children will recognize. After saying each word, invite the children to replace the last sound to make a new word. Encourage the discovery of many new options.

- Say a selection of words that have more than one ending consonant sound (e.g., *cast, mask, lint*). After saying each word, invite children to replace the last sounds make a new word.

▶ Connect with Home

Send home four or five pictures that children can name. Have them explain to their families how they can change last sound of each word to make new words.

Glossary

accented syllable A syllable that is given emphasis in pronunciation. See also *syllable, stress*.

affix A letter or group of letters added to the beginning or ending of a base or root word to change its meaning or function (a *prefix* or a *suffix*).

alphabet book / ABC book A book that helps children develop the concept and sequence of the alphabet by pairing alphabet letters with pictures of people, animals, or objects with labels related to the letters.

alphabet linking chart A chart containing uppercase and lowercase letters of the alphabet paired with pictures representing words beginning with each letter (*a, apple*).

alphabetic principle The concept that there is a relationship between the spoken sounds in oral language and the graphic forms in written language.

analogy The resemblance of a known word to an unknown word that helps you solve the unknown word's meaning. Often an analogy shows the relationship between two pairs of words.

antonym A word that has the opposite meaning from another word: e.g., *cold* versus *hot*.

assessment A means for gathering information or data that reveals what learners control, partially control, or do not yet control consistently.

automaticity Rapid, accurate, fluent word decoding without conscious effort or attention.

base word A word in its simplest form, which can be modified by adding affixes: e.g., *read; reread, reading*. A base word has meaning, can stand on its own, and is easily apparent in the language. Compare to *word root*.

behavior An observable action.

blend To combine sounds or word parts.

capitalization The use of capital letters, usually the first letter in a word, as a convention of written language (for example, for proper names and to begin sentences).

closed syllable A syllable that ends in a consonant: e.g., *lem*-on.

concept book A book organized to develop an understanding of an abstract or generic idea or categorization.

concept word A word that represents an abstract idea or name. Categories of concept words include color names, number words, days of the week, months of the year, seasons, and so on.

consonant A speech sound made by partial or complete closure of the airflow that causes friction at one or more points in the breath channel. The consonant sounds are represented by the letters *b, c, d, f, g, h, j, k, l, m, n, p, qu, r, s, t, v, w, y*, and *z*.

consonant blend Two or more consonant letters that often appear together in words and represent sounds that are smoothly joined, although each of the sounds can be heard in the word: e.g., *tr*im.

consonant digraph Two consonant letters that appear together and represent a single sound that is different from the sound of either letter: e.g., sh*ell*.

contraction A shortened form of one or more words. A letter or letters are left out, and an apostrophe takes the place of the missing letter or letters.

decoding Using letter-sound relationships to translate a word from a series of symbols to a unit of meaning.

dialect A regional variety of a language. In most languages, including English and Spanish, dialects are mutually intelligible; the differences are actually minor.

directionality The orientation of print (in the English language, from left to right).

distinctive letter features Visual features that make each letter of the alphabet different from every other letter.

early literacy concepts Very early understandings related to how written language or print is organized and used—how it works.

English language learner A person whose native language is not English and who is acquiring English as an additional language.

fluency In reading, this term names the ability to read continuous text with good momentum, phrasing, appropriate pausing, intonation, and stress. In word solving, this term names the ability to solve words with speed, accuracy, and flexibility.

grammar Complex rules by which people can generate an unlimited number of phrases, sentences, and longer texts in that language. Conventional grammar refers to the accepted grammatical conventions in a society.

grapheme A letter or cluster of letters representing a single sound, or phoneme: e.g., *a, eigh, ay*.

graphophonic relationship The relationship between the oral sounds of the language and the written letters or clusters of letters. See also *semantic system, syntactic system*.

have a try To write a word, notice that it doesn't look quite right, try it two or three other ways, and decide which construction looks right; to make an attempt and self-check.

high-frequency words Words that occur often in the spoken and written language.

homograph One of two or more words spelled alike but different in meaning, derivation, or pronunciation: e.g., the *bat* flew away, he swung the *bat*; take a *bow, bow* and arrow.

homonym One of two or more words spelled and pronounced alike but different in meaning: e.g., we had *quail* for dinner; I would *quail* in fear. A homonym is a type of homograph.

homophone One of two or more words pronounced alike but different in spelling and meaning: e.g., *meat, meet; bear, bare*.

idiom A phrase with meaning that cannot be derived from the conjoined meanings of its elements: e.g., *raining cats and dogs*.

inflectional ending A suffix added to a base word to show tense, plurality, possession, or comparison: e.g., dark-*er*.

interactive read-aloud A teaching context in which students are actively listening and responding to an oral reading of a text.

interactive writing A teaching context in which the teacher and students cooperatively plan, compose, and write a group text; the teacher acts as a scribe but invites individual students to contribute some writing for letters or words that have high instructional value.

letter knowledge The ability to recognize and label the graphic symbols of language.

letter-sound relationships The correspondence of letter(s) and sound(s) in written or spoken language.

letters Graphic symbols representing the sounds in a language. Each letter has particular distinctive features and may be identified by letter name or sound.

lexicon Words that make up language.

long vowel The elongated vowel sound that is the same as the name of the vowel. It is sometimes represented by two or more letters: e.g., c*a*ke, *ei*ght, m*ai*l. Another term for long vowel is *lax vowel*.

lowercase letter A small letter form that is usually different from its corresponding capital or uppercase form.

morpheme The smallest unit of meaning in a language. Morphemes may be free or bound. For example, *run* is a unit of meaning that can stand alone (a free morpheme). In *runs* and *running*, the added -*s* and -*ing* are also units of meaning. They cannot stand alone but add meaning to the free morpheme. The -*s* and -*ing* are examples of bound morphemes.

morphemic strategies Ways of solving words by discovering meaning through the combination of significant word parts or morphemes: e.g., *happy, happiest; run, runner, running*.

morphological system Rules by which morphemes (building blocks of vocabulary) fit together into meaningful words, phrases, and sentences.

morphology The combination of morphemes (building blocks of meaning) to form words; the rules by which words are formed from free and bound morphemes—for example, root words, prefixes, and suffixes.

multiple-meaning word A word that means something different depending on the way it is used: e.g., *run—home run, run in your stocking, run down the street, a run of bad luck*.

multisyllable word A word that contains more than one syllable.

onset In a syllable, the part (consonant, consonant cluster, or consonant digraph) that comes before the vowel: e.g., the *cr* in *cream*. See also *rime*.

onset-rime segmentation The identification and separation of the onset (first part) and rime (last part, containing the vowel) in a word: e.g., *dr-ip*.

open syllable A syllable that ends in a vowel sound: e.g., *ho*-tel.

orthographic awareness The knowledge of the visual features of written language, including distinctive features of letters as well as spelling patterns in words.

orthography The representation of the sounds of a language with the proper letters according to standard usage (spelling).

phoneme The smallest unit of sound in spoken language. There are forty-four units of speech sounds in English.

phoneme addition To add a beginning or ending sound to a word: e.g., /h/ + *and*; *an* + /t/.

phoneme blending To identify individual sounds and then to put them together smoothly to make a word: e.g., /k//a//t/ = *cat*.

phoneme deletion To omit a beginning, middle, or ending sound of a word: e.g., /k//a//s//k/ - /k/ = *ask*.

phoneme-grapheme correspondence The relationship between the sounds (phonemes) and letters (graphemes) of a language.

phoneme isolation The identification of an individual sound—beginning, middle, or end—in a word.

phoneme manipulation The movement of sounds from one place in a word to another.

phoneme reversal The exchange of the first and last sounds of a word to make a different word.

phoneme substitution The replacement of the beginning, middle, or ending sound of a word with a new sound.

phonemic (or phoneme) awareness The ability to hear individual sounds in words and to identify particular sounds.

phonemic strategies Ways of solving words that use how words sound and relationships between letters and letter clusters and phonemes in those words.

phonetics The scientific study of speech sounds—how the sounds are made vocally and the relation of speech sounds to the total language process.

phonics The knowledge of letter-sound relationships and how they are used in reading and writing. Teaching phonics refers to helping children acquire this body of knowledge about the oral and written language systems; additionally, teaching phonics helps children use phonics knowledge as part of a reading and writing process. Phonics instruction uses a small portion of the body of knowledge that makes up phonetics.

phonogram A phonetic element represented by graphic characters or symbols. In word recognition, words containing a graphic sequence composed of a vowel grapheme and an ending consonant grapheme (such as *an* or *it*) are sometimes called a word family.

phonological awareness The awareness of words, rhyming words, onsets and rimes, syllables, and individual sounds (phonemes).

phonological system The sounds of the language and how they work together in ways that are meaningful to the speakers of the language.

plural Of, relating to, or constituting more than one.

prefix A group of letters placed in front of a base word to change its meaning: e.g., *pre*plan.

principle In phonics, a generalization or a sound-spelling relationship that is predictable.

punctuation Marks used in written text to clarify meaning and separate structural units. The comma and the period are common punctuation marks.

r-controlled vowel sound The modified or *r*-influenced sound of a vowel when it is followed by *r* in a syllable: e.g., *hurt*.

related words Words that are related because of sound, spelling, category, or meaning. See also *synonym, antonym, homophone, homograph, analogy.*

rhyme The repetition of vowel and consonant sounds in the stressed syllables of words in verse, especially at the ends of lines.

rime In a syllable, the ending part containing the letters that represent the vowel sound and the consonant letters that follow: i.e., dr-*eam*. See also *onset.*

root See *word root.*

schwa The sound of the middle vowel in an unstressed syllable (the *e* in *happen* and the sound between the *k* and *l* in *freckle*).

segment To divide into parts: e.g., *to/ma/to.*

semantic system The system by which speakers of a language communicate meaning through language. See also *graphophonic relationship, syntactic system.*

shared reading An instructional context in which the teacher involves a group of students in the reading of a particular big book or other enlarged text in order to introduce aspects of literacy (such as print conventions), develop reading strategies (such as decoding or predicting), and teach vocabulary.

shared writing An instructional context in which the teacher involves a group of students in the composing of a coherent text together. The teacher writes an enlarged text while scaffolding children's language and ideas.

short vowel A brief-duration sound represented by a vowel letter: e.g, the /a/ in *cat.*

silent e The final *e* in a spelling pattern that usually signals a long vowel sound in the word and that does not represent a sound itself: e.g., *make.*

solving words (as a strategic action) Using a range of strategies to take words apart and understand their meaning(s).

spelling patterns Beginning letters (onsets) and common phonograms (rimes), which form the basis for the English syllable. Knowing these patterns, a student can build countless words.

stress The emphasis given to some syllables or words in pronunciation. See also *accented syllable.*

suffix A group of letters added at the end of a base word or word root to change its function or meaning: e.g., hand*ful*, hope*less*.

syllabication The division of words into syllables.

syllable A minimal unit of sequential speech sounds composed of a vowel sound or a consonant-vowel combination. A syllable always contains a vowel or vowel-like speech sound: e.g., *pen/ny*.

synonym One of two or more words that have different sounds but the same meaning: e.g., *high, tall*.

syntactic awareness The knowledge of grammatical patterns or structures.

syntactic system Rules that govern the ways in which morphemes and words work together in sentence patterns. This system is not the same as proper grammar, which refers to the accepted grammatical conventions. See also *graphophonic relationship, semantic system*.

syntax The way sentences are formed with words and phrases and the grammatical rules that govern their formation.

visual strategies Ways of solving words that use knowledge of how words look, including the clusters and patterns of the letters in words.

vocabulary Words and their meanings. See also *word meaning/vocabulary*.

vowel A speech sound or phoneme made without stoppage of or friction in the airflow. The vowel sounds are represented by *a, e, i, o, u*, and sometimes *y*.

vowel combination See *letter combination*.

word A unit of meaning in language.

word analysis To break apart words into parts or individual sounds in order to parse them.

word boundaries The white space that appears before the first letter and after the last letter of a word and that defines the letter or letters as a word. It is important for young readers to learn to recognize word boundaries.

word-by-word matching Usually applied to a beginning reader's ability to match one spoken word with one printed word while reading. Younger readers learn by pointing. In older readers, the eyes take over the process.

word family A term often used to designate words that are connected by phonograms or rimes (e.g., *hot, not, pot, shot*). A word family can also be a series of words connected by meaning (e.g., *baseless, baseline, baseboard*).

word meaning/vocabulary *Word meaning* refers to the commonly accepted meaning of a word in oral or written language. *Vocabulary* often refers to the words one knows in oral or written language.

word root A word part, usually from another language, that carries the essential meaning of and is the basis for an English word: e.g., *flect, reflect*. Most word roots cannot stand on their own as English words. Some word roots can be combined with affixes to create English words. Compare to *base word*.

word structure The parts that make up a word.

words (as a text characteristic) Decodability of words in a text; phonetic and structural features of words.

word-solving actions The strategies a reader uses to recognize words and understand their meaning(s).

References

Adams, M.J. 1990. *Beginning to Read: Thinking and Learning about Print.* Cambridge, MA: MIT Press.

Allington, R. 1991. "Children Who Find Learning to Read Difficult: School Responses to Diversity." In *Literacy for a Diverse Society: Perspectives, Practices, and Policies*, edited by E.H. Hiebert. New York: Teachers College Press.

Armbruster, B.B., F. Lehr, and J. Osborn. 2001. *Put Reading First: The Research Building Blocks for Teaching Children to Read: Kindergarten Through Grade 3.* Jessup, MD: National Institute for Literacy.

Ball, E.W., and B.A. Blachman. 1991. "Does Phoneme Awareness Training in Kindergarten Make a Difference in Early World Recognition and Developmental Spelling?" *Reading Research Quarterly* 26 (1): 49–66.

Biemiller, A. 1970. "The Development of the Use of Graphic and Contextual Information as Children Learn to Read." *Reading Research Quarterly* 6 (1): 75–96.

Blachman, B. 1984. "The Relationships of Rapid Naming Ability and Language Analysis Skills to Kindergarten and First-Grade Reading Achievement." *Journal of Educational Psychology* 76 (4): 610–22.

Blanchard, J.S. 1980. "Preliminary Investigation of Transfer Between Single-Word Decoding Ability and Contextual Reading Comprehension of Poor Readers in Grade Six." *Perceptual and Motor Skills* 51:1271–81.

Bradley, L., and P.E. Bryant. 1983. "Categorizing Sounds and Learning to Read-A Causal Connection." *Nature* 301:419–21.

Bryant, P.E., M. MacLean, L.L. Bradley, and J. Crossland. 1990. "Rhyme and Alliteration, Phoneme Detection, and Learning to Read." *Developmental Psychology* 26 (3): 429–38.

———. 1989. "Nursery Rhymes, Phonological Skills and Reading." *Journal of Child Language* 16 (2): 407–28.

Ceprano, M.A. 1980. "A Review of Selected Research on Methods of Teaching Sight Words." *The Reading Teacher* 35 (3): 314–22.

Chall, J.S. 1989. "Learning to Read: The Great Debate. 20 Years Later." *Phi Delta Kappan* 70 (7): 521–38.

Clay, M.M. 2001. *Change Over Time in Children's Literacy Development.* Portsmouth, NH: Heinemann.

———. 1998. *By Different Paths to Common Outcomes.* York, ME: Stenhouse Publishers.

———. 1991. *Becoming Literate: The Construction of Inner Control.* Portsmouth, NH: Heinemann.

Daneman, M. 1991. "Individual Difference in Reading Skills." In *Handbook of Reading Research*, edited by R. Barr, M.L. Kamil, P. Mosenthal, and P.D. Pearson, 512–38. New York: Longman.

Ehri, L.C. 1991. "Development of the Ability to Read Words." In *Handbook of Reading Research*, edited by R. Barr, M.L. Kamil, P. Mosenthal, and P.D. Pearson, 383–417. New York: Longman.

Ehri, L.C., and S. McCormick. 1998. "Phases of Word Learning: Implications for Instruction With Delayed and Disabled Readers." *Reading and Writing Quarterly* 14 (2): 135–63.

Fountas, I.C., and G.S. Pinnell. 2018. *Fountas & Pinnell Classroom*. Portsmouth, NH: Heinemann.

———. 2018. *Fountas & Pinnell Classroom™ Guided Reading Collection, Kindergarten*. Portsmouth, NH: Heinemann.

———. 2018. *Fountas & Pinnell Classroom™ Independent Reading Collection, Kindergarten*. Portsmouth, NH: Heinemann.

———. 2018. *Fountas & Pinnell Classroom™ Interactive Read-Aloud Collection, Kindergarten*. Portsmouth, NH: Heinemann.

———. 2018. *Fountas & Pinnell Classroom™ Shared Reading Collection, Kindergarten*. Portsmouth, NH: Heinemann.

———. 2018. *Fountas & Pinnell Classroom™ Words That Sing, Kindergarten*. Portsmouth, NH: Heinemann.

———. 2018. *Sing a Song of Poetry: A Teaching Resource for Phonemic Awareness, Phonics, and Fluency, Kindergarten*. Portsmouth, NH: Heinemann.

———. 2017. *Guided Reading: Responsive Teaching Across the Grades*, 2d ed. Portsmouth, NH: Heinemann.

———. 2017. *The Fountas & Pinnell Literacy Continuum: A Tool for Assessment, Planning, and Teaching, Expanded Edition*. Portsmouth, NH: Heinemann.

———. 2017. *Comprehensive Phonics, Spelling, and Word Study Guide*. Portsmouth, NH: Heinemann.

———. 2014. *Fountas & Pinnell Select Collection, Kindergarten*. Portsmouth, NH: Heinemann.

———. 2011. *Literacy Beginnings: A Prekindergarten Handbook*. Portsmouth, NH: Heinemann.

———. 1999. *Voices on Word Matters: Learning about Phonics and Spelling in the Literacy Classroom*. Portsmouth, NH: Heinemann.

———. 1998. *Word Matters: Teaching Phonics and Spelling in the Reading/Writing Classroom*. Portsmouth, NH: Heinemann.

Fox, B., and K.D. Routh. 1984. "Phonemic Analysis and Synthesis as Word-Attack Skills: Revisited." *Journal of Educational Psychology* 76 (6): 1059–64.

Hohn, W., and L. Ehri. 1983. "Do Alphabet Letters Help Prereaders Acquire Phonemic Segmentation Skill?" *Journal of Educational Psychology* 75 (5): 752–62.

Holdaway, D. 1987. *The Foundations of Literacy*. Portsmouth, NH: Heinemann.

Hundley, S., and D. Powell. 1999. In *Voices on Word Matters*, edited by I.C. Fountas and G.S. Pinnell, 159–64. Portsmouth, NH: Heinemann.

Juel, C. 1988. "Learning to Read and Write: A Longitudinal Study of 54 Children from First Through Fourth Grades." *Journal of Educational Psychology* 80 (4): 437–47.

Juel, C., P.L. Griffith, and P.B. Gough. 1986. "Acquisition of Literacy: A Longitudinal Study of Children in First and Second Grade." *Journal of Educational Psychology* 78 (4): 243–55.

Lesgold, A.M., L.B. Resnick, and K. Hammond. 1985. "Learning to Read: A Longitudinal Study of Word Skill Development in Two Curricula." In *Reading Research: Advances in Theory and Practice*, edited by G.E. MacKinnon and T.G. Walker, 107–38. New York: Academic Press.

Liberman, I., D. Shankweile, and A. Liberman. 1985. *The Alphabetic Principle and Learning to Read*. U.S. Department of Health and Human Services. Reprinted with permission from The University of Michigan Press by the National Institute of Child Health and Human Development. Adapted from "Phonology and the Problems of Learning to Read and Write. *Remedial and Special Education* 6:8–17.

Liberman, I.Y., D. Shankweiler, F.W. Fischer, and B. Carter. 1974. "Explicit Syllable and Phoneme Segmentation in the Young Child." *Journal of Experimental Child Psychology* 18 (2): 201–12.

Lundberg, I., J. Frost, and O.P. Petersen. 1988. "Effects of an Extensive Program for Stimulating Phonological Awareness in Preschool Children." *Reading Research Quarterly* 23 (3): 263–84.

McCarrier, A.M., G.S. Pinnell, and I.C. Fountas. 2000. *Interactive Writing: How Language and Literacy Come Together*. Portsmouth, NH: Heinemann.

Moats, L.C. 2000. *Speech to Print: Language Essentials for Teachers*. Baltimore, MD: Paul H. Brookes.

Nagy, W.E., R.C. Anderson, M. Schommer, J. Scott, and A. Stallman. 1989. "Morphological Families in the Internal Lexicon." *Reading Research Quarterly* 24 (3): 262–82.

National Institute of Child Health and Human Development. 2001. Report of the National Reading Panel: "Teaching Children to Read: An Evidence-Based Assessment of the Scientific Research Literature on Reading and Its Implications for Reading Instruction." *Reports of the Subgroups*. Washington, DC: National Institutes of Health.

New Standards Primary Literacy Committee. 1999. *Reading and Writing: Grade by Grade*. Washington, DC: National Center on Education and the Economy and the University of Pittsburgh.

Perfetti, C.A., I. Beck, L. Bell, and C. Hughes. 1987. "Children's Reading and the Development of Phonological Awareness." *Merrill Palmer Quarterly* 33 (3): 39–75.

Pinnell, G.S., J.J. Pikulski, K.K. Wixson, J.R. Campbell, P.B. Gough, and A.S. Beatty. 1995. *Listening to Children Read Aloud: Data from NAEP's Integrated Reading Performance Record (IRPR) at Grade 4*. Princeton, NJ: Educational Testing Service, National Assessment of Educational Progress.

Pressley, M. 1998. Reading Instruction That Works: The Case for Balanced Teaching. New York: The Guilford Press.

Read, C. 1971. "Pre-School Children's Knowledge of English Phonology." *Harvard Educational Review* 41 (1): 1–34.

Snow, C.E., M.S. Burns, and P. Griffin, eds. 1998. *Preventing Reading Difficulties in Young Children.* Washington, DC: Committee on the Prevention of Reading Difficulties in Young Children, Commission on Behavioral and Social Sciences and Education, National Research Council.

Treiman, R. 1985. "Onsets and Rimes as Units of Spoken Syllables: Evidence from Children." *Journal of Experimental Child Psychology* 39 (1): 161–81.

Vellutino, F.R., and M.B. Denckla. 1991. "Cognitive and Neuropsychological Foundations of Word Identification in Poor and Normally Developing Readers." In *Handbook of Reading Research*, edited by R. Barr, M.L. Kamil, P. Mosenthal, and P.D. Pearson, 571–608. New York: Longman.

Vellutino, F.R., and D.M. Scanlon. 1987. "Phonological Coding, Phonological Awareness, and Reading Ability: Evidence from Longitudinal and Experimental Study." *Merrill Palmer Quarterly* 33 (3): 321–63.

Vellutino, F.R., D.M. Scanlon, E.R. Sipay, S.G. Small, A. Pratt, R. Chen, and M.B. Denckla. 1996. "Cognitive Profiles of Difficult-to-Remediate and Readily Remediated Poor Readers: Early Intervention as a Vehicle for Distinguishing Between Cognitive and Experiential Deficits as Basic Causes of Specific Reading Disability." *Journal of Educational Psychology* 88 (4): 601–38.